CONTENTS

VOCATIONAL A LEVEL BUSINESS

RG Bywaters
JE Evans-Pritchard
AJ Glaser
EZ Mayer
LE Gillman

Longman

Edinburgh Gate
Harlow, Essex

Pearson Education Limited
Edinburgh Gate
Harlow
Essex
CM20 2JE
England and Associated Companies throughout the World.

ISBN 0 582 40635 8

First published 2000
Third impression 2003

Printed in Singapore (B & JO)

The Publisher's policy is to use paper manufactured from sustainable forests.

UNIT 1

Business at work

Organisational Objectives

In this chapter you will learn about the objectives of public and private businesses, about goods and services, people's needs and wants, and business attitudes and cultures.

Introduction

First of all, let us be quite clear about the meaning of the word 'business'.

Business – any kind of commercial activity, including production, selling and buying.

This definition of business explains the term in its widest sense. There is another meaning, however, this time concerned with businesses in general.

A business – an organisation whose purpose is to provide goods and services to satisfy customers' needs and wants.

Needs and wants

In the past, it was quite easy to define needs and wants. 'Needs' referred to what people had to have to live; 'wants' were things people liked, or wanted to have, but which were not needed to maintain life. Thus food, clothing and shelter were, and still are, basic 'needs' – without them, we would perish.

'Wants' are also sometimes called luxuries. We could describe them as the icing on the cake. Whereas staple foods, such as rice, potatoes, pasta or bread, have always been considered necessities, exotic imported fruit or Belgian chocolates are lovely to eat, but we can do very well without them, so they truly are 'luxuries'.

In the second half of the twentieth century, with the growth of new industries and the invention of a number of modern appliances, the dividing line between 'wants' and 'needs' became rather blurred. If we all only wanted what we absolutely need, many modern industries would never exist. As economies developed, and the standard of living kept rising, people's expectations, their 'wants', also multiplied. Today, in countries such as the UK, we believe that we now need things that some years ago would have been classed as luxuries. For example, when first introduced, electric lighting was a luxury, affordable only by the very rich. The same was true of the first motor cars. Now we regard both as necessities of life.

We should remember, however, that in many countries, goods and services which we consider to be really basic are still unobtainable for a large part of the population. Furthermore, as new industries flood the market with new goods, demand for these is created until everyone 'wants' them as a matter of course. Not so long ago, very few British people took holidays abroad, or owned their own computers, freezers or mobile phones. Today, these goods and services are no longer considered to be luxuries.

Whatever the definition of 'wants' and 'needs', they have to be satisfied somehow. Some are provided by government agencies or public corporations, but the vast majority are produced by business organisations.

To sum up, if we, the consumers, were not prepared and able to buy goods and services, business activity would cease. We must now look more closely at the different types of organisations that provide the public with the whole range of what it needs and wants.

There are many thousands of businesses in the UK. Some are small, others employ many people. Some manufacture goods for sale, while others sell goods made by somebody else. Today, more and more businesses do not deal in goods at all – they provide **services**.

Goods

> **Goods** – these are tangible and are manufactured, grown or mined.

Goods are items that we can see and touch. There are three main categories of goods – **consumer goods**, **durable goods** and **capital goods**.

> **Consumer goods** – those goods that we buy for everyday use. They are used (consumed) relatively quickly.

> **Durable goods** – goods that last much longer and are not bought so frequently.

Anything that we, as consumers, buy falls into one of the above two categories of goods. We must all eat and drink to stay alive; we also need clothing and footwear. We need to furnish our houses, and most of us want to have television sets, VCRs, washing machines and radios.

Goods that we buy are manufactured, processed or constructed from raw materials.

In order to manufacture or process goods that individuals can buy, the manufacturers need machinery and equipment. For example, a maker of washing machines needs various cutting, shaping and bending machines. Today, many factories use robots in the production of their goods. These machines are called **capital goods**.

Capital goods – robots at work on the factory floor

Customers and consumers do not usually have direct contact with the producers of goods. They normally deal with retail organisations that sell the products.

The structure of business organisations also varies. In this unit, you will learn about different legal types of business organisations, from the sole trader to a public limited company. In this chapter, we shall examine the objectives of different organisations: profit and non-profit making, privately owned and state run or controlled.

CASE STUDY

What do we need?

Marianna Gillespie and Iris French have been friends since their schooldays. They went to school together, to college together, and married within six months of each other. Today, they are both in their mid-thirties, still live close to each other, and meet several times a week. Although each has two children, their situations are vastly different. Marianna's husband, Jake, is a successful businessman, and Marianna has never had to go to work. Her friend Iris has not been so fortunate. Her husband, Mike, had a good job as a manager in a large clothing factory, but was made redundant five years ago, and has not been able to find a permanent job since. Iris works part-time as a dentist's receptionist, and Mike does casual jobs, but money is tight, and they have trouble making ends meet.

Last week, Marianna and Iris met in Marianna's large, beautifully furnished house, and began to talk about Christmas, now only a few weeks away.

'The children want new bicycles,' said Marianna, 'and we shall have to buy them new designer trainers, because all their friends have some. Also, Jake has promised me a new car, because my Escort is already three years old, and past its best!'

'I wish we could have a car,' said Iris wistfully. 'You know that we had to sell it when Mike lost his job …'

'Yes, yes,' said Marianna, 'but you don't really need one, do you? You live so close to your work, and to the children's school.'

Iris sighed. 'You're probably right, but I do wish I could buy the children some new clothes for Christmas. They are growing out of their shoes, and I can't afford to buy new ones this month.'

Marianna wasn't listening. 'Jake has said that I can either have a new car, or a new three-piece suite. I really need both, but he won't listen!'

Iris thought of her old furniture, and began to wonder whether Marianna was really the good friend she had believed her to be for so many years.

Services

> **Services** – intangible facilities which people need and want and are prepared to buy.

Services, therefore, are all the things which cannot be classified as goods. Goods, we noted, are tangible, but services are not, as they are not manufactured. In the UK, as in other developed countries, the service industries have grown rapidly in the last forty or fifty years. They range from education, health, selling houses and insurance to hairdressing and the entertainment industry.

Activity

Look carefully at the list of goods given below. Some are consumer goods, while others are durable or capital goods. Sort the goods into their correct categories, and present the result in table format.

- cup of tea in the college canteen
- pair of shoes
- lathe
- dishwasher
- personal computer
- industrial sewing machine
- mobile phone
- printing press
- potatoes
- perfume
- refrigerator
- rolling mill (sheet metal)
- camera
- fly press (e.g. for producing washers)
- writing paper
- weaving frame
- soap
- bottling plant
- freezer
- hamburgers

It is interesting to note that, although, overall, the manufacturing industries declined in the course of the twentieth century, we now have many completely new service industries, some of them created as a direct result of the manufacture of goods which we now consider commonplace, but which were not even thought of a hundred years ago. For example, new technology in its various forms needs repairs and maintenance, so jobs such as computer programmer or trouble-shooter have emerged as a direct result of the ever-growing importance of computers both in industrial and personal use.

The basic principle of business is that it is carried on for profit. Whatever its business activity, the aim is to exchange goods or services for payment. However, the aims of organisations in the **private sector** are somewhat different from those in the **public sector**. Before we look at the private sector, however, we must know something about the large variety of organisations that are not in private ownership.

Public sector organisations

Public sector organisations are those that are run by or controlled directly or indirectly by the government. This is done to ensure that everyone is provided with essential goods and services.

In recent years, many state-run organisations have been **privatised** (sold off to private shareholders). British Telecom, British Aerospace, British Steel, British Gas, Rolls-Royce, British Coal, British Airways, National Power, PowerGen and British Rail have all been privatised since 1979. The reasons for privatisation included the belief that, once in private hands, these industries would have to become more efficient as they would have to cope with competition.

Some industries, however, still remain in the private sector. These are:

- the nuclear industry
- the Civil Aviation Authority (CAA)
- defence (including all armed forces)
- National Health Service (NHS).

In addition, all government departments belong in the public sector.

If we look carefully at the organisations in the public sector, we can see that the services they provide should not be in private ownership, because of:

- national security
- the need to ensure that these services are provided for everyone, not only those who can afford them.

Imagine what might happen if the army, the air force and the navy were run by individuals whose aim was only to make a profit, or if there was no nationwide provision of health services for every citizen.

Government departments

Government departments oversee a very wide range of activities which affect all of us. For example, the Department for Education co-ordinates full-time education for all children up to the age of 16, and further and higher education for those over that age. The Foreign and Commonwealth Office is in charge of embassies and consulates all over the world, and promotes British interests and looks after British citizens abroad. The Home Office looks after internal affairs, such as immigration, and is responsible for police, prisons and the probation service. The Department of Social Security operates the social security and benefits system, which includes the implementation of family credits, income support and child benefits.

The departments mentioned above are examples of the wide scope of activities undertaken by government departments. As you can see, all the services that they provide are important to the nation as a whole, although we often take them for granted.

Governmental organisations also include local authorities. These are all controlled by elected representatives. The Home Secretary, for instance, is head of the Home Office, while the Social Services department of your local council is controlled by one of the council's elected councillors.

Public corporations

Public corporations are simply state-owned industries. As you already know, most of these have now been privatised in the UK. Public corporations are like business organisations because they sell goods and services to the community. However, their main aim is to run the industry for the good of the public, and not just to make a profit.

Quangos (Quasi-autonomous non-governmental organisations)

This very complicated name refers to public organisations which are not run directly by the state, but by specially appointed boards. The Training Agency and regional health authorities are quangos, as is the Civil Aviation Authority (CAA).

The public sector also differs from the private sector in one very important aspect. Making a profit is not its main aim. This does not mean that public sector organisations do not have to keep to their budgets or that they can spend as much as they like. Many receive funding from the government. This funding comes from government resources which are made up from money collected through various taxes, including Corporation Tax, VAT and Income Tax. Since we all pay taxes when we work, we can say that we all own the public sector organisations. This is why they are ultimately answerable to us – the public – for the way in which they carry out their responsibilities.

The private sector and its objectives

- BHS
- Thomas Cook
- A restaurant
- PDSA (People's Dispensary for Sick Animals)
- NUS (National Union of Students)
- Your local estate agent
- ICRF (Imperial Cancer Research Fund)
- St Mungo's (charity looking after young homeless people)
- A school or college
- PC World

The 10 organisations listed above are all in the private sector, but not all of them have profit as their main objective. Charity organisations exist to raise funds to support special causes. ICRF, for example, raises money for research into cancer through its shops and various other projects. Educational establishments must operate efficiently within their budgets, but their main aim is to provide the students with the best courses and teaching possible. The PDSA was set up to provide veterinary care for animals whose owners cannot afford to pay for it. St Mungo's supports homeless young people, and raises cash, through donations etc., to provide shelters, food and long-term help and advice for those who have no one else to help them. The NUS is a trade union, established to help its members and to liaise with the Department for Education and various education authorities to try to protect the rights of all students.

Only five organisations in the list are business organisations in the fullest sense, and these are all quite different. British Home Stores and Thomas Cook are well established businesses, while PC World is a very successful but fairly recent chain of stores selling everything needed by the owners of personal computers. The local estate agent deals with buying and selling of property in a particular area, while the restaurant aims to attract people living or working in its vicinity.

To survive, all five must make enough money. A business that consistently makes a loss will, eventually, have to close. It is not true, however, that every business

organisation always sets out to make a profit, or to keep expanding. Businesses which do want to do this are said to aim at achieving **profit maximisation**.

Profit maximisation – making as much profit as possible.

A firm which wants to maximise its profit can do one of several things to achieve its objective.

- It can try to save as much as possible on its factors of production – in other words, to use the cheapest premises, labour and machinery. Nowadays, firms often find that using machines is cheaper than employing people, and so they invest in machinery and reduce their workforce.

- It can concentrate on making goods or providing services for which demand is growing. This needs very careful planning, and can sometimes result in too many companies all providing the same goods and services.

- It can work out the level of production at which the levels of profit are greatest, and remain at that level of production.

- A very large business organisation can adjust its prices or the amount it produces in order to achieve the highest profits.

- In order to stay ahead of competitors, it can try to provide new products. This can be done through a research and development programme and is very expensive, so only very large organisations can do this. A good example is the pharmaceutical industry in which such giants as Glaxo-Wellcome carry out massive research programmes in the hope that they will be able to put new and better products on the market.

Brand leadership

Business organisations know very well that a brand name that has become well known and is recognised everywhere as being good value for money is a great asset for the business. The Body Shop brand name is an example of this. Coca-Cola is another. A leading brand can give a company dominance in a particular market.

Market domination

This means that a business has become so important in its marketplace that it is able to lead the field as far as quality, quantity and price are concerned. A company in this position has stability and security. To achieve market domination, sales must be increased. This sometimes is done through cutting prices (and therefore profits) for a time, hoping that this policy will get rid of competitors. If this is successful, the company can then increase prices and increase profitability.

Growth

A business can grow in different ways. The quickest is the **take-over** route.

> **Take-over** – the process in which a stronger company buys a weaker company.

Another way of growth is through diversification, or introducing new products or services. Growth can also be achieved by expanding existing markets, as we have seen.

Growth is quite often difficult, often risky and usually requires large investment. Sometimes, even when this increase in size is achieved, it does not result in profit maximisation. If the new goods introduced are cheaper and therefore less profitable, overall profits might fall.

It is also a mistake to believe that all businesses always want to grow bigger and bigger.

Surviving

Many businesses do not aim at making a profit, only at making enough to enable them to continue being in business. This is often true of small businesses, such as sole traders. In times of economic difficulties, survival becomes important for many organisations. During the recession of recent years, the building industry was very hard hit, and many building firms simply tried to stay in business, hoping that in a few years the situation would improve.

If surviving is the aim, the business hopes to **break even**. For a relatively short period of time, it might even operate below that point, but no business can go on losing money indefinitely.

> **Break-even point** – a situation in which the income of a business is equal to all its expenditure.

Loss making

This objective sounds quite absurd in business terms, but it does exist. A very large group of companies, most of which make high profits, might be prepared to continue with a loss making member company for two reasons.

1 The high profits earned by the other members will be heavily taxed and the loss maker will help to lower the tax burden on the group as a whole.

2 The loss maker might provide goods or services which the others need and which would cost more if they had to be bought in from an outside supplier.

CASE STUDY

Decision time

Thaddeus Cowper is Chairman of the Board of Directors of Cowper's Garden Centres plc. The company, based in the Midlands, has five garden centres and sells its products directly to the public. Its biggest competitor is Beautiful Gardens plc, with seven centres scattered over the same area. Cowper's Garden Centres' best selling item is its own-brand horticultural multi-purpose fertiliser, sold under the brand name of 'Cowper's Wonder'.

The Board of Directors has recently reviewed the finances of the company, and agreed in principle that the time has come for the firm to expand. However, the directors could not agree how this should be achieved. Here are the views of some of the members of the Board.

- Philip Kirk, Head of Finance, thought that Cowper's Garden Centres should consolidate its position, and concentrate on producing and selling the most profitable lines. He argued that, as interest in gardening has been steadily increasing in recent years, partly as a result of popular gardening TV programmes, the company would maximise its profits by concentrating on 'Cowper's Wonder'. In his opinion, a change in the method of production of the fertiliser would bring down production costs, thus increasing the profits even further.

- Tricia Long, in charge of Sales and Marketing, disagreed strongly with Philip. She was in favour of growth, and suggested that if Cowper's Garden Centres took over Flowers and Stuff Ltd, it would achieve a dominant position in the market, which could then be exploited to increase profits. Flowers and Stuff Ltd, also based in the Midlands, has five garden centres, but is rather old-fashioned, and has not been doing too well in recent years. Tricia is confident that Flowers and Stuff could be acquired at a reasonable price.

- Words of caution came from General Manager, Jonathan Duff. Jonathan said that, in his opinion, the increased demand for gardening products was not likely to continue, and that the best way forward for the company was to continue as it was.

No agreement was reached, and the meeting was adjourned. Thaddeus Cowper now has the task of analysing the suggestions made by his senior staff, and he is not yet sure which is likely to be the best for the firm in the long run.

We have already looked at some businesses which are not profit maximising. There are others which, although structured like commercial ventures, do not list profits as their main objective. One of these is the Big Issue organisation which publishes a weekly magazine sold by the homeless in London, Birmingham and other cities. While the Big Issue tries to make a profit, a large proportion of which is used to provide accommodation and support for the vendors, its main objective is to give the long-term homeless unemployed a way back to work, through selling the magazine and earning money.

Environmental issues

The last decades of the twentieth century brought about a great surge of interest in environmental problems. We all know about global warming, and the dangers of pollution, and more and more people are aware of the need to look after the environment, including dangers to wildlife, and the need to try and provide ourselves and our families with a healthy lifestyle, including a healthy, balanced diet.

The Body Shop, already mentioned on page 7, is the first, and best known, cosmetics manufacturer which guarantees that none of its products have been tested on animals. It also makes sure that the products and raw materials that it buys overseas are grown naturally, and that the people involved in their production are not exploited. Today, many other companies have followed the Body Shop's example.

Even more recent is the public concern resulting from the introduction of GM (genetically modified) foods. A number of large food distributors and manufacturers have decided not to sell GM foodstuffs because of the potential risks to consumers. Opting out of selling GM foods means that the businesses concerned also opt out of raising their profits.

Social factors

Some business organisations have always considered that their prime objectives had to be social, rather than purely profit-orientated. The Consumer Co-operative Movement (CCM) was established not just to sell goods but to improve the lives of all its members. In 1985, the biggest Co-op, the Co-operative Retail Services (CRS) formulated its social goals for the next century. They include:

- offering high quality goods and services at the lowest possible prices
- providing fair return to the members on their investment
- encouraging employees to participate in the democratic structure of the CRS, and providing them with broad training facilities and best possible working conditions
- giving support to voluntary and self-help organisations
- doing everything in its power to protect the environment
- working towards the maintenance of peace.

As you can see, these objectives are much wider than just trying to achieve the greatest possible commercial success.

While very many business organisations do not include social issues in their mission statements, more and more are beginning to include general or specific social aims

in their objectives. In some cases these consist of support for their local communities, sports sponsorships and so on.

To sum up, it is important to remember that although profit figures very largely in the activities of business organisations, it is by no means the only objective.

Other objectives

There are other objectives that many business organisations recognise as important, and include in their list of aims.

Producing high quality products or providing high quality service

Not all organisations wish, or even need, to produce goods of high quality. Some decide to supply cheaper, less well-made goods for which there is a demand. High quality goods carry a high price tag, and not everybody can afford to buy Rolex watches or Rolls-Royce motor cars. There is always demand for goods in a lower price range, which is not to say that these are not of good quality.

High quality service has now become a top priority with many suppliers. Customer care is a recognised area of training, and more and more business organisations realise that the help, information and aftersales service provided leads to customer loyalty and is therefore of prime importance. Big providers, like British Telecom, make customer service an important part of their package of services, and today a large number of organisations ensure that customers' queries and complaints are dealt with promptly and efficiently by skilled staff.

Ensuring that the workforce is skilled and efficient

Most employers today understand that labour is a most important factor of production and also that to get the most out of their workers they must provide training and incentives other than just the wages. In the changing economic climate of the twenty-first century, skill requirements are constantly changing, and workers must be given the opportunity to train and retrain.

It has also been proved (see Chapter 3, page 35) that workers who are valued by their employers are much more likely to be interested in their jobs, and to achieve more. Later on in this unit you will learn about some of the ways in which employers can improve the efficiency of their employees.

Conclusion

All organisations exist for a purpose, and business organisations exist to satisfy our needs and wants. In a complex economy such as ours, there are many kinds of organisations, some private, some public, with many different objectives. Although it is true to say that profit is the most important objective of business organisations, it is not the only one, as we have seen. The order of priority in which a business puts its objectives influences the way the company operates and its attitudes to its employees and its customers. These attitudes are known as business cultures, and you will learn more about them later on.

Revision Questions

1 What is meant by the term 'basic needs'?
(1 mark)

2 Why are some people's 'needs' other people's 'luxuries'? (4 marks)

3 Give three examples of goods that we now consider necessities but which would have been thought of as luxuries 50 years ago. (3 marks)

4 Why do we buy consumer goods much more often than we buy durable goods? (2 marks)

5 What are capital goods? Give two examples.
(2 marks)

6 What is meant by a service? (1 mark)

7 Why do we need more services today than our grandparents did 50 or 60 years ago?
(3 marks)

8 Name two service industries that satisfy a need, and two that satisfy a want. (4 marks)

9 What is privatisation, and why were many British public sector industries privatised?
(6 marks)

10 Why should the armed forces not be in private ownership? (2 marks)

11 What is a quango? Give three examples.
(2 marks)

12 How does the Government fund the public sector? (2 marks)

13 Name three types of organisations in the private sector which do not have profit as their main objective. (3 marks)

14 How can a business try to maximise its profits?
(4 marks)

15 What does 'brand leadership' mean? Give four examples. (3 marks)

16 Why is growth often risky for a business organisation? (8 marks)

17 Why do some businesses aim only at breaking even? (2 marks)

18 With reference to the case study 'Decision Time', what advice would you give to Thaddeus Cowper? (10 marks)

19 Why have environmental and social issues become important to business organisations?
(3 marks)

20 How can employers ensure that their workers are skilled and efficient? (2 marks)

CHAPTER 2

Types of Business

KEY TERMS:

unlimited liability

limited liability

incorporated

unincorporated

co-operative

recession

turnover

venture capital

downsize

In this chapter you will learn about:

- the difference between the private sector, the public sector, and charities

- aspects of the different types of business ownership: sole traders, partnerships, private and public limited companies, franchises, and co-operatives

- the difference between businesses in terms of the liability of their owners, the use of profits and sources of finance.

Introduction

There are a number of ways of classifying a business. It could be in the private sector, as more than 3.5 million UK businesses are; in which case it has making a profit as one of its main objectives. Or, if we accept the very broad definition of a business organisation, as set out in the first chapter of this section, it could be in the public sector. In that case its purpose will be to provide a service for the whole community, a service which will be paid for out of taxation, at either a local or national level. A business may also be in the voluntary sector, which is usually regarded as a branch of the private sector. Charities obviously fall under this heading as they are a separate group – they are not profit making organisations in the sense that a private sector enterprise is, nor are they state owned. They are, however, regulated by the state.

Business organisations can also be classified in one of the following industrial sectors:

- primary

- secondary

- tertiary or service.

Which of the these classifications is appropriate in any given case will depend on what is being done at that stage with the product or service. The oil industry, for example, spans all three sectors. Drilling for crude oil is an extractive enterprise and is part of the primary sector. When it is refined into petrol, crude oil is processed and this is a secondary sector activity. The distribution and selling of petrol is clearly in the service sector. The business activities of a company like British Petroleum cover all three sectors as it is engaged in extracting, processing and selling.

If we examine private businesses more closely, we see that they are not all established or organised in the same way, so someone who might be considering starting a business would have to make a number of decisions:

1 What are the aims and objectives of the business?

2 How will it be financed?

3 What type of legal status should it have?

As we shall see in the course of this chapter, question 3 is a rather important choice to make.

CASE STUDY

BERNARD MATTHEWS

Bernard Matthews created the business which bears his name. Starting with a few turkeys and a very small investment, Bernard Matthews has gone from strength to strength, and today his company dominates the pre-packed sliced meat market in the UK.

In the view of the organisation's founder, the most important aspect is that it operates through vertical integration. The company owns its poultry farms and processing and packaging plants, so all stages of production can be controlled. This has contributed to the high standard of the final product.

A business organisation's legal status can be recognised by its name. It is not only misleading, but inaccurate, to use such terms as company, firm, organisation, and partnership as if they were interchangeable. They each have a precise legal meaning. An understanding of the different types of private businesses is necessary before an informed choice can be made about business types. Realistically, however, someone starting a business is unlikely to look beyond the first three types listed below:

- sole trader
- partnership
- private limited company
- public limited company
- co-operative
- charity, or not-for-profit organisation
- franchise.

Sole trader

When the term 'sole trader' is used in connection with a business, it describes the status and legal ownership of the enterprise. It simply means that the firm is owned by one person who is self-employed. He or she conducts the business on his or her own behalf and not in conjunction with anyone else. As 'sole trader' is a legal term, it tells us nothing about the size of the enterprise, although the vast majority are very small firms. Typically, one person runs the whole business, perhaps with the help of one or two employees.

In 1971 the government set up the Bolton Committee and asked it to report on the importance and place of small firms in the UK economy. One of the committee's problems was to reach agreement on an acceptable definition of the term 'small firm'. It eventually suggested that the majority of small firms had the following characteristics:

- a small share of the market
- managed personally by their owners rather than through a management structure
- independent; the owners make all major decisions.

On the other hand, the 1985 Companies Act defines a small firm as one with a **turnover** below £1.4 million and having fewer than 50 employees. These particular characteristics could, of course, apply equally to sole traders, partnerships or private limited companies.

> **Turnover** – the amount of money taken in a business; the total sales of the business in a year.

The sole trader is the most common form of business organisation in the UK. It is often found in the craft occupations. These include shoe-repairers, electricians and plumbers; but you will also find that market-stall holders and the person running the local corner-shop are likely to be sole traders. We will also see that they play an important role in the start-up of the newer high-tech industries. Fig. 1.2.1 places sole trader occupation in industrial groupings. As you will note, it covers a wide range of activities.

Figure 1.2.1 Sole traders by industrial groupings

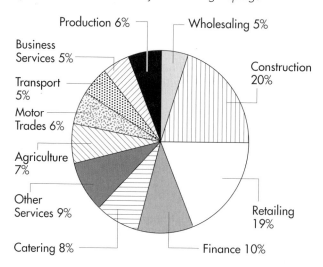

Essentially, a sole trader's business operates at a local level. The business is usually financed from the owner's savings, with additional borrowings from family and friends. Banks and other traditional lenders in the UK are often unwilling to make loans to such businesses. This reluctance has been identified as a real weakness in our economy, as it has the effect of stifling emerging enterprise, which is very bad news for Britain. The difficulty of raising finance, either to start a new business or to expand an existing one, is a problem experienced not only by sole traders but also by partnerships and private limited companies.

The situation in the USA is, however, markedly different. There, the attitude of banks and **venture capital** institutions to new business propositions is positive and supportive, particularly if the proposal is in the area of high technology. A recent study found that the percentage of the population involved in business start-ups in the whole of Europe was only a quarter of that in the US. As a consequence, Europe in general, and the UK in particular, suffer from a shortage of so-called 'gazelles' (rapidly growing, profitable, small firms). These companies are estimated to have created 80 per cent of new jobs in the USA in recent years.

Venture capital – risk capital, usually supplied in the form of a loan, as an investment in a small or medium sized business.

Nevertheless, there has been growth in the small-firm sector in the UK, but it has come about as a result of structural changes in our economy, particularly over the past 30 years. For example:

- The service sector, in contrast to the primary and secondary sectors, has grown and it is particularly well suited to small business.

- An increasing number of large manufacturing and service organisations, both private and public, have subcontracted many of their products and processes. Small firms have sprung up to take advantage of the new opportunities this has presented.

- The continuing tendency of large firms to **downsize** has resulted in redundancies, especially among middle-level managers. They have often used their redundancy payment as start-up capital for new ventures after having difficulty in finding other employment. In periods of **recession**, like the early 1990s, the move into self-employment was particularly marked.

Downsize – to reduce the number of people employed by a business.

Recession – a period in which there is a decline in economic activity, trade and prosperity, usually accompanied by growing unemployment.

A serious disadvantage of operating as a sole trader is that while the proprietor keeps all the profits generated by the business, he or she also has to accept **unlimited liability** with regard to any losses and, in the event of the business becoming insolvent, must bear the losses personally. This could lead to the sole trader having to sell off personal assets, such as a house or a car, to satisfy creditors' demands. It follows, then, that this form of business carries high risks and is only appropriate for a person who wants to have complete control of an enterprise and intends to keep it relatively small in scale.

Unlimited liability – the type of liability in which the owners of a business (usually a sole trader or a partner) are responsible for all business losses.

To summarise: running a business as a sole trader has both advantages and disadvantages. Among the advantages are:

- The owner is free to manage the business as he or she sees fit and also has the freedom of being his or her own boss.

- There are no legal requirements before starting the business.

- Annual accounts do not need to be audited by a chartered accountant and business affairs can be kept private.

- The owner enjoys all the profit generated by the business.

- Business decisions are made very quickly.

Among the disadvantages are:

- Unlimited liability means that if the business fails, the owner is personally responsible for all debts.

- Lack of continuity means that, on the death or retirement of the owner, the business ceases to exist.

- There may be difficulty in raising outside capital to start the business (banks are also hesitant to lend money at reasonable rates even when the business is already up and running).

- One person has to take the whole responsibility for making decisions.

- The hours of work are very long and this has an effect on the proprietor's health and family life.

Partnerships

Forming a partnership is one possible solution to overcoming some of the disadvantages associated with running a business as a sole trader. A partnership is a way of sharing the problems, risks, hard work, and, indeed, the isolation which will always be a part of trying to manage all aspects of a business of your own. Of course, an important concern is finding the right partner(s) to work with, because, legally, each partner could find him or herself responsible for the whole debt

of the business partnership if it becomes insolvent. This means that if one partner, perhaps as the result of an unfortunate business decision, involves the partnership in a large debt, each of the other partners is liable (responsible) for it because partners, like sole traders, have unlimited liability for the debts of a business.

Starting up a partnership is neither very involved nor particularly expensive. The Partnership Act 1890 states that a partnership comes into being when 'between two and twenty people agree to supply capital and work together in a business with the purpose of making a profit'. In the eyes of the law the partners themselves are *the* business, in the same way that the sole trader is *the* business. Legally, both of these types of business are **unincorporated**.

Unincorporated – a legal term which applies to a sole trader or a partnership in which the actual business and its owner(s) are treated by the courts as if they were the same, i.e. have **unlimited liability**.

Firms of doctors, accountants, veterinary surgeons and solicitors are invariably partnerships. In fact, if these professionals wish to work together as a group, they have little choice but to operate as partners as there are legal restrictions to them operating as a limited company, a form of business which we will examine next. Partnerships are also found in the retail, catering and building industries, but are by no means restricted to these areas, as can be seen in Figure 1.2.2.

Figure 1.2.2 Partnerships by industrial groupings

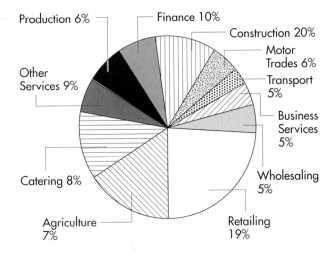

Activity

Make a list of 12 small businesses in the neighbourhood in which you live. Enter the information you have gathered in a table like the one below:

Name of business	Type of business	Product or service	Number of employees	When established

You may have to find some of the answers by asking the owner or someone working in the business.

When the table is completed, answer the following questions.

1 To which sector of production do the 12 businesses belong?

2 Did any of them require a very large initial capital outlay?

3 Have any been operating for 10 years or more?

Whereas sole traders usually carry on their businesses locally, partnerships, in particular solicitors and accountants, often operate nationally. The headquarters of the practice might be in London and have branches in the provinces. Nor does it end there: the vital importance to the UK of the European Union (EU), with which it has more than half of its trade, has led to the need for solicitors and accountants to establish offices in Brussels and in other major towns throughout the EU. This international dispersal is now a necessity if solicitors etc. are to provide the on-the-spot services demanded by clients who themselves have international interests.

Figure 1.2.2

Ambitious Lawyers & Partners

There are people out there who say you can't build a high-level law firm from scratch. That the most exciting work and biggest names will always stay with the magic circle. These are the same people who maintain you can fully service the biggest of today's corporate clients without being able to offer a full range of professional services.

Some people believe in recognising the future and some don't. The believers are the founding partners of KLegal. They have seen that the globalisation of business necessitates a fundamental shift in the nature of the practice of law, and have created a new firm to embrace this challenge. KLegal's support comes from the highest levels of KPMG, but our structure,

client base and future success will be created in their entirety by you.

Take a fresh look and help build a firm that will shape the future of law. We are looking for ambitious lawyers and partners in Banking, Corporate, Employment, Intellectual Property, IT/Telecoms and Property with experience gained in a leading City practice. For a confidential discussion please call Yvonne Smyth or Debbie Cochrane at ZMB on 0171 523 3838 (evenings/weekends 0181 374 8455) Fax: 0171 523 3839. Alternatively write to them at ZMB, 37 Sun Street, London EC2M 2PL.
Email: debbie.cochrane@zarakgroup.com

KLegal, solicitors: associated law firm of KPMG

A whole new world.

As we have mentioned, partnerships are regulated by the Partnership Act 1890. It is sensible, however, for them to conduct their business in line with the terms of a **partnership agreement**, a form of contract drawn up by solicitors. This document sets out details of the capital to be contributed by each partner, their voting rights, the share of profits (and losses) and the procedure to be followed in the event of partnership disputes. Prudent partners will certainly insist on a partnership agreement being put in place before they commence business.

The advantages of a partnership include:

• the potential to raise more capital than a sole trader, because there are more individuals to contribute funds

• a greater range of skills and the sharing of responsibilities

• no necessity to make financial accounts publicly available (unlike a limited company).

Among the disadvantages of a partnership are:

• unlimited liability – each partner being liable for the whole debt of the partnership and risking personal bankruptcy if the business becomes insolvent

• disagreements among partners which sometimes result in the dissolution of the partnership and the business

• business decisions take longer to make, as a wrong decision can have serious consequences for all the partners.

CASE STUDY

Decisions

Liam, Annette, Jatinder, and Luke have been friends for several years. Having completed their Vocational A Level Business, they have now decided to set up in business. This decision has not proved popular with most of their parents who thought that going to university would be a better option. However, the friends are determined, but are finding it difficult to agree on the type of business.

As they do not have a lot of money, they know that their business must be one that does not need a large capital investment. They have talked over several ideas:

1   Jatinder and Liam are very keen to start a motorcycle courier service. They both have motorcycles of their own, and think that such a venture needs nothing more than a telephone number for customers to use. They want Luke to take his motorcycle driving test as soon as possible (he is already learning) and Annette to look after the customer enquiries, etc.

2   Annette and Luke do not like the courier service idea. They consider it very risky as there is already so much well established competition in the city. They have done a bit of research and have come to the conclusion that a small sandwich bar in the city centre would be a good idea. There are many students and office workers in the area and not many fast food places. Annette has suggested that they could utilise the motorcycling skills of their two friends by offering a sandwich delivery service. She herself is quite capable of organising the food and drink side of the business. Luke and Annette realise that the initial outlay would be much greater.

Limited liability companies

What is a company? A company is set up to run a business. Unlike a sole trader or a partnership, which are unincorporated businesses, it has to be registered before it can start to operate, but once all the paperwork is completed and approved, the company becomes registered as a legal body.

Unlike a sole trader or partnership, a limited liability company is also a separate legal entity and is recognised as being distinct from its owners. It is owned by shareholders and managed by directors who run the company in the shareholders' interest. Put another way, ownership of the business and management of the business are separate from each other. Due to the protection given by **limited liability**, shareholders are not personally liable for the company's debts. In the event of the business failing, their loss is limited to the amount of money which they invested in the company. This is obviously an important advantage. However, limited liability comes at a price and, to deter the possibility of fraud, the company is subject to a number of legal and administrative requirements from the time the business is set up. These are regulations that unincorporated firms like sole traders and partnerships are able to avoid.

Limited liability – the type of liability in which a shareholder of a private limited company or public limited company is only liable for the amount of money invested in the business.

Incorporated – a legal term which applies to private and public limited companies where the business and its owners, the shareholders, are regarded as separate, i.e. the shareholders have **limited liability**.

There are two forms of limited company:

*   the private limited company (Ltd)
*   the public limited company (plc).

The private limited company

Many small to medium sized businesses trade as private limited companies. This is also the path often followed by sole traders and partnerships when they wish to expand their operations but still retain control of the business. Private limited companies are usually family businesses with the company's shares owned by family members. These shares cannot be sold to the public, which obviously limits the firm's ability to raise finance. They can, however, be transferred and sold to other shareholders within the company. The shareholders and directors of private limited companies are invariably the same people.

Private limited companies far outnumber public limited companies (see later). There are approximately 500,000 in the UK, mostly modest in size, but quite important, considering the numbers of people they employ. Furthermore, they have the potential to innovate and grow. Many plcs which, today, are household names started life as private limited companies. Mostly, private limited companies operate locally from a single site, but many also supply their products and services nationally or even internationally.

Advantages of private limited companies:

- limited liability for shareholders
- greater potential to raise capital
- benefits of economies of scale and use of specialist staff.

Disadvantages of private limited companies:

- the expense of setting up, especially the legal costs
- the accounts have to be audited and this is expensive
- increased paperwork associated with the legal requirements to submit annual returns and financial statements
- details of the company's accounts must be published annually and consequently become available for inspection by competitors, customers and suppliers.

Small firms as creators of jobs

We have already made reference to the role of small firms as 'seed beds' for high-technology industries. Traditionally, they have also been seen as important generators of new jobs. Support for this view has come from the highest level of government. In 1996, John Major, the Conservative Prime Minister, said, 'Small businesses are the backbone of our economy and the main source of future jobs.' This opinion is shared by the present Labour Government, whose spokesman was reported as saying, '… we know small businesses are big job creators'. However, a recent report of the Trades Union Congress (TUC) seriously challenges this view. When it undertook its own investigation the TUC found that the number of jobs created by small firms had been greatly overstated.

The report examined the statistics set out in Tables 1.2.3, 1.2.4 and 1.2.5 and showed that although micro firms (i.e. those with no employees, the self-employed), plus small firms, constituted between them 99 per cent of all businesses, they accounted for only about 48 per cent of all employment and only 28 per cent of total sales. On the other hand, medium and large companies, which comprise the remaining 1 per cent of firms, contributed 52 per cent to overall employment and nearly three-quarters of all sales. These findings demonstrate the overwhelming importance to the UK economy of medium and large businesses, in terms both of employment and output.

In addition, there is evidence that small firms are responsible for as many job losses as job gains. According to figures supplied by a leading bank, in 1995 1,227 new businesses were started each day in Britain – and there were 1,205 closures – a net daily gain of only 22. On an annual basis this amounted to around 8,000 new businesses, the overwhelming majority of which were one-person businesses. This is not an impressive record, especially when it is realised that the majority of jobs in small firms tend to be insecure, low skilled and generally poorly paid. Serious, long-term, skilled jobs are most likely to be generated by relatively small numbers of rapidly growing large companies.

Table 1.2.1

Number of businesses by size of firm, 1994	
Total number of businesses in the UK	3.7 million
Micro firms (0–9 employees) (of which those with no employees, i.e. self-employed)	3.5 million (94%) 2.4 million (67%)
Small firms (10–49 employees)	171,000 (5%)
Medium firms (50–249 employees)	26,000 (0.7%)
Large firms (250+ employees)	6,200 (0.2%)

Table 1.2.2

Share of UK employment by size of firm, 1994	
Size of firm	**%**
Micro	32
Small	16
Medium	13
Large	39

Table 1.2.3

Turnover contribution by size of firm, 1994	
Contribution	**% of total turnover**
Micro	12
Small	16
Medium	25
Large	47

Public limited companies

Plcs are similar to private limited companies, but are usually much larger. They are able to raise capital by selling their shares on the London Stock Exchange if they are listed. The shares of some of the largest plcs are also traded on the New York and Tokyo stock exchanges. This enables plcs to raise very large sums of money in a way that is much cheaper than borrowing from banks which is the only channel, apart from personal funds, available to the other types of businesses we have investigated. There is a risk, however, that the original shareholders can lose control of their business if large quantities of its shares are purchased as part of a hostile takeover bid.

Public limited companies were created by the Companies Act 1980 and, by law, must have the words 'public limited company', or, more usually, the abbreviation 'plc', after the name of the company. Their right to trade shares and raise money on the Stock Exchange are features that, in recent years, have made them a very attractive form of business organisation to some building societies and even football clubs, in particular to the owners of these organisations. Both have been keen to exchange their present legal form of ownership for the more flexible and potentially profitable 'plc'. There are a number of reasons why some building societies are especially keen to adopt the plc status:

1   They say that customers now demand a wider range of financial services, similar to those provided by banks.

2   Building societies need to be able to grow if they are to be able to compete profitably with banks, and only plc status will allow them to achieve this.

3   The rules under which building societies operate are too restrictive. The managements of building societies claim that while these rules may have been acceptable for most of the last hundred years, during which period the desire for home ownership, as opposed to renting, was being satisfied, in the new century the building societies will need a more flexible form of organisation. In their opinion the best way of exploiting future opportunities in the financial world is by way of the plc.

Could there also be a conflict of interest between the needs of building societies and Premier League clubs and the fact that the managers and owners stand to gain financially from their organisations converting to plcs?

21

CASE STUDY

ABBEY NATIONAL

Converting to a Public Limited Company

Abbey National is the UK's second largest mortgage lender, helping over 2 million people to buy their homes. The lending is funded through the savings and investment accounts of some 10 million customers and through money raised on the wholesale lending markets.

As well as mortgage and savings operations, Abbey National offers a range of personal financial services, including pensions and insurance. Abbey National's origins go back to the building society movement of the nineteenth century, when a group of people would club together and pool their funds in order to buy every member of the group a home. The early societies were known as 'terminating societies', and would break up when every member had a house.

The next step was the development of 'permanent societies', where there were two groups of people: savers and borrowers. Savers put their money into the society and earned interest on the savings. Borrowers took out loans to buy houses (mortgages) and repaid them, with interest, over a period of 20 to 25 years.

Abbey National was formed in 1944 by a merger of two other societies: Abbey Road Building Society and National Building Society.

Background to plc

The 1980s and 1990s have been a period of profound change in the financial services market. To understand Abbey National's decision to convert to a plc, it is important to understand the major forces for change.

1   Financial deregulation removed some previously existing restrictions on what the various financial institutions were allowed to do – most importantly, banks were now allowed into the mortgage market.

2   Abbey National wanted to expand and, to do this, had to be able to raise more funding than that obtained from building society funds.

3   The 1986 Building Societies Act allowed building societies to become plcs.

Decision

Abbey National realised that if it was going to thrive in the twenty-first century, it would need the freedom of action to diversify and to make more use of wholesale funding. Building societies might be left behind if they remained essentially 'one product' home loans businesses when banks were moving into their market. Abbey National wanted the freedom to compete with the banks on a level playing field – which it could not do as a building society.

Going public

Before Abbey National became a plc, a number of hurdles had to be cleared:

1   A majority of members (there were 5 million at the time) had to support the change, with at least 20% of members voting.

2   The Bank of England had to authorise the change of status to a bank.

3   The Building Societies Commission, which regulates building societies, had to approve the conversion.

The decision to convert was made in 1989, after a massive vote in favour by Abbey National's members. All the members were given an equal number of shares in the new plc, and the right to buy additional shares.

The Bank of England and the Building Societies Commission both approved the conversion. Today, it has been proved that the decision was the right one. The company's pre-tax profit in 1994 was £932 million, almost double 1989's figure of £501 million. On 30 June 1995 Abbey National was the fourth largest bank in the UK, with assets of £94 billion.

Source: The Abbey National Group

Some experts say that, these days, the plc is the only viable form of large-business organisation as it has many legal advantages over all other types of business. One of the most important of these is limited liability, the other is its ability to raise substantial sums of money. There are strong arguments in support of the view that, without these advantages, many businesses would not have grown to the size that is necessary in order to operate economically and profitably. The risks to investors and owners would have been too great.

It should be understood that although the plc is the dominant form of business organisation in Europe and the USA, it is not universal. In Japan large business structures, known as **keiretsu**, are the norm. Among the best known of these are Mitsubishi and Mitsui. In South Korea, the **chaebol**, a very large, tightly controlled family business, is preferred. Daewoo, the car maker, is an example of this form.

However, as we have seen, plcs are a very important part of the UK economy – without doubt the most important in terms of the wealth and employment they create. Many are household names, e.g. Marks & Spencer, Barclays, BP, Tesco, British Airways, British Gas, and British Telecom. The last three were once nationalised businesses, managed by the state on behalf of the public. Over the last 20 years they have been privatised and, like all other private companies, are now owned by shareholders and run with the main purpose of making profits for their owners. We will examine the role of public sector organisations later in this chapter.

Table 1.2.4 The advantages and disadvantages of public limited companies (plcs)

Advantages	Disadvantages
• The shareholders (owners) have limited liability	• The founder owners can lose control of the company because its shares can be readily bought on the stock exchange
• The shares in the company can be freely bought and sold	
• The company can more easily raise the substantial amounds of capital (money) which it needs for expansion and development	• Starting a plc is expensive compared with other types of business and requires a great deal of documentation
• Banks and other financial institutions are more willing to lend the company money, usually at preferential rates of interest	• Large organisations can become difficult to manage efficiently; staff often feel ignored by a remote management
• The company's continued existence does not depend on the founders of the business	• Detailed financial accounts must be published each year, providing valuable information to competitors and prospective take-over companies
• As large organisations, plcs benefit from economies of scale, for instance cheaper borrowing and bulk purchasing	

The co-operative

The **co-operative** is a form of business in which people join together to make decisions, share the work and share any profits. There are two types of co-operative trading organisations:

- a retail co-operative society, which is set up under the terms of the Industrial and Provident Societies Acts
- producer or worker co-operatives in which a group of people come together to produce goods or provide a service.

Retail co-operative societies

There were about 80 co-operatives in the UK by the 1990s. The best known example of a retail co-operative is 'the Co-op', which now operates the Leo's supermarket chain. These are regional stores, usually found in traditional industrial areas and, in the past two decades, they have been in decline. This is mainly because of the intense competition in the retail sector from companies such as Sainsbury's, Tesco, Waitrose and Asda. A number of smaller co-operatives still pay dividends to customers, but the majority of the larger ones use profits to improve facilities and to make prices more competitive.

Today, in addition to retail outlets, the co-operative movement includes the Co-operative Bank, milk and delivery services, funeral services and the Co-operative Insurance Society.

Producer or worker co-operatives

Producer co-operatives have been reasonably successful in agriculture, where groups of farmers have banded together and shared marketing and production costs. The wine co-operatives of southern France are an example of this. Agricultural co-operative movements are also to be found in Denmark, New Zealand and Israel.

Worker co-operatives came to prominence in Britain in the 1970s. This was a time of rising unemployment when many employees were made redundant. Faced with the certain prospect of losing their jobs, the threatened workers banded together and, collectively, used their redundancy money to take over the running of their failing firms. These enterprises then became worker co-operatives. Initially, the workers accepted reduced wages because they expected eventually to share in the company's profits. Some were successful, but many were not. One example of a successful venture was the Tower Colliery.

The Tower Colliery in South Wales was closed by British Coal in 1994. Although it was profitable, its owners believed that the uncertainty of future demand for coal, particularly from the electricity-generating industry, meant that the colliery's long-term future was in doubt. There was then little chance of alternative employment for miners in the South Wales valleys, particularly if they were middle-aged, as many of them were. The prospect of spending the rest of their working lives on the dole provided the powerful incentive to establish a worker co-operative. New capital was raised from a number of sources and the business was restructured, new markets found, and, in due course, a successful business was rebuilt.

Employee share ownership

A variation of the worker co-operative idea is the Employee Share Ownership Plan (ESOP). This is a way of enabling staff to share in a company's financial success. In addition to a salary, the employee receives a percentage of the firm's profits. ESOPs have proved very popular in America, but have been much slower to catch on in Britain. An example of a successful British ESOP is the Baxi Partnership, the country's largest staff owned manufacturer and one of the top domestic boiler and central heating firms.

The franchise

This is a fairly recent but fast growing form of business ownership in the UK. It works this way. A well known company with a successful product or service gives another firm the right to make, service or sell its products in a particular area. The idea originated in the USA where nearly 40 per cent of all retail business is done on a franchise basis.

The firm that sells the franchise is called the franchiser. The person or firm that buys the franchise is referred to as the franchisee. The franchiser helps the franchisee to set up the business by providing training and business advice, supplying equipment and materials, and sometimes even helping to find a suitable location. Of great importance is that the franchiser usually takes responsibility for promoting and marketing the product. In exchange for all this support the franchiser

At the coal face – Tower Colliery workers take control

The miners of Tower Colliery, the last deep mine in South Wales, marched back to work on January 3rd, not only as owners of their own pit but also apparently vindicated in their belief that there is a long-term market for the anthracite coal that they produce.

Perched near the bleak upland moors of the Brecon Beacons, Tower was closed last April by British Coal. Despite consistently making a profit, British Coal seemed to believe that uncertainty over demand from the nearby Aberthaw power station meant that Tower's long-term future was shaky. Now, however, the pit's future has been secured with £70m-worth of contracts over the next five years. Goitre Tower Anthracite, a new company formed by the men, has already sold the 430,000 tonnes it will produce in the next 12 months in deals worth about £20m. A leader of the workers' buy-out, Tyrone O'Sullivan, the pit's former union secretary and now the firm's personnel director, says Tower recently turned down an offer from a German company to buy 500,000 tonnes of coal. Mr O'Sullivan claims that British Coal was also anxious to close the mine quickly to make it easier to sell to the pit's managers, rather than its miners. 'Our campaign of resistance to the closure made the management buy-out politically impossible,' he recalls. Miners refused a £9000 redundancy package and insisted that the pit be put into the government's lengthy closure-review procedure. British Coal agreed not to close the pit, but only on condition that the miners accepted 12-hour working days, six-day weeks and the loss of redundancy pay.

Faced with this pressure the men voted to accept closure but launched their own buy-out with the redundancy money they received: 228 miners and 11 managers each put up £8000. Price Waterhouse assembled a roster of institutional investors, headed by Barclays Bank, to lend money to the new firm. The miners' bid, thought to amount to about £3m, beat those from PowerGen and Wimpey.

An 11-strong team of worker-managers will run the pit from day to day. It has appointed three of the firm's five board directors, including Cliff Jones, the new boss of the pit and a former British Coal pit manager. The workers have directly elected the two remaining directors. The company's unpaid, non-executive, non-voting chairman is the respected former director of the South Wales Region of British Coal, 74-year-old Philip Weekes. 'The miners know best how to work the pit,' he says.

Output will be controlled to ensure long-term job security. On British Coal's own estimate, there are enough reserves to last at least ten years at the projected rate of exploitation. British Coal's bonus-pay system is being replaced with an across-the-board basic wage. This will curb overtime but provide a £70-a-week general increase, taking wages to between £15,000 and £18,000 a year. 'We aim to demonstrate that we can improve safety and run a company without old-fashioned conflict and low wages,' says Mr O'Sullivan. Sounds wonderful.

Source: The Economist, January 5 1995

charges a fee for its services and also, each year, after allowing a suitable period for the new business to get established, takes a percentage of the franchisee's turnover.

Examples of franchises are to be found in all Britain's high streets. Most often these are fast food outlets, for example, McDonald's, KFC and Pizza Hut. Non-food franchises include printing services (Prontaprint) and petrol stations (Shell). Probably the best known British franchiser is The Body Shop, which has in excess of 900 franchisees worldwide.

A franchise agreement allows a trader to become his or her own boss by avoiding some of the attendant risks of setting up a business from scratch (you will remember that eight out of 10 new businesses fail within the first two years of operation). However, the reduction of risk comes at a price. A well known and much sought-after franchise, like McDonald's, in a big city location, will cost the franchisee at least £250,000 – and that's just for the licence.

What is on offer with a Prontaprint franchise?

Prontaprint is the UK's largest network of franchised design, print and copy business service centres, with 220 outlets. It offers franchisees:

- training and other start-up support
- innovative technology that allows the franchisee to be highly competitive
- central marketing with advertising and promotion that ensure that the Prontaprint name is the leader in the field
- central buying that allows outlets to keep their costs low
- financial support in starting the business.

For an established business to become a Prontaprint franchisee, the following finances and terms are typical:

Total start-up costs		£100,000
Contribution paid by franchisee		£40,000
Royalties to be paid by franchisee		10%
Contract period		10 years
Typical turnover	1st year	£200,000
	2nd year	£250,000
Profits	1st year	£24,000
	2nd year	£45,000

Charities

Charities are not primarily profit making organisations, but, as previously stated, they do form part of the private sector, and exist for the purpose of helping people and promoting special causes. They therefore have a somewhat different approach to business than that of the other organisations we have examined.

It would be giving the wrong impression if this suggests that the best known charities are in any way 'amateurish' organisations. Many are run in a very professional manner, employ well paid fundraisers and public relations staff, and organise nationwide and sometimes worldwide advertising campaigns.

Figure 1.2.3

FUNDRAISING   MARKETING   COMMUNICATIONS

TRINITY HOSPICE
Specialists in Palliative Care

Does a job that involves this mix excite and challenge you? Then read on...

Director of Fundraising & Marketing

Based: Clapham Common

Salary up to £40,000

Trinity Hospice is a leading centre for the care of patients with progressive advanced illness and limited prognosis. We provide the highest quality of holistic care in an environment that reflects our patients' special needs. With 30 in-patient beds, day care facilities and highly developed support for patients at home, Trinity has pioneered the provision of seamless palliative care.

Following the recent appointment of a new Chief Executive, we are on the threshold of exciting developments. This new role will be a pivotal one on the Senior Management Team, involved in overall strategic planning, increasing awareness, developing our supporter base and launching a capital appeal.

The current income is £1.5m (excluding trading), with the potential to double this in 3 years.

We require someone with a successful track record of fundraising, combined with creative marketing and internal and external communications skills, who will review and rejuvenate marketing and communications in an innovative way.

If you are inspired by the opportunity to think laterally, to deliver a radical fundraising strategy, and to position a positive marketing image for this fabulous hospice contact our Consultant: Adele Bird, Director, Charity Recruitment, 40 Rosebery Avenue, London EC1R 4RX, fax: 0171 833 0188, e-mail: ab@charityrec.source.co.uk for further information.

Closing date for applications: 29 October 1999. First interviews 4 and 5 November.
Final interviews on 17 November. For additional details see charityopps.com

Currently, Britain has approximately 200,000 registered charities with assets amounting to £25 billion. Technically speaking they operate as **trusts**, which is a legal arrangement in which people called trustees are responsible for holding funds and other assets which have been donated to the charity by the public. Recent legislation has allowed the trustees of charities greater freedom to invest their assets on the stock market.

Figure 1.2.4

Charities to get investment boost

By Gavin Lumsden

THE £25 billion charity sector is poised to be given wider investment powers which could substantially increase the amount charities can invest in the stock market.

The Charity Commission will today signal that it is prepared to take a more flexible approach to the investment policies used by charities.

Under the Trustee Investment Act of 1961 the bulk of the charitable sector has been barred from putting more than 75 per cent of its assets into equities.

Although less than half the sector's funds are actually invested in shares, this ruling has restricted many charitable foundations.

Michael Carpenter, the Commission's legal commissioner, will today tell a conference that the organisation is prepared to take a more lenient approach to requests from charities that want to adopt more profitable investment strategies.

Mr Carpenter said: "We are aware that our policies need to be regularly refreshed and we have been reviewing our response to wider investment powers, and we expect to settle and revise a new policy very soon."

Commentary, page 35

Source: The Times, October 20 1999

A charitable trust can be set up for any of the following purposes:

- to relieve poverty (e.g. Oxfam, War on Want)
- to advance education (e.g. a private school)
- to promote religion (e.g. the maintenance of places of worship)
- to protect the environment (e.g. Nature Conservancy Trust, Greenpeace).

An organisation with charitable status is exempt from many of the legal obligations to which other organisations are subject. This applies in particular to matters of taxation. A charity must, however, comply with other legal requirements such as health and safety and employment legislation. It must also keep accurate records, just like a company, and if, due to incompetence or misuse of funds, it became bankrupt, the trustees would be held both legally and financially responsible.

Businesses also give to charities. Their donations attract special tax concessions. Many firms take part in a scheme that promotes the idea that these companies should give 1 per cent of their profits to charity. However, this has proved to be an over-ambitious goal, as Figure 1.2.5 illustrates. To date, only one company has met the target.

Figure 1.2.5 Top givers (as a percentage of their pre-tax profit)

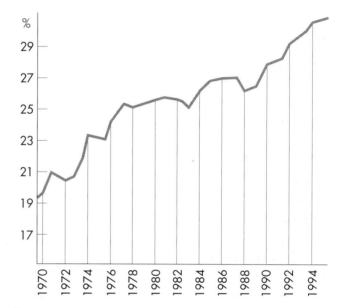

Source for figures: Accounting & Business Magazine, Corporate Survey, March 1999.

International and global business

Earnings from exports are a very significant part of the UK's gross national product (GNP). In 1995 this amounted to £153 billion and was an important contribution to the nation's standard of living and quality of life. Currently, about 30 per cent of the UK GNP comes from export activities. This is one of the highest percentages of any country in the world.

Figure 1.2.6 Percentage of UK GNP earned from exports

Many of the businesses that we have examined are involved in the export of goods and services. Initially, a business may only be concerned with using up spare production capacity, but it soon realises that trading overseas will, in many cases, help it to gain in other ways. The following are some of the advantages:

- higher earnings – profit margins in some overseas markets can exceed those in the home market
- spreading risks – a downturn in home markets may be compensated for by an upturn in export markets
- the benefits of economies of scale – larger production runs by manufacturing businesses help to reduce unit costs.

The international business environment has changed greatly during the last decade. This is a change that has been labelled by some writers as a truly global shift. They already recognise a world in which business is rapidly progressing away from localised, national and regional markets towards a system where markets are combining into one vast global market place in which national tastes, fashions and choices are all beginning to merge. A McDonald's restaurant is as easy to find in London, Berlin and Bangkok as it is in New York or other towns in the USA. A large proportion of the world's youth drink Coca-Cola and Pepsi, own a Sony Walkman and wear Levi jeans, all of which are global brands.

Coca-Cola is the product which perhaps best exemplifies the global brand. Its trademark is recognised by 94 per cent of the world's population and it can be found everywhere on all five continents.

There are generally agreed to be two main causes of this trend towards the globalisation of markets. These are:

1   **The progressive removal of barriers to the free movement of goods, services, and capital.** The World Trade Organisation (WTO), which replaced the General Agreement on Tariffs and Trade (GATT) in 1994, has been successful in creating freer trade between countries by reducing tariffs and gradually removing other barriers to international trade. By the late 1990s 120 countries were members of the WTO. Between them they accounted for 90 per cent of all world trade.

2   **The spectacular developments in communication, information, and transport technology.** Global communication has been changed out of all recognition by recent developments in satellite TV and this has helped to spread global brands. Also, the microprocessor now allows information to be transmitted instantly along the worldwide electronic highway. In addition, superfreighters and containerisation have greatly improved the distribution and transportation of goods. Today, the speed and ease with which international trade takes place have had the effect of shrinking the globe.

The Economist magazine has pointed out that globalisation today is all about steeply falling telecommunications costs, thanks to satellites, fibreoptics and the internet. These technologies allow companies to locate different parts of their production, research and marketing in different countries, but still tie them together through computers and teleconferencing. But the essential element is the cheapness of communication. In the 1930s, a three minute telephone call between London and New York would have cost nearly £200 at today's prices. Today, through the internet, it is almost free.

The public sector

The public sector consists of all those businesses that are either directly owned or controlled by the state (the government) or by local authorities (local government). All other businesses form part of the private sector and are owned and controlled by private individuals. The principal public sector organisations are traditionally divided into three broad categories:

1   the central government and its departments or ministries, e.g. the Ministry of Defence, the Department of Health

2   public corporations, often referred to nationalised industries

3   local authorities.

The public sector is very important. It accounts for almost half of the UK's economic activity. Just one of its organisations, the National Health Service (NHS), is the largest single employer in the UK and is also the largest employer in the EU. Local authorities are also significant employers of staff. They are often the biggest employer in their particular area. The London Borough of Ealing, for example, directly employs over 7,000 people.

All public service organisations and the services they provide are paid for by taxation which the government collects on our behalf through income tax, VAT, corporation tax and the various excise duties levied on alcohol, petrol and tobacco. The total money raised by tax and spent by the public sector each year is enormous. In the financial year 1999–2000 it is projected, according to Treasury estimates, to be in the region of £350 billion. This amounts to £6,000 for every man, woman and child in the UK.

Figure 1.2.7

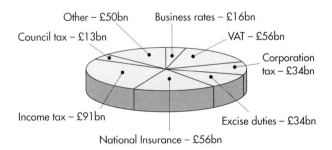

Where taxes come from

Note: 1999–2000 figures. *Source:* HM Treasury.

Figure 1.2.8

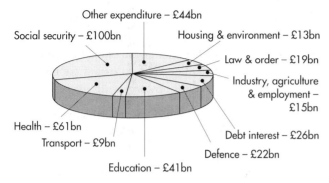

Where taxpayers' money is spent

Other expenditure – £44bn

Social security – £100bn

Housing & environment – £13bn

Law & order – £19bn

Industry, agriculture & employment – £15bn

Health – £61bn

Transport – £9bn

Debt interest – £26bn

Defence – £22bn

Education – £41bn

Note: 1999–2000 figures. *Source: HM Treasury.*

The public sector exists because most of us think that there are some services to which everyone is entitled, irrespective of whether they can afford to pay for them out of their own personal income. It is generally considered that the most important of these services are:

- education
- health care
- social welfare, e.g. unemployment and sickness benefit.

It is also generally accepted that services such as defence and policing can be properly provided only by the state. It is just not sensible for these to be provided privately. Until recently, the prison service would also have been included in this category, but some prisons are now managed by the private sector. Not everyone agrees with this development.

State or government ownership and control of public organisations has decreased significantly since 1979. This is due to the policy of **privatisation** (see Chapter 1 of this unit), once pursued with vigour by the conservative Government headed by Margaret Thatcher as Prime Minister. The policy has, however, been continued by successive governments. The New Labour administration, which came to power in May 1997, seems keen on following the same policy at least in some areas and has plans for involving private sector finance in the modernisation of the London Underground. The privatisation of air traffic control is also being considered. These proposals do not have the support of all Labour MPs, many Labour supporters or large numbers of the electorate.

The policy of privatisation, pioneered in Britain, has found favour in other European countries. Where Britain led, others are following. Nevertheless, in spite of the programme of privatisation, the public sector remains very large and has a significant effect on all aspects of our lives. We must now examine the various forms of public sector organisations more closely.

Central government

Government ministers are the political heads of the various departments of state, e.g. the Treasury (Chancellor of the Exchequer), the Home Office (Home Secretary) and the Ministry of Defence (Secretary of State for Defence). Ministers are selected by the Prime Minister from among the most prominent MPs in the majority party following a general election and the 20 or so most important of them form the Cabinet which is presided over by the Prime Minister. The Cabinet is the committee that makes and carries out government policy. Ministers are helped in the running of their ministerial departments by civil servants who give them advice and generally oversee the carrying out of government policy. In addition to the ministries, the government also controls other departments which provide various services. Among them are the Central Office of Information (COI) which prepares publicity and promotional material about Britain, the Royal Mint, located in South Wales, which produces the country's coins and bank notes, and the Forestry Commission which oversees the supply of timber from state-owned forests. These are some of the better known ones but there are others.

Public corporations

Those organisations which are government owned and run on behalf of the country are called public corporations. They are often referred to as nationalised industries. As they are part of the public sector, the people appointed to manage them are accountable to the government, usually to government ministers.

Twenty years ago making a profit would not have been among a public corporation's main objectives. This is not so today. Public corporations are now set financial targets that they are expected to meet and they can no longer, as in the pre-Thatcher times, depend on receiving help out of general taxation should they get into financial trouble.

Since the policy of privatisation has become such a central feature of all government economic policy, the number of public sector corporations has declined. The Post Office and the British Broadcasting Corporation (BBC) are probably the best known remaining examples. Before privatisation, nationalised industries composed quite a big proportion of the public sector (see Chapter 1). As previously mentioned, many have now been transformed into very large and profitable plcs.

Local government

The UK is served by more than 400 local authorities (councils). These authorities are controlled by elected councillors who are, for the most part, representatives of the main political parties. There are, however, significant numbers of independent local councillors who have no political affiliations. Following local council elections, which take place every four years, the political group with the largest number of councillors is elected. They make policy and run council services, such as granting building planning permission and maintaining parks, libraries and the fire service. The day-to-day work is carried out by professional council employees. A large London borough like Ealing employed more than 7,000 in people 1998–99, nearly 6,000 of whom were operational fire staff. Almost 1,000 were administrative and clerical staff. The councillors themselves do not receive salaries but are paid expenses for attending council meetings and committees.

The majority of council income is received from the Department for the Environment as a central government grant. Taking again the example of the London Borough of Ealing, the council estimated that it would require £293 million to provide council services in the year 1999–2000. £160 million of this would come from the central government grant – money raised by general taxation. The local council tax, which is paid by each household in the borough, contributes nearly £75 million, and a further £61 million would come from business rates.

In recent years, many local authorities have **contracted out** some of their services, such as refuse collection, park maintenance and parking services (including the collection of parking fees and fines), to private sector organisations that tender competitively for the contract. The company which convinces the council that it offers the best service and price obtains the contract. This practice amounts to a form of privatisation at a local level, but the private contract company does not, of course, 'own' the service. Every few years the service must be tendered for again. Some councils allow their employees to take part in the tendering process.

Revision Questions

1 How are the services provided by the public sector paid for? (1 mark)

2 In which industrial sector do the following belong:

- a bakery
- a motorway service station
- a fleet of fishing boats
- a house-building company
- a satellite television company. (5 marks)

3 'Sole trader' is a legal term; it tells us nothing about the size of an enterprise. Explain why this is so. (5 marks)

4 Give three reasons for the growth of small firms since 1970. (4 marks)

5 Explain the link between downsizing, recession, and the growth of self-employment. (6 marks)

6 The consequences of running a business which has unlimited liability could, in certain circumstances, be quite serious. Why, then, are small firms prepared to take the risk? (5 marks)

7 From a legal point of view, sole traders and partners are *the* business. Which term is used to describe their status? (1 mark)

8 What is the value and purpose of a partnership agreement? Is it compulsory? (3 marks)

9 Who owns limited liability companies? (1 mark)

10 Explain the following statement: 'In a private limited company the shareholders have limited liability'. (4 marks)

11 What are the advantages for the shareholders of converting from a private limited company to a public limited company? What is the risk for the original owners of the company? (3 marks)

12 Why are workers in producer co-operatives often initially prepared to accept lower wages? (2 marks)

13 Buying a popular franchise is not cheap. What are the benefits for the franchisee and what does the franchiser gain? (3 marks)

14 For what purposes are charities established? (2 marks)

15 A national firm, an international firm, a global firm; how do you distinguish between them? Give examples of each. (5 points)

16 The growth of global markets depends on at least two important developments. Explain. (5 marks)

17 Public sector organisations and public limited companies have very different objectives. Explain. (6 marks)

18 Why is it not sensible for the army and the police to be organised and run by private companies? (4 marks)

CHAPTER 3

Organisational Structures and Functions

KEY TERMS:

organisation	management by objectives	autocratic
motivation	business culture	consultative
hierarchy	business structure	organisational function
manager	delegation	
democratic	matrix	

In this chapter you will learn about the different structures of business organisations, and how the structure depends on the type, size and culture of the business. You will also learn about business functions that must be carried out, and why.

Introduction

First, we must answer the question: 'What is an **organisation**?'

Organisation – a group of individuals working together for a specific purpose.

Whenever three or more people decide to come together for a specific purpose, a group is formed. The reasons for establishing groups are many – the aim may be to complete a certain task, to carry out social or sporting activities, or for business purposes. Thus, we can say that all the following are examples of groups:

- a football club
- a charity shop
- the corner shop
- the BBC
- Marks & Spencer
- a high street bank
- a hospital.

Although these are all groups, they are very different. Some groups are formally organised – you will find business organisations in this category – others are informal, e.g. several mothers of young children who meet up once a week for coffee and a chat. Some groups are temporary. For example, a group of parents getting together to campaign for a zebra crossing outside their children's school will continue to exist only until the local council has agreed to their demands. Football clubs, colleges, schools, clinics and, of course, businesses are all groups with long-term objectives.

Business structures

Business structure – the way in which a business is organised internally.

In this chapter we shall examine groups within business organisations, and also different ways in which the organisations are structured.

If you look at the chart below, you will see that in a large organisation the divisions between different groups are very clearly marked. Each department is a group of individuals working together. Although the jobs within the group might be different (an accounts

Figure 1.3.1

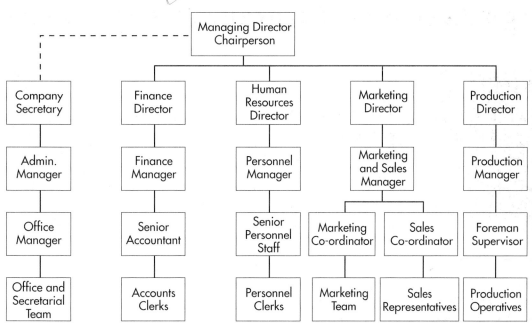

clerk's work and responsibilities cannot be compared to those of his or her departmental manager), they all have the same general aim. In the case of an accounts department, the aim is to ensure that the accounting function of the firm is working efficiently and communicating with other departments and the management.

Every group must have a leader. In an informal, temporary group, the leader might not be appointed – someone usually just takes over the role without any formalities. In a business organisation group leaders are appointed, and have very clear and comprehensive job descriptions so that they know exactly what is expected of them.

In the chart above, you will see that, working upwards:

1 A group of operatives is led by a charge hand/ supervisor or foreman.

2 All supervisors in a department are led by a departmental manager.

3 Departmental managers are led by the departmental director.

4 The chairperson of the board, who is often the managing director, heads the departmental directors who form the members of the board.

Organisational structures

However, not all organisations are structured in the same way. The structure depends on the way in which its activities are arranged or grouped. It is only sensible that people who do similar work should be grouped together. This is simple in a small organisation, but has to be formally arranged in a large company otherwise time and money would be wasted.

CASE STUDY

Chaos at Front Gates Ltd

Front Gates Ltd started as a small family business in 1990. It specialised in custom-made outside doors and gates, and was run by two brothers, Bill and Jack O'Donald. In the beginning, they employed only two skilled carpenters. As the business grew, they took on more and more operatives who all worked in the factory and were supervised by Jack, when he had the time. The brothers were kept busy, looking after clients, sending out quotations, talking to and chasing suppliers and dealing with any matter that needed attention.

In 1995, after a very successful year of trading, the brothers registered the business as a private limited company. By mutual agreement, Bill became the managing director, with Jack taking on the job of general manager. They did not, however, write their own job descriptions. They did not think it necessary, so quite often they would both carry out the same task which was time wasting and often irritating.

By 1996, there were 48 people working on the shop floor. None of them had a job description, and Jack did not allocate specific jobs to any of them. As a result, jobs started by one person were frequently left unfinished as the operative had been called away to do something else.

A similar situation arose in the office. John, the secretary, was never quite sure of his responsibilities and duties. He was also frustrated by Bill, who would deal with enquiries and correspondence without telling John or at least giving him copies of the letters etc. As a result of this, when customers rang with enquiries or complaints John could

never be sure what had already happened, and what he was supposed to do.

Narinder Gopal, a friend of the brothers, and a successful businessman himself, suggested to Jack and Bill that they should organise the firm into some kind of formal structure, but they did not like the idea.

'It's not necessary,' said Bill, 'we are doing all right as it is. A formal structure is for very large companies, not for a friendly, family firm like Front Gates.'

Soon afterwards, things began to go wrong. There were arguments on the shop floor, with the operatives all wanting to do things the way they liked. Many left without giving an explanation. Customer complaints increased.

Bill and Jack blamed it all on John. The Inland Revenue and the VAT office sent final warnings.

Bill and Jack could not understand what was happening. The last straw came when John gave in his notice. The brothers were astonished.

'Aren't you happy here?' they asked.' We know there have been differences between us but we treated you as a friend, almost a member of the family!'

'Friendship is one thing,' said John, 'but in business you must be organised. I'm sorry, but I can no longer work in this chaos. And, because I do think of both of you as friends, I must tell you that if you don't want to go out of business you'll have to do something about it very soon!'

Reasons for different structures

All businesses are different and the way they are organised internally depends on a number of factors:

- size
- number of employees
- type of business – manufacturing or service
- type of work
- scope of activities – local, national or international.

Furthermore, the structure can also depend on the way in which the management wants the company to be run. In recent years, many large companies have come to realise that the traditional structure was not 'employee friendly'. Often, the workers never saw any of the managers, certainly not the senior ones, and this meant that the employees found it very difficult to feel loyalty towards, and interest in, the activities of the firm. This realisation has led to a number of firms simplifying their structure and getting rid of some layers of management.

Motivation

Motivation – stimulating people's interest in what they do, so that they are more willing to work hard to achieve their goals.

In the past, employers were not very much concerned with motivating their workers. Money was considered to be the only reason why people went to work and, as long as their wages were paid, employees were expected to work as well and as hard as they were able. This view has changed gradually until, today, we know that, while the wages are the main reason why people work, many other aspects of employment can motivate or de-motivate them. Security, prospects of promotion, interest in the job itself, additional perks and facilities such as bonuses, company cars and company shares are all motivating factors for the workforce.

The study of motivation includes the work of Frederick W. Taylor, Elton Mayo, Maslow (see page 45) and McGregor. All of them contributed to modern techniques of management, and all of them concentrated on the human factor at work.

F. W. Taylor

In his work *The Principles of Scientific Management*, published in 1911, **F. W. Taylor** laid down some rules for resolving differences between management and workers. At that time, there was little training in factories and workshops, and foremen and chargehands made their own rules about hiring, laying off and conditions of work.

Taylor wanted to improve the system by bringing about agreement between management and workers, so that common objectives could be set. He was still of the opinion that money is the only motivator at work, but he tried to establish by experiment the best way of carrying out a job, and the time needed to complete it. Once this was done, he was certain that his 'scientific' method would prove beneficial to business organisations. He was not very interested in differences between individuals or in their individual needs and wishes.

Elton Mayo

Working in the 1930s, **Elton Mayo** and his collaborators introduced the idea that human relations were of importance at the workplace. Mayo's ideas are not surprising to us today but they were startling when first published. Mayo stressed that management must communicate with the workers and involve them in the decision-making process. He suggested that informal groups be formed which would then discuss their own ideas with the management. This idea has now been successfully used for many years in many different industries. One of the best known examples is the experiment carried out by the Volvo car company in Sweden in 1989. In Volvo's new plant in Uddevalla in Sweden, workers were put in groups of eight to 10 people. Each group decided how to organise its own work, and was responsible for producing a complete car. At the original Volvo plant in Gothenburg, a traditional production line system was used. Volvo managers wanted to find out whether the new system would help to reduce absenteeism, which at Gothenburg averaged 25 per cent. In the Uddevalla plant, absenteeism did not rise above 8 per cent, confirming that workers able to make their own decisions felt more involved in their work, and suffered less from the monotony of repetitive jobs.

While Mayo's contribution was very important, it did not always work in practice. If the workers are not inspired by the company's vision and policy, they will not respond. In addition, close co-operation between workers and managers can lead to dissatisfaction on the part of the workers, particularly when they get to know in detail about the managers' level of pay and working conditions.

Douglas McGregor

Douglas McGregor is best remembered for his 'Theory X and Theory Y'. In 1960, he published *The Human Side of Enterprise*, an attempt to apply the principles introduced by Taylor, Maslow and Mayo to business. He set out the reasons why people work, as follows:

McGregor's two theories describe two extreme opposites – the lazy worker, who must be controlled, and the well motivated, hard working worker who only needs to be treated well and encouraged. The large majority of employees fall somewhere between the two, but it is now generally accepted that Theory Y is more likely to yield good results than Theory X. Even today, however, many employers, while paying lip service to Theory Y, still treat some workers, particularly those in lower positions, in accordance with Theory X.

Although none of the ideas outlined above can be called really scientific – simply because people are not machines, and no two individuals respond to any situation in exactly the same way – they were all instrumental in changing the way in which those who manage regard those whom they manage.

Whatever the approach of those in charge, the structure of a business organisation greatly influences how it operates and its management.

Table 1.3.1 McGregor's Theory X and Theory Y

Theory X	Theory Y
Workers are motivated by money.	Workers have many needs which can motivate them.
Workers dislike work and are lazy.	Workers can enjoy work.
Workers are selfish, lack ambition, avoid responsibility and ignore needs of the organisation.	Workers are prepared to organise themselves and take responsibility, if they are motivated.
Workers must be directed and controlled.	Workers should be allowed by management to show creativity and apply their job knowledge.

CASE STUDY

The New Broom

The operatives at Conway Brushes Ltd have never been unionised. The company, which manufactures brushes, brooms and a range of household cleaning implements, was set up in the 1960s by Joseph Conway, and he stayed on as Managing Director until his recent retirement.

Joseph Conway's management style was autocratic. He saw no need to consult his workers on any matter pertaining to the firm. He made his own decisions, and often did not even consult the other members of the management team. His son, Joseph Jr, who came into the firm on leaving college, often tried to persuade his father that the workers would be happier, and therefore more efficient, if they felt that their views and opinions were regarded as important. Joseph Conway Sr would have none of it.

'Nonsense,' he said. 'I know what's good for the firm and what's good for the firm is good for them, isn't it? Look how well we are doing!'

'But, Father,' Joseph Jr tried to explain, 'according to Taylor and Mayo and ...'

'Don't give me any of that rubbish,' the older man said. 'We don't need it. And if they don't like it, they can go somewhere else!'

And soon, this is what the workers did. Staff turnover grew from year to year. Except for a core of workers who had been with the company from the very beginning, none was interested in what was going on in the business. The more ambitious moved on to other jobs as soon as they could. Joseph Jr was very concerned about this but when he tried to talk to the employees the only answer he got was a shrug and a comment about the lack of prospects at Conway Brushes.

In addition, other problems have arisen. The quality of products, always the main selling point, has fallen sharply. As a result, there has been a steep rise in the number of customer complaints, and some distributors have now withdrawn orders.

Joseph Jr, who studied various management styles while at college, is convinced that his father's autocratic approach is the cause of all the troubles. When his father decided to retire, Joseph Jr took over as Managing Director and resolved to change the way in which Conway Brushes was managed. He was not sure, however, which style would suit the company best.

Types of structure

Tall or hierarchical

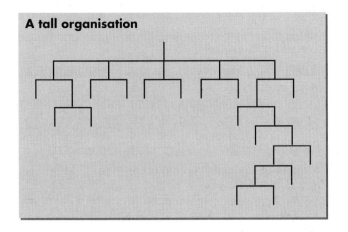

A tall organisation

Hierarchical – structure in which there are many levels.

In this type of structure, which looks tall when it is drawn as a diagram, jobs are specialised and each group of people has a person designated as supervisor. It is a very formal structure, with lines of communication carefully arranged. A company organised like this usually has many official procedures and rules. Every member of staff has a detailed job description, knows precisely who is his or her manager, and has been taken on after a formal interview.

The reasons for this are the need to ensure fair treatment of all employees, and to set standards for employees and for customers.

A tall structure is sometimes called a 'pyramid' structure, because it also looks like a pyramid. At the top, there is only the chief executive, whatever his or her title. At each level below there are more and more employees. Some 'pyramids' are steeper than others, depending on the number of 'layers'.

Flat structure

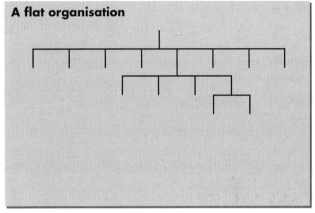

A flat organisation

A flat structure is one with only two or three levels. It is usually found in relatively small organisations, and it has several advantages. There is less formality, and fewer rules and procedures. The staff know each other, and the managers know the staff. Communication can be easier and quicker which is of importance if decisions have to be acted on quickly.

CASE STUDY

Young Veterinary Partnership

In 1950, Mr Michael Young bought an existing veterinary practice, situated in the residential centre of Ealing, West London. Today, the Young Partnership is well established, and has four clinics. In addition to the original one, there are now two others, serving other West London locations, as well a franchise in a PETs MART store, acquired in 1992.

After the retirement of the founder, the practice was taken over by his son, Mr Anthony Young. Recently, he has taken on a partner and changed the status of the practice into a partnership, with himself as senior partner.

The practice deals mainly with small domestic animals and is required to provide 24-hour cover in case of emergencies. This means that the veterinary surgeons work weekend and night rotas.

Management

The running of the practice is divided equally between the two partners, who rely on regular meetings as a means of efficient communication. One of the partners is in charge of staff recruitment, while the other looks after the financial and administrative side of the business.

The head nurse line-manages the veterinary nurses, and the head receptionist is in charge of the reception staff. Their line manager is the junior partner.

Employees

- 6 veterinary surgeons (this includes both the partners)
- 11 nurses (4 fully qualified)
- 5 receptionists (full-time)
- 2 receptionists (part-time)
- 1 administrative manager
- 2 Saturday helpers

In addition, holiday locums are employed when needed and some administrative and receptionist duties are carried out by the wives of the partners, as is quite often the case in family businesses.

Hours and conditions of work

Because of the requirement to provide round-the-clock service, all staff work rotating shifts. The nurses work a 37.5 hour week, as do full-time receptionists, with part-time workers being employed on a pro-rata basis.

As already mentioned, both the partners also work as veterinary surgeons and this, together with their other duties, brings their average weekly work load to about 56–65 hours a week.

All staff are paid their salaries by bank transfer, and the holiday entitlement for full-time employees is four weeks a year.

Training and job opportunities

- Partly qualified nurses receive on-the-job training in the practice, and also attend Berkshire College of Agriculture on a day-release basis.

- Qualified nurses can gain additional qualifications, such as that of surgical nurse, and can become practice managers.

- Veterinary surgeons can progress through specialisation.

Advertising and publicity

The partnership does advertise in *Yellow Pages*, but mostly it relies on word of mouth. Its steady growth can be explained by its well established reputation in the West London area.

Difficulties and future plans

As already mentioned, the main difficulty is the restraint on growth because of the need to provide 24-hour cover. Very strict Control of Substances Hazardous to Health (COSHH) regulations apply to the practice and these are exceedingly time consuming.

The practice is well regarded and doing well in its present size and structure. The partners hope that in the future they will be able to bring in more specialisms, in addition to the generalist service now provided.

Activity

The Young Veterinary Partnership

1 Draw an organisational chart for the partnership.

2 Is the chart a 'tall' one or a flat one?

3 Now draw another chart, showing what would happen if the two partners decided to:

- employ a full-time secretary

- take on eight more veterinary nurses

- promote three nurses to nurse-supervisor.

4 How does the second chart differ from the first? Explain the changes.

Matrix structure

Matrix – a business structure grouping together workers from different areas for a specific project.

In this structure, people with specialised knowledge and skills are put into project teams. This means that team leaders can choose the right people for a particular project, and allows employees in lower positions to participate. Every individual is responsible for his or her own work, and the line manager is the person responsible for the current project.

For example, if a confectionery manufacturer decided to produce a new chocolate bar, the manager responsible for the project would select a team drawn from various departments, including production, marketing, sales and finance.

The matrix system motivates workers, and fits in with McGregor's Theory Y. It is, however, costly as each project needs additional secretarial and administrative support. Another disadvantage is the difficulty of creating a team that will work together if all the members come from different departments and do not understand the objectives of other sections of the company.

Hierarchical, centralised and decentralised structures

Hierarchy – a system in which grades of authority are ranked one above the other.

Any business structure, tall or flat, in which there is a clear path from top management to the lowest position in the firm, i.e. the operatives, is a hierarchy.

A centralised structure is one in which a top manager makes all the decisions and has total control over the way in which the operational plans are carried out. We can say, therefore, that a centralised system does not allow for delegation. There are some advantages of such a system. Senior managers are more likely to take an overall view of the business and its needs, whereas their subordinates might be concerned only with their own part of the company.

The decentralised system is the direct opposite. Decentralisation means delegating certain tasks to others. Some delegation cannot be avoided, even in an organisation that operates a centralised system, because senior managers cannot carry out all procedures and duties. If a company decides to delegate more responsibility than absolutely necessary, the benefits can include greater motivation of staff, and increased flexibility and reduced response time. For example, if a decision regarding the introduction of overtime for a specific period can be taken only by the Managing Director, some time will elapse before it is agreed. This might mean that a vital order is not completed on time. In a decentralised system, the Production Manager can make such decisions quickly, avoiding unnecessary delay.

Managers

> **Manager** – a person who is responsible for the operations of a business, or part of a business. Some managers look after people, others look after tasks.

Senior managers are often heads of departments, while middle managers are responsible for smaller parts of the organisation. In a hierarchical structure, the parts are often subdivided into smaller sections, each in the charge of a junior manager.

When looking at an organisational chart, you will notice that the vertical columns show separate functions of departments, e.g. finance, production, marketing or human resources. Horizontal levels show the level of responsibility and importance within the organisation.

Span of control

In a hierarchical structure, the span of control of managers is narrow – in other words, they are responsible only for those directly under them. In a flat structure, the span of control tends to be broader as those in charge are responsible for more activities within the organisation.

Levels of authority

Instructions are passed down the line of authority, i.e. from the highest to the lowest level.

Complaints and disciplinary matters are passed upwards, in the first instance to the next higher level.

Problems are also passed upwards to the next level. If they are not resolved, they can be taken to the level above.

CASE STUDY

Ultra Electronics

Ultra Electronics is an international group of businesses specialising in the design and manufacture of products for aerospace markets worldwide, as well as providing specialist equipment for ships and submarines, and for land fighting vehicles.

Ultra was founded in 1920, and has gone through many changes over the years. In 1977, Ultra was bought by Dowty which was itself acquired by the TI Group in 1992.

In 1993, as a result of a management buy-out, Ultra Electronics Ltd was formed and, thanks to good management, has since gone from strength to strength.

Ultra Electronics Holdings plc was floated on the Stock Exchange in 1996 and, in the same year, the company was awarded the Queen's Award for Technology.

The company has been growing steadily over the last few years, and now has businesses in Canada and the USA as well as the UK. Currently, Ultra has 13 sites and employs over 2,000 people. Of these, 823 work in engineering and 861 in production, while administration and sales account for the rest.

Both sales and profits increased in the years 1994–98.

Among its customers are such very important organisations as Airbus Industries, the Ministry of Defence, British Aerospace and Rolls-Royce.

The management structure of the Ultra Group is flat, with head office consisting of only eight people. Authority and responsibility is given to the divisions, one of which is described below.

The Controls Division

The Controls Division, situated in Greenford, West London, is not typical of Ultra as a whole because it is concerned with civil aerospace products, rather than defence electronics.

The managing director is in charge of the division and runs it with little interference from head office. He has, however, to work in accordance with the agreed strategy and to an agreed budget, and the aim of the division is always to 'meet or beat' the budget.

Figure 1.3.2

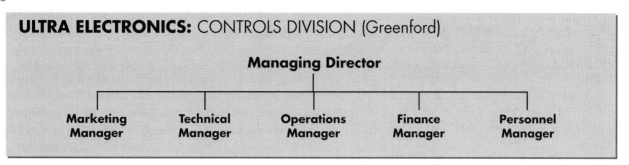

The MD's role

- to win new business (this involves a lot of travel)

- to develop new products (in this industry, this takes four to five years)

- to ensure support for existing products (repairs, spares)

- to ensure the high level of quality control which is vital in Ultra's business

- working with his five heads of departments.

The MD ensures that he is in regular contact with all his workers, which contributes to employees' interest and loyalty.

Figure 1.3.3

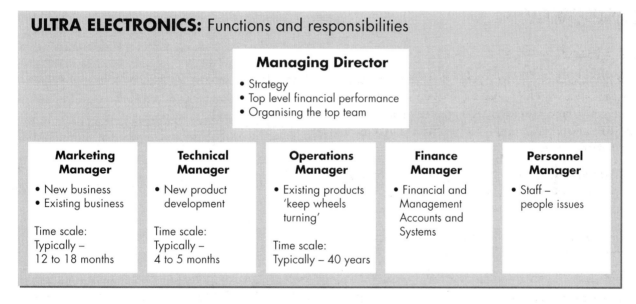

Figure 1.3.4

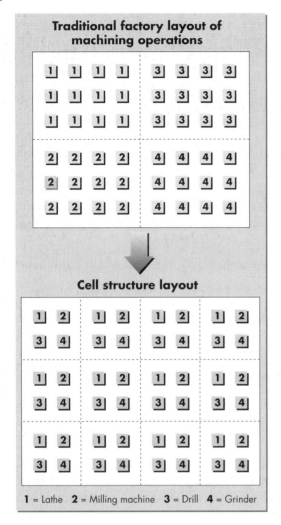

Workforce

The Controls Division is organised into a **manufacturing cells structure**.

The workers used to be allocated to separate sections. Now the manufacturing cells system means that workers can be shifted from one cell to another. This gives them more interest in the job, and leads to job enrichment. Working closely together, workers learn from each other and acquire additional skills. This leads to greater flexibility.

About 95 per cent of the workers are full-time. All undergo a three-month trial period, and have six-monthly reviews. Training and retraining is carried out as required and is the responsibility of managers and supervisors, supported by the division's personnel manager. In 1999 the training budget was set at £160,000. This means an average of three and a half days per person, apart from the engineers who will each receive on average five days' training.

Because many production processes are semi-automated, the division no longer needs to have workers on regular round-the-clock shifts but workers do additional shifts when required. All employees are willing to be flexible with respect to working patterns when customer demand requires it.

The division, as is normal within Ultra Group, is not unionised. It has a very low worker turnover, indicating good management–worker relationships.

Figure 1.3.5

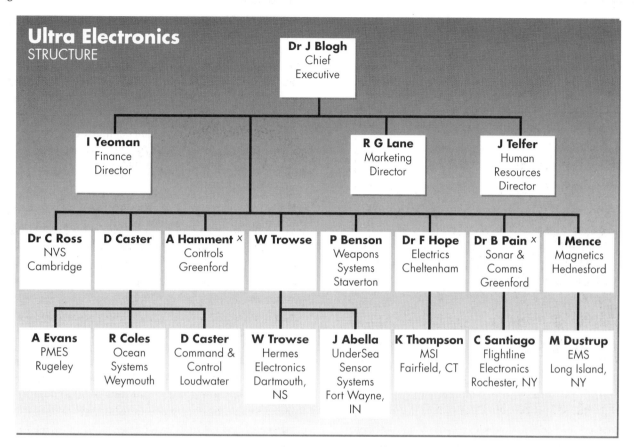

Payments

All workers are paid a monthly salary by direct debit. Depending on the division's financial performance, all employees qualify for an annual bonus. They also receive free shares in the company and have an option to join a share save scheme within which additional shares can be bought at below market price.

ACTIVITY

1 Explain why it is necessary for Ultra Electronics to have a formal organisational structure.

2 How many levels of management are there at Ultra?

3 How many levels of management are there in Ultra's Controls and Systems Division?

4 To whom would an operative at the division take a problem or a complaint?

Delegation

> **Delegation** – giving others the responsibility for certain tasks.

It has been said that delegation is an art which many managers find very difficult, if not impossible, to learn. If you talk to people who have worked for several managers or supervisors, you will probably find that they have tales to tell of their bosses' inability to 'let go' and to delegate.

The principle of delegation in management is quite simple. A person in charge of a group is not there to do all the work. If he or she has sound judgement and good knowledge of the staff, it should be possible to decide which parts of the job can be passed on, or delegated, to others. Simple or not, there often are difficulties. Some people in positions of authority feel that they are the only ones who can do the job properly. If this is true, then they either have not recruited and trained their workers properly, or do not trust them. Other managers feel that because the ultimate responsibility still lies with them, they are the only ones who should do the job. Whatever the reason, the inability to delegate is bad management practice. If we look at any organisational chart, we will see that efficient delegation of responsibility is the main cornerstone of all business structures. The board of directors decides on the strategic plan and delegate its implementation to the senior managers who, in turn, entrust certain parts of the plan to middle managers. Middle managers then pass some tasks to supervisors.

CASE STUDY

To delegate, or not to delegate?

Malcolm Briner had worked in the Human Resources Department of Foods Galore plc, a large food distributor, for a number of years. He was competent and conscientious and was well liked by his colleagues. Malcolm was quite happy in his job, and did not seek promotion. Last year his line manager, Nigel Green, retired, and the head of department, Angelica Burton, suggested to Malcolm that he should apply for the vacancy. Malcolm was flattered by her encouragement, applied, was interviewed, and was offered the position. He now had his own office and his own personal assistant and a long list of matters outstanding. He was confident that he could prove himself in his new position, as he knew exactly what to do.

After a few weeks, Malcolm found that the workload of his new job was more than he had expected. He never left the office before eight in the evening, and always took work home with him at weekends, yet he was failing to complete the work. To make sure that everything was done properly, Malcolm checked on the work of his colleagues. All important matters he handled himself.

Malcolm could not understand why his staff seemed dissatisfied, and became very disillusioned. When his first performance review came round, he was ready to complain about the incompetence of the other employees and was very surprised when Angelica told him firmly that the fault lay in his tendency to try and do everything himself.

When the performance interview was over, Malcolm went back to his office and sat with his head in his hands. Everything had gone wrong and he did not know why.

Lucy, his personal assistant, found him sitting there. 'Are you all right?' she said, 'Can I do anything?'

'I'm a failure,' moaned Malcolm, 'I work so hard and nobody appreciates me, and the section is doing badly ...'

'I'm not surprised', said Lucy. 'You shouldn't be doing everything yourself. You have good staff – trust them. Give them more responsibility and see what they can do. That's what Nigel did, don't you remember? That's how you learned when he was your manager.'

Management styles

The structure of a business organisation is closely linked with its management. There are several quite distinct styles of management, each with its own advantages and disadvantages. The most common are:

- autocratic
- democratic
- consultative
- by objectives.

Autocratic

Autocratic – one person (or group) having absolute power.

In an organisation with an autocratic management style, the manager or managers make all the decisions without any consultation with the workers. The employees must obey instructions without question. As a result, the workers often become unhappy and feel that they and their views are not important to the management. However, we must remember that in some situations this management style is vital. Think what might be the outcome if members of the army did not obey orders unless they had been consulted about their superiors' decisions!

The autocratic style has the advantage of enabling decisions to be made quickly, with no time wasted on discussion.

Democratic

Democratic – a system based on equality of all members of a community.

In a democratic management style, employees are encouraged to participate in decision making. This encourages the employees and makes them feel that they are real stakeholders in the business. Another positive factor of this style is the contribution made by workers at different levels. Unlike the autocratic manager, the democratic leader listens to his or her staff, and is prepared to take their suggestions and ideas on board.

While this management style does motivate the workers much more, it is more difficult to implement. In order to enable the employees to participate in decision making, they must be well informed about the company, its aims and objectives, and its plans.

Consultative

Consultative – this management style takes the democratic principle even further, with workers being asked for their opinions as a matter of course.

Here, before any decision is taken, the manager will consult his or her team. The employees are given a chance to discuss the problem in question, and their views are taken into consideration. Although, at the end, the manager is the one who makes the decision, it is based on conclusions reached by the group as a whole.

This system also acts as a good motivator but, like the democratic style, it is time consuming.

Management by objectives

Management by objectives – joint setting of objectives and a joint review of achievements.

Maslow's theory

This management style is based on the theory of human needs formulated by an American psychologist called Maslow. He stated that all objectives exist in response to various needs, and he divided the needs into five distinct categories, from the lowest, most basic ones, to the highest.

Figure 1.3.6 Maslow's hierarchy of needs

You will see that Maslow's theory states that:

1   First of all, we all must satisfy our basic or physiological needs – in other words, we all need food, drink and shelter just to stay alive.

2   When these needs are satisfied, we begin to make plans for safety and security. In the past, this meant simply ensuring that our basic needs would be taken care of, but today we also need security of employment and provision of many services.

3   The next level of need is to belong to a group. With a few exceptions, humans need the companionship of other humans. Such groups include family, friends and, of course, business organisations.

4   Self-esteem, or the feeling that we are of some worth, comes next. Individuals vary in what they want to achieve. Some want power, others seek promotion at work, and many want more and more material possessions. This need motivates people to work harder and makes them ambitious.

5   The highest level of need, according to Maslow, is the drive to achieve as much as possible. In a business organisation, it is found in top level management and in highly qualified professionals and skilled craftsmen.

Maslow's theory is a hierarchy, with a progression from the lowest to the highest needs. In a business organisation, most people, once they have achieved a certain objective, want to move up to the next one. This might be a better job, more money, a bigger office or a managerial position. Management by objectives attempts to encourage employees to improve their own performance in line with their own goals. This should help them to fulfil their own needs, and will also make the company more efficient.

It is a complicated system, because employees must be encouraged to set objectives together with their line managers, and to review performance regularly. The objectives set must conform to the objectives of the business as a whole.

The advantages of this management style include an increase in the efficiency of the individuals and of the business, greater motivation and better training for workers, and a control system, as well as good internal communications. It will not work, however, if it is not well organised, and is not suitable for businesses in which jobs held by individuals are highly structured. Some critics of this style say that it also allows management to hold too much control.

You have now learnt that there are several quite distinct types of business structures, and also different styles of management. In many organisations, the work involved in production and the size of the firm necessitate a particular structure. However, the preferred style of management often influences the structure. In recent years there has been a marked trend towards a form of management which is consultative rather than autocratic. This has meant that in many cases the structure has had to be changed.

Business cultures

Culture in organisations is often described as the set of values, beliefs and attitudes of both employees and management that helps to influence decision making and, ultimately, behaviour within the organisations. Each organisation has a unique culture.

Andrew Boden

Source: Business Review, Sept. 1999

Business structures are blueprints on the basis of which firms are organised. As we have seen, experts such as Maslow, Taylor and others have attempted to define these structures in accordance with scientific principles. However, organisations are composed of people, and the behaviour of people is never scientific. Individuals react to the behaviour of others; their behaviour changes according to circumstances. This is why the way that an organisation works depends on the 'set of values, beliefs and attitudes' mentioned in Andrew Boden's quotation. Since people are all different, organisations are all different too.

You will remember McGregor's Theory X and Theory Y. He believed that workers respond to management's attitude to them, and that managers who treat their workers in line with Theory Y are much more likely to influence them positively. A good example of the implementation of Theory Y is Sir Richard Branson's Virgin Atlantic, an organisation that allows individuals freedom of action.

Whatever the attitude of management, it always has a significant impact on the culture of the organisation. In a tall structure, the influence of the top management might not reach the shop floor operatives, while in a flat structure all employees are directly influenced by the attitudes and beliefs of management.

Categories of business culture range from the negative, in which there is little co-operation between managers and workers, to the dynamic culture, with enthusiastic managers and employees working together to implement positive changes and innovations.

Look carefully at the business cultures shown below.

The differences between different cultures might not be as clear cut as in the diagram. A positive culture is often a dynamic/innovative one, and a bureaucratic one often becomes negative, but it is possible to identify a company's culture by examining its management structure and management style.

Organisational functions

All business organisations exist either to manufacture goods or to provide a service (sometimes, a single organisation does both) in order to make a profit. All business activity requires the use of **factors of production**, and all businesses must ensure that they have the requisite factors of production, and that these are used effectively. This requires the organisation to ensure that all its parts carry out their functions.

We shall now look in detail at the various business functions necessary for a business to succeed. You will see that the structure of the business and the functions are very closely linked.

Figure 1.3.7 Business cultures differ

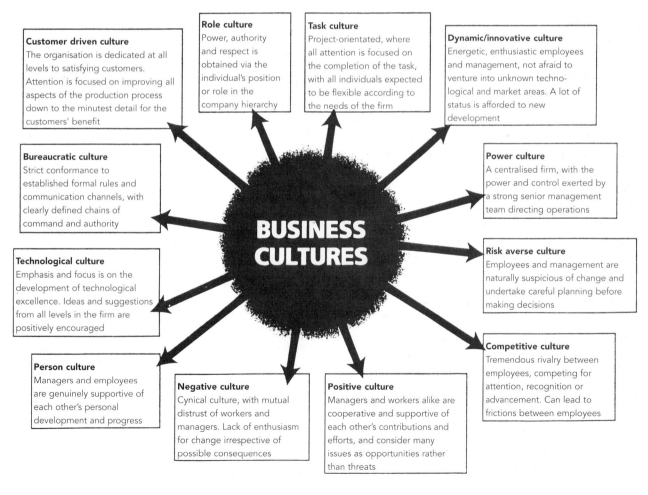

Customer driven culture
The organisation is dedicated at all levels to satisfying customers. Attention is focused on improving all aspects of the production process down to the minutest detail for the customers' benefit

Role culture
Power, authority and respect is obtained via the individual's position or role in the company hierarchy

Task culture
Project-orientated, where all attention is focused on the completion of the task, with all individuals expected to be flexible according to the needs of the firm

Dynamic/innovative culture
Energetic, enthusiastic employees and management, not afraid to venture into unknown techno-logical and market areas. A lot of status is afforded to new development

Bureaucratic culture
Strict conformance to established formal rules and communication channels, with clearly defined chains of command and authority

Power culture
A centralised firm, with the power and control exerted by a strong senior management team directing operations

Technological culture
Emphasis and focus is on the development of technological excellence. Ideas and suggestions from all levels in the firm are positively encouraged

Risk averse culture
Employees and management are naturally suspicious of change and undertake careful planning before making decisions

Person culture
Managers and employees are genuinely supportive of each other's personal development and progress

Negative culture
Cynical culture, with mutual distrust of workers and managers. Lack of enthusiasm for change irrespective of possible consequences

Positive culture
Managers and workers alike are cooperative and supportive of each other's contributions and efforts, and consider many issues as opportunities rather than threats

Competitive culture
Tremendous rivalry between employees, competing for attention, recognition or advancement. Can lead to frictions between employees

BUSINESS CULTURES

Factors of production

Before looking at the functions of a business, it is a good idea to look again at the factors of production.

1 **Land** – this factor includes not only the premises of a business and the actual land on which a factory or a shop stands, but also natural resources – rivers, forests, coal, metal ores and the soil itself. Some businesses need large areas of land, while others use only a small building or part of a building.

2 **Capital** – this is the money used to set up and run a business, and also includes all equipment and machinery used.

3 **Labour** – this resource is people, without whom no business activity could take place. Everyone in a business organisation, from the shop floor workers to the managing director is part of this factor of production.

4 **Enterprise** – this factor of production is unlike the others in that it is intangible. It refers to the way in which those who start businesses, the entrepreneurs, formulate policies and carry them out. Entrepreneurs take a risk that their venture might fail, in which case they will lose their investment. If the venture is successful, the surplus of money made – the profit – goes to the entrepreneurs.

CASE STUDY

Who dares wins!

Organisations do not become successful by sticking rigidly to a tried and tested formula. Of course, they stick to and cement in their core strengths, but in a turbulent and dynamic marketplace they also adapt and become agents for change.

Successful individuals and companies have to keep succeeding, keep challenging themselves to do better to increase their lead.

Today, with hindsight, people at Coca-Cola recognise that the company has not always been prepared to take the risks that were required to achieve success. In the 1960s and 1970s, for example, the organisation was somewhat conservative. It became reluctant to take risks or even initiate change in the core business.

The 1980s heralded an era of change for Coca-Cola. On the 8th of July 1982, Diet Coke was launched in the United States, starting a new period in which Coca-Cola was prepared to take risks by bringing in new products in the soft drinks sector. Within a year it had become the largest selling low-calorie soft drink in America.

Source: Times 100

All organisations must carry out a number of separate functions. These functions put together constitute the business system of the organisation. In a small business, as we already know, there might not be a formal structure, and one or two people might carry out a number of functions. In a large company, each section or department specialises in carrying out a particular function.

In most businesses there are six organisational functions, and they are all very closely related.

① Purchasing – Pg 23 other Book

1 Production

The function of production is to use materials to manufacture goods, or to supply a service. If production fails, the organisation as a whole will fail.

No business can survive if it does not produce enough goods or services to satisfy the needs of customers.

2 Finance

All businesses must control their expenditure. To achieve this, the Finance Department must record all transactions, produce all financial documents and reports and deal with incoming and outgoing payments.

3 Marketing

The function of marketing is to identify and anticipate customer needs (see Unit 3, Chapter 1). This is done through a variety of activities, including market research, advertising, promotion, packaging, pricing and distribution.

4 Research & development

The R&D function is usually found only in large organisations which try to maintain or increase their market share by introducing new products or by changing and improving existing ones. In a competitive market companies try to stay at least one step ahead of their competitors, and the job of R&D is to enable them to do so.

5 Human resources

Previously known as Personnel, this function of a business is concerned with the labour factor. It deals with all aspects of recruitment, selection and training of the workforce. It is also responsible for implementing health and safety legislation at work, and for looking after the welfare of the employees. Another aspect of this function is dealing with training of staff, employee appraisal, and any disputes, complaints or grievances that might arise.

6 Administration

This department's function is to communicate with the workforce, produce all necessary documentation, keep all records apart from financial ones, and deal with all enquiries.

It is easy to see that, with the exception of R&D, these functions are vital to the efficient working of any organisation. They are easy to identify in a large company – you only have to look at an organisational chart giving information of its business structure. A small business, as already mentioned, might not designate the functions in the same way. This does not mean, however, that they do not exist.

CASE STUDY

Lunching Out

Jatinder and Tracy have been friends since their schooldays. They both went to college where Jatinder did a catering course, while Tracy studied business management. They both wanted to be their own bosses and decided to open a small shop selling hot soup, rolls, sandwiches and soft drinks. Having done some research, they were confident that such an outlet, located in a busy high street, would attract business people in the morning and at lunchtime.

Lunching Out is proving a successful venture, and the two partners are happy but very busy. Jatinder's father, himself a successful businessman, has told the girls that they should now take on someone who would look after the financial side of the business, and perhaps another person to carry out the marketing function.

'We don't need anything like that,' said Jatinder. 'We are not a huge company, which needs marketing and finance departments!'

Her father did not agree. 'Every business needs those things,' he said. 'You might not realise it, but between you you are actually carrying out these business functions.'

Tracy and Jatinder were not convinced but agreed to write down exactly the tasks which each one of them has taken on, in order to see who is right. Here are their lists:

Jatinder

1   buys all supplies at the cash-and-carry

2   prices all products

3   helps their two assistants prepare the food

4   is responsible for the assistants and the part-time cleaner.

Tracy

1   keeps all accounts

2   deals with correspondence, enquiries and telephone calls

3   deals with any matters concerning local regulations

4   drafts advertisements to put in the local paper and runs off and distributes door-to-door leaflets.

Revision Questions

1 What is the main difference between a formal and an informal organisation? (2 marks)

2 All organisations have objectives. What are the objectives of:

i) Oxfam

ii) the Scout Movement

iii) the BBC

iv) a trade union

v) Age Concern. (5 marks)

3 Why do large business organisations have clearly defined departments? (3 marks)

4 Explain what is wrong with the structure of Front Gates Ltd, and suggest ways of improving it. (5 marks)

5 Why is it important to motivate workers? (2 marks)

6 What was the most important contribution of Elton Mayo to the theory of management? (3 marks)

7 McGregor's Theory X states that most workers are lazy and will work only if they are directed and controlled. Do you think that this theory is largely true, or is it more likely that Theory Y describes most people more accurately? Give reasons for your answer. (6 marks)

8 What are the advantages of the autocratic style of management? (3 marks)

9 Why does a flat structure of management allow for better communication within the organisation? (3 marks)

10 What are the difficulties of implementing a matrix structure? (3 marks)

11 It has been said that a good manager must be able to delegate. Explain. (2 marks)

12 How is management by objectives linked to Maslow's theory of human needs? (4 marks)

13 Why is the study of business structures not, strictly speaking, a science? (2 marks)

14 What is meant by business culture, and how can management introduce a particular culture into the workplace? (5 marks)

15 Why do many businesses not need the R&D function? (2 marks)

16 With reference to the Lunching Out case study, indicate which functions are the responsibility of each of the partners. Suggest ways in which they could organise their responsibilities better. (6 marks)

Communication in Business

In this chapter you will learn what communication is, and why an efficient business must have a good system of communication. You will also learn to identify the communication channels within businesses, and their effect on the quality of communication.

We now have to consider the nature and importance of communications in a business environment. Business organisations, as you well know, are run by people for people, and their diverse activities require individuals and groups within the organisations, and those outside, to communicate as efficiently as possible. In this chapter, we shall examine both the **internal** and the **external channels** necessary in a business.

Introduction

Communication – transmitting and receiving information.

The ability to communicate with others is one of the most important qualities of humans. We communicate from a very early age – even young babies manage to let their parents know what they want, what they do not like and what makes them happy. Without language, however, it is difficult to communicate fully. As soon as a child learns to speak, its ability to receive and react to information, and to give information to others, increases dramatically. The next step is reading and writing, then using the telephone and, nowadays, using the computer. By the time we leave school, we are all communicating in a variety of ways, although we may, perhaps, not have defined what we are doing in exactly those terms.

A person living completely alone on a desert island, like Robinson Crusoe, would not have the need or the opportunity to communicate with anyone, but there are very few people in such an isolated situation.

Communication channels

Internal communication – sending information and receiving feedback within the business.

External communication – the ways in which a business communicates with other organisations, and with individuals outside the business.

Both internal and external communication can be oral, paper-based or electronic.

Oral communication

This includes communication by word of mouth, which can be face-to-face, by telephone, through meetings and conferences and by presentations.

Paper-based communication

Informal notes, internal memoranda, formal business letters and business reports are included in this method of communication.

Electronic communication

The business world and the way it operates have changed greatly in recent years, largely due to new technology. Today, most organisations use the following communication methods as a matter of course:

Facsimile machine (fax)

Sending and receiving fax messages is easy, fast and inexpensive. It also has the advantages of the message sent being recorded (unlike a telephone conversation), and the possibility of transmitting it even when the recipient is not available.

E-mail (correspondence from computer to computer)

Twenty years ago even the most forward-looking entrepreneurs could not have imagined that e-mail would ever become a worldwide international communication tool. Nowadays, it is widely used by individuals and organisations alike.

Enhanced telephone systems

Traditional telephone conversations and fax messages are still two of the main ways of communicating, but fibre optics technology has brought new lines which can carry much more information than the standard ones.

Thanks to new technology, businesses now have access to such facilities as:

Videoconferencing

People in different parts of the world can now see each other and hold conversations without having to meet in one location. This saves time and money, such as the cost of hotels and travel, and can be set up quickly, which is an additional advantage.

MIS (management information services)

All the up-to-date statistical information which management requires, including all financial data, can be obtained quickly and accurately.

The internet

Already used by millions of people all over the world, the uses of the internet in business are constantly expanding, allowing organisations to link with others, to inform potential customers of its products and services, and to receive information in return.

Information technology has had a dramatic effect on the way communication takes place throughout the business world. Like many innovations, however, it has its negative as well as positive side.

Positive effects of changes in communication technology

- Improved speed – information about any aspect of an organisation or its activities can now be sorted, analysed and retrieved almost immediately.

- Information can be transmitted to or received from thousands of organisations within minutes.

- Improved access – vast amounts of data can be stored on computers, providing companies with easy access to a wealth of details.

- Wider audiences – the internet and satellite communication networks reach many more people than had ever been possible before.

Negative effects of changes in communication technology

- Cost – initial investment in hardware and software can be very substantial and on-going costs are also high. A small company might find the purchase of even one or two computers and basic software very expensive, while installing new systems in a large organisation requires a large outlay and considerable sums spent on upkeep.

- Incompatible equipment – this can be a serious problem with IT. Different manufacturers produce different products, both as hardware and, in particular, software.

- Threats to security from hackers – some organisations give this as a reason for not using the internet or EDI.

- The danger of deliberately introduced computer viruses, like the 'ILOVEYOU' virus, which was started in the Philippines in May 2000 and quickly spread around the world. It destroyed information held on computer databases, causing billions of pounds worth of damage both to commercial organisations and to governments.

Internal communication

In order to establish an effective system of communications at work, it is necessary for management to be quite definite about what people must know.

In very small organisations, ensuring effective communication is usually quite simple. A small firm employing half a dozen or so people under one roof, and with only the owner/manager in charge, has no need to set up a complicated structure of communication. The boss has easy access to all his employees, individually or as a team, and can decide what to tell them, and when. The employees also can approach him or her directly for additional information or with a suggestion or a complaint. In a big organisation, things are not so simple.

CASE STUDY

Talking is not enough

Marvin Tait is a successful businessman. Now in his thirties, he opened his first garage 10 years ago, and soon became known in the neighbourhood as a reliable and honest provider of car maintenance and repairs services. Marvin employed four mechanics and one junior apprentice, and ran the business on his own. He firmly believed that well informed employees were happy and efficient employees, and did everything he could to make them feel part of the business. The mechanics knew they could always approach Marvin with any problems that arose, and he encouraged them to suggest ways of improving the firm's operations.

The success of the garage encouraged Marvin to acquire another garage, a few miles away. This meant that he now had to divide his time between the two locations and so was not as easily accessible to his employees. This situation became even more pronounced when further expansion took place. At present, Marvin owns a chain of garages specialising in high quality repair work. He has changed the status of the business from a sole trader to a private limited company, and now employs between 80 and 90 mechanics, 10 managers, a dozen apprentices and a full-time accountant, as well as receptionists, administrators and drivers.

Marvin still thinks that personal contact with his workers is important, and tries to visit each garage at least once a fortnight, but he has no time to talk to the workers individually, or to tell them what is going on in the business. He has left it to the managers to inform their teams of what is necessary, and now spends his time attending to more pressing matters.

Marvin has noticed that, recently, staff turnover at all his garages has risen sharply. Although the work is still coming in, there have been complaints about unsatisfactory repairs and the lack of interest shown by the employees. Marvin is at a loss and has no idea what has gone wrong.

Last week, he was airing his complaints to his wife, Jenny.

'I don't know what is going on,' he said. 'I pay them well, give them bonuses at Christmas, they have plenty of work, and yet they seem to have lost interest. When I think of the old days, when we were like one happy family …'

'Just a minute,' said Jenny. 'Don't you think this is just what has gone wrong. You can't run the business now as if it still was a family. You haven't got the time. Your employees hardly know you now. They certainly don't have the opportunity to come directly to you with their problems or ideas.'

'True,' said Marvin, 'but the managers are supposed to do all that.'

'Have you instructed the managers exactly how to communicate with their teams?' asked Jenny.

'Well, no,' answered Marvin sheepishly. 'I just assumed that if I let them know things, they would pass on what is necessary.'

'You shouldn't have assumed that,' said Jenny. 'When I was working for that large company before we were married, there were very clear channels of communication between all the levels of management. Everyone was informed of what was going on as a matter of course, and everyone knew whom to approach with problems or suggestions. You really have to think of putting in a clear communication structure, and all your problems will go away!'

'Oh dear,' said Marvin, 'I suppose you're right. And I thought that all I had to do to run a garage business was to know about motor vehicles!'

Downward communication

Management must inform subordinates about company policy and the decisions made in the form of an operational plan. It is now recognised that good managers also consult the workforce before decisions are made, and give the workers a chance to discuss any proposals and to put forward suggestions and ideas.

> **Downward communication** – sent from higher to lower layers of employers.

If you look at the chart, you will see that the Chairperson of the Board of Directors, usually the Managing Director, can transmit information in several ways.

- If it is necessary to everyone to know it, it must be sent to all employees.

- If it is of importance only to senior managers, they will be the only ones to receive it.

- Some information might be necessary for senior and middle managers but not for others.

Figure 1.4.1 Organisational chart of a large company, showing channels of communication

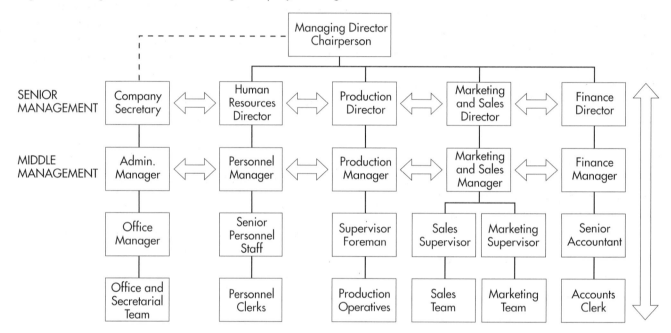

In the same way, departmental managers will send information to their supervisors, or to whole departments. In every situation, it is vital that people are not only informed of decisions made, but have the reasons for those decisions explained to them.

Upward communication

> **Upward communication** – a system which allows workers to communicate effectively with their superiors.

Downward communication used to be the only channel used in most business organisations. It led to an autocratic system of management (see Chapter 3, page 45). It meant that the workers were never consulted about the company's policies and plans, and that they had no opportunity to air their views or offer suggestions. This is now considered a very negative way of management, and it has been proved that, to be effective, communication must be two way. The upward channel of communication gives all employees the chance to express their views, ask for clarification and participate to some extent in the way in which the business is run. Most progressive organisations now have built-in systems allowing people to communicate with their line managers and, if necessary, higher management. See Fig. 1.4.1.

In both upward and downward communication, the methods vary from formal to informal.

Both the upward and the downward channels of communication are known as **vertical**, as the information is passed from the top to the bottom of the organisational 'tree', or from the bottom to the top.

Another form of internal communication is the **lateral**, or sideways, channel. This refers to information or instructions passed from department to department, or between members of staff who are on the same level in the company. See Fig. 1.4.1.

The most effective method of communication is face-to-face verbal communication, supported by written information. Line managers should hold regular briefing meetings with their teams. Such meetings combine both downward and upward communication – the managers pass information down, and receive immediate upward feedback from their workers. This feedback can then be taken further up the line if necessary.

Formal communication

Formal communication – going through established channels, usually in written form.

Formal communication can be addressed to the staff as a whole, to selected groups of employees or to an individual in the company.

Here are some examples of formal communication:

- all communication involved in the recruitment process, including job descriptions and specifications, the conditions of employment and the contract itself

- company policies on such matters as the equal opportunities policy, grievance procedure, complaints procedure and health and safety

- decisions reached by management

- job appraisal procedures

- reports

- consultative documents.

The objective of progressive companies is to involve the employees, irrespective of their position, in everything that is going on in the business. When workers are involved, they feel valued, and this is not just good for them, it is good for the business. (See reference to Elton Mayo, page 35). To achieve this, communication must be transmitted to them on certain topics.

- All workers must be informed about:
  - organisational policies
  - appointments and promotions
  - changes in pay and/or conditions
  - future plans and current achievements.

- Some information might be important only to individual workers or departments, e.g.:
  - budgets (for budget holders, usually departmental heads)
  - sales figures
  - details of profitability etc.

CASE STUDY

Communications – the key to success!

The FKI Group

The FKI Group is a multinational group of companies engaged mainly in engineering. It has member companies in the UK, the USA and Europe. The independently managed companies within the group are involved in the design, manufacture and supply of a wide range of high tech solutions to engineering production and services to the material handling, hardware and automotive engineering industries. FKI member companies have customers throughout the world and have earned an international reputation as leaders in their field. Building and maintaining a reputation such as this is gained by dedication to quality and technical excellence – a clear priority when meeting customer needs.

Managers throughout FKI companies acknowledge that success comes through people at all levels working as a team – working together to solve problems. If they are to do this successfully, they need to communicate properly. This means *talking*!

Talking

Communication needs to flow in all directions in a successful organisation. The board needs to communicate its objectives through management to all employees but, equally, also needs to be able to receive ideas and input from all corners of the business. Here are some of the ways businesses communicate:

Annual reports

Each employee receives an annual statement from the managing director of his or her company, which summarises company successes or problems in the previous year. It provides an outline of changes planned for the year ahead and how these fit into the company strategy for the medium and long term. It also summarises the financial progress of the company.

Team briefings

Messages about new developments and changes in production methods or the solutions to problems can be rapidly cascaded by team briefings – a regular and

systematic provision of up-to-date information. The board agrees key messages, these are communicated face-to-face with managers, managers pass these on in face-to-face meetings with supervisors and they, in turn, pass on the messages through similar meetings with production teams.

Working groups

'Quality improvement teams'

Sometimes a problem can be solved or change achieved by bringing together people from different departments and different levels to deal with a specific issue. It might be the introduction of a different manufacturing process or a problem with defective products, missed deadlines or customer complaints. The group is brought together to discuss a particular issue for a specified period, it makes recommendations and then disbands.

Quality Circles

These are groups of people meeting to deal with problems of quality which they have identified in their day-to-day work. The groups are retained on an on-going basis. Membership is voluntary, meetings are held during normal working hours and the group itself sets priorities for the topics it will cover. See also chapter 5 of this unit.

Notice boards

This is an old, and far from 'high tech', technique but, if used properly, posters and notice boards can provide accurate and speedy information on production achievements, safety records and quality performance. This can help to correct some of the misinformed and exaggerated stories which flourish on the unofficial 'grapevine' in every workplace.

Job appraisal

All employees agree with their immediate manager the scope of their job. This job description means that the objectives, duties required, responsibilities and performance levels expected are understood and can be used as a basis for regular appraisals. At appraisals, the manager can give feedback to employees on how well they are performing against job requirements, the employees can express any ideas they might have for improving their performance and, together, they might identify any training needs that ought to be met.

Suggestion schemes

Employees are encouraged to produce ideas – in writing or orally – on how products, processes or administrative procedures could be improved. Sometimes cash awards are made for ideas which, when adopted, can help the organisation to save money or improve customer services without additional costs.

In addition to the above, the FKI Group has adopted the following strategies:

- weekly meetings of directors and middle managers

- a team enterprise approach – authority is delegated to production teams

- project teams are formed for short periods to address cross-company issues

- directors also address the entire workforce together at a quarterly meeting which provides an explanation of business plans, progress and problems. Questions and suggestions are encouraged.

Informal communication

Informal communication – unofficial, outside formal channels.

The FKI Group case study gives all the ways of communication within the group the general title of 'talking'. In this case, 'talking' means a two-way communication process in all its forms. Strictly speaking, talking, whether face-to-face or on the telephone, is part of informal communication. It is, as it has always been, one of the main ways in which instructions, ideas, suggestions and comments can be exchanged quickly. To be effective, oral communication needs some rules and we shall look at these later in some detail.

It is also important to recognise that all unofficial, unplanned communication which takes place outside the organisation's formal channels merits the name of informal communication. It may happen, for example, via the '**grapevine**', over lunch or on social occasions. In other words, such communication is outside the control and the structure of the organisation.

'Grapevine' – a term used to describe rumours and general gossip in the workplace. It can be inaccurate, and may distort the real situation.

The dangers of the 'grapevine' can be largely avoided by more open communication through the formal channels.

Feedback

Feedback is a feature of the democratic style of management (see page 45). It is a built-in system of two-way communication in the workplace and is important as it ensures that a message has been fully understood and also enables subordinates to contribute to the decision making process. In theory, if it works well it should bind the two sides more closely together. Unfortunately, in some organisations, although the workers are asked for their comments and suggestions on various issues, their response is generally ignored. Eventually this lack of real communication is bound to lead to workers' disillusionment and dissatisfaction.

Restricted communication

For reasons of confidentiality, some information is passed to only a selected number of people. Sometimes this type of communication, known as 'telling only those who need to know' is used for reasons of efficiency.

Open communication

Information placed in the public domain, to which everyone has access, is called open communication. Open channels can be traditional or electronic:

- traditional – a notice board, newsletter, tannoy message, staff meetings, etc.
- electronic – MIS which can be adjusted to send information to all users.

External communication

As we have seen, a business organisation must have good internal communication channels in place if it is to function efficiently. Equally important are the ways in which a business deals with the world outside.

CASE STUDY

In need of a system?

Stephanie has just started work in the office of Paul Stetting, Managing Director of Just Games Ltd, a medium sized firm which manufactures board games. At her interview, Stephanie was asked about the business course she had just completed. When she was offered the job, her new boss told her that he had been impressed by her answer to a question about the importance of communication in the workplace.

'I'm looking forward to working with you,' he enthused. 'In this company, we are very keen to ensure that our channels of communication, both internal and external, are efficient, and that our employees feel they are important to the firm!'

Stephanie was rather surprised to find that, in spite of what Paul had said, communication in the company seemed rather haphazard. For example, the managers did not hold any meetings with their teams. When asked why, one of them told her: 'If they want to know what's going on, they can ask. If they don't ask, obviously they are not interested, so it would be a waste of time to call

meetings and tell them things that they do not need to know to do their job.'

One of Stephanie's responsibilities was the supervision of six people in the general office. To her astonishment, although the office was fully equipped with the most up-to-date new technology, none of the workers had been trained to use e-mail or the internet. Even worse, the filing system was so disorganised that customers' letters, memos from other departments and other written communications could not be located, making follow-up problems very difficult to deal with.

Stephanie was horrified to hear some of the juniors answering the telephone in an off-hand manner, often while chewing gum or eating their lunch.

At the first opportunity, Stephanie spoke to Paul about her concerns. He, however, did not seem unduly perturbed by her comments. 'If you think something is wrong, put it right. I do think communication is important, but too many rules and regulations get in the way of real work. We are doing all right as we are, and I must remind you that, after all, you're not a member of the managing team.'

Stephanie was very upset.

As you know, a business organisation exists to provide goods or services, and it must make a profit in order to survive. However efficient its internal communication, it will fail if it does not communicate efficiently with outside agencies or individuals. Methods used in external communication are frequently the same as those used within the organisation, but the recipients are quite different.

Organisations must communicate with:

- their suppliers

- their customers
- local authorities
- the Inland Revenue
- the VAT office
- banks and insurance companies
- other organisations, e.g. insurance brokers, solicitors, market research specialists.

For example, communicating with suppliers is of great importance. Wrong materials can wreck a product and delays in delivery often cost large amounts of money. Even when dealing with a long established supplier, communications must be clear, adequate and in the correct format. When buying in materials or parts, a company will:

- ask for a catalogue or a price list
- send a letter of enquiry
- receive a reply, usually in the form of a quotation
- place an order
- receive an invoice
- send payment.

You can see from this that even one transaction entails a number of communications between the company and the supplier. All of them are necessary, although nowadays various methods can be used. For example, an enquiry can be made by telephone, by letter, through fax or e-mail.

Similarly, communicating with customers can be done in different ways. If a company deals directly with individuals, a letter or the telephone is still the most common method. If the company sells to wholesalers or retailers, it often sends sales representatives to meet with the bulk purchaser face-to-face, as well as using the telephone, the fax and e-mail.

Each department in a large organisation communicates with different external agencies and should have an efficient system in place to enable it to do so.

More about oral communication

We have already examined the various methods through which we communicate. Most business organisations spend much time and money putting their communication channels into place. They are aware of the need for written, or otherwise recorded, messages to be clear, unambiguous and suitable for the purpose for which they are to be used. However, the most basic and direct form – oral communication – is often overlooked by individuals and organisations alike. It is frequently assumed, albeit wrongly, that 'everyone can talk'. To be effective when communicating orally, we need to understand what it entails. Another aspect of interpersonal communication is body language. We shall now look in some detail at what makes for effectiveness in oral and written communications.

Oral communication is the most basic and easiest form of communication between people. We all talk to many people – friends, family, shop assistants and even those we meet casually in the street. People at work also communicate in this way. A supervisor might give verbal instructions to members of his or her team. If the instructions need clarification, the workers might ask for extra details that are also given verbally. Managers at all levels talk to their subordinates, and also to each other. For such communication to be effective in a business situation some rules must be adhered to.

- The language used must be suitable for the purpose – using highly technical expressions when explaining something to a very young and inexperienced worker is not likely to help him or her.
- A clear and distinct speaking voice is very important – mumbled information is not easily understood.
- The speaker should be able to put people at their ease.
- Finally, it is not enough to be able to talk to others; it is also very important to listen to what they have to say, as verbal communication is a two-way process.

Body language

In face-to-face communication, body language is also important. By body language, we mean facial expressions, gestures and movement or body posture. For example, employees who meet members of the public are trained to smile and look interested, and not to sound bored or to slouch. If you have ever had an interview, perhaps for a job or for a college place, you will know that candidates are advised to appear interested, speak clearly, and show interest and enthusiasm.

Written communication

This channel is of great importance and has the advantage that the information it contains is recorded and can be referred to later. This avoids misunderstandings. On the other hand, limiting communication with people to memos only, for example, has some disadvantages. Individuals might misinterpret the contents of a memo and draw different conclusions from the message it contains.

In the workplace, in addition to memos, there are several other forms of written information, such as:

- newsletters
- handbooks
- bulletins
- circulars
- notices posted on notice boards.

Telephone communication

Talking on the telephone is a method of business communication used very frequently and for many reasons. It is still oral but since those talking cannot see each other, the tone of voice used and clarity of expression are even more vital. At some time we have probably all had to deal with someone in a business organisation who does not seem to know anything, and does not seem to care. Often the person on the other end of the telephone is the first contact of a customer with the organisation. If he or she is impatient, impolite or ignorant, the customer might decide to have nothing more to do with that particular company.

Communication is only successful when the intended result is achieved. This effectiveness is dependent on the choice of recipient, the clarity of the message and the choice of the communication medium.

Source: Times 100

It is important to understand the close relationship between effective communication and the achievement of business objectives. Managers devote a large percentage of their working day to communicating. On average, 75 per cent of management time is spent talking; at the highest levels of management this rises to 90 per cent. Communication is the process by which planning, organising, leading, directing and controlling are carried out in all organisations. Good communications should reduce conflict and prevent avoidable misunderstandings. Some would argue that it is the solution to all conflicts within organisations. While this is really too sweeping a statement, the importance of good communications is very great.

Revision Questions

1   Give three examples of internal business communication. (3 marks)

2   Give three examples of external business communication. (3 marks)

3   What is meant by electronic communication? Give examples. (6 marks)

4   What are the advantages of electronic communication to a business? (4 marks)

5   Why are some companies not using electronic communication? (3 marks)

6   Why should a large firm have a well established system of communication channels? (2 marks)

7   Explain, with reference to an organisational chart of a company, the difference between upward and downward communication. (5 marks)

8   Why is feedback an important part of communication? (2 marks)

9   With reference to the 'Talking is not enough' case study, what advice would you give to Marvin to improve his relationship with his workers? (5 marks)

10   What is meant by 'lateral flow of information'? (2 marks)

11   Why is some information in a business sent only to 'those who need to know'? (2 marks)

12   Why are all matters concerned with staff recruitment and selection dealt with through formal communication? (3 marks)

13   In the case study 'The FKI Group', why is 'talking' used to mean all channels of communication? (2 marks)

14   Why can the 'grapevine' communication channels do harm to a business organisation? (3 marks)

15   How, and by what means, should a customer service department deal most effectively with a customer who has twice not received goods ordered six weeks ago, after a promise from the company that delivery would be within 10 days? (4 marks)

16   Why in oral communication is it as important to be a good listener as it is to be a good speaker? (3 marks)

17   Why do managers spend a large part of their working days talking? (2 marks)

CHAPTER 5

Production and Quality

KEY TERMS:

production	kaban system	just-in-time (JIT)
added value	cell working	quality circles
efficiency	quality control	lead time
productivity	quality assurance	benchmarking
lean production	total quality management (TQM)	

In this chapter you will be introduced to the concept of production of both goods and services, how the production process aims at adding value to products, and why all organisations, both public and private, consider this to be important. You will also examine various Japanese production improvement methods, including lean production and just-in-time, and consider the crucial importance of quality to companies by investigating the ideas and cultures underpinning quality control, quality assurance, and total quality management.

Introduction – what is production?

Production – the provision of goods and services by private and public organisations.

An understanding of the concept of added value is central to an understanding of the term 'production'. However, before we examine the various ways that businesses add value to their products, it is appropriate to look at some of the popular misconceptions surrounding the term 'production'.

In the first place, the word 'production', as used in economic textbooks, is a broad, comprehensive notion. It not only refers to the manufacture of products like cars and computers, but also to such intangible services as advertising, distributing, and selling cars and computers. The term also includes the goods and services provided by public sector organisations, e.g. the central government and local authorities, as well as those supplied by the profit making private sector.

The concept of added value

Added value – (i) the difference between the cost of producing a product or service and the selling price; or

(ii) the additional benefit offered to a buyer, e.g. the increased quality that persuades him or her to purchase.

Production is essentially about adding value to goods and services. Added value is one of the most important economic ideas you will encounter on your course. It is therefore vital that you gain an understanding of what it means, both for the success of organisations and, indeed, for the economic well-being of the country.

Let us look briefly at how a company involved in the oil industry might go about adding value to its product.

1 Crude oil, which is lying thousands of metres below the desert of Saudi Arabia, certainly has potential value (companies are, after all, willing to pay millions of pounds to be granted a concession to explore for it). Value is added when the oil, which is unusable as crude, is discovered and brought to the surface.

2 Its value will increase after it is pumped through pipelines to the coast, loaded on to oil tankers, and transported to Europe for processing.

3 The value of the product will be further enhanced when the crude oil is refined, by means of a cracking plant, into petrol.

4 It will undergo another significant addition of value at the next stage, when it is distributed to the petrol service stations for sale to the public.

You should note that at each stage in our example value has been added to the product.

A company like BP Amoco, which is involved at every stage of the production of petrol, will aim to maximise added value at each stage. It recognises that business success is achieved by adding the maximum amount of value to the product.

All businesses search for new ways to add value to their products. This may be achieved by trying to make them more reliable, so that the public will be prepared to pay higher prices. You will discover later in this chapter that the customer's perception of a product's quality is now seen as the most important factor in deciding whether the product or service, and indeed the business, will be successful.

Yet another, increasingly important, way of adding value is by providing service. Very sensibly, companies aim at establishing good customer relationships, whether the customer is the public or another company in the chain of production. Relationships are built and maintained by attentive aftersales service – an added value which is essential for complicated technical products such as computers and mobile telephones.

The concept of added value can therefore be seen as much more than simply changing the physical nature of a product. These days, it must also include excellent service which further enhances value by creating favourable impressions of both the product and the company. Advertising certainly has a role to play here. It can add to the product's value as it is perceived by the customer, but this perception can be maintained only if the product or service advertised is genuinely a quality product.

Organisations that provide services are also very interested in adding value to their products.

Figure 1.5.1 Adding value to oil

Let us take as an example a further education college. It might try to add value to its courses (the product) by providing, in addition to the basic teaching programme, the following add-on services:

- a personal one-to-one tutorial system
- a counselling service
- work experience placements for vocational courses
- overseas educational visits
- state-of-the-art sports and recreational facilities
- a crèche for the children of parents returning to education.

Students are likely to find some of these additional services both valuable and attractive. The college will be keen to offer them because it hopes, by doing so, to attract and retain more and better students who will complete their studies with high grades. This should enhance the college's reputation locally, which will, in turn, encourage other students to apply for its courses. A successful college is better able to attract increased funding from the government and consolidate its position. Thus it will have become stronger as a result of having added value to its basic product.

Adding value by quality assurance

Value is added by companies offering customers the reliability and quality that they want. On page 68 you will see that quality expert Tom Peters argues the greater importance of quality over price in determining demand for the majority of goods and services. He contends that at a time when customers' incomes and expectations are rising, they will always consider paying extra for superior quality. Later in this chapter you will learn the ways in which companies approach the issue of quality.

Adding value by improving productivity

Private companies seek to maximise their profits. In a competitive market, the option of raising prices to increase profits is not a realistic possibility. Companies must therefore look for other ways to achieve this. The obvious way is to improve **efficiency** and, by improving efficiency, improve **productivity**.

Efficiency – producing results effectively and with little waste of effort.

Productivity – a measurement of the efficiency with which a firm turns production inputs, e.g. labour and raw materials, into outputs.

Although efficiency and productivity are not identical terms (see the definition boxes), for our purpose of illustrating the increased value that the company can achieve by being more productive, they will be treated on this occasion as if they are the same.

If a firm is able to increase its production (outputs) while still using the same quantity of **factors of production** (inputs), then it will have improved its productivity. By achieving the same value of sales at a lower cost, it will also have increased the added value of production. A firm will also improve its productivity if it can achieve the same value of output with fewer or cheaper factors of production. Businesses will always seek the most efficient ways to produce and this invariably means the cheapest. Increases in the price of one factor will quickly persuade the business to substitute it with a less costly factor. There is little doubt that the more expensive labour becomes – on average it accounts for more than two-thirds of total manufacturing costs – the more management will switch to automated production and away from labour-intensive production. Examples of this development are to be found in modern car-assembly plants, where unskilled and semiskilled workers have been replaced by computer-controlled robots.

Robots in use at a modern car-assembly plant

Using human resources to add value

Reduced stock levels which result from the introduction of just-in-time production methods (see below) will improve a company's quality and this improved quality will add value to the product being produced. However, such a system requires well trained, flexible and preferably multiskilled labour to operate it efficiently. Training labour to this standard results in additional costs, which British management has traditionally been reluctant to incur. Indeed, according to an article in *The Economist* magazine (17 May 1997) many British bosses are generally unconvinced of the merits of training. A survey of British business people, carried out by the Institute of Personnel and Development, found that almost half preferred to poach trained workers from other companies, rather than to train their own workers; and more than a third worried that, once trained, people were more likely to leave the company.

Furthermore, half of British companies failed to spend their annual training budgets. Compared with Germany, France, Japan and the USA, British companies spend a much smaller percentage of their resources on training. This unwillingness to invest in training programmes is short-sighted, as a well trained workforce will almost certainly bring greater productivity and profitability.

Just-in-time production (JIT)

> 'The JIT idea is very simple; produce and deliver finished goods just in time to be sold, subassemblies just in time to be assembled into finished goods, fabricated parts just in time to go into subassemblies and purchased materials just in time to be transformed into fabricated parts.'
>
> *Source*: *Japanese Manufacturing Techniques*, by R. Schonberger

The JIT method of production had its origins in the Japanese car company Toyota. The method was developed and refined throughout the 1960s and 1970s when it was popularly referred to as the Toyota Manufacturing System. It was enthusiastically taken up by other Japanese manufacturers and came to be recognised in the USA and Europe as part of the explanation for Japan's industrial success. The system made use of a series of cards as part of the control mechanism which was known in the West as the **kaban** system ('kaban' is Japanese for 'card'). This is somewhat misleading, as the system depended on more than the use of cards for its operation.

Kaban system – an integral part of JIT production that was developed in Japan in the 1960s and 1970s. It involves each stage of the production process holding only a minimum stock of work-in-progress. This reduces the likelihood of extensive production faults and also reduces the amount of money tied up in work-in-progress.

The JIT approach aims to reduce production costs by keeping stocks of material, components, and work-in-progress at minimum levels, and to produce finished goods just before they are due to be sold. In addition, the components required to complete the finished product, whether they are produced in-house or bought in, are very tightly scheduled, so that they arrive at final assembly just as they are needed. Typically, the assembly plant will aim at keeping no more than a half-day's stock in its stores. Obviously, to operate the system successfully requires very careful planning and right-first-time quality; otherwise the whole production operation very quickly comes to a stop.

Another important idea underpinning JIT production is the elimination, wherever possible, of 'waste', as the term is understood in its widest possible sense. Here 'waste' means 'anything other than the minimum amount of equipment, materials, parts, space, and workers' time which are absolutely essential to add value to the product'.

This approach requires that the production process is carefully examined to see at which points value is added and, more significantly, where unnecessary non-value-added activities take place. Non-value costs are usually added at the following production stages:

- storage
- quality inspection
- rework of faulty materials and parts
- work movement.

All the above stages are part of the standard production process.

By focusing efforts on cutting out waste as it is defined above, a company increases its productivity and profitability. The JIT approach, then, will ideally concentrate on such non-value-added activities as:

- improving the production layout flow of components through the plants
- reducing batch sizes because large batch sizes lead to high costs and often low quality
- increasing the reliability and quality of suppliers
- reducing the total number of suppliers and working closely with these preferred subcontractors
- creating a culture of continuous improvement.

A reliable measure of the amount of waste in a production process can be obtained by looking closely at stock levels. Invariably, high stock levels tend to hide quality problems, machine downtime (the time when the machine is idle), and late deliveries. A JIT system will bring these problems to light.

Lean production

Lean production – economical and efficient production which does not use more inputs (resources) than are absolutely necessary to produce the final product.

Lean production is the name given to a series of measures, originally developed and practised in Japan, that are designed to reduce waste, improve quality, and increase profits. Table 1.5.1 sets out the essential differences between lean and traditional methods of production.

Table 1.5.1

Typical features of traditional vs lean methods of production		
	Traditional	**Lean**
Stock	Large	Small
Set-ups	Slow, infrequent	Fast, frequent
Quality	Statistically based methods to identify defective goods for reworking	Quality products first time
Batch size	Large	Small
Management	By edict (order)	By agreement
Worker skill	Single function – routine	Multi-function
Suppliers	Seen as adversaries/many sources	Seen as partners/few sources
Deliveries	Few	Many
Communication	Vertical and mainly downward	Multiple
Consultation	Limited	Extensive

Source: 'Lean Production', by Bruce Jewel, in *Business Education Today*, March–April 1998

Who is lean production for?

Who benefits if British firms adopt lean production techniques?

1. The firm – adopting lean production should benefit the firm. Cost will be cut, quality will improve, workers will be more motivated. As a system of production, there will have to be a direct benefit to the firm if there is to be any internal motivation to adopt such changes.

2. Customers – the recognition of the importance of the consumer to a business places the customer at the heart of all that the organisation does. By presenting the customer with a better quality product and allowing the firm to be more responsive to changes in customer demands, lean production ought to lead to greater customer satisfaction.

3. The economy – by creating a more efficient use of resources, the economy as a whole ought to become more competitive with other countries.

Source: 'Are we Heading for Lean Times?', by Ian Swift, in *Business Review*, November 1997

It is now time to consider what is involved when a company adopts a lean production practice. Its introduction necessitates the following:

- just-in-time approaches to production and stock-holding (see above)
- time-based competition, involving shorter product development and shorter **lead times**

Lead time – the time taken by a firm between receiving an order for a product or service and delivering it.

- **Quality circles** – these can be regarded as productivity improvement groups (see page 70)

Quality circles – discussion groups that meet regularly to identify quality problems, consider alternative solutions and recommend them to management.

- autonomous team-working
- enabling workers to take decisions and solve problems
- flexible methods of manufacturing, involving computer-controlled machines and a multiskilled workforce
- flexible working methods
- **cell working**.

Cell working – the logical arrangement of equipment into groups of machines to process families of parts.

With the exception of time-based competition, the other lean production methods are investigated elsewhere in this unit. It is worth looking at time-based competition in detail now, as it brings to light some surprising facts about traditional production practices.

This is what happens when a pair of spectacles is ordered: a customer has an eye test, receives a prescription, chooses a frame, places an order, and, perhaps after a couple of weeks, the order is delivered. However, the manufacturer does not work on the spectacles for the whole of this period. For most of the time the order waits in a queue and the part-finished product waits to be completed. So, for 99 per cent of the time nothing is done to complete the order and, as value is not being added, this is unproductive time. Value is added only during the brief period that the lenses are being made and fitted into the frame.

Source: 'Lean Production' by Bruce Jewell, in *Business Education Today*, March-April 1998.

This example illustrates the rather startling statistic that productive time can be as little as 1 per cent of the time taken to complete an order. If companies can reduce this unproductive time, they can gain a competitive advantage. This opportunity was seized on by firms such as Vision Express who offer a high-speed service in which spectacles are made on the premises within an hour.

Time-based competition emphasises the old adage that 'time is money'.

In their book *Competing Against Time-based Competition is Reshaping Global Markets*, George Stalk and Thomas Hout use the example of the 'H-Y War'. This explains how Honda defeated their competition, Yamaha, by the speed of their product development (60 new models of motorcycles in one year and a further 113 in 18 months). These authors invented the '0.5 to 5 rule', according to which value is only added to products during 0.5 per cent to 5 per cent of the time taken to manufacture them. The remaining time is unproductive because no value is being added. By eliminating this wasted time, it has been estimated that manufacturers can get their product to the market between 20 and 200 times faster.

Quality

Few will take issue with the statement that quality is an important factor throughout the production process. This applies as much to the provision of services as it does to the production of goods and is as true of the public sector as it is of the private sector. The importance of quality is not a new development. Organisations have always endeavoured to produce reliable goods to specification and to provide a satisfactory, reliable service. If nothing else, the existence of private sector competitors ready to poach their markets always provided the spur, were it needed, to 'get things right'.

What is a relatively new development is the current overwhelming importance that quality has assumed in the minds of consumers. They now expect, even demand, a very high degree of reliability in the products and services they buy. Companies unable to supply to these expected standards are extremely unlikely to survive. In today's world, a business that lacks quality products will simply not continue to exist and, furthermore, a local authority that fails to provide efficient services will be subjected to a constant barrage of criticism and, following the next local election, probable replacement.

The importance of quality

In his book *Thriving on Chaos*, the business and quality guru Tom Peters claims that how consumers perceive the quality of products and services is the *most* important factor in deciding whether the product or service will be successful in the marketplace and, by implication, whether the business which provides them will itself be successful.

Quality is now regarded by consumers as more important than price in determining the demand for a wide range of goods and services. Customers are prepared to pay more for a quality product. According to Tom Peters' analysis, consumer quality involves the following:

- It must give consumer satisfaction.
- It must exceed consumers' expectations and, in doing so,
- It must *delight* the consumer.

It should be obvious from the foregoing that what the customer wants is of supreme importance, whether the customer is a member of the public or another business in the 'chain' of production. Focus on the customer's needs is a crucial feature of **total quality management** (TQM), a concept which we will be examining in more detail later in this chapter.

At this point, we must understand that customer focus involves a business being prepared to change in line with constantly changing customer requirements. This may include changing fashion, tastes and designs or anything else. It is even an advantage, naturally, if the business is able to anticipate changes and, where possible, exceed customers' expectations.

Quality systems

Three stages have been identified in the development of quality systems over the past 50 years. They are:

- quality control (QC)
- quality assurance (QA)
- total quality management (TQM).

Quality control

Quality control has been a feature of production of British industry for many years. Perhaps it is best

Quality control – a system of detecting faults in products and services and keeping the faults within acceptable limits by a process of inspection.

understood as it is applied to manufacturing processes, but it is also used in service organisations. The QC approach to reliability is based on a business accepting that errors are bound to happen when goods are produced and that it is the responsibility of the firm's inspection department to find and remove faulty products before they are dispatched to the customer. QC therefore concentrates the inspection effort on fault detection. The noteworthy feature of the process is that it takes place after the goods have been produced and money has already been expended on their manufacture. This approach to quality cannot avoid wasting time and materials, with the result that the organisation must incur additional costs, i.e. the cost of inspection time spent detecting the faults, reworking the components where this is possible, or, if not, the cost of scrapping them.

Quality control is undertaken by inspectors using a range of inspection and test equipment. Some inspectors patrol the production areas, checking parts as they are made, while others check the final product. Obviously, the earlier in the production process faults are discovered, the less waste and cost are incurred by the company. Nevertheless, the business accepts a percentage of waste; it is an unavoidable aspect of operating a quality control system. As a matter of course a wastage factor is built into the original estimate of the cost of producing the product.

Quality assurance

Quality assurance – attempting to assure that quality standards are maintained throughout all areas of an organisation. The system aims at achieving zero defects, i.e. perfect quality.

The quality assurance (QA) concept takes quality control an important step further. It is concerned with preventing faults from happening in the first place by aiming at producing zero defects, whereas QC tries only to limit defects to an acceptable percentage.

While the operation of QC is the responsibility of the inspection department, QA is, by contrast, an organisation-wide approach that places responsibility for quality on the *whole* workforce, particularly the front-line operators who actually make the product. Operators carry out their own scheduled quality checks, involving a technique called statistical process control which uses various inspection instruments and inspection gauges. The operators are required by management to keep records of the inspection check and, in some companies, are given the additional authority to stop their section of the production process if the part they are making is 'out of tolerance', i.e. outside the limits of accuracy established by statistical process control.

> 'Toyota is the only car-manufacturing company that empowers its members to hold up the production line if something goes wrong. This takes a lot of courage. On the assembly line, a car is made every 88 seconds. So, halting the production line for a minute and a half costs £15,000 – the price of an Avensis car.' (Assistant General Manager of Quality Assurance, David Hurst)
>
> *Source*: 'Making a Lean Machine', by Lee Knight, in *Business Education Today*, May–June 1998

Although in the operation of a QA system a large measure of the responsibility for product quality is transferred from the inspection department to the worker/operator, inspectors still retain an important role in the process. Initially, it is they who set up the QA system and establish, from the outset, the quality standard expected. It is also their responsibility to see that the standards are maintained both inside the factory and also by the subcontractors that supply the factory.

This is particularly important where QA is applied to goods inward inspection. If the bought-in materials used in production are of an unsatisfactory standard there is little or no chance that the finished article will be a quality product. This will also have important repercussions on the company's relationship with the subcontractor. Failure to supply correctly may well jeopardise the whole production process, with far-reaching adverse consequences for the subcontractor, the company and the company's customers.

CASE STUDY

Lucas

Computer system helps to achieve zero defects

With a little help from their computer system, buyers at the Lucas brake factory at Cwmbran in South Wales have secured a major improvement in their suppliers' quality levels. In the 12 months to October 1994, the proportion of goods received which were rejected fell to 2,500 per million. And the number of concessions – goods received out of specification but accepted into production – fell more than fivefold. 'We are confident that by prevention rather than detection we can achieve zero defects,' says purchasing agent Martyn Brown. To improve their monitoring of supplier performance, buyers of Cwmbran developed a system on an IBM database. It can generate a wide range of comparative reports. Assessing quality levels, it can compare one supplier against another, or one supplier against commodity or industry standard performance; it can compare suppliers by a particular item; it can immediately generate virtually any report a buyer wants, covering any time period required. 'The system is providing us with the type of information that we and our suppliers need to achieve zero defects,' says Brown. 'We now communicate performance data electronically to our suppliers monthly, advising them of progress towards their agreed targets. It helps us and our quality engineers to focus on the real problem areas.'

Source: Bnet

Total quality management

TQM could be described as an attitude of mind. An attitude which aims at achieving continuous quality, efficiency and reliability creates improvements throughout the whole organisation. It is an approach which takes the level of the reliability and quality concept beyond QA. It is concerned with creating an organisation-wide culture of quality which permeates every aspect and every department of the business. Quality should become as much the concern of the lowest paid worker as it is of the chief executive.

Essential to an understanding of the concept is the notion that organisations must put customers and consumers and clients at the very centre of the production and service process. This is a key issue for all organisations, in both the private and public sectors, as business life becomes increasingly more difficult. In the private sector, competition grows more fierce all the time; in the public sector the level of service demanded by the taxpayer continues to rise. Successful organisations will be those that are able to meet, and aim at excelling, their customers' needs all the time, every time. Consistently delighting customers, as Tom Peters informs us, is today's number one business objective. It is, after all, the customer who ultimately pays the wages.

It is now time to examine the various control and assurance systems that, when combined with the organisation's focus on the quality requirements of the customer, constitute TQM.

Quality circles

Quality circles form an important part of a company's programme of continuous improvement and make a notable contribution to the goal of TQM. The particular features of quality circles may be summarised as follows:

- They are a small group of workers who meet voluntarily and appoint their own group leader.
- They meet on a regular basis, often after work.
- They are usually from the same work area.
- Their purpose is to identify, investigate, analyse, and solve work-related problems.
- They present their solutions to the management.

- They are actively involved in implementing and monitoring the effectiveness of the suggested solutions.

The participants of a quality circle are in it by choice and they select which work problems are to be tackled – these aspects are the essential characteristics of a circle – these, and the experience and enthusiasm that each member of the group brings to the tasks. The problems they tackle are not just restricted to quality but include anything connected with operations in the workplace. However, issues such as pay and working conditions are avoided.

The benefits of quality circles

The introduction into a company of quality circles invariably leads to the correction of faults and to increased reliability of products and services. This, in turn, enhances employees' job satisfaction and their pride in good workmanship. In itself, this then leads to enhanced quality, to an increased awareness of the importance of quality matters in the organisation and, most significantly, to fostering an attitude which seeks

to implement continuous improvement. Another benefit to the organisation is improved two-way communication. Management and staff become more aware of and sympathetic to each other's problems. Furthermore, communications between departments also improve and, as circles attempt to solve the problems of their own area, other, previously hidden difficulties are revealed in associated processes and areas.

The management structure and training which are necessary for quality circles to operate is the same as that needed for the installation of the Quality Standard ISO 9000, which is, as we shall see on page 72, also an important and necessary part of a total quality management programme.

The commitment to improvement demonstrated by quality circles reassures customers and, although the companies implementing quality circles usually do not have financial gain as their principal goal, they often find that the financial benefits of the scheme significantly outweigh the costs.

CASE STUDY

Paragon Laundry

Since quality circles have been in place, many problems have been solved.

The Paragon Laundry Group has 10 outlets in the South West of England and South Wales. The outlets provide a full cross-section of services, from laundry and dry cleaning for the domestic customer, to garment rental and linen hire to industry, businesses and hotels.

These areas all demand a high degree of quality if collection, processing and delivery are to take place at the right time, in the right number, and to the right standard.

Paragon's first exposure to quality circles came when Managing Director Derek Stevens attended a seminar on the subject. Convinced that this was something that fitted into the company's overall philosophy, he immediately organised a further seminar for all the laundry's general managers.

A pilot scheme was launched in those laundries where general managers were most enthusiastic. Progress was swift, and in no time members of staff, many of whom had probably never before spoken in a meeting, were standing up before their managing director to make points. It was an eye opener on what circles could do for individual self-development. They were also solving real problems and beginning to think about the job they were doing. Another advantage of the circles, soon discovered by Paragon, was that a fair number of 'problems' solved themselves in minutes once they had been raised and discussed within the circle.

Since quality circles have been in place at Paragon, many problems relating to the workplace have been solved, from improvements in layout to communication with customers and installing new phone systems. Not all circles have survived, and there is sometimes a right time to rest a circle, but Mr Stevens is pleased to note that they usually start up again with new members once there is a new problem to solve. In fact, the number of circles within the group has continued to grow.

Once a year there is a quality circle get-together to which everyone involved in quality circles is invited, and where one or two quality circles make presentations, along with outside guest speakers.

Quality circles are now an integral part of life at Paragon Laundry. No doubt, over the years the practice and methodology will evolve, but in their basic outlook they are essential to the company's total quality philosophy.

Source: Bnet

ISO 9000

Using formal quality standards and systems to ensure consistently reliable supplies had its origins in the armed services after the Second World War. The services developed specific defence standards for the manufacture of munitions. These were later taken up, modified appropriately and used in other sectors of engineering and manufacturing industry. Following on from this, in 1979 the British Standards Institute (BSI) published BS5750, which further contributed to the raising of quality throughout UK industry. This standard was later adopted internationally (hence the letters ISO, which stand for International Standards Organisation), and developed into the ISO 9000 series which is now used by over 100,000 organisations in 70 countries. The provisions of ISO 9000 are now being adapted and used by non-commercial organisations such as hospitals, educational institutions and local government.

ISO 9000 offers three standards:

- ISO 9001 – a model for quality assurance in design, development, production, installation, and servicing

- ISO 9002 – a model for quality assurance in production, installation, and servicing

- ISO 9003 – a model for quality assurance in final inspection and testing.

A company needs to adopt only one of these standards and the nature of the business will determine which is chosen. Thus, if the business is a design-and-build contractor, a manufacturer of custom-designed products or a professional organisation, it will choose ISO 9001. The key factor in this decision is that there is a design element in what it produces. If the business is, for example, a manufacturer of standard products, or an estate agent, or an installer of burglar alarms, it will consider ISO 9002. If, on the other hand, the business supplies simple products or services, where the customer can easily check its quality, as in the case of the service performed by a window cleaner or shoe repairer, then ISO 9003 will be the appropriate standard.

The underlying principles of ISO 9000 are applicable to large and small businesses. The standards are flexible and adaptable to the particular needs of all companies. Should the firm be small and have a fairly straightforward product or service, then a short and simple quality system would be sufficient to meet its needs.

CASE STUDY

Stelmax

Stelmax employs 12 people and makes high quality, PVC-based adhesives and sealants. Founder Pat Martin has always run a tight ship and wanted the company to remain small and profitable.

'I used to think that ISO 9000 was just for the big fish in the sea,' she said.

'But I increasingly recognised that quality is important to all firms, large, medium and small. Although I understood that ISO 9000 would not change the quality of the products, I did know that it could guarantee their consistency, a factor that was likely to become more and more important in an increasingly competitive market at home and abroad.

'Do not be put off by some of the language of the standards which may appear a bit complicated. The standards have to be precise, because each requirement has to be understood in the same way by independent experts in many countries.'

Source: Bnet

The benefits of ISO 9000

ISO 9000 can help an organisation to:

- examine its business and improve its systems, methods and procedures. This often leads to significant cost savings
- involve and motivate staff to raise their performance, introduce further improvements, and to do things right first time
- ensure that orders are delivered consistently on time
- highlight product or service deficiencies and develop design/process improvements
- make sure that any quality failures and customer complaints are recorded and investigated and prompt action is taken to prevent recurrence.

CASE STUDY

Glossop Carton and Print Ltd

The company achieved ISO 9000 certification in spring 1992. Since then its gross profit has risen and the company is producing goods more efficiently than before, thereby achieving important savings. When things go wrong, the causes can now be pinpointed more easily.

The firm, which manufactures printed and plain cartons, trays and blister cards for the DIY and car accessory industries, has seen the benefits of implementing ISO 9000 spread throughout the 28-strong organisation.

One of the company's directors claims: 'Because of our feedback to our employees, they can see what has gone wrong. We are proud of our system. Everybody in the company is involved. We feel this is the only attitude that works. The standard is not a piece of paper, it is a tool to be used. When used properly, the company reaps the rewards.'

Source: Bnet

ISO 9000 is an important part of TQM as it aims to develop a culture of continuous improvement throughout the organisation.

Benchmarking

Benchmarking – a continuous systematic process for evaluating the products, services, and work processes of organisations that are recognised as representing best practices for the purpose of organisational improvement.

Ambitious companies strive to be successful; they want to be the best at what they do, or, at the very least, as good as the best in their particular area of business. One way of discovering how they match up to the opposition is by measuring their efforts and achievements against rival companies that operate in the same sector of industry. The method that is used to do this is called **best practice benchmarking** (BPB). It is a technique increasingly used by successful companies around the world in all types of business, both manufacturing and service, to help them become as good as or better than the best.

Many of the companies which make use of this technique are household names: Ford, ICI and Nissan are examples. Others are quite small, employing only a few people. What all have in common is the realisation that success and profitability result in part from understanding how the business is performing, not only when it is judged against the previous year's accounts, but when it is measured against those who are recognised as the best performers in their industry.

Best practice benchmarking involves a combination of the following:

- deciding what, in the perception of their customers, is the essential difference between ordinary producers and outstanding producers
- setting standards which are in line with the best practice that can be found
- discovering and analysing how the best companies achieve the highest standards

- applying both other companies' experience together with their own ideas to meet and, where possible, exceed, the standard.

BPB is not about trying to become exactly like another company, nor is it simply measurement for measurement's sake. The aim is, rather, to build upon the success of others, so as to improve future performance. By benchmarking on a continuous basis, companies are benefiting from current best practice, not out-of-date concepts. Benchmarking is always carried out with the purpose of putting improvements into action and, as such, forms an important part of the philosophy of total quality management.

There are, then, serious gains to be made by a company from a BPB approach:

- better understanding of their customers and their competitors
- fewer complaints and more satisfied customers
- reduction in waste, quality problems and reworking
- faster awareness of important innovations and how they can be applied profitably
- enhanced reputation within their markets
- as a result of the above, increased profits and turnover.

Furthermore, the technique allows companies to learn from the experience and errors of others and also saves them the cost of making mistakes.

America is far ahead of Europe in implementing BPB. A major study into industrial productivity, carried out in 1990 by the Massachusetts Institute of Technology, concluded that:

'A characteristic of all the best-practice American firms we observed, large or small, is an emphasis on competitive benchmarking: comparing the performance of their products and processes with those of world leaders in order to achieve improvement and to measure progress.'

Revision Questions

1   Why do firms aim at adding value to goods and services? (4 marks)

2   Production is essentially about adding value to goods and services. Explain what this statement means, with reference to the oil industry example on page 62. (6 marks)

3   Give two examples of how an airline might add value to its basic service. (3 marks)

4   Give two examples of how a garage which repairs and services cars could add value to its operation. (3 marks)

5   Quality is replacing price as the main reason why some people buy certain products and services rather than others. Give one reason for this development. (1 mark)

6   Name three industries, other than the car industry, where automated production has replaced, or is replacing, labour-intensive production. (3 marks)

7   How does the introduction of JIT production save a company money? (3 marks)

8   The JIT method aims to reduce production costs by keeping stocks and work-in-progress at minimum levels. How will this improve the quality of products? (4 marks)

9   What is meant by the term 'lean production'? (2 marks)

10 Why does 'lean production' require that workers are multiskilled? (2 marks)

11 Explain the term 'non-productive time'. (2 mark)

12 Companies gain a competitive advantage by reducing non-productive time. Explain. (3 marks)

13 What will happen to private companies that are unable to produce quality products and services? (1 mark)

14 Focus on customers' needs is the essential ingredient for an organisation's success. Explain. (7 marks)

15 On what is the quality control (QC) approach to reliability based? (2 marks)

16 Which groups of workers are central to the operation of a QC system? (1 mark)

17 Quality assurance (QA) is all about preventing faults happening. How does an organisation go about achieving this? (6 marks)

18 Prevention, rather than detection, is the way to zero defects. Explain what this means with reference to quality systems. (8 marks)

19 Total quality management (TQM) is as much the concern of the lowest paid worker as it is of the chief executive. Why? (5 marks)

20 How does the introduction of quality circles into an organisation lead to the correction of faults and to increased reliability? (4 marks)

21 Successful TQM depends on an organisation placing the needs of its customers at the very heart of its production process. Why is this so? (4 marks)

22 If benchmarking is not about becoming exactly like another company, what is it about? (5 marks)

CASE STUDY

Phones Galore Ltd

Phones Galore Ltd, as the name implies, is a company that manufacturers a wide range of telephones. It is a family business and was established in 1977 by two brothers, Nick and Arthur Dawley. In the early years, the business was run as a partnership, on a 50:50 basis. Both brothers put in an equal amount of money at the start, and agreed to divide the profits equally. They did not bother with any written agreement as they did not think this was necessary. At the time, they manufactured domestic and office telephone units.

For the first five or six years all went well. Orders kept coming in, and the brothers managed to run the business by dividing the work between them.

In 1983, Nick accepted a large order from Metacom plc without checking that the partnership had sufficient resources available. When Phones Galore failed to deliver on time, Metacom plc invoked a penalty clause and this nearly caused Phones Galore to go bankrupt.

Arthur was very angry with his brother and demanded that Nick should cover the losses from his own assets. Nick refused, saying that they had agreed to share both profits and losses equally. Eventually, Arthur agreed, on condition that in future all decisions were to be taken by both of them.

Arthur wanted to put everything in writing at this stage, but it soon became apparent that if the firm was to continue, a number of other, major changes, would have to be made, including a new management structure and changing the status of the business.

In 1985, Phones Galore became a private limited company, with the brothers as directors, and a new production manager, Walter Slaker, was appointed.

When mobile telephones were first introduced, the brothers extended their range of products to include mobiles. This proved so successful that by the mid-1990s mobile phones accounted for 80 per cent of production.

Today, Phones Galore Ltd employs about 90 people, and, last year, it had a turnover of £5 million, with a net profit of £250,000.

Nick has now retired from the business, but recently his son, Damian, has joined the firm. Damian is 22, has completed a Vocational A Level Business course, and is very keen to show that he is capable of improving things at Phones Galore Ltd. He is particularly concerned with the style of management and the structure of the business.

Damian has been asked by his uncle to organise a sales section, as Arthur finds that he is now too busy to be in charge of that operation, and recognises that the sales reps do not really know who is in charge of them.

He thinks that the way the business is structured is not very efficient, and has already jotted down some ideas as to how it could be rearranged.

Damian is also very concerned about the management style adopted by his uncle. Arthur has told him that Phones Galore Ltd is like 'one happy family', but Damian feels that this view is incorrect. He has noticed that the turnover among the workforce is very high, and has tried to find out the reasons for this. Although the workers are rather cautious when talking to the boss's nephew, some of them have said that Arthur, although quite fair, runs the business in a very autocratic fashion.

Mel, one of the foremen in production, has become friendly with Damian and now feels that Damian can be trusted. 'The problem is,' Mel told Damian last week over a pint in the local pub, 'that your uncle's word always has to be law. Even people like Lynn and Nerys must do what

Figure 1.A.1 Organisational chart of Phones Galore Ltd.

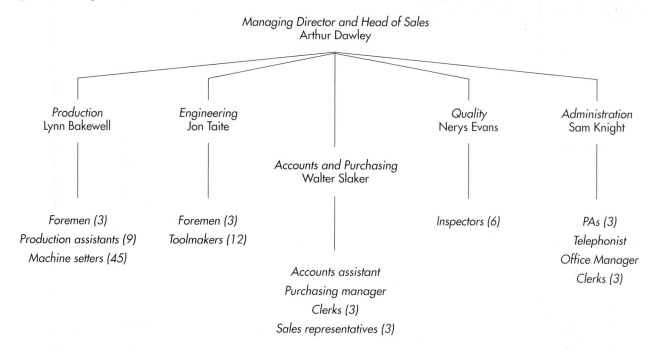

he says. The only person to whom he listens sometimes is old Walter, who has been here forever.'

'What about involving people, asking for their suggestions?' asked Damian.

'You must be joking,' said Mel. 'We're never told anything, we don't know what's going on. Whether it's good or bad, he just expects us to do our jobs, collect our pay and go home. No wonder those who can, leave. I'm looking for another job myself!'

'How about training schemes, and appraisals?'

'Your uncle doesn't believe in them. And now the grapevine has it that he is thinking of ways of improving the quality of our products, but he has not informed us of anything that this might mean. Anyway, no surprise there – he never visits the factory floor, and certainly doesn't ask for our opinions!'

Damian was very perturbed by his conversation with Mel. He realises that the whole culture of the business must change if Phones Galore is to continue, and perhaps even increase its market share. He has some ideas and intends to talk to his uncle about them, but is aware that it is going to be very difficult to persuade Arthur to change the way in which he has run the business for so many years.

Although Phones Galore does have a quality control section, Damian thinks that the way forward for the firm is to introduce TQM. He would like to try out the various methods he has been taught about, like RFT and JIT production. He is confident that, with a change in communication within the business, once the top-down method is replaced by consultation and discussion, the workers will become much happier and, therefore, more reliable and efficient and less likely to leave as soon as they are fully trained.

Damian has already tried talking to Arthur about the importance of added value in the production of goods, but Arthur laughed at the idea. 'We make a good product and don't need those new-fangled ideas of yours!' he said.

It was, therefore, a great surprise to Damian when, a few days ago, Arthur called him in and told him to prepare some suggestions to be put to the rest of the managers next week.

'It's not that I agree with all that textbook nonsense,' he said, 'but I am a bit worried. Telephones for All Co. Ltd, which, as you know, is our biggest competitor, seems to be taking away a lot of our business, and I do know that they have introduced all these strange methods. All I want is to make a decent profit, and now I have to take on these JITs and TQMs ...'

Damian knows that this is his big chance to persuade Arthur to 'bring Phones Galore into the new millennium' – which is Damian's overall aim. However, to do this, he must prepare himself before the meeting.

As Damian, you now must carry out several tasks in readiness for next week's meeting.

Task 1

1   Make an appointment for an interview with a manager of a local business. During the interview, try to find out how the management of the business:

- communicates with workers

- ensures worker co-operation

- deals with quality problems

- helps the local community

- addresses added value issues.

You should prepare a short questionnaire to ensure that you do not forget any questions and do not waste the manager's time.

2   Write a short report on your findings.

Task 2

You are concerned that Phones Galore Ltd has no marketing function in its organisational structure. You have checked and have found out that Telephones for All Co. Ltd has recently appointed a marketing manager. Collect as much marketing material, produced by different business organisations, as you can so that you can show this to the managers of Phones Galore.

Task 3

You are also concerned that there is no one responsible for human resources in your uncle's firm, and you suspect that this might be another reason why workers at Phones Galore are unhappy. Write a memo to your uncle, explaining why a human resource function is necessary.

Task 4

You are now ready to draw up a new organisational chart for Phones Galore. When you have done so, write a comprehensive set of notes explaining the reasons for all the changes that you would like to introduce.

Task 5

Arthur has made it clear that he now realises the need to introduce TQM, but you know he is not convinced about its value. Prepare a concise written statement, setting down the reasons for TQM and the best ways in which TQM can be introduced.

Task 6

Everyone in Phones Galore is used to communications coming only in the form of orders from above. Prepare some notes on the various ways in which communication in the firm can be improved. You should include an explanation of different channels of communication, as well as different methods, such as meetings, newsletters, notice boards, etc.

Task 7

You remember that Arthur has told you that all that he wants is to make a profit. He does not seem to be clear how he wants to achieve this. Write some notes explaining the difference between growth, increased sales and increased volume of sales.

Task 8

You now have to prepare to speak to Arthur and the other managers about your proposals, and the reasons why you think they should be introduced.

Using all the material from Tasks 1–7, draw up a set of notes for your presentation.

The presentation should last 10–15 minutes, and you must use diagrams, charts, etc. to illustrate your talk.

You must be prepared to answer questions from your audience.

Task 9

Imagine that two years have passed. Your suggestions have been accepted and Phones Galore now has a new organisational structure and a new management style. You have now been appointed as head of Human Resources.

As a result of the changes, turnover for the last financial year has increased to £7 million, and net profit to £400,000. The workforce is now 112. Arthur is delighted with the way things are going, and has asked you to write a detailed report on the firm as it is today.

He has also admitted that he had been wrong in saying that profit was all he wanted. He finds great satisfaction in knowing that his customers are happy and that his workers consider Phones Galore the best firm to work for.

Write a report entitled: How change has been beneficial for Phones Galore Ltd.

UNIT 2

The Competitive Business Environment

CHAPTER 1

How Competition in the Market Affects Business – An Introduction

KEY TERMS:

competition

In this chapter you will be given a brief introduction to why competition is so important in the world of business. Chapters 2, 3 and 4 will explore what causes competition in greater depth, and how businesses react to this competition.

The top selling ice cream products of 1999

Traditionally, tubs of ice cream have been the largest selling ice cream products in the UK. But times have changed. Now it is the branded products that compete most aggressively for the title of market leader. In 1999 the highest sellers were:

Figure 2.1.1

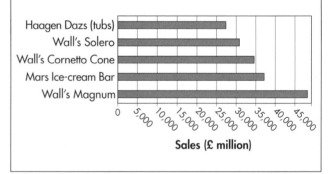

Introduction

All businesses are affected by competition. In many cases the competition is obvious. Coca-Cola is in close competition with Pepsi Cola, but it is also in competition with Virgin Cola, the supermarkets' own brands and a range of other cola brands such as Panda. But Coca-Cola is also in competition with other fizzy soft drinks, such as Fanta, 7-UP, Sprite, supermarkets' own brands and minor brands of these drinks. It is also in competition with non-fizzy soft drinks such as Sunny Delight (see page 91).

Less obvious competition is also going on. When most people go shopping they put aside a certain amount of money that they are willing to spend. If we take the example of the weekly shop at the supermarket we will find that, for many people, buying Coca-Cola is not just an alternative to buying Pepsi Cola, or other soft drinks. It is also in competition with buying bread, or meat or even a National Lottery scratch card. In the end all products are in competition with other products because the potential customers have a limited income to spend.

Competition in business does not arise just because there are other products that customers can buy. There is also competition between businesses for the best raw materials, the most skilled labour and for the best location to set up the business. Each of these will affect how a business is able to produce goods or services and the quality of the final product. Businesses compete for all of the following reasons:

- to gain or keep customers
- to employ the best labour, raw materials, premises, land, finance, etc.
- to find the best location

- to occupy the best places and times with their advertising and promotion
- to gain the right to sell in certain countries
- to be number one in the industry
- to be seen as more environmentally friendly than other businesses.

It not just the businesses that compete.

- Customers will compete with other customers to get the products that they want, especially if they are scarce.
- People will compete with other people for jobs, especially when there are high levels of unemployment.

- Shareholders may compete with customers because lower prices for customers may mean less profits for the owners.
- The needs and wishes of the community may compete with the aims and objectives of businesses, e.g. when the owners of rural public houses want to sell them off for private housing and the locals want their pubs to stay.

All of this competition affects business directly and indirectly.

The following chapters will be looking at what makes customers buy one product rather than another, and how businesses can try to ensure that it is their products that the customers will want to buy.

How supply and demand affect markets

In this chapter you will learn what supply and demand are and how they interact to determine the price of a product and the number of units of that product that are sold. This chapter will look in detail at:

- the meaning of supply and demand

- how supply and demand interact to determine the price and the quantity that are sold of a product

- what conditions cause supply and demand to change

- what determines how much the price and quantity of a product will change by when the conditions of supply or demand change.

business students to predict what will happen if the conditions change.

Figure 2.2.1 A basic supply and demand graph for Product A

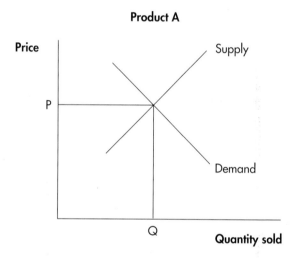

In this chapter we will consider how this graph is built up, what it means and how it can be used to help work out why businesses behave in the way that they do. By studying how supply and demand interact we can also work out:

- what will make the price and output of a product change

- what will happen to demand if a business changes its prices

- which products will allow the business to make most profit

- how businesses will be affected by what their competitors do

Supply and demand of products

Supply and demand are at the heart of all business and all trade. The producers **supply** the products and the customers **demand** them. Both sides are needed. If there was no supply there would be no products, even if customers wanted them. If there was no demand the businesses could produce the products but they would be unable to sell them. Soon the businesses would be forced to give up producing them or go bankrupt.

Supply and demand also act together to determine what the price of a product will be and how much of it will be produced and sold. The easiest way to show how this happens is to use graphs. This allows businesses and

- why businesses can charge different prices to different customers
- why we get shortages and surpluses
- why the government taxes some products and not others.

First we look at why the supply and demand graph has the shape that it does and why this dictates the price and the output of products.

Demand, supply, price and quantity

These four factors are all connected and create the graph shown above. The main factor that determines how much will be supplied or demanded is the price.

That is why price is plotted on the vertical axis of the graph. When we change the price the supply and demand lines will tell us how this will affect the quantity that producers want to supply and the quantity that customers want to buy.

Demand

> **Demand** – the willingness to buy something backed by the ability to pay for it.

Demand occurs because people need or want goods and services. For most products the producers expect to be paid and demand therefore has to be backed with money that the customers are willing to spend on the product.

The demand for a product depends on various factors, the most important of which is its price. Generally, the higher the price of the product the less of it will be purchased. This is because people have only a limited income to spend and they have a great many things that they could spend it on. If the price of a Big Mac is put up too much people will simply go to Burger King and buy a Whopper instead. And if all burgers rise in price people will buy pizzas, kebabs or fish and chips instead.

Figure 2.2.2 Effect of price rise on McDonald's and Burger King

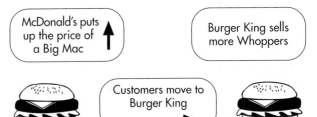

Common sense tells us that as price rises, demand will fall and that as price goes down, more people will buy a product. This can be confirmed by checking what people actually do.

A survey was carried out in a shopping precinct near London. Shoppers were offered a taste of organic peanut butter flavoured with pine nuts and asked, among other questions, how much they would be willing to pay for a 340 g jar. Table 2.2.1 shows the results of the survey. Figure 2.2.3 shows the results plotted on a graph.

Table 2.2.1 Demand for peanut and pine nut butter

Price	Number of jars people were willing to buy at this price or less
£2.50	31
£2.25	39
£2.00	60
£1.75	94
£1.50	142
£1.25	198
£1.00	259

Figure 2.2.3 Demand curve for peanut and pine nut butter

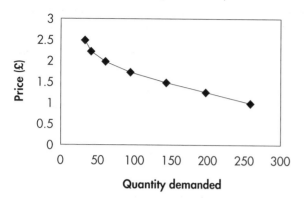

Figure 2.2.3 shows a fairly typical demand curve with the line sloping downwards from the left to the right. This shows that as the price is lowered, more of the product will be demanded. This will be true for most products and can be confirmed by carrying out your own questionnaire.

Supply

> **Supply** – the willingness to produce and sell products at particular prices.

Producers supply products so that they can meet their business objectives. One major objective that businesses have is to make profits, and in order to do this they must cover their costs. This is why businesses will be willing to supply products only if the price is high enough.

As the price of a product rises more producers will be able to cover their costs so the quantity supplied to a market will rise as the price rises. This is shown in Figure 2.2.4.

Figure 2.2.4 A typical supply curve

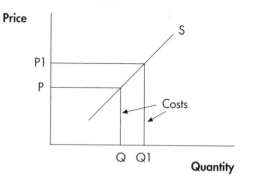

The supply curve shows how much will be supplied at each price. If the price rises from P to P1 more producers will be able to cover costs of production and so the quantity that is supplied to the market will rise from Q to Q1. When prices fall some producers are unable to cover their costs and will be forced out of the market.

Supply and demand interacting to determine price and quantity

> **Equilibrium price** – the price at which the quantity that suppliers wish to supply will be exactly the same as the quantity that customers wish to buy.

Figure 2.2.5 shows a typical supply and demand graph, with a price of P. At this price, the quantity that people wish to buy, as shown by the demand curve, is Q units. At the same time, the amount of the product that the producers wish to supply at this price of P, as shown by the supply curve, is also Q units. At this price, the supply and demand are equal, so both suppliers and customers are happy. This is called the **equilibrium price**.

Figure 2.2.5 A basic supply and demand graph for Product A

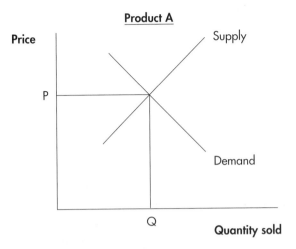

The two graphs below show what would happen if the wrong price was set and why the market would also go back to the price where supply and demand were equal.

Figure 2.2.6 What will happen if the price is set too high?

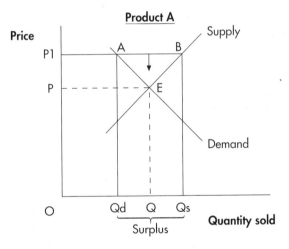

If the price was set at P1 then, by drawing a line across on the graph, we can see what would happen. The price line would hit the demand curve at A and only Qd units would be demanded. But because the price is high, producers would want to produce Qs units of the product. The price line hits the supply curve at B.

This would cause a surplus AB (or Qs – Qd) which, at this price, the producers would be unable to sell. The only way they could sell the surplus would be to lower the price to P. As they do this more people will buy the product. Demand will expand from A to E. At the same time fewer producers will want to supply the product

and supply will contract from B to E. At point E, the equilibrium point, Q units will be demanded and supplied so there will be no surplus.

Figure 2.2.7 What will happen if the price is set too low?

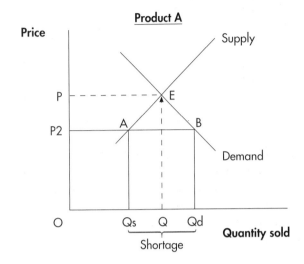

If the price was set too low, at P2, this would cause a shortage. At this price suppliers will only be willing to sell Qs units of the product but customers will want to buy Qd units. The shortage will be AB (or Qd – Qs).

Many customers will be unable to buy the product even if they wish to. As businesses see this situation they will raise the price, up to P. This will earn them more profits, but at the same time it will stop some people buying. Demand will contract from B to E. Because the price is higher, new businesses will be attracted into the market and supply will expand from A to E. At the equilibrium price of P, customers will want to buy Q units of the product and the producers will want to sell Q units. The shortage will disappear.

Only at the equilibrium price will there be no shortages and no surpluses. This is the position that the market will naturally finish up at.

The conditions of demand and supply

So far we have looked only at price and how this affects demand and supply. Price determines the slope of the supply and demand lines. There are, however, other very important conditions and these will determine *where* the supply and demand lines are drawn on the graph.

Figure 2.2.8 shows what would happen if, say, Jaguar started to win many of the Formula One Grand Prix races in 2000. Many more people might be encouraged to buy Jaguar cars for driving on the roads and this would cause the whole of the demand curve to shift to the right, from D to D1. This is an increase in demand and shows that at all prices more people are now willing to buy the cars.

Figure 2.2.8 How a change in the conditions of demand will change the price and output

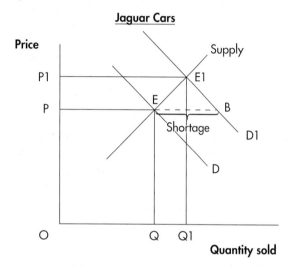

Initially, at price P, there will be more demand than supply so there will be a shortage, from E to B. But, as was shown above, the market will then be forced to the new equilibrium point E1 so that the shortage is removed.

When the conditions of supply or demand change, this will create a different price (P to P1) and a different quantity will be sold (Q to Q1).

The conditions of demand

Five major factors that affect demand are:

- population
- income
- the price and availability of substitutes
- taste and fashion (including advertising)
- what people expect to happen to prices and output in the future.

All of these will change the whole market condition and the demand curve will be in a different position on the graph. In other words, more or less will be demanded at each price. This is shown in Figure 2.2.9 below.

Figure 2.2.9 Changing conditions of demand

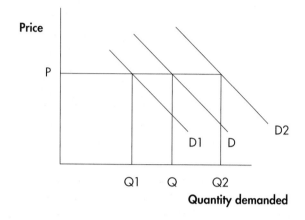

If, for example, there was a very successful advertising campaign demand would increase from D to D2, even though the price was still at P. The amount that people would be willing to buy would rise from Q to Q2.

If there was some negative publicity the demand would decrease from D to D1, and at the price of P only Q1 would be purchased.

We will look in turn at each of the conditions that can cause the demand curve to move.

Population

Population refers to the number of potential buyers in the market. The population in the UK has been rising by about 0.3 per cent each year for the past 20 years. That is equivalent to nearly 200,000 extra people every year and all of them will need feeding, somewhere to live, clothes, health care, etc.

The total population for individual businesses can also increase as they move into new markets. If they move from being local businesses to being national businesses, the potential population will be increased. The same is true as businesses move from being national to being international and multinational.

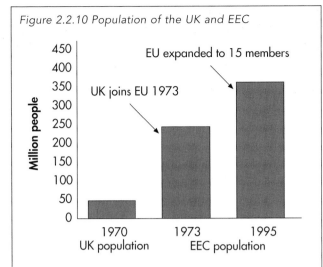

Figure 2.2.10 Population of the UK and EEC

EU expanded to 15 members

UK joins EU 1973

Million people

450
400
350
300
250
200
150
100
50
0

1970
UK population

1973

1995
EEC population

A major factor that encouraged the UK to join the EEC in 1973 was the fact that this would open up a market of more than 250 million people. Since we joined, the EU has increased from 9 to 15 countries and to more than 370 million people. Twelve other countries are being considered for membership.

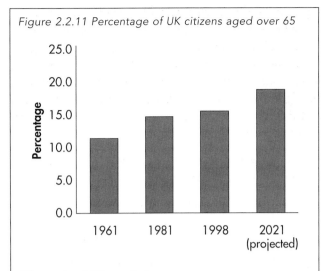

Figure 2.2.11 Percentage of UK citizens aged over 65

Percentage

25.0

20.0

15.0

10.0

5.0

0.0

1961   1981   1998   2021
(projected)

The ageing UK population

As the population of the UK has grown, from 52.8 million in 1961 to 59.2 million in 1998, the greatest area of growth has been in the 65+ age group. This group has grown from 6.2 million to 9.3 million. The general population has grown by just over 12 per cent. The 65+ age group has grown by 50 per cent. And the forecast for 2021 is for a further 2.8 million people in this age group.

It is not just the total population that is important. Most of the increase in population comes from births, although there is some immigration. As babies are born it is the demand for health care, cots, prams, baby food and clothes that experiences the greatest increase. Later, as the children grow up, it is the toy market and education etc. that are affected.

All of the following characteristics of population will also affect the demand for products.

- **Age** – This will affect, food, clothes, medical treatment, cars, alcohol, etc. The demand for all of these changes with age.

- **Gender** – This will affect clothes, cosmetics, sports equipment, magazines, etc., many of which still have a gender bias.

- **Location** – This will affect where people want their shops, transport systems, business services, etc. Most people are located in cities and towns but a growing number are moving out of city centres and into the countryside.

Income

Income in the UK has been rising, in real terms, by about 22 per cent every decade for the last 30 years. This means that people have more money to spend and this increases demand for a wide range of products.

As people buy necessities first it is the luxury products that have experienced the greatest increase in demand. The kinds of product that people buy with their additional incomes are holidays, leisure and entertainment, eating out, additional pension cover, second cars, and electrical household equipment such as dishwashers, microwaves and hi-fi systems.

Increasing demand for leisure services

Between 1989 and 1999 the sector of consumer expenditure that grew fastest was the leisure services industry. In 1989 it took less than 3 per cent of consumer expenditure. By 1999 this had risen to more than 6 per cent.

This high increase in demand could not be fully met by providers of these services because new leisure facilities take time to build. The result has been a very large rise in prices (see Figure 2.2.13). This is also what the theory would predict.

Figure 2.2.12 Rising prices for leisure services, UK 1989–99

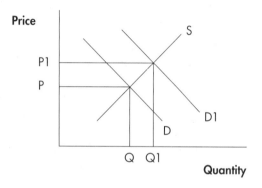

As demand increases from D to D1 the businesses raise their prices P to P1 to cover their additional costs and to make higher profits.

Sales rise from Q to Q1 because people really want these services and they have the additional income needed to pay for them, even at the higher price.

Figure 2.2.13 Rising prices for leisure services, UK 1989–99

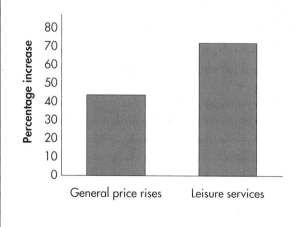

Substitutes

Substitutes affect the demand for products in three ways.

- When the **price of the substitute** is changed – if Eurostar puts up the price of its tickets from London to Paris, more people will consider flying or even taking the ferry instead.

- When the **amount being offered for sale** is changed – as new computer games are brought out existing computer games tend to lose sales.

- When the **quality being offered for sale** is changed – as new products like CDs are brought out the demand for old-style products like cassettes decreases.

Recovery of motorbike and scooter sales

In 1993 motorbike and scooter sales had dropped to just 47,724. By 1997 the sales had recovered to 93,289. In the first 11 months of 1999 figures had exceeded 147,809.

The recovery reflects the fact that people are getting fed up with the alternatives. Cars get stuck in traffic jams and public transport is overcrowded and unreliable. Motorbikes and scooters have also become more affordable at a time when the prices of cars and public transport have been rising.

Products with many close substitutes, such as lemonade or mobile phones, are more likely to be affected by this than products with few or no close substitutes, such as Microsoft Windows or milk. (See also details on elasticity on pages 97 & 98.)

Taste and fashion

Taste and fashion cover a wide range of factors that affect demand. The most obvious are advertising and promotion. They are specifically designed to affect demand and to change the way we think about products. Some advertising is so powerful that customers will buy the product even before it has been produced, as with tickets for the Millennium Dome.

Taste and fashion also change because:

- people want to try new things – as with the growth of adventure holidays

- the producers stop producing the old products and bring out news designs – as with clothes, cars and toys

- conditions change over the year – as with the demand for ice cream, suntan oil and salads (See the changing demand for potatoes on page 92.)

- general conditions change – as with traffic congestion (see the inset above on motorbikes), more home security because of rising crime rates and more childminders as more people go out to work.

Number 1 soft drink

Sunny Delight has become the top selling non-carbonated soft drink in the UK.

This has been achieved through an aggressive advertising campaign, and promotional offers such as 'two for the price of one', coupons and samples.

Sales	1998	1999	Percentage increase
Sunny Delight	£72,336	£136,258	88.4%
Coca-Cola (bottles)	£95,144	£121,414	27.6%

This is a good example of how marketing can increase the demand for a product, but it should be remembered that bottled Coke is only one of Coca-Cola's products and it remains the biggest producer of soft drinks in the UK.

Expectations

Expectations of what is going to happen in the future often affect what we do now. This will change demand for two reasons:

- if people think the price of a product is going to change

- if people think the supply of a product is going to change.

If people think the price of alcoholic drinks or tobacco is going to be put up in the Budget they will often go out the day before and stock up on cigarettes, whisky, beer, etc. If people think the price of video players or toys or clothes will come down immediately after Christmas in the sales, they may put off buying these things until after Christmas.

If people think that there is going to be a shortage of, say, turkeys just before Christmas, they will buy theirs early and put it in the freezer. If they think that more of a product will be supplied later, and the price will come down, they may put off their purchases until later. Many people will wait for new books to come out in paperback, at which time they are often only 25 per cent or 20 per cent of the hardback price.

The conditions of supply

As with demand, price is the most important factor that affects supply because businesses need to cover their costs. There are, however, other very important factors that affect how much is supplied. These include:

- physical and natural conditions

- the effects of political decisions and the actions of society

- indirect taxation such as VAT

- technology

- the cost of the factors of production.

With each change in these conditions of supply the whole supply curve will be shifted to the left (a decrease) or to the right (an increase). This is shown in Figure 2.2.14.

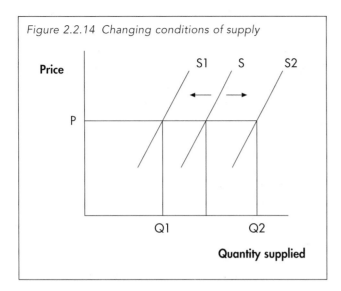

Figure 2.2.14 Changing conditions of supply

If, for example, there was a bad harvest which affected all producers of apples, the whole supply curve would move to the left, S to S1. Even at a price of P the farmers would be able to supply only Q1 apples and still cover their costs.

If there was a very good harvest, farmers would be able to supply Q2 apples even if the price remained at P.

We will look in turn at each of the conditions that can cause the supply curve to move.

Physical and natural conditions

Physical and natural conditions affect nearly every product. Sometimes this is fairly obvious, as with agricultural products. For other products the effects of these conditions are less obvious, but they are still there. The examples given below show how wide these effects can be.

- Weather conditions – affecting the production of crops, disrupting transport systems and slowing down the production of goods produced outdoors such as houses
- Natural disasters such as earthquakes – destroying factories, roads, communications, etc.
- Disease – affecting both crops and lifestock
- Illness – affecting humans and stopping them from working
- Finite resources running out – ending coal, tin and iron ore production in certain pits.

Changing supply and demand for potatoes

Figure 2.2.15 Potatoes provided to meet UK consumption

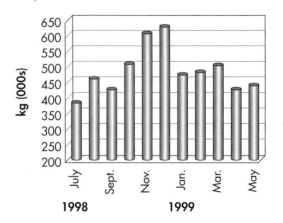

In the UK the supply and demand for potatoes causes a significant difference in how many are supplied to the UK market in different months.

On the supply side, the main harvesting season is October and November, although additional potatoes are supplied from imports. Potatoes can also be stored fairly cheaply and will last throughout the winter.

On the demand side, more potatoes are eaten during the winter months, when people want hot filling meals. In warmer weather, people eat fewer carbohydrates, preferring light meals such as salads.

Potatoes reach their highest price in May and June, when those that were stored from the previous year have run out and the current year's crop has not yet been harvested.

Political and civil actions

Political and civil actions can affect businesses dramatically. It is the government that imposes bans on the production and sale of certain drugs, insists on safety features in cars, and limits the number of public houses a brewery can own. Each of these actions affects supply in some way, either limiting what can be supplied or increasing the costs for the producers.

Metrication laws

On 1 January 2000 it became an offence to sell loose products, such as fruit, vegetables, meat, petrol, in anything other than metric measures, i.e. kilograms, litres, centimetres, etc. Draught beer and cider can still be sold in pints, as can milk if it is in a returnable bottle. Other milk must be sold in litres. A fine of up to £2,000 can be imposed on any business which does not comply with the new law.

The Department of Trade has estimated that it will cost businesses up to £33 million to convert their weighing machines, and pumps, etc. Businesses have estimated the cost at anywhere between £60 and £10,000 for a small business and very much higher for businesses with many machines, pumps, etc., to convert.

On the civil side the trade unions have often been the main factor affecting supply. They can limit supply by going on strike, working to rule, refusing to do overtime, etc. They can increase costs by negotiating higher pay levels.

Civil actions also include disturbances such as demonstrations and riots. These may affect supply by disrupting transport routes, damaging property and even making businesses change the way that they produce.

Indirect taxation

Indirect tax – a tax placed on the production of a good or a service and is an additional cost for the producer.

Indirect taxation affects most goods that are produced because at some stage in their production they are usually transported. All petrol and diesel fuels have a hydrocarbon tax placed on them, so all transport using cars, lorries, ships and aircraft has to cover this tax.

The major taxes that are placed on specific products are:

- hydrocarbon taxes – placed on petrol, diesel, paraffin, methylated spirits, etc.

- alcohol taxes – placed on spirits, wines, beers, ciders, etc.

Days lost through labour disputes

After progressive declines in trade union membership in the UK, which have reduced membership by over 40 per cent, 1999 saw the first increase for 20 years. As membership has fallen the power of the unions has also fallen, but this has not removed all the effects of strikes, work to rule, and other actions that have lost working days in industry.

Some industries suffer more than others. The industries with the greatest number of days lost are shown on the graph below.

Figure 2.2.16

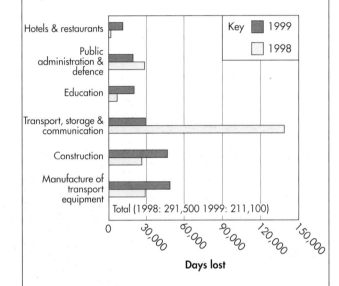

In 1999 the four major causes of these lost days were:

- Pay   65.3%
- Disputes over redundancy plans   17.2%
- Working conditions & supervisors   6.9%
- Dismissal and other disciplinary concerns   4.7%

- tobacco taxes – placed on cigarettes, cigars, pipe tobacco, snuff, etc.

- betting taxes – placed on the football pools, horse racing, bingo, etc.

- import duties – placed on products from outside the EU, such as Swiss chocolate, American consol games, Japanese cars, etc.

The other major indirect tax is **value added tax** (VAT). This is placed on a very wide range of products sold in the UK. The current standard rate is 17.5 per cent, which is paid by any business which adds value to its products. The rate for domestic fuel is unusual as it is only 5 per cent.

In 1998 the government raised the following taxes from the sale of goods and services:

Figure 2.2.17

Betting	
Hydrocarbons	
Tobacco	
Alcohol	
VAT	

0   20   40   60

£ billion

Government subsidies will have the opposite effect to taxes. Subsidies are given to firms to reduce their costs and this will increase the supply, helping businesses to lower their prices for customers. Examples of subsidies are:

- payments made under the Common Agricultural Policy (CAP) to help EU farmers (see page 176)

- payments made to businesses under Regional Policy when firms set up in certain areas (see page 153)

- payments made to support sporting and cultural projects, as with the good causes grants from the National Lottery

- grants from charitable organisations, such as The Prince's Trust which helps people between 18 and 30 years old to set up in business and gives grants to allow ideas to be tested in the market.

How different taxes affect the supply curve

If a firm adds £2.00 of value to a product it will have to pay 35p in VAT. If it adds £4.00 of value it will have to pay 70p in VAT. The amount of tax paid rises as the price rises, so when this is drawn on a graph the supply lines diverge. (This is called an **ad valorem tax**.) Other taxes, such as the tax on cider, will be the same whatever the price is. In this case the supply curve will be parallel to the original supply line. (This is called a **specific tax**.)

Figure 2.2.18

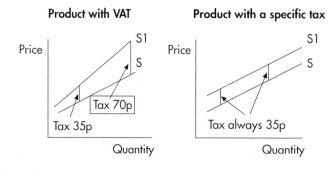

Technology

New technology is introduced by firms so that they can improve their production, either by improving the quality of the product or by producing at lower costs. Lowering the costs will cause the supply to increase.

Because of the widespread use of computers in both goods and service industries, practically every business in the country is affected by technology in one way or another. Examples include:

- automated production lines – car manufacturing, printing, bottling drinks, etc.
- computer technology – for data collection, retrieval and reproduction, EPOS and EFTPOS systems, internet shopping, etc.
- genetic engineering – increasing the yields of crops, improving medical treatment, etc.
- new machinery, tools and equipment – faster computers, multi-task machines such as combine harvesters, specialised tools speeding up tasks, ergonomically designed equipment causing less stress and injury to workers, etc.
- faster communications systems – modems and the internet, mobile phones, pagers, optical fibres, etc.

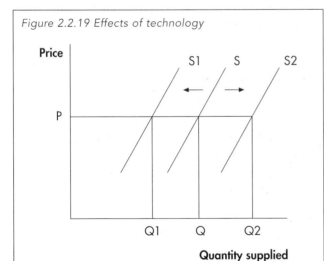

Figure 2.2.19 Effects of technology

Successful new technology will increase supply from S to S2 and more will be produced, Q to Q2.

When machines etc. get old and become less efficient they will produce less and cost more to run. This will cause the supply curve to shift to the left, S to S1, and less will be produced, Q to Q1.

Costs of the factors of production

Four factors are used to produce all products, and each has its own cost. These are:

- land – rent
- labour – wages
- capital – interest
- enterprise – normal profit.

When any of these change, the costs of production will change and that will change the position of the supply curve. We will look at the effects of the cost of borrowing – **interest** – to make the point.

In the UK the general interest rates are determined by the Bank of England. Each time they are changed the cost of borrowing money changes, and businesses which have borrowed money are faced with higher or lower costs on their borrowing.

Figure 2.2.20 shows how this will affect the supply curve and hence the prices and quantities sold. Table 2.2.2 shows how often the main interest rate of the Bank of England has been changed between 1997 and 1999. Each time the interest rate changed, the costs of borrowing for businesses changed, and so did the basic supply curve.

Similar changes will occur if any other costs, rent, wages or normal profit increased or decreased.

Figure 2.2.20 The effect that changing interest rates has on production

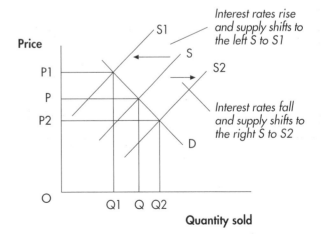

Table 2.2.2 Changing UK interest rates, 1997–99

	Date	Interest rate		Date	Interest rate
1997	1 Jan.	6.00		5 Nov.	6.75
	6 May	6.25		10 Dec.	6.25
	9 June	6.50	1999	7 Jan.	6.00
	10 July	6.75		4 Feb.	5.50
	7 Aug.	7.00		8 Apr.	5.25
	6 Nov.	7.25		10 June	5.00
1998	4 June	7.50		10 Sep.	5.25
	8 Oct.	7.25		5 Nov.	5.50

The effect of supply and demand changes on markets

When real world markets are examined the effects of supply and demand are fairly complex. We will see some of these effects in Chapter 4 when we look at different types of market and how businesses actually price their products, react to competition, and change the conditions of supply and demand so that their businesses will benefit.

A good example of how real markets are more complex than has so far been covered is the concept of **elasticity**. This is covered on pages 97 to 101. But even with something as apparently simple as advertising there are complications in the real world.

Figure 2.2.21 Effect of advertising on Product A

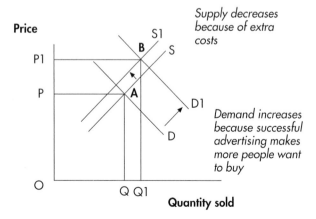

Businesses advertise in order to increase demand D to D1 on Figure 2.2.21, but advertising also has a cost. The advertisements have to be made and the television stations, magazines, etc. need to be paid before they will show them. These additional costs will cause the supply curve to decrease, S to S1. The overall effect of advertising is shown, with the new equilibrium being where D1 and S1 cross, at point B.

Elasticity

Elasticity is a very important concept in business and helps to explain why a great many business practices go on. Below we will look at the major forms of elasticity and consider how they affect the way that businesses behave. We will look at:

- price elasticity of demand
- condition elasticity of demand (e.g. income elasticity of demand)
- price elasticity of supply.

Elasticity shows what will happen when one of the conditions that affect the market is changed. If we are looking at 'price elasticity of demand' the elasticity will tell us the answer to this basic question:

If a business puts its prices up, what will happen to the quantity of the product that customers are willing to buy?

We will now look at each of the major elasticities in turn.

Price elasticity of demand

> **Price elasticity of demand** – this shows how much the quantity demanded of a product will change when the price is changed.

When a business changes the price of its product it is important that it knows what effect this will have on the demand from its customers. Price elasticity of demand will tell the business what is likely to happen.

Figure 2.2.22 shows what would happen if products had different price elasticities of demand. With both lines the price has been raised from P to P1. With the inelastic demand curve, Di, there is little effect on the quantity demanded and sales only fall to Qi. With the elastic demand curve De, however, there is a very great effect on demand. Many customers will not be prepared to pay the higher price and the quantity sold will fall to Qe.

Figure 2.2.22 Different price elasticities of demand

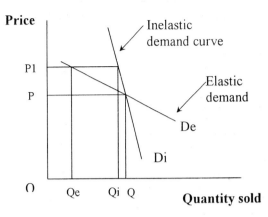

Whether the price elasticity of demand for a product is elastic or inelastic will depend on a number of factors. These are listed in Table 2.2.3, with examples of products that have these characteristics.

Many products have factors that make them both price elastic and price inelastic. If your car has just broken down and is not worth repairing, another car may be a necessity (and hence inelastic) even though it will cost you a large proportion of income (and hence elastic).

The elasticity of demand may also be different for different people (see price discrimination, page 128). For commuters taking the train from Salisbury to London this will be a necessity (inelastic) and there will be few practical alternatives (inelastic). For a family who have decided to go up to London for the day there would be a lot of alternatives (elastic) such as going to the seaside instead, taking the car, going by coach.

Knowing the price elasticity of demand of a product will allow all of the following decisions to be made:

Table 2.2.3

Elastic	Inelastic	Examples
Many/close substitutes	Few/distant substitutes	**Elastic:** fresh fruit and vegetables, banking services, petrol, hens' eggs, accountancy services **Inelastic:** specialist fishing equipment shops, the Severn Bridge, Microsoft Windows, letter post
Luxuries	Necessities	**Elastic:** yachts, fast cars, expensive chocolates, swordfish, platinum jewellery **Inelastic:** salt, bread, telephones for most businesses, electricity
High proportion of income spent	Low proportion of income spent	**Elastic:** holidays, new houses, new cars, pension provision, a three-piece suite **Inelastic:** matches, pepper, plastic rulers, local telephone calls from a phone box
Long time is available to find substitutes	Little time is available to find substitutes	**Elastic:** when the price is put up and customers have a long time to find alternatives, they will not buy the product **Inelastic:** when the price is put up and customers are in a hurry, they will continue to buy the product
Large price rise	Small price rise	**Elastic:** hundreds of pounds on a holiday, a pound on a jar of coffee, 10p on a can of Coca-Cola **Inelastic:** £30 or £40 on a new car, a pound on the price of a cross-Channel ferry trip, 1p on a pint of bitter

- Which product to choose as a loss leader. The products chosen will be very elastic so that many extra customers will come into the shop and buy other goods as well.

- When to charge people different prices for the same product, as with train tickets or cinema tickets (see also page 128).

- Which products to put a tax on if the government wants to raise revenue. Tobacco, alcohol and petrol all have inelastic demands so when the price is raised customers will continue to buy them and the government will continue to get its taxes.

- How to make a product inelastic. If a business can convince its customers that its products are necessities (and hence inelastic) it can raise the price without losing many of its customers.

Income elasticity of demand

> **Income elasticity of demand** – this shows how much the quantity demanded of a product will change when incomes change.

Income elasticity of demand shows how different products respond to a change in income. If, say, incomes in the UK rose by 10 per cent, the demand for different products would be affected in different ways. Figure 2.2.23 shows what might happen to these different products.

- **Income elastic** products will experience a big increase in demand, D to De. These will tend to be luxuries like second holidays, eating out and sports cars.

- **Income inelastic** products will experience little increase in demand (D to Di), or even no increase in demand (D stays at D). These products will tend to be necessities such as basic food, household cleaning products, and transport to work. People will have already set money aside to buy necessities so when they get an increase in their incomes they do not want to buy more necessities.

- **Inferior goods** are products that experience a decrease in demand (D to Dn) when incomes rise. The demand decreases because customers can now afford to buy better quality products, e.g. new cars instead of second hand cars, designer label clothes and holidays in Bali rather than in Spain.

Figure 2.2.23 Different income elasticities of demand

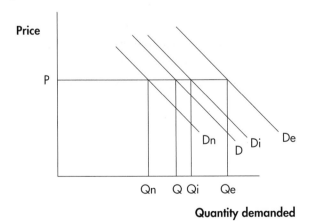

As has already been mentioned, real income in the UK has risen by over 20 per cent in each of the last three decades. All businesses should know what these increases in income are likely to do to the demand for their products. If the business has an elastic product it will need to prepare for the increase in demand that will be coming. If the business has a product with an inelastic demand it will need to decide if it is happy with its sales and profits, and if not it will have to move into income elastic products. If the business has an inferior product it will need to get out of the market and move to a better quality product.

The successful businesses of the next decade will include those entrepreneurs who have worked out what it is that we will be spending our extra income on in the future, i.e. those products with high income elasticity of demand.

Figure 2.2.24 shows how disposable incomes and expenditure have changed in the UK over eight years. Real disposable income rose every year (in 1998 it rose by 0.01%). In 1991, however, UK residents decided to spend 1.8% less than in 1990, even though their incomes had risen.

Figure 2.2.24 Percentage change in real personal disposable income and final expenditure on consumption, UK 1990–98.

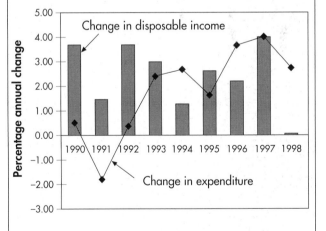

The up and down patterns of expenditure, and disposable income, show how hard it is for businesses to predict what is going to happen in the future, and it also stresses how important it is for them to understand the income elasticity for their own products. The graph shows the overall patterns, but for individual products the patterns are quite different.

Cross-elasticity of demand

> **Cross-elasticity of demand** – this shows how much the quantity demanded of one product will change when the price of another product changes.

Cross-elasticity of demand shows how products are related to each other. If the price of coffee is raised by the producers, some people will stop buying it and buy tea instead. The extra demand for tea will cause the price of tea to rise. At the same time, if less coffee is being bought then less Coffeemate, which is used with coffee, will be bought. The decrease in the demand for Coffeemate will cause it to fall in price.

Figure 2.2.25

What is being shown here is the cross-elasticity of demand. This shows which products are substitutes, and how close these substitutes are. It also shows which products are complements to other products, like fish and chips, gin and tonic, etc., and how much each relies upon the other. Tea and milk are complements, but if people drank coffee instead, most people would still take milk with their coffee.

Knowing what the cross-elasticity of demand is for their products is vital for businesses. They must know:

- what will happen to the demand for their products if a competitor changes its prices

- how many customers they will lose or gain if they change their prices

- how changes in the price or demand for other products will affect the demand for their products, i.e.

 i. which products are substitutes for their products

 ii. which products their products are complements to.

Price elasticity of supply

> **Price elasticity of supply** – this shows how much supply will change when there is a change in the price of a product.

As with the price elasticity of demand, the price elasticity of supply dictates what shape the supply curve will have, i.e. how steep the line will be. When it is very steep it will be inelastic.

Figure 2.2.26 shows what would happen if products had different price elasticities of supply. In both cases the price has been raised from P to P1. With the inelastic supply curve, Si, producers will be able to provide only a small amount of additional output (Q to Qi), but with the elastic supply curve, Se, they will be able to provide a great deal more output (Q to Qe).

Figure 2.2.26 Different price elasticities of supply

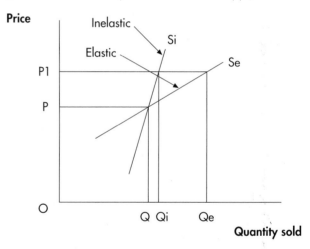

The price elasticity of supply will be determined mainly by the time that the producer has to produce extra products. In the short run the producer can provide only what has already been produced. With more time more goods and services can be produced, extra staff can be taken on, additional goods can be imported. In the long run new factories can be built. The longer the time available, the more elastic the supply will be.

How elasticity is measured

When a business is going to choose a product to act as a loss leader it needs to choose a product that has an elastic price elasticity of demand. Unfortunately, the

The changing elasticity of potatoes

At point **A** producers have already sent potatoes to the shops so the quantity is fixed, even if demand and price rise.

With more time, line **B**, more potatoes can be provided by wholesalers and from stocks that farmers keep.

With additional time, line **C**, additional potatoes can be imported.

In the long run, line **D**, farmers will plant more potatoes and a great many more can be supplied. In the UK, that will take up to a year.

Figure 2.2.27

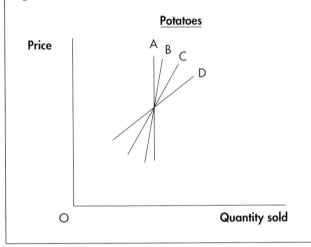

Example: A business has worked out that if it lowered the price of its potted plants from £2.50 to £2.00 this would cause sales to rise from 200 to 300. The price elasticity of demand would then be:

$$\text{Price elasticity of demand} = \frac{50\%}{-20\%} = -2.5$$

$$\text{or} = \frac{100}{200} \div \frac{-0.50}{2.50} = -2.5$$

Price elasticity will be a minus figure because demand rises as price falls. A figure of more than −1, e.g. −2, −2.5, etc., is elastic. The figure −2.5 means that for every 1 per cent fall in price the quantity demanded will rise by 2.5 per cent.

A figure below −1, e.g. −0.5 or −0.2, is inelastic, and means that demand does not change very much as the price is changed.

All of the elasticities are measured using a similar formula, as shown below.

$$\textbf{Price elasticity of supply} = \frac{\%\ \text{change in } \textbf{supply}}{\%\ \text{change in } \textbf{price}}$$

$$\text{or} = \frac{\text{change in supply}}{\text{original supply}} \div \frac{\text{change in price}}{\text{original price}}$$

$$\textbf{Income elasticity of demand} = \frac{\%\ \text{change in } \textbf{demand}}{\%\ \text{change in } \textbf{income}}$$

$$\text{or} = \frac{\text{change in demand}}{\text{original demand}} \div \frac{\text{change in income}}{\text{original income}}$$

$$\textbf{Cross-elasticity of demand} = \frac{\%\ \text{change in } \textbf{demand for product A}}{\%\ \text{change in } \textbf{price of product B}}$$

$$\text{or} = \frac{\text{change in demand of product A}}{\text{original demand for product A}} \div \frac{\text{change in price of product B}}{\text{original price of product B}}$$

products in stores all have different prices and different quantities of sales. It is not, therefore, immediately obvious which product is more elastic. To calculate elasticity a formula is used:

$$\textbf{Price elasticity of demand} = \frac{\%\ \text{change in demand}}{\%\ \text{change in price}}$$

$$\text{or} = \frac{\text{change in demand}}{\text{original demand}} \div \frac{\text{change in price}}{\text{original price}}$$

In the following chapters we will see how important elasticity is in deciding what pricing policy to adopt, how to react to competitors, which firms will be most affected by interest rate rises, etc.

Further Study

Although some examples have been given of how supply, demand and elasticity affect real businesses it is important to check for yourself what is going on in the real world. This will help you to understand the theory and why supply and demand are so important to business.

Confirming the shape of the demand curve

1   Select a product. The best product to select would be something that is fairly new.

2   Ask a range of people what would be the maximum price they would pay for the product. The more people you ask, the more reliable the results will be.

3   Put the results into a table with a range of prices. For each price you should put down the number of people who would pay that price or more.

4   Plot the data from the table on to a graph and build up a demand curve.

Confirming the shape of the supply curve

This is more difficult to do because you are unlikely to be actually producing something. You do, however, supply your own labour when you work and this fact can be used to build up a supply curve.

1   Select a job, e.g. window cleaning or working in a fast food restaurant.

2   Ask a range of people what would be the minimum wage that they would need to receive in order to do the job. The more people you ask, the more reliable the results will be.

3   Put the results into a table with a range of wages. For each wage you should put down the number of people who would work for that wage or for less.

4   Plot the data from the table on to a graph to build up a supply curve.

Checking the conditions of demand

1   Select a variety of products, some goods and some services.

2   For each of these products check the conditions of demand that are likely to affect them:

   i)   Which aspects of population will be important – age, gender, total number of people, location, etc.?

   ii)   How will changes in income affect the demand?

   iii) What are the main substitutes and how close are they?

   iv)   Is the product one that is affected by changing tastes and fashion?

   v)   Do prices or quantities change suddenly and make people hedge against price rises or shortages?

Checking the conditions of supply

1 Select a variety of goods and services.

2 For each of these products check the conditions of supply and list the ones that are likely to affect the product:

    i)   Which physical and natural conditions will affect the ability of the producers to provide their products?

    ii)   Are the products affected by any political decisions such as a ban in some countries? How active are trade unions in the industry?

    iii) Are the products subject to a tax? What is the rate of the tax? How often is the rate of tax changed?

    iv) What technological changes are being made to how the product is made?

    v)   Which are the most important costs for the product – rent, interest, wages or the profit that the producers insist on receiving?

Checking elasticities

1 With the products that you have studied above, consider the factors that affect elasticity and decide if the product is elastic or inelastic.

2 For price elasticity of demand, consider if it is a necessity or luxury, and how close the substitutes are, etc.

3 For income elasticity of demand, consider if the product is a necessity or luxury, whether it is an inferior or a superior good, etc.

4 For cross-elasticity of demand, consider what the nature of the product is and how it relates to other products. Does it have substitutes? Is it a complement?

5 For price elasticity of supply, consider how easily the producers could respond to an increase in demand. How important is time? How easily could they get hold of more workers/staff? Do they need to be trained?

6 Try some calculations, using the formulae given above, to try to work out what the elasticities might be and whether the answers make them elastic or inelastic.

Noting changes in the real world

The conditions of supply and demand are changing all the time and you need to think about what these changes are and how they will affect businesses. Check news programmes, magazines, etc., which make comments on price changes or the quantities being sold. Work out which conditions of demand or supply have caused the changes.

Revision Questions

1 Define 'effective demand'. (1 mark)

2 Explain why the supply curve slopes upwards from the left to the right as price is increased. (3 marks)

3 If the demand for a product increases because of successful advertising, what will happen to the price and quantity sold? (2 marks)

4 Which two of the following will cause the supply curve to shift rather than the demand curve?
  i) higher temperatures making people want to buy more ice creams
  ii) higher temperatures causing a drought that affects producers of milk
  iii) lower incomes affecting the market for new cars
  iv) higher wages affecting how many employees firms can take on. (2 marks)

5 Draw a fully labelled supply and demand graph that shows the effects on the market for ordinary CD players as more DVD systems are produced and sold. (3 marks)

6 For each of the following population factors give an example of a product(s) that you feel is most likely to be affected by it. Explain clearly why you think it will be affected by this factor.
  i) age
  ii) gender
  iii) whether people live in the north or the south of the UK
  iv) if people are married or single
  v) what religion people belong to. (10 marks)

7 Name five pairs of different products that you think are in competition with each other, e.g. tea and coffee. (5 marks)

8 Which businesses do think are most likely to be affected by strikes? Justify your answers. (4 marks)

9 Give details of one business that you have studied that has introduced new technology to reduce its costs. Draw a supply and demand graph to show how this will affect the market, the price of the final product and the quantity sold. (5 marks)

10 Explain what conditions of supply and demand might have changed to cause the equilibrium point on the following graph to move from point A to point B. (4 marks)

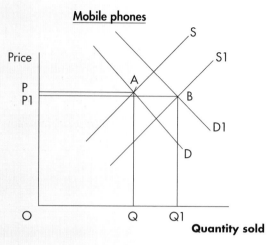

Mobile phones

11 List five factors that will have an effect on the price elasticity of demand. (5 marks)

12 Calculate the income elasticity of demand for a product whose sales increase from 2,500 items per week to 3,000 items per week as a result of a 10 per cent increase in people's incomes. (1 mark)

13 Draw a graph that shows a product with a high price elasticity of supply. (2 marks)

14 Incomes will rise by about 20 per cent in the next 10 years. List three products that you think will rise in demand by at least 20 per cent in the next 10 years and explain why you think the demand for each of these products will be affected so much. (6 marks)

15 Give **three** examples of products and list one product that is a complement to each of them, e.g. houses and household insurance. (6 marks)

16 Give **two** different reasons why the demand shown on the graph below might have shifted from D to D1. (2 marks)

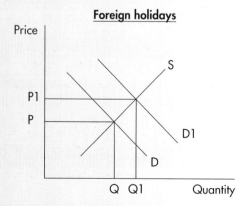

Foreign holidays

CHAPTER 3

Products and Markets

KEY TERMS:

products   markets   commodities

consumer products   capital products   industrial products

goods and services   internal markets

This chapter will look at:

- the different types of goods and services that businesses produce and how the markets in which these products are sold differ

- how business is broken down into primary, secondary and tertiary sectors and how these have been changing.

Introduction

All products are either **goods** or **services**. They are called '**products**' because businesses have '**produced**' them.

> **Product** – something that is produced by a business for the benefit of its customers.

Goods are products that can be seen and felt and, if the owner wants, even passed on to someone else. They include all of our basic household products such as food, drinks, cosmetics, electrical goods, cars and houses. They also include raw materials like cotton and iron ore as well as machines, equipment and factories used by businesses to make their products.

> **Goods** – products that can be seen and touched.
> **Services** – products that do something for customers but cannot be touched.

Services are products that are difficult to see and touch and, generally, they cannot be passed on to anyone else. Services include the services that we as consumers receive, such as accommodation in a hotel, having our hair cut, and being entertained in a cinema. They also include services that businesses receive and which help them to produce goods. Business services include wholesaling, advertising, insurance, banking and transport.

Goods, services and markets

There can be some confusion about what is a service and what is a good. When we go to the supermarket and buy tins of cat food, bottles of beer or boxes of soap powder, we are actually buying both goods and services.

The goods are provided by firms which usually specialise in the production of particular types of good. Spillers, Pedigree and Quakers make cat food; Carlsberg, Whitbread, Heineken make beer; and Unilever and Procter & Gamble make soap powders. The supermarkets make none of these products. Even their own brands are generally made for them by other producers. What the supermarkets do provide, however, is a place where consumers can see the goods displayed, collect them in trolleys, pay for them, or even sometimes have them delivered. The supermarkets provide the service of retailing.

Consumer products and capital products

The terms 'capital' and 'consumer' are used to describe goods and services in terms of who finishes up getting them. If they are capital goods or services, businesses finish up with them. If they are consumer goods or services, private individuals, couples or families finish up with them.

Capital goods and services – products made by one business for other businesses to use.

Capital goods and services are used by businesses to help them produce other goods and services.

Capital goods include:

* tools
* machines
* delivery vehicles
* factories
* furniture in offices.

Capital services include:

* a service contract to repair and maintain machinery or vehicles
* the telephone connections provided by BT and Mercury that allow businesses to talk to their suppliers and customers
* the services of a security firm which provides regular checks through the night to ensure that offices and shops are not broken into.

Consumer goods and services – products made by businesses for people who are not in businesses to use.

Consumer goods and services are those products which are received by the end users, the consumers. They are not being used to help produce anything else that will then be sold by a business. Sometimes they are referred to as **end products**.

Consumer goods include:

* family cars
* fruit and vegetables for personal consumption
* home computers bought for use by an individual or family.

Consumer services include:

* entertainment at a cinema
* the retailing provided by shops
* the service of your local GP or hospital.

Sometimes the same product can be both a capital product and a consumer product. It depends on who is receiving it and what it is being used for. If a father buys a PC for his children, this will be a consumer good. If a business buys the same computer so that it can be used to keep records of its customers and do accounts more easily, the new computer will be a capital good.

Capital goods and services get turned into consumer products as they are used up. A producer of pottery mugs and plates, etc. will buy a potting wheel, a kiln and clay. These are all capital goods because they will help the producer make the pottery items. As the mugs and plates are made and are ready to be sold to us as consumer goods, the clay is being turned from a capital good into a consumer good. And as the potting wheel and kiln get older, and finally have to be replaced, they are also being turned into consumer goods. Each year these long-lasting capital goods will depreciate, and it is this depreciation that is being turned into the end product.

....

CASE STUDY

The Great Wall of China (Fish & Chip shop and Chinese Takeaway)

The Great Wall of China serves takeaway meals every evening, providing its customers with **consumer goods** in the form of food and drinks. It also provides **consumer services** by cooking, serving, and wrapping the food.

In order to provide these goods and services the Great Wall of China needs various capital goods and services.

The **capital goods** include the pots, pans, woks, spoons, spatulas, bowls, etc. needed to cook the food. They also include the ovens, grills, refrigerators and heated display cabinets. For customers waiting for their food, seats and a slot machine are provided – also capital goods. There is also the shop itself. Raw materials, the uncooked foods, spices, soft drinks, etc., are capital goods when they are bought, but they will be used up fairly quickly and turned into the end product.

The **capital services** include the telephone link which allows customers to ring up and order meals, the insurance against fire and injury to customers and a contract with a firm that removes the dirty cooking oil, cleans it, and returns it to be used again.

....

Industrial goods

> **Industrial goods** – goods that are produced exclusively for use by other businesses.

Industrial goods are really just another name for capital goods. They are made in order to be sold to other businesses. Sometimes the term is used more specifically to refer to capital goods that will be used over a medium or long term to produce other goods. Examples would include:

- machinery – e.g. an automated welding system in a car production plant
- equipment – e.g. a mainframe computer network for operating communications
- vehicles – e.g. a combine harvester used on an arable farm
- buildings – e.g. a classroom, an assembly hall and a sports block in a school
- power systems such as generators – e.g. as a back-up system in a hospital
- furniture – e.g. tiered seating in a football stadium.

The main characteristic of industrial goods, which distinguishes them from some other types of capital goods, is that they are designed for use only by businesses. Many goods, such as personal computers, cars, mobile phones, hammers and four-poster beds, may be used by businesses but they may also be bought and used by consumers. Industrial goods are very rarely bought and used by consumers. Consumers do not, generally, buy combine harvesters, mainframe computers or football stadiums.

Many industrial goods are tailor-made for the needs of a particular business. When the Channel Tunnel was built, giant cutting rigs were created that would carve through the rock and allow the tunnels to be constructed behind them. When new Lego toys are made, each part will be formed using an injection-moulding tool that has been specially made for the job.

Commodities

> **Commodities** – unprocessed or partially processed goods from the primary sector which form the raw materials of secondary industry.

The term 'commodity' is potentially very wide and includes all goods. There is also a more specific meaning for this term that refers to what is sold on the 'commodity markets'. In these markets **commodities** are the raw materials for businesses that process primary products into secondary products. The commodities, such as coffee beans, grain, wool, fish, timber and crude oil, have all been produced in the primary sector from farming, forestry, fishing or mining. Producers of jars of coffee, cornflakes, woollen jumpers, fish fingers, paper or petrol buy these raw materials and process them into the finished products that we buy.

A major characteristic of commodities is that when one producer supplies a good, e.g. grain, it is very similar to the grain that is being supplied by all the other producers. It may vary in type and/or price but each type of grain will be competing against products that are, essentially, identical. Commodities markets are, therefore, very competitive.

Internal markets

> **Internal markets** – markets where parts of a single business bid against other parts of the same business to provide goods or services to the business.

Internal markets are created inside businesses. Instead of individual parts of the business working together, they are allowed to compete against each other. This creates a competitive environment in which it is hoped that the business will become more efficient.

This competition can take various forms:

- Separate parts of the business may compete with each other to provide another part of the business with goods or services. An example would be where a business has three factories all preparing raw materials that are used in a fourth factory to produce consumer goods. The firm may ask each of the three factories to work out how cheaply they could provide raw materials for a new product that the business wishes to make. The business would then ask the factory with the cheapest costs, or the best service, to produce the raw materials.

- Individual parts of the business may decide to buy from other parts of the business or may buy from firms outside the businesses.

- Parts of the business may decide to sell outside the business rather than sell to the business itself.

Essentially, each part of the business is allowed to operate as though it were an independent firm.

The reason why a business will do this is to encourage all of the separate parts to produce at the lowest cost, to find the most efficient method of production and to offer the best services. The units that succeed will ensure employment for their staff and probably a bonus for their manager.

These kinds of markets are quite different from the other markets we have considered because, in the end, the whole business wants to survive, grow, make more profits, etc., and it does not really want to destroy one of its parts unless this will help the whole business.

CASE STUDY

The internal market in the NHS

In the 1980s and 1990s an internal market was set up for the National Health Service. As part of this internal market general practitioners (GPs) were given funds from the government which they could then use to buy the health services of whichever hospital they wanted to.

Where hospitals had good, fast and cheap medical services they were in high demand and received extra funds.

Unfortunately, other hospitals lost funds and were unable to provide the services expected by people living in the area.

This kind of internal market was abandoned in the NHS in the late 1990s.

Figure 2.3.1

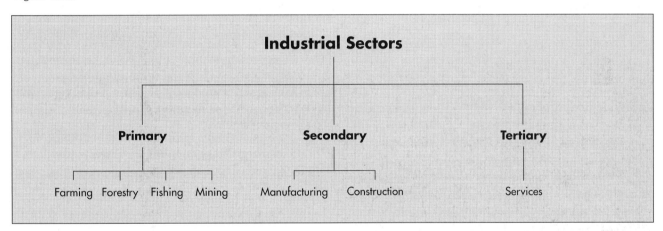

Primary, secondary and tertiary industry

Goods and services can also be divided into primary, secondary and tertiary products on the basis of what stage of the production process a business is involved in. Most of the goods that we receive have gone through three distinct stages of production.

Figure 2.3.2

As the names themselves suggest, this division classifies business by the stage of production involved. Primary will come before secondary and then there will be tertiary.

Primary industry

Primary industry covers the production of **farming**, **forestry**, **fishing** and **mining**. For many products, such as fish fingers, this will be the first stage of a product which will then be sold on for processing at the secondary stage. Many of these products will be sold for processing through the commodity markets.

- Fish are caught ready for making into fish fingers.
- Grapes are grown ready for making into wine.
- Iron ore is mined ready for making into steel.

Secondary industry

Secondary industry covers the **manufacturing** of goods such as steel, electricity, cars, televisions and tinned food. It also includes **construction** of factories, houses, roads, etc. Secondary industry processes the goods that come from primary industry and turns them into something that people want.

- Fish ⇒ **processing factory** ⇒ fish fingers.
- Wood ⇒ **timber mill** ⇒ **furniture manufacturer** ⇒ tables.
- Clay ⇒ **brick manufacturer** ⇒ **builder** ⇒ houses.

Tertiary industry

Tertiary industry covers **services**.

- Wholesaling, retailing, banking and insurance, all of which help businesses in the primary and secondary industries to sell their goods.
- Direct services, which are provided to the general public. Examples include hairdressing, hotels and restaurants.
- Government services such as health and education.

Sometimes a business is producing in more than one sector.

- Farmers may produce products in the primary sector and sell them through wholesalers to other businesses.
- Some farmers manufacture their own secondary products, as when milk farmers produce butter or cheese, or owners of vineyards produce their own wine.
- Some farmers will rent out cottages to holiday makers as well as running their own farms. They will then be producing in both the primary and tertiary sectors.

With many larger businesses this is quite common because they are producing a range of different products, as in the case of Pepsi.

The Coca-Cola and Pepsi companies are both known primarily as manufacturers of cola and other soft drinks. As well as colas they produce Nestea (Coke), Lipton (Pepsi), Powderade (Coke), All Sport (Pepsi), Sprite (Coke) and 7 Up (Pepsi).

In 1996 Coca-Cola sold £8.5 billion of soft drinks and £1.1 billion of juices and foods. All were manufactured by Coca-Cola and were part of **secondary** industry. The firm produced nothing else.

In 1996 Pepsi sold £6.4 billion of soft drinks and £5.9 billion of snack foods, both part of **secondary** industry. The highest part of their sales, however, came from their fast food restaurants (Kentucky Fried Chicken, Taco Bell and Pizza Hut), which earned the company £6.9 billion of sales. These restaurants are part of **tertiary** industry.

How has the size of the sectors changed over time?

Gross domestic product (GDP) measures everything that is produced in the UK. If we consider what percentage of GDP is produced by each sector of industry, we can see a significant change in the percentage figures over time. The changes in these relative figures are shown in Figure 2.3.3, from 1969 to 1989 and to 1999.

Figure 2.3.3 Changes in output from primary, secondary and tertiary sectors in the UK (1969, 1989 and 1999)

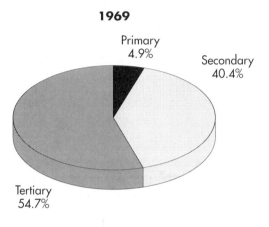

1969

Primary
4.9%

Secondary
40.4%

Tertiary
54.7%

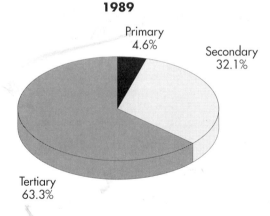

1989

Primary
4.6%

Secondary
32.1%

Tertiary
63.3%

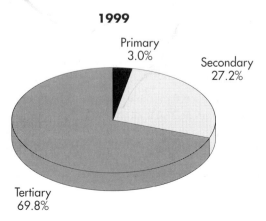

1999

Primary
3.0%

Secondary
27.2%

Tertiary
69.8%

> **Gross domestic product (GDP)** – the total amount of production produced by a country in a particular period of time (e.g. a year).

But these pie charts tell only part of the story. Total GDP in the UK increased, in real terms (i.e. after inflation had been taken into account), by 80 per cent between 1969 and 1999. That means that the UK produced more in every sector. However, some sectors grew faster than other sectors. If we take the actual real value of what was produced in 1969 and in 1999, we can see how each sector grew.

Figure 2.3.4 Percentage real growth in industrial sectors in the UK, 1969–99

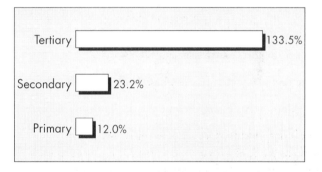

Tertiary 133.5%

Secondary 23.2%

Primary 12.0%

The growth in the tertiary sector is huge compared to the other sectors. The reasons why it is so large, and the others are comparatively small, can be explained by looking at the supply and demand factors involved.

The relatively **low growth of the primary sector** is explained by, among other things:

- Food is a necessity so when we get extra income we do not buy more food. It is income inelastic.

- We have been producing too much food. This has occurred because farmers were receiving subsidies and other support from the EU through the Common Agricultural Policy. In recent years farmers have been paid not to produce, through schemes such as 'set aside'.

- Many of the coal pits in the UK have been closed and we are importing coal instead.

The **medium growth in the secondary sector** is explained by the fact that some industries have expanded and some have contracted. For example:

- Electrical equipment went up by nearly 25 per cent in the last 10 years. This is because of the increase in demand for computers, microwaves, mobile phones, etc., all of which have a high income elasticity of demand.

- Chemicals rose by nearly 20 per cent in the last 10 years. Chemicals are used to make plastics, medicines, etc., and there has been a large increase in demand for these because many more products are now made of plastic and we care a great deal more about our health. Also, there are many more elderly people.

- Leather and textiles have both fallen by more than 15 per cent in the last 10 years. A decrease in demand for home produced goods has occurred because there are now cheaper, and sometimes better quality, imports available. The value of the pound is very high and this has made imports cheaper and our exports more expensive.

The **tertiary sector has increased substantially** because:

- Many services are income elastic. They are luxuries and this is what we spend our extra income on. We eat out more instead of preparing our own meals. We take more holidays and are prepared to pay more for them.

- We have more income and more time and we want to buy different and new services. Leisure and recreation services have grown considerably as we watch more television, play more computer games, join more golf clubs and go out to discos, cinemas and bowling alleys.

- The communications industry has grown by over 70 per cent in the last 10 years. On the supply side the industry has created a wide range of new products, such as satellite communication, the internet, mobile phones and telephone banking. At the same time customers have demanded better communications, e.g. businesses requiring EPOS and EFTPOS systems that connect retail outlets with the banking system, and consumers wanting to be able to buy shares on the internet.

All of the examples given above are fairly general. Ultimately, the changes that occur in any individual firm depend upon a range of factors that are very specific to that firm.

> Sir Clive Sinclair invented the home computer in the UK in 1980. Most homes now have a home computer, and for a time that made Sinclair very rich. Unfortunately he also invented the C5 motor car, a single-seater battery-operated car, which very few people wanted to buy and his business had to be sold to Amstrad.

> Sheep farmers in Wales in 1999 found that the price of lamb was so low that they could not cover the costs of producing the lamb when they sold it. This happened because too much lamb was on the market and the CAP support had been cut. Many individual farmers had to sell their farms and find other employment.

Markets

> **Market** – a place or process, which brings together buyers and sellers so that products can be sold.

Everything that is sold is sold through one kind of market or another. Markets bring buyers and sellers together and any process that brings buyers and sellers together is a market.

Above we looked at different types of goods and services. For each of these there will be a market that allows those who want the product to buy it and those who produce the product to sell it. Each of these markets will have different characteristics and will operate in different ways.

Consumer goods and services

These have traditionally been sold through retail shops, with customers visiting the shops in order to buy their goods or receive their services. Some services, such as education and health, sport and leisure, are provided in specialised locations. Other services, such as window cleaning, gardening, gas and electricity supplies are provided in the home. Today an increasing number of goods and services are provided in the home through technology, e.g. telephone banking and internet shopping.

Capital goods and services

These tend to be sold by businesses making direct contact with other businesses. Capital services, such as maintenance of machinery and security services, will be provided at the office or factory; other services, such as accountancy, legal advice or banking, will be provided at the offices of the supplier.

Capital goods, and especially **industrial goods**, are often sold through catalogues, exhibitions, or through representatives visiting the businesses. Many capital goods are tailor-made for the business and will be agreed after careful discussion between the two businesses. The market here may involve visits to both businesses, discussions on the telephone, faxes and e-mails.

Commodities

These are often sold through commodity markets. These are markets that specialise in particular types of commodities, where many sellers offer their products and a wide range of different grades of one type of good is available to the buyers. London is a major centre for the sale of gold, fur, metals, petroleum, rubber and tea.

Commodities are nearly always traded without the goods actually being seen. The goods can be brought at **spot**, which means that the goods are available to be taken away immediately and used by the purchaser. Commodities can also be bought as **futures**, where the purchaser buys goods that have not yet been produced and will receive them later when they have been produced. A buyer may, for example, buy coffee futures in, say, June, but not receive the actual coffee until it is harvested in Kenya or Brazil in December or January.

Because commodities can be bought as futures it is possible that the price will change between the 'futures' price, say, in June and the 'spot' price in the following January. There are, therefore, some people who buy futures purely in the hope that their price will rise and that they can sell their rights to the coffee, tea, rubber, etc. to someone else at a higher price. These speculators do not actually want the commodities at all.

Specialist markets

These are markets which sell only one type of product. These include commodity markets but there are many others, including:

- the **Stock Exchange** – selling stocks and shares and government bonds to businesses and to the general public

Futures for Coffee

	Price $/tonne	Volume (5 tonnes)
Mar	1075	2,661
May	1091	2,023
Jul	1114	371
Sep	1137	87
Nov	1159	31
Jan	1182	–

As the table shows, most futures will rise in price, although this does depend on the season and how much of the product is expected to be produced in the future months. A main reason why prices rise in the future is that there is more risk involved when you are buying something that has not yet been produced, or is in stock somewhere. It could go up in price even more and by buying futures the buyers are making sure that they get stocks of coffee before anyone else. For producers like Nestlé or Maxwell House that is very important.

- the **Baltic Exchange** – selling transportation on ships to business customers who need their products transported by sea
- **Billingsgate** – selling fresh fish mainly to fishmongers and supermarkets
- **livestock markets** – selling live animals mainly to the farming community and to businesses that will slaughter the livestock and produce food products
- **Harrogate Toy Fair** – selling toys and games once a year to retailers who will then offer them for sale to the general public
- the **London Metal Exchange** – selling a range of common metals such as aluminium, lead, nickel, tin, zinc and copper
- the **London Bullion Exchange** – selling precious metals such as gold, silver, platinum and palladium.

Market structure

Market structure also affects how markets behave. We will look at typical market structures, e.g. monopolies, oligopolies, competitive markets, in the next chapter.

Further Study

Many different types of products are around us all the time. We buy consumer goods and services ourselves, and as we travel about we see capital goods, such as buildings, machines and checkout tills. We also see many capital services, such as delivery vans, security guards and business internet services. Other capital goods and services will be seen only by visiting businesses, watching videos, etc. You may come across internal markets only through researching particular businesses. It is possible to visit the commodity markets, but again these may be most easily researched through articles, videos and the internet.

Observing products and markets

This can be done on several occasions when you go out.

1   Select a couple of shops for your survey.

2   Note, as you go round them, if they are selling goods or services, or, as with most retailers, a mixture of both.

3   Also note down the capital goods that they are using to help them sell their goods or services, e.g. fixtures and fittings, buildings, machinery and equipment.

4   You may be able to observe the capital services that they have, such as a security guard provided by a shopping precinct, but you will probably have to ask a manager in order to find out what services businesses pay for.

Checking other markets for consumer goods and services

A growing number of consumer goods and services, as well as products for business, can now be purchased through access from home, school or college. The suppliers are usually very keen to inform potential customers about these services. You can collect details in the following ways:

1   downloading details from the internet

2   picking up brochures from stores, banks, travel agents, etc. which offer on-line services

3   phoning businesses that offer on-line services. Many of these businesses have freephone numbers and will supply you with details by post

4   check the on-line services that allow individuals and businesses to buy and sell shares, trade in commodities, buy properties at home and abroad, etc.

Visiting businesses

To understand the nature of the different markets for goods and services, how buyers and sellers are brought together, what products are available, how customers contact particular businesses, etc., it is often best to visit the actual businesses involved. At the consumer level that is easy because you are consumers and you can arrange to visit shops. In the case of the other markets – businesses selling to other businesses, commodity markets and internal markets – it is very useful to arrange a visit to these markets and to speak to the people involved. When you approach businesses you should consider the following general rules:

1   The best contacts are usually made through people you know, e.g. family or friends.

2   They have their businesses to run, jobs to do, etc., and you should make it clear what you would like to see, but at the same time be prepared to fit in with what is easiest for them.

3   As you go round the business, make a note of the plant, equipment, tools and machinery that are being used. Ask what services are provided by outside agencies, and ask them if they have internal markets.

4   If you are offered any brochures, leaflets, etc., about the business, take them. They are likely to be useful to some part of your study.

5   Always write a letter of thanks to the person/people involved in arranging your visit. This will help to ensure that they will help other students in the future.

Revision Questions

1 Explain the difference between a good and a service, giving examples of each. (4 marks)

2 Give two examples of capital goods and two examples of capital services that would be used by:

 a) a bakery

 b) a bank

 c) a car manufacturer

  (12 marks)

3 Give one example of when each of the following would be a capital item and when it would be a consumer item:

 a) a television

 b) the services of a bank

 c) a haircut

  (6 marks)

4 How do industrial goods differ from other capital goods? (2 marks)

5 Explain why commodity markets are so competitive. (4 marks)

6 Describe how an internal market operates in a business you have studied. (4 marks)

7 Describe how the relative importance of primary, secondary and tertiary industry has changed in the UK in the last 30 years and explain why these changes have occurred. (9 marks)

8 Give details of a firm that you have studied that produces with each of the following combinations. Explain what they produce and why they are in both sectors of industry.

 a) the primary and tertiary sectors

 b) the secondary and tertiary sectors

 c) the primary and secondary sectors

  (9 marks)

CHAPTER 4

Market Structures and How Businesses Become More Competitive

KEY TERMS:

perfect competition	monopoly	oligopoly
integration	contestable markets	price makers and price takers
non-price competition	kinked demand curve	added value
product differentiation	competitive pricing	skimming
destroyer pricing	penetration pricing	price wars
stakeholders	price discrimination	mergers and takeovers

In this chapter you will learn how competition affects the way that businesses behave and how businesses react to competition in order to meet their objectives.

Introduction

This chapter will look at:

- the different types of goods and services that businesses produce and how the markets in which these products are sold differ

- what conditions affect how much of a product is supplied and how much is demanded

- how different types of market structure, such as monopoly, affect businesses

- what actions businesses take to increase their competitiveness and their control over the markets in which they operate

- how the actions of businesses affect their stakeholders.

Market structures

A major factor that determines how markets operate is the amount of competition there is in the market. The amount of competition is affected by how many firms are competing. At one end there are many firms competing and at the other end there is only one firm.

Competitive markets

Price takers – firms that have to accept the current market price when they sell their products.
Price makers – firms that dictate the price in the market and all other firms have to accept these prices.

Really competitive markets will have the five conditions listed in Table 2.4.1.

- There will be a large number of firms selling and also a great many people buying. This makes it very difficult for one firm to control the market. Firms will have to accept the price that is standard for the market. They will be **price takers**.

- The firms will all be selling the same products. The products will be **homogeneous**, i.e. all of the same kind. This means that it does not matter which firm customers go to as they will always get the same types of product.

- There will be **free entry** and **free exit** from the market. Any business that wants to enter the market will be able to do so with little cost. This means that if businesses are seen to be making high profits, other firms will join the market.

Table 2.4.1 The main types of market structure

	Highly competitive market	Competitive market	Oligopoly	Monopoly
1. Number of firms in the market	Very many	Many	Few	One
2. Similar products	Very similar	Similar	Similar but branded	Unique
3. How easy is it for firms to enter and leave the market?	Very easy	Easy but there are some restrictions	Difficult, costs are high	Impossible
4. Good knowledge of what is happening in the market	Customers and firms know everything	Customers and firms know most things	Firms use branding to pretend products are different	Customers know of nowhere else to buy products
5. Easy for customers to move to other sellers	Customers can move with little or no cost	Customers can move but it takes time	Customers will move if prices are changed	Customers cannot move, there is no other market

- There will be good knowledge of the market. Everyone will know the prices in different firms, where they are selling, etc. If one firm offers a better deal than the other firms, the customers will simply move to that firm.

- It will also be easy for customers to move from one seller to another and for businesses to find employees, raw materials, etc. when they need them. There will be **good mobility** for customers and for the factors of production.

These conditions combine to make this market highly competitive. Price will be the same and customers and businesses can move in and out of the market easily.

Examples of highly competitive markets

1 The commodity markets tend to be highly competitive because there are a great many businesses all trying to sell products that are very similar.

2 The Stock Exchange is also an example of a highly competitive market because there are many buyers and sellers of shares and computers link the market together so that everyone knows all the prices.

3 Personal computer manufacturers are highly competitive. There are some big well known companies like Dell and IBM who make their own computers but there are also hundreds of small producers who buy their parts from the big producers and make up their own computers.

Contestable markets

Contestable market – a market with very low entry and exit costs so firms can enter when profits are high and leave when profits fall.

In some markets firms will enter and leave fairly quickly. They will enter when they see that the businesses already in the market are making large profits. They will set their prices at or below the existing market price, and compete with the existing businesses. This will cause the prices to start to fall and the profits will get smaller and smaller.

Eventually the owners of these new firms will decide that they are not getting enough profit and move into a new market where the profits are still high. Because they enter the markets, take the profits, compete the prices down and then leave, they are described as '**hit and run**' businesses.

Firms will be able to behave in this way only if the following conditions exist in the market:

- There are **low entry costs**. This means that the firms can set up with few costs. They will not need expensive factories, premises, machines, stocks, etc. Staff will need little or no training.

- There are **low exit costs**. This means that the firms can leave the market will few costs. There will be low levels of stock, or they will be able to sell it to someone else easily. Any machinery or equipment can be easily sold with little loss. The lease will be paid on a weekly or monthly basis. There will be no redundancy payments to be made to employees because they will not have worked in the firm for very long.

- There will be **high levels of profit** in the market. This allows the businesses to enter, charge lower prices to capture customers, and still make good profits for themselves.

Winchester's Christmas Shops

Each year at least one shop opens about six weeks before Christmas to offer the public last-minute stocking fillers. The goods on sale are usually cheap and cheerful and available in many other shops. The goods can be bought cheaply from local wholesalers and they tend to have high mark-ups. The shops open in empty premises which are waiting for more permanent businesses to take up the leases. They have very basic shelving, a cash till and little else.

Typical products on offer for 1999 were:

- a range of coloured candles
- metal and glass candle holders
- road maps of Great Britain
- opaque drinking glasses in many different colours
- bottles of perfume
- Christmas decorations.

Before Christmas Day the shops have sold out and are gone.

Examples of contestable markets

1 Christmas shops which only open for a few weeks up to Christmas, selling decorations, cheap diaries, etc.

2 New ideas that are then copied by other firms. Initially one firm may be earning high profits but then these are competed away by new firms, some of which may be 'hit and run' businesses. This happened with *Trivial Pursuit*, when for a short time, many firms produced books of questions on different topics.

Monopolies

Monopoly – a market in which there is only one firm or where one firm completely controls the market.

The government defines a monopoly as a firm which has 25 per cent or more of the output of the market.

In theory a monopoly means that there is only one firm in a market. A more important definition is that one firm has *control* of the market. There may be other firms in the industry but the one firm behaves as though it were the only firm and the other firms are unable to do anything about it. Microsoft Windows is a good example of a product which is so dominant in the market that it is essentially a monopoly even though other firms are also producing operating systems.

There are many reasons why monopolies occur, but all of them in some way prevent other firms from competing.

- **Natural monopolies** occur when there is only room for one business in the market. This occurs with village shops or a betting office in a parade of shops. It also occurs with sports centres and multiplex cinemas where, usually, there is not enough demand for two in the same place.

- Legal protection, such as copyright and patents, prevent other firms from producing similar products.

- Some businesses cost a great deal of money to set up, like the Channel Tunnel, and other firms are unlikely to be able to set up and compete against the existing firm.

- Some businesses become monopolies by merging with or taking over other firms. Other businesses become monopolies by forcing their competitors out of business (see destroyer pricing on page 127).

- Some businesses become monopolies through branding. If their branding is very successful customers will not consider any other product as a substitute. There are no real substitutes for Marmite, Lucozade or tennis at Wimbledon.

Because it dominates its markets the monopoly can choose what the price will be. Monopolies are therefore **price makers**.

Examples of monopolies

1 Many of the firms that used to be state owned monopolies have become privately owned monopolies, although there is a growing amount of competition for some of them. Most private households can get their water only from their local water board. On many rail routes there is only one train operator.

2 Some attractions are unique and are therefore natural monopolies, such as the complex at Land's End or the Blackpool Tower.

3 Specialist shops are often monopolists within certain areas. It is rare to get more than one taxidermist, fishing tackle shop or gunsmith in most towns.

Consumer monopolies in Whitchurch

Whitchurch in Hampshire has a population of about 4,000 people and it is expanding fairly rapidly as over one hundred houses are built each year. Despite the increase, the number of shops and services is declining and in many types of business there is only one supplier for the town. These include only one:

doctor's practice	dentist
secondary school	supermarket
betting office	florist
butcher's shop	bank
DIY shop	chemist

Oligopolies

> **Oligopoly** – a market in which there are only a few firms producing similar products and competing with non-price competition.

An **oligopoly** is a market with only a few firms. That is what the word 'oligopoly' means. There are, however, very specific characteristics which make markets oligopolistic. These are:

- There are only a **few main firms** in the market. There are only two major producers of soap powder: Procter & Gamble and Unilever. There are only three main producers of pet foods: Spillers, Quaker and Pedigree.

- The firms are selling, essentially, **the same product**. Most soap powders are almost identical, as are most brands of petrol, most tins of cat food and most of the standard range of products sold by supermarkets.

- The businesses have what is called a **kinked demand curve** and therefore they usually compete by using **non-price competition**.

- They are **interdependent** and are affected very strongly by what any of their competitors do. See the inset on Asda and Tesco on page 128.

- There are **high entry costs** so the number of firms in the industry does not change very much. Most oligopolies, such as petrol companies, pet food producers and washing powder manufacturers, have had the same firms competing for decades.

With oligopolies the demand curve has two different shapes depending on whether the price is being raised or being lowered. These are shown in figures 2.4.2 and 2.4.3 below.

Figure 2.4.2 What happens if one firm raises its prices?

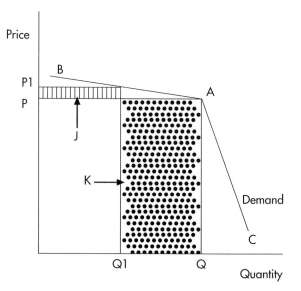

Figure 2.4.3 What happens if one firm lowers its prices?

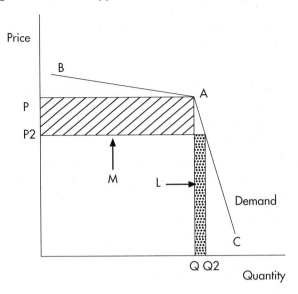

To explain the kinked demand curve we will use the example of petrol stations. There is very little difference between one brand of petrol and the next – Shell, Esso, Texaco, or the supermarkets' petrol.

If one firm tried to put up the price by itself, from P to P1, it would find that the demand curve, between A and B, was very elastic. Customers would simply go to other petrol stations. They might gain some additional

revenue (area 'J') from the customers who stayed loyal, but they would lose much more revenue (area 'K') because they were selling Q to Q1 fewer products.

On the other hand, if the firm tried to gain extra customers by lowering the price from P to P2 it would be faced with a very inelastic demand curve between A and C. The other petrol stations know that this firm could capture extra sales by lowering the price so they immediately prevent this by lowering their own prices as well. The firm may gain a few extra sales and revenue (area 'L'), but it will have lowered its prices for all its customers and it will have lost a great deal of revenue (area 'M').

Non-price competition – all competitive strategies that do not involve changing the price of the products.

Oligopolies cannot easily change their prices because they will lose revenue and hence profits. They therefore compete by using **non-price competition**. The kind of non-price competition used is shown in the inset on supermarkets below, but many of these strategies could be applied to petrol stations, pet foods and other oligopolies.

CASE STUDY

Non-price competition in supermarkets

Sometimes supermarkets do get into price wars and this can be very damaging. In the mid-1990s Gateway tried to capture a bigger share of the market by lowering its prices. The price war that followed almost put it out of business. Generally, supermarkets feel it is safer to compete by using non-price competition. In recent years they have used all of the following strategies.

- **Product differentiation** – This has included the introduction of organic products, new meat products such as ostrich, and, recently, even computers.

- **Advertising** – This is carried out on a regular basis on the television, in magazines, in the stores themselves, on carrier bags, etc.

- **Quality** – When supermarkets first produced their own brands they were inferior to the main brands. Today supermarkets' own brands are often as good as if not better than the main brands. The supermarkets also compete in the quality of the services they provide with wider aisles, smooth trolleys, self scanners and regularly filled shelves.

- **Special services** – Many supermarkets now offer free delivery, loyalty schemes, cash back, free parking, childminding, opening 24 hours a day, etc.

- **Other attractions** – These are not directly related to the supermarkets but they do help to attract customers. They include restaurants and cafés, play areas for children and petrol services. For Tesco and Sainsbury's the petrol stations have now become important sources of revenue themselves.

- **Special offer –** Many special offers are really price competition, such as 'buy-one-get-one-free' or discounts on future purchases. These actually compete by lowering the price of products.

- **Promotions** – Supermarkets are constantly trying to find ways to bring their services to the notice of the public. Promotions include running competitions, loyalty cards, air miles.

- **Customer service** – This includes information on food labelling, refund policies, credit facilities, help desks, internet shopping.

You'll find that we help you achieve healthy eating in many ways...

...looking at labels can make your shopping easier and your food choices healthier

Healthy Balance Symbol

For instant help to improve the balance in your diet, just look for the Sainsbury's Healthy Balance symbol.

Foods carrying this symbol are suitable for healthy eating because they are generally low in fat, particularly saturated fats, and have a limited amount of added sugar and sodium (salt). These foods also have a good mix of other nutrients such as protein, starch, vitamins and fibre, which make up a balanced diet.

On a few high fat foods, such as vegetable oils and spreads, the symbol highlights the healthiest option. These foods should be eaten in small amounts.

Labelling

A blue panel at the base of the nutrition label, found on most products shows you how many calories and grams of fat there are in each serving.

NUTRITION INFORMATION		
TYPICAL VALUES (COOKED AS PER INSTRUCTIONS)		
	PER ½ PACK	PER 100g
ENERGY	1138 k J.	481 k J.
	296 k cal	115 k cal
PROTEIN	20.1g	7.9g
CARBOHYDRATE	28.3g	11.1g
of which sugars	7.4g	2.9g
of which starch	20.9g	8.2g
FAT	19.4g	7.6g
of which saturates	7.7g	3.0g
of which mono-unsaturates	9.1g	3.2g
FIBRE	less than 0.1g	less than 0.1g
SODIUM	less than 0.1g	less than 0.1g
PER ½ PACK	296 CAL	19.4g FAT
GUIDELINE DAILY AMOUNTS		
EACH DAY	WOMEN	MEN
CALORIES	2000	2500
FAT	70g	95g
OFFICIAL UK GOVERNMENT FIGURES FOR AVERAGE ADULTS		

Looking at labels can help you choose foods containing less fat. These claims highlight lower fat options:

Low fat - less than 5 grams of fat in 100 grams and in a serving*

Reduced fat - at least 25% less fat than the standard product

99% fat free - less than 1g fat in 100g   **98% fat free** - less than 2g fat in 100g

97% fat free - less than 3g fat in 100g   **96% fat free** - less than 4g fat in 100g

95% fat free - less than 5g fat in 100g

Low in saturates - less than 3g saturated fat in 100g

or in a serving*

*if the typical serving is larger than 100g

A Sainsbury's leaflet with information about food labelling

Other market types

No two markets are exactly the same and the types of markets described above are general types which show general characteristics, such as few competitors, free entry, homogeneous products, low costs and high profits. In the real world markets often have some characteristics from one type of market and other characteristics from completely different types of markets and this makes it difficult to say exactly what type of markets they are.

South West Trains has a monopoly of rail transport from Salisbury to Waterloo, but it is possible to take a coach, a taxi, a private car or even an aeroplane. Village shops have monopolies in their villages but most people have cars and can drive to the supermarkets and shops in the nearby towns.

The egg market

The market for eggs has been considered, by many people, to be very competitive. Most eggs are very similar and in many cases the market is competitive. (i) There are hundreds and hundreds of producers, (ii) eggs are for sale in many places, (iii) they all appear to be much the same.

However, the egg market is less competitive than it at first seems. There is one major producer, Tames Valley Eggs, which produces more than a quarter of all the eggs. New niche markets have been established. At first they were for free range eggs and now they are for organic eggs.

How businesses seek to change their own competitiveness

There are essentially two ways in which businesses can compete more effectively in the marketplace:

1 change their production or marketing so that their products become more appealing to the customers

2 change the market so that there is less competition from other businesses.

We will consider both of these but it is not always easy to separate them. Lowering prices should make a business more competitive. At the same time it may drive other businesses out of the market so there is less competition.

Added value – the value of a product increases as it is produced.

In many cases the products become more competitive because value has been added to them. Value can be added to products in a great many ways, such as advertising, correct pricing, better quality, etc., and we will look at these below. In some cases, however, value is simply added by charging the customer a higher price and that does not usually make the business more competitive.

Figure 2.4.4 Adding value

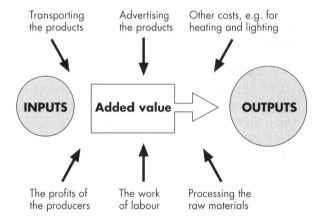

Improving quality

As people's incomes rise and they have more leisure time, the quality of what they buy becomes more and more important. Most businesses recognise this and also recognise that if they cannot give the customer the quality of products that they want the customers will go elsewhere.

Figure 2.4.5 Ways in which businesses can improve quality

The quality of products can be improved in a great many different ways. Some general ways are shown on Figure 2.4.5. The most appropriate way in which quality can be improved will depend on what type of product is being produced. Table 2.4.2 shows some of the improvements that have been made in the quality of two specific products over the last few years.

Although there are regular improvements in quality, many businesses do not go as far as they could. If they did they would lose sales in the future. For a long time now it has been possible to make light bulbs that would last 10 or 15 years, and the same is true of exhaust systems for cars. However, the manufacturers have decided not to make these quality improvements because replacement sales would plummet.

Table 2.4.2 Quality improvements in (i) cars and (ii) travel services

Family cars	Travel services
• More safety features, e.g. seat belts, ABS, air bags and roll bars	• Wider choice of destinations
• Better petrol consumption	• Services and holidays backed by ABTA
• More environmentally friendly features, e.g. unleaded petrol and catalytic converters	• Computerised facilities for rapid confirmation of bookings
• More comfort features as standard, e.g. electric windows, cassette or CD player and air conditioning	• Insurance facilities offered by the travel agency
• More durable product with galvanised metal, reinforced glass, flexible wing mirrors	• Additional hotel accommodation, ferry crossings, etc., booked through the travel agency
• Manufacturer's warranty as standard	• Brochures etc. sent by post so that clients can read and decide at their leisure
	• Internet facilities for booking from home

CASE STUDY

Differentiation in fruit drinks

It is not just the brand name that makes fruit drinks different. A quick check of the ingredients on the label also reveals that the drinks are made in different ways and contain different quantities of fresh juice.

- At the bottom of the price range are drinks made of water mixed with juice concentrates and added sugar.

- The middle range is made from concentrated juice revitalised with water but nothing else.

- At the top of the range, and with the highest prices, is freshly squeezed juice, chilled and ready to serve.

Product differentiation

> **Product differentiation** – products in the same, or similar, markets have features that make them different, or appear to be different.

Product differentiation can be real or imagined. In the sparkling soft drinks market Lucozade is a different product to Coca-Cola because it has a different flavour and is made from different ingredients.

On the other hand, Pepsi Cola and Coca-Cola are very similar in taste and appearance. Nevertheless, many consumers believe that Pepsi and Coke are different because the producers spend millions of pounds on advertisements telling them that they are different. The product differentiation for these two colas has been created through cleaver advertising and **branding**. This aggressive branding has helped to make and keep Pepsi and Coca-Cola the two giants of the soft drinks market.

Sometimes product differentiation is also used to make minor changes to products so that the businesses involved can charge different prices to different groups of customers. (See price discrimination on page 128.)

Advertising and promotion

Advertising and promotion are covered in detail in Unit 3 chapter 4. Promotion has two basic objectives: to inform and to persuade. Providing information about new products, how to use products, where to find the products, etc., is vital but, frequently, the primary objective of many promotional activities is to change customers' behaviour and make them want to buy the business's products. Promotion has become a necessary part of competition.

Businesses use advertising either to challenge their competitors directly or to make it clear to the target audience that there are no significant substitutes for their products. This is shown very clearly by the words they choose to put across their messages.

- 'It's the real thing' (Coca-Cola).
- 'You can't do better than a Kwik-Fit Fitter'
- 'There's nothing quite like a McDonald's'
- 'Beans means Heinz'
- 'Never knowingly undersold' (John Lewis Partnership)
- 'Millions are better off with BT Together'

Pricing strategies

The price of a product is frequently the major factor that decides whether or not customers will buy a product. Businesses have therefore come up with a range of different pricing strategies that will help them to be, or appear to be, more competitive than other businesses. There are also pricing strategies that help businesses to reduce the level of competition in the market.

Competitive pricing

> **Competitive pricing** – this occurs when one firm fixes its prices at the same rate as its competitors.

There are very few products that are not in competition with other, similar products. The prices chosen by the individual businesses reflect this and most of the pricing strategies covered below show some degree of competitive pricing.

Competitive pricing or **competition based pricing** occurs when there is a high degree of competition in a market and the individual businesses do not want to create a price war. They therefore price their products at the current market price. This allows them to compete against other similar products, because they have the same prices. At the same time, they do not pose a major threat to existing firms because there is already a high level of competition in the market.

Penetration pricing

> **Penetration pricing** – this occurs when a new product is launched at a price significantly below the current market price so that it can enter the market.

Penetration pricing is frequently used when new firms enter the market or when a new product is launched on to the market. Initially, the price of the new product is set below the current market price. This encourages people to try the product. After an introductory period the price is put up to the normal market price. Putting the price up fairly quickly helps to ensure that existing businesses will not retaliate and put their prices down as well. If this happened, the new product might never make it into the market.

Figure 2.4.6 Original demand for the product

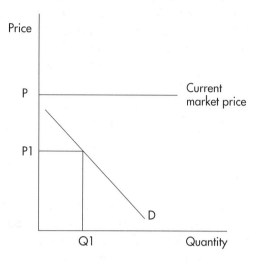

Figure 2.4.7 Demand and sales after penetration pricing has been used

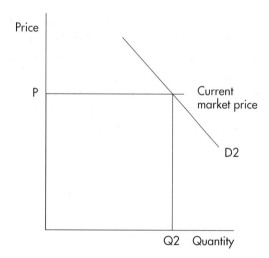

Figures 2.4.6 and 2.4.7 show what happens to the demand for and sales of these kinds of new products. At the current market price of P there may not even be enough demand to sell any of the new product. If the price is put at P1 it will encourage people to try the product and sales of Q1 will be possible.

If the customers like the product they will keep on buying it and they will tell other people about it. This will change the demand from D to D2. The firm will now be able to put the price back to the normal market price and still sell their product. If the penetration pricing has been successful the business will sell many more products, Q2.

This way of pricing new products is common practice in many markets including those for magazines, confectionery, breakfast cereals, soft drinks and ice cream products.

Skimming

> **Skimming** – this occurs when the price of a new product is set very high in order to gain additional revenue from customers who are prepared to pay a high price for the product.

Skimming, also known as **price creaming**, is used by businesses to gain additional revenue from their customers. Figure 2.4.8 shows how they are able to get the extra revenue.

If the product was sold at the normal market price of P1, the business would sell Q1 products and gain the revenue shown by the shaded areas X and Z.

Figure 2.4.8 Gaining additional revenue through skimming

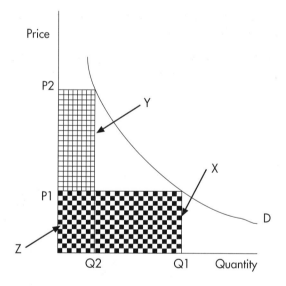

If, on the other hand, the price was put at P2, to start with the business would sell Q2 products and gain the revenue shown by the shaded areas Y and Z. Once these products had been sold they could then lower the price to P1 and sell the other products between Q2 and Q1. The business would then receive the revenue shown by the shaded area X.

By skimming, the business makes more revenue (in this case Y more revenue) than if it did not use skimming. It must, however, be careful that it does not annoy the customers who paid the higher price. With many products, such as new Playstation or Nintendo games, this is achieved by waiting for a few months before the price is dropped. With books it is achieved by changing the product very slightly, i.e. producing a hardback copy first. The paperback copy is then released some seven months later. In both cases, the customers who really want the product now are prepared to pay more for it.

Destroyer pricing

Destroyer (or destruction) pricing – this occurs when one business puts its prices down in order to drive competitors out of the market.

Destroyer pricing is used by businesses to get rid of competitors and capture their customers. For a business to be able to use destroyer pricing it must:

- have lower costs than its competitors, or be able to lose money itself while it is destroying

- be able to dictate what the market price will be. This usually means that it has monopoly power and is the price maker.

Before destroyer pricing is used, both firms can survive because the market price of P is above their costs, AC1 and AC2. The destroyer then lowers the price to P1, which is below the competitor's costs of AC2. The competitor cannot compete at that price and is driven out of the business.

The customers now have nowhere else to buy the product so they buy from the destroyer. The demand increases from D to D2 and sales increase from Q to Q2. The destroyer now makes a great deal more revenue and profits.

This used to be quite a common practice in the UK but there are now strict laws on anti-competitive practices and so it now tends to be done only by smaller businesses who are not covered by the law.

Price wars

Sometimes businesses do compete aggressively on the basis of price, especially when it is difficult to attract customers. Occasionally, this leads to an all out price war where competing firms progressively lower their prices until some of the firms are driven out of the market. This increases the demand for the goods of the firms that are left in the market and they then stop the price war.

Figure 2.4.9 Destroyer's product

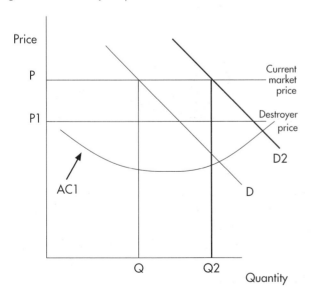

Figure 2.4.10 Competitor's product

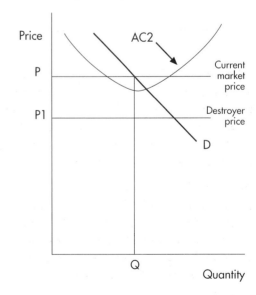

CASE STUDY

Is another price war starting between the supermarkets?

As the new millennium starts a new round of price cuts has begun in the supermarkets. The first step came in 1999 following Wal-Mart's takeover of the Asda supermarket chain. Following its practice in the United States, Wal-Mart cut over 4,000 prices by the end of 1999 and it has announced that it intends to reduce further 6,000 prices in 2000.

Tesco, the UK's largest supermarket chain, has responded quickly and aggressively. It has announced plans to bring down the price of over 1,000 items during 2000 and some prices will fall by as much as 20 per cent. Sainsbury's will soon follow suit.

Profits have been high for the main players in the supermarket sector and they can afford to lower their prices. Consumers will benefit, at least in the short run.

For the smaller supermarkets this aggressive reduction of prices is not such good news. Somerfield was struggling to keep customers and cover costs throughout 1999 and some stores were finally taken over by the John Lewis Partnership in January 2000. John Lewis owns Waitrose, but that is also a fairly small supermarket chain. As the giants compete for their share of the market, it will be the small players who finally pay for the price war, and some may pay with the closure of their businesses.

Price discrimination

> **Price discrimination** – the setting of different prices for different customers for what is essentially the same product.

We have already seen one example of price discrimination with skimming when two different groups of customers are charged different prices for the same product. For businesses to be able to price discriminate successfully four basic conditions have to be met.

- The business must have monopoly power in the market.
- It must be possible to keep the different customers apart.
- It must not cost too much to keep them apart.
- The different groups of customers must have different price elasticities of demand.

Why these conditions are important should become obvious as we look at the example of price discrimination on trains. There is, in fact, a lot of discrimination in rail travel, e.g. in:

- first and second class tickets

- child and adult fares
- special rates for the unemployed and for students
- different charges for peak and non-peak travel.

If peak and off-peak travel is looked at, we can see how and why the conditions apply.

On many routes the individual train operator has a monopoly. This means that if it put up the prices at peak times the customers could not go to a competitor because there is none.

It is possible to keep the two sets of customers apart because the cheaper off-peak tickets can be used only after a certain time of day. The cost of keeping the two sets of customers apart is also easy and cheap. There are guards on the trains checking the tickets already so there is no extra cost.

The price elasticities of demand are different because the commuters have to get to work by a certain time. For them rail travel is a necessity, there are few substitutes and the travel is seen as a low proportion of the income they will earn at work. For the off-peak user, say, going to London for the day, the demand is elastic. They do not have to go to London, they could go by car, they could go to the seaside or stay at home. There are many alternatives.

It is the different elasticities that explain why businesses use price discrimination. This is shown in Figures 2.4.11 and 2.4.12.

Figure 2.4.11 Peak travel

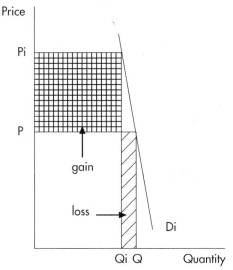

Figure 2.4.12 Off-peak travel

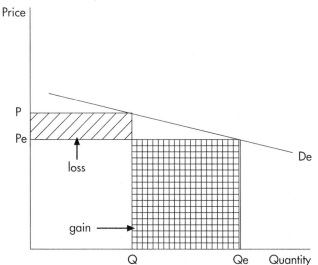

If the original price was P for all customers the train operators can make additional revenue (and profits) by moving the prices in different directions. For peak travel the price is put up. This will stop a few people from travelling and the number of sales will drop from Q to Qi, causing a loss of revenue as shown in Figure 2.4.11. However, most commuters will continue to travel and pay the higher price of Pi. This will bring in additional revenue as shown by the checked area on the graph. The gain will be very much larger than the loss, so total revenue will increase.

For off-peak travel the price will be put down to Pe and this will attract a great many more customers. The gain in revenue from the extra sales, Q to Qe, is shown by the checked area on Figure 2.4.12. There will be some loss of revenue, shown by the hashed area, because customers who would have travelled and paid a price of P are now only being asked to pay Pe. Overall, however, the gain is far greater than the loss.

Discrimination of this kind is very widespread. Table 2.4.3 gives some examples.

Mergers and take-overs

Merger – this occurs when two firms join together to become one business with shared ownership.
Take-over – this occurs when one firm buys up another firm and becomes the sole owner of the new firm.

The difference between a merger and a take-over is one of ownership. In a merger, the two firms agree to become one and the new firm is then owned by all the original owners. In a take-over, one firm buys out the other firm and takes over ownership.

Mergers and take-overs are very common. The joint firms have more power in the market and this either helps them to compete or allows them to dominate the market completely. As they join together they are 'integrated'. The benefits of integration include:

- When businesses merge or are taken over in the same industry (**horizontal integration**), they gain greater market share and therefore more power in the market.

- This can be used to remove competitors from the market.

- Where jobs, factories, shops, etc. are duplicated, some of them can be removed. This saves costs and makes the joint business more competitive.

- The joint business can gain economies of scale because it is larger.

- For businesses that wish to expand this is a much quicker method than internal growth.

- This integration can be used to join up with suppliers (**backward integration**) or with customers

Table 2.4.3 Examples of price discrimination

The market	How price discrimination is used
Electricity	• Different prices for consumers and for businesses • Different rates at different times of day • Different rates if bills are paid early • Different rates if you buy other services, like gas supply, from the same provider
Cinemas	• Different rates for adults and children • Different rates at different times of day • Special rates for season ticket holders
Cross-Channel ferries	• Different rates for car passengers and foot passengers • Different rates at different times of the year • Different rates for customers who have loyalty cards • Different rates for people who book and for people who turn up on stand-by

(**forward integration**). This will help to ensure that the business gets the raw materials that it needs or that it has a place in which it can sell.

- Businesses may join together that are not in the same market (**conglomerate integration**). This helps to spread risk. If one part is doing badly, the other part can support it.

There are also disadvantages with integration, including:

- The businesses may have different management styles and this can cause friction.

- Where there is duplication, some staff will have to go and this can cause resentment and a feeling of insecurity.

- Where one firm has bought out another against its wishes (a **hostile take-over**), the staff of the firm that has been taken over may not wish to co-operate.

- Sometimes businesses are only taken over so that they can be split up and the parts sold off (**asset stripping**). This can put large numbers of people out of work and destroy perfectly good businesses.

- Integration can give the business monopoly power and this may be used to exploit its position in the market, e.g. putting up prices to consumers, forcing suppliers to lower their prices.

Vodafone and Mannesmann agree the largest merger of all time

After months of bitter exchanges between Vodafone AirTouch and the German telecom company Mannesmann, the two companies have finally agreed to merge. If there are no objections from the European Commission, this integration will represent the largest merger ever and will make the combined company the fifth largest in the world.

Figure 2.4.13 Market value of top five world companies

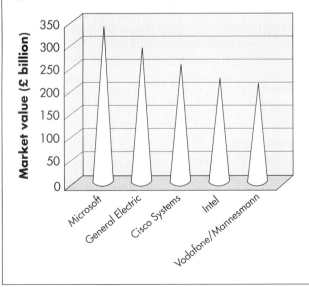

How do competition and businesses' actions to reduce competition affect stakeholders?

The details given in this chapter have already shown how many of the stakeholders will be affected by the way that businesses behave. If, for example, a business decided to take over another business and then cut back surplus staff, this would affect stakeholders in the following ways:

- The **employees** who were laid off would suffer, but possibly those who remained might have more work and better pay.

- The **suppliers** would now have larger orders, but the suppliers to the firm that had been taken over might lose sales.

- If the take-over led to economies of scale and lower costs, the **customers** might benefit from lower prices. If the take-over gave the new business more power, prices might be raised and the customers would suffer.

- If the new firm could reduce costs and sell more products, then the **shareholders** would receive more profits.

- If the take-over led to employees being laid off, then the **community** might have to pay for increased unemployment benefits or for retraining.

- If the take-over had to be paid for out of cash and funds, this might leave less to pay **creditors** with and they would be paid later.

To see the full effects on the stakeholders of any business action it is necessary to study the changes that have been made very carefully. They will be different for each business. Some general examples are given below.

Customers

Customers will usually be affected by changes in the price of products, the range that is on offer or the quality.

Table 2.4.4

Business action	Beneficial effects	Negative effects
Advertising	Customers know what products are on sale	Prices may rise to cover the cost of advertising
Product differentiation	A wider choice of products	Prices may be put up simply because of minor differences
Price discrimination	Customers with inelastic demand will pay more	Customers with elastic demand will pay less
Destroyer pricing	Customers benefit from lower prices while the destruction is taking place	In the long run prices rise and there is less choice for the customer

Employees

Employees are likely to be affected by more or less work, changes in their rates of pay and the work load.

Table 2.4.5

Business action	Beneficial effects	Negative effects
Destroyer pricing	Employees in the successful firm will have more secure jobs	Employees in the destroyed firm will lose their jobs
Improving quality	Staff have a better product to sell and may need to be trained in new skills	Unskilled workers may be replaced and the work load may increase
Creating a monopoly	May make the jobs of existing employees more secure	Employees have no alternative firms to move to if they are unhappy where they are

Creditors and suppliers

Monopsonist – a single buyer in a market.

These will include suppliers who have sold raw materials to the business but also financial institutions that have lent money and the tax authorities who are waiting for VAT payments, etc. When firms become very big and powerful they may be the only firm that suppliers sell to. When this happens the firms have become **monopsonists**.

Table 2.4.6

Business action	Beneficial effects	Negative effects
Increased levels of competition	May increase total sales and this will provide more money to pay creditors	Will lower prices and may reduce profits and cash flow so creditors are paid later
Creating a monopoly	Should provide more funds to pay creditors	Large firms can become monopsonists and they can then dictate terms to the suppliers
Penetration pricing	This allows another firm into the market and should increase orders to suppliers	This may take custom away from other businesses and reduce demand to their supplier
Hit and run actions	Temporary increase in demand as businesses compete	Suppliers may build up stocks and then find their customers have left the market

Shareholders

Shareholders are most likely to be affected by the level of profits that the businesses make, but they will also be affected by how much the business is worth.

Table 2.4.7

Business action	Beneficial effects	Negative effects
Price wars	Increased profits for the owners of the businesses that win and survive	Falling profits during the war and the loss of their businesses for those who lose
Advertising	Increased profits if the advertising is successful	Lower profits if the advertising is unsuccessful or if it is just used because competitors are advertising
Hit and run actions	Easy profits for the businesses that are entering the market	Existing businesses have their profit levels competed away

The community

The community will be affected by the levels of employment and the knock-on effects of employees spending their incomes in the community. It will also be affected by efforts to make products more environmentally friendly, etc.

Table 2.4.8

Business action	Beneficial effects	Negative effects
Increased environmental quality of the products	Less pollution in the community, fewer accidents, etc.	Higher costs for products and this may mean less income for spending in the community
Destroyer pricing	This may benefit the community if the destroyer firm is located there	The community will lose income and have more unemployed people to pay for if the destroyed firm is located there
Advertising	This may increase sales and employment in the area and provide more incomes to spend	The advertisements may be large hoardings or big displays that destroy the atmosphere of the area

Furter Study

The best way to see how these market structures work and how businesses actually compete is to study real businesses. This will confirm the examples given in this chapter but it will also add a great deal more detail and many points that have not been covered above.

Studying real market structures

This can be done easily by checking the following sources.

1   Note the number of shops that are selling the same kind of goods or providing the same services in your local town. Decide if they are monopolies, oligopolies or competitive.

2   Check goods on sale in supermarkets. Check the labels to see who actually makes the branded products. Frequently, as with pet foods, there is a very limited number of producers.

3   Check details in libraries on particular markets. Try to find out what market share they have. Details will be given in specialist magazines such as *The Grocer* and *Marketing Weekly* or in government publications on markets. Details are also reported by specialist research firms, such as Mintel.

Checking actions used by businesses to become more competitive or gain more market power

These strategies are going on around us all the time. You need to check what is being done and work out why the businesses are behaving in this way.

Check advertisements and try to work out if they are trying to gain new customers or simply retaliating against another business's advertising.

Check the business press for details on mergers and takeover bids. These are reported regularly and the reports give details of why they are occurring and the likely effects on the market.

Note any changes in pricing for specific products and try to work out which pricing strategy is being used.

For price discrimination, skimming, penetration pricing etc., note down when these are used and which products they are typically used for.

The effects on stakeholders

To study the effects on stakeholders you need to look carefully at what change has been made and then consider the likely effects. Sometimes press reports do clearly state how certain stakeholders will be affected, especially if it is going to lead to more or fewer jobs.

Revision Questions

1 From the conditions given below select those that will go with (a) a highly competitive market and (b) a monopoly.

    i) price maker
    ii) price taker
    iii) free entry
    iv) homogeneous product
    v) no substitutes
    vi) unique product

                       (6 marks)

2 Explain what a contestable market is and what conditions are necessary for these markets to exist.   (6 marks)

3 Give **four** reasons why monopolies occur, and for each reason give an example from UK business.   (8 marks)

4 Explain, using diagrams, why oligopolies will not put the price of their products either up or down.   (12 marks)

5 Give five examples of how petrol stations use non-price competition to attract customers.   (5 marks)

6 How has each of the following products improved in quality in recent years?

    a) games consoles
    b) telephone services
    c) clothes shops

                       (6 marks)

7 Explain what is mean by product differentiation and give examples from products you have studied.   (5 marks)

8 The figure shows the position of a business entering a market and using penetration pricing.

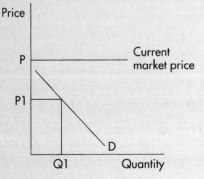

a) Explain the diagram and how this action helps the business to enter the market.

b) Draw another graph to show what will happen in the long run and explain the new graph.

                       (6 marks)

9 Explain what skimming is and why businesses use it.   (6 marks)

10 Give **three** reasons why many firms use competition (or competitor) pricing.   (3 marks)

11 **a)** List the four conditions that are necessary before a business can use price discrimination effectively.   (4 marks)

  b) How do cinemas use price discrimination?   (2 marks)

  c) Explain how each of the four conditions you listed in (a) apply to a cinema.   (4 marks)

12 Explain the difference between a merger and a take-over.   (2 marks)

13 **a)** What is the difference between "horizontal" and "vertical" integration?

  b) Explain the benefits of each sort of integration to the firms involved.   (8 marks)

14 Identify who the listed stakeholders are for the following businesses (a) a plumber, (b) a green grocer, and (c) a coal mine.

    i) the suppliers
    ii) the employees
    iii) the customers
    iv) the community

                       (8 marks)

15 Explain how a rise in the price of raw materials might affect each of the following stakeholders of a petrol company:

    i) the suppliers
    ii) the shareholders
    iii) the customers
    iv) the employees
    v) the community

                       (5 marks)

How Business is Affected by Government Policy

In this chapter you will learn how government actions affect businesses. Sometimes this is deliberate and is done because governments do not approve of the way that businesses behave. Sometimes governments have other objectives for their actions, such as managing the economy, but their actions still have an impact upon businesses.

Introduction

This chapter will look at:

- why governments intervene to control the way that businesses operate
- how governments control what businesses do
- the effects of government controls on businesses and how these controls affect the businesses' stakeholders
- the main agencies that control and monitor how businesses operate
- the influence of European Union institutions and laws on UK businesses
- the way that governments manage the economy and how this affects businesses and their stakeholders.

Why do governments intervene to control how businesses operate?

The primary objective of most private business remains that of making a profit. Profits can be made only if the producer charges more for the product than it costs to make. The greater the profit, the greater the gap between costs and the price at which the products are sold. With many businesses the desire for more profit means that they are prepared to exploit their stakeholders in order to achieve personal gain. This is why the government needs to intervene – to protect stakeholders who have less power than the business.

How to maximise your profits in 10 easy steps (A guide to unscrupulous business practices)

1 Pay your workers a subsistence wage and threaten them with the sack if they will not work for this wage.

2 Charge customers as much as you can.

3 Pretend in your advertising that your product will do anything. The public are too stupid to know that you are telling them lies.

4 Destroy the competition so that customers have to pay your prices.

5 Use cheap materials so that goods do not last and customers will have to come back to buy more goods.

6 Provide no health and safety features: they cost money and if employees are hurt, it is their fault.

---

7   Don't pay your bills but ask for more raw materials on credit. After all, the supplier needs you for his custom. You can always go to another supplier.

8   If your factory/shop causes pollution, don't worry. The community will clear it up.

9   Claim expenses for eating out, holidays, etc. This will reduce your declared profits so there will be less tax to pay and less profit to pass on to other shareholders.

10 Do not declare what you are doing to the tax office. You can then avoid paying tax altogether.

It would be nice to believe that firms, left completely uncontrolled, would run their businesses in an ethical way. But they do not, and that is why government needs to step in and set acceptable standards, and to ensure, through the law, that these standards are met.

The main reasons why government intervenes to control business are:

- to ensure that businesses trade fairly and honestly

- to protect the stakeholders from practices that would harm them

- to increase competition that is beneficial to customers and competitors

- to ensure that business activity helps to support the major government economic objectives of full employment, low inflation, economic growth and a positive balance of payments

- to ensure that businesses do not cause environmental or social damage to the country or to individual communities.

These are very general objectives. The examples given throughout the rest of this chapter will help to clarify what these general objectives are and also show how wide they can be.

Table 2.5.1 Features of competition

Good features	Bad features
• Keeps prices down	• Can lead to price wars and the destruction of good businesses
• Makes businesses more efficient	• Allows dominant firms to become monopolists
• Gets rid of weak businesses	• Gives no protection to new firms
• Encourages the development of new and better products	• Allows businesses to steal and use other businesses' ideas
• Prevents businesses from making unacceptably high profits	

Controlling competition

Competition has both good and bad features.

The government, therefore, needs to create rules that will support the good features of competition and prevent the bad ones. It has done this by passing a great many different laws. The Competition Act was passed to ensure that anti-competitive practices were prevented in businesses with a turnover of more than £10 million. The Patents Act and Copyright Acts were passed to ensure that inventors and creators of new ideas would not have them stolen and used by competitors.

Control of anti-competitive practices

In 1948 the Monopolies and Restrictive Practices Act set up a commission to ensure that the anti-competitive features of monopolies and other restrictive business actions would be investigated and, where necessary, stopped. In 1956 the two parts were split with the Director General of Fair Trading and the Restrictive Practices Court dealing with restrictive practices, and what was to become the Monopolies and Mergers Commission (MMC) dealing with monopolies. The Competition Act 1998 replaced the MMC with the **Competition Commission**.

The institutions involved in controlling anti-competitive behaviour are shown in Figure 2.5.1.

Figure 2.5.1 Control of anti-competitive practices

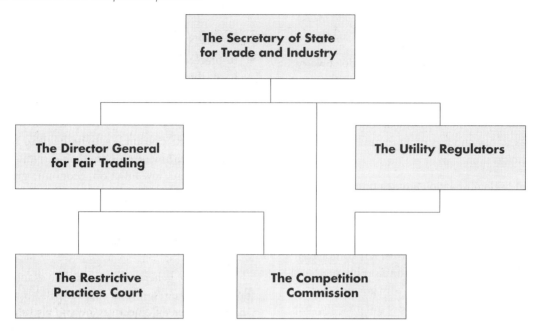

The basic role of each of these bodies in controlling anti-competitive behaviour is as explained below.

The **Secretary of State for Trade and Industry** has ultimate responsibility for ensuring that anti-competitive actions by businesses do not take place. He is responsible for appointing the Director General of Fair Trading, the Utility Regulators and the members of the Competition Commission. He can also refer businesses to the Competition Commission for investigation. The decisions of the Competition Commission will be referred back to the Secretary of State and he or she will decide what action needs to be taken.

The **Director General of Fair Trading** (DGFT) is the head of the Office of Fair Trading and responsible for enforcing competition law and consumer protection. The DGFT can refer businesses to the Competition Commission. He also has the role of monitoring restrictive practices and decides when businesses should be referred to the Restrictive Practices Court.

The **Utility Regulators** are responsible for ensuring that businesses in their particular sectors of industry do not behave in an anti-competitive way. They can also refer businesses to the Competition Commission. They also have some rights to take action against restrictive practices. There are regulators for gas, electricity, water, telecommunications, railways and airports.

The main competition laws

The Fair Trading Act 1973 deals with mergers and monopolies.

The Restrictive Trade Practices Act 1976 deals with agreements between individuals and businesses that restrict trade in some way.

The Resale Prices Act 1976 makes it illegal, except in very limited circumstances, for a business to dictate what the final selling price of its products will be.

The Competition Act 1980 deals with anti-competitive practices by businesses in general.

The Competition Act 1998 has replaced the three previous Acts and strengthened competition law in the UK by introducing two additional prohibitions:

a) anti-competitive agreements
b) abusing a dominant market position.

These prohibitions follow EU legislation as laid down in the Treaty of Rome.

The **Restrictive Practices Court** decides on cases of restrictive practices that are referred to it by the DGFT. Businesses which are found to be breaking the Restrictive Trade Practices Act will be ordered to change their ways.

The **Competition Commission** has the role of investigating mergers, monopolies and anti-competitive practices. It can only investigate cases which have been referred to it by the Secretary of State, the DGFT or the Utility Regulators. It investigates merger and monopoly cases on the basis of whether or not they are against the public interest. It examines cases on anti-competitive practices only on the basis of whether or not they restrict competition. Recommendations for action are made by the Commission to the Secretary of State, who then decides what will be done.

You can access the Competition Commission's website at:

www.competitioncommission.gov.uk

Controlling restrictive and anti-competitive business practices

A restrictive practice is an agreement between individuals or organisations that restricts competition. Some agreements are permitted but these need to be registered with and approved by the Office of Fair Trading. When the OFT considers these agreements it will be looking for two criteria:

- Does the agreement act against the public interest? If it does, it is illegal unless it meets one of the 'gateways' that allow it to continue.

- Are there other reasons, known as 'gateways', why the agreement should be allowed? These gateways include:

  1 agreements that protect the public against injury

  2 agreements that counteract anti-competitive behaviour by other businesses

  3 agreements that help to maintain levels of employment or exports.

Businesses with turnovers of less that £50 million do not have to register their agreements with the OFT unless they are price-fixing agreements.

Figure 2.5.2 General procedures for dealing with restrictive practices and anti-competitive practices

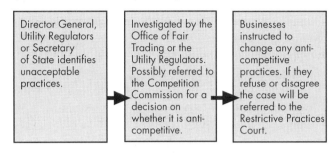

Mergers and monopolies

It is mainly the role of the Director General of Fair Trading to monitor mergers, monopolies and anti-competitive practices, but the Secretary of State and the Utility Regulators may also recommend investigations. Monopolies and mergers will be investigated only if the monopoly, by itself or by merging firms together, has 25 per cent or more of the market. Anti-competitive practices will be investigated only if the business has an annual turnover of at least £10 million and 25 per cent of the market.

Where businesses are found to be abusing their monopoly power they will be ordered to cease such activities. Where the existence of a monopoly is considered to be very anti-competitive, the monopoly can be broken up. Where a merger would form monopolies that would be against the public interest, the Secretary of State can prevent the merger from going ahead.

Figure 2.5.3 General procedures for dealing with mergers and monopolies

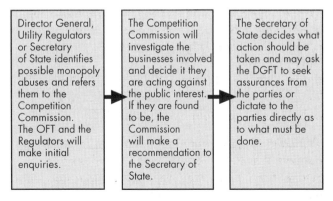

Examples of laws that regulate trading in the UK

Agricultural Produce (Grading and Marking) Act 1928
Misrepresentation Act 1967
Development of Tourism Act 1969
European Communities Act 1972
Fair Trading Act 1973
Control of Pollution Act 1974
Health and Safety at Work Act 1974
Prices Act 1975
Torts (Interference with Goods) Act 1977
Unfair Contract Terms Act 1977
Sale of Goods Act 1979
Supply of Goods and Services Act 1982
County Courts Act 1984
Companies Act 1985
Food and Environment Protection Act 1985
Consumer Protection Act 1987
Scotch Whisky Act 1988
Pesticides (Fees and Enforcement) Act 1989
Environmental Protection Act 1990
Food Safety Act 1990
Cheques Act 1992
Timeshare Act 1992
Clean Air Act 1993
Sale and Supply of Goods Act 1994
Sale of Goods (Amendment) Act 1995

Consumer protection

Most businesses operate in a fair and safe way, but there is a very significant minority who do not, and an even greater number of businesses who would treat the consumer unfairly if they thought they could get away with it. This is why government has introduced legislation to force businesses to behave as society expects them to.

The range of government interference in trading is vast, as the examples of legislation given in the inset show. There are, however, certain widely recognised Acts of Parliament that give certain fundamental rights and protections to the consumer. These include:

The Weights and Measures Act 1963 which makes it illegal for businesses:

- to sell goods as weights or measures that are less than they have stated

- not to state or display what the weight or measure of a good is

- to sell certain products in measures other than those permitted by law, e.g. most liquids must be sold in litres or millilitres.

The Trade Descriptions Act 1968 which makes it illegal to:

- make inaccurate descriptions about products

- make misleading claims in advertisements

- claim a product is in a sale unless it has been at the higher price for at least 28 days previously.

The Consumer Credit Act 1974 which specifically protects consumers when they buy on credit and insists that:

- businesses offering credit or advising on credit facilities must have a licence

- charges for providing credit must be reasonable

- charges for providing credit must be clearly stated on all advertisements.

The Sale of Goods Act 1979 which states that:

- goods must be of 'merchantable quality', i.e. good enough to sell without any major flaws, not damaged, etc.

- goods must 'fit the purpose' - i.e. be able to do what they are claimed to be able to do. For example, if a seller of the car claims that the car will be able to carry a family of four comfortably, it must be able to do this

- goods must 'fit the description given', e.g. if a car salesperson claims that a car has seat belts for all passengers, it must have them.

The Consumer Protection Act 1987 which makes it illegal to:

- supply goods which are unsafe.

The Food Safety Act 1990 which requires that:

- all food is prepared and stored in hygienic conditions

- pre-packed food lists ingredients clearly and accurately.

Consumers are also protected by laws and codes which insist that businesses have proper safety procedures, adequate insurance cover, truthful advertising, etc.

Protecting the environment and the community

Internal, external and social costs and benefits

Winners and losers!

Now that the Newbury bypass has been built the traffic in the centre of Newbury is less congested and people living in the town can get to work more quickly. Drivers using the A34 to get from the South up to Oxford and the Midlands can now travel from Southampton to the M40 on dual carriageway all the way.

But inside the town some businesses, especially those on the old A34 route, now find that they have fewer customers. And outside the town the new A34 runs through countryside that was unspoilt forest and farmland.

When businesses produce goods they are primarily interested in their own costs, revenue and profits. They do not always consider how their production might affect people who are not their customers or how it will affect the community as a whole. Two examples should make this clear.

1 If a business wants to increase its profits it may decide to cut costs by reducing the workforce. This will give the business more profit but it will also cause unemployment. The local community, not the business itself, will have to pay for this unemployment, either in unemployment benefits or in retraining.

2 If a business which receives its raw materials in cardboard boxes cannot be bothered with the time and cost of recycling, it may simply burn them. This may cause air pollution and affect people in the neighbourhood who never buy this firm's products.

The government is interested in both the costs and benefits (**internal**) of the firms and the costs and benefits (**external**) of people who have nothing to do with the firms. When these are considered together (internal and external), they give **social** costs and benefits. If the social costs of producing something are greater than the social benefits, then the products should not be produced.

Figure 2.5.4 Examples of legislation to protect the public and the cosumer in the car industry

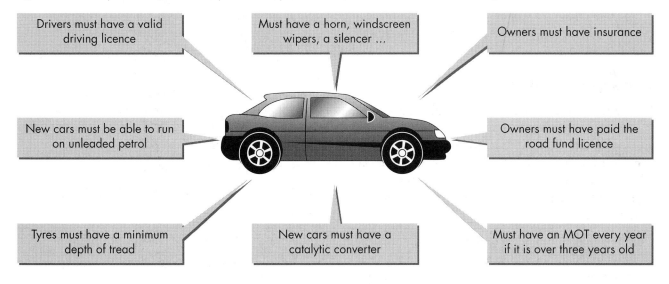

Drivers must have a valid driving licence

Must have a horn, windscreen wipers, a silencer ...

Owners must have insurance

New cars must be able to run on unleaded petrol

Owners must have paid the road fund licence

Tyres must have a minimum depth of tread

New cars must have a catalytic converter

Must have an MOT every year if it is over three years old

Internal costs and benefits – those which the firm has to pay or receives.
External costs and benefits – those which people who have nothing to do with the firm have to pay or receive.
Social costs and benefits – the combination of internal and external costs and benefits.

The government has introduced a great many laws in order to try to make certain that businesses do not create external costs, e.g.:

- It is illegal to pollute the air by driving vehicles with leaded petrol.

- Nightclubs are not allowed to play music too loudly.

- Green belts are created to stop factories being built right next to residential housing.

- If employees have been working for more than two years the business must pay them redundancy money if they lose their job simply because the business wishes to reduce staff levels. This lessens the need for the community to support people who are redundant.

- The testing and introduction of new medicines or agricultural products such as genetically modified foods must follow very strict guidelines.

CASE STUDY

The GM debate is affecting how producers can market their goods

After considerable debate about genetically modified (GM) foods the government has agreed to further restrictions on GM foods.

- The commercial growing of GM crops will be banned for another three years. Crops will not be allowed to be sold for profit.

- Any GM crops that might be used for animal feed, and thus enter the human food chain, will have to be traced, and the final foods will have to be labelled as containing GM material.

These changes have been forced on the industry by the general public's opposition to GM foods. A spokesman for one firm heavily committed to GM crops stated:

> 'I don't think anyone ever underestimated the ability of opponents to generate public concern. What did catch us out was the ferocity of the campaign.'

Nov. 1999

How the government manages the economy and how this affects business

An important function of modern government is to control the economy so that its citizens become wealthier and have a better standard of living. In order to achieve this the government sets itself certain objectives:

Table 2.5.2 Government's objectives

Objective	What this means	Why the government has this objective
Full employment	Everyone who wants a job and can work has a job	• People at work produce valuable goods and services. • Work provides people with incomes and they can support themselves. • When people spend their income they help to keep other people employed. • Unemployed people have to be provided for by the state and taxes need to be increased to pay for this.
Economic growth	More goods and services are produced. This is measured by a rise, or fall, in the **Gross Domestic Product** (GDP)	• This provides us with more of what we need and want. • More goods and services raise our standard of living. • We will have more products to sell abroad and can earn money to buy the imports we need. • More production creates more jobs and raises incomes and profits.
Low inflation	General prices do not rise by very much each year	• High inflation in the UK will stop people buying our exports and encourage us to buy more imports. This harms UK firms. • People on fixed incomes will not be able to buy as much. • Inflation causes cash flow problems for businesses. • Inflation encourages employees to ask for higher wages and that causes more inflation.
A positive balance of payments	More money is coming in from selling exports than is being paid to buy imports	• Makes the UK richer. • Helps to keep the value of the pound high which makes the price of imports cheaper and this helps to keep inflation low. • If the value of the pound is strong interest rates do not need to be high to protect it.
A stable economy	The indicators such as inflation, unemployment, growth, interest rates, etc., do not fluctuate wildly	• This makes it easier for businesses to plan for the future. • People will not suddenly be threatened with unemployment, higher prices, etc. • People and businesses who borrow money will know exactly how much this will cost. • Foreign investors will be willing to invest in the UK because they know that the value of their investments will not change simply because the value of the pound changes.

How governments control the economy

Gross domestic product – the total amount of goods and services produced in the country in a specific period of time, usually one year.

When governments control the economy they normally do this by changing the conditions of supply or demand. It is therefore easiest to see how the controls work by using supply and demand graphs. The graphs will be for everything that is produced in the country, i.e. the **gross domestic product** (GDP). Figures 2.5.5 and 2.5.6 show how the government policies work and how they affect the objectives listed above.

Figure 2.5.5 How a change in demand will affect the economy

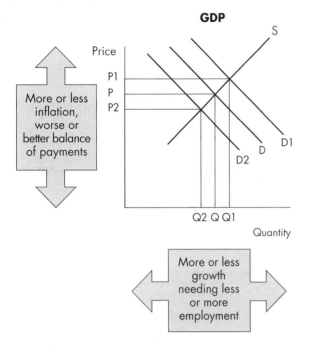

The government can stimulate the economy and increase demand D to D1. This is called **reflation**. It will increase output Q to Q1 and this will create more growth and increase employment because more people will be needed to produce the goods and services.

> **Reflation** – this occurs when the economy is affected by an increase in demand.
> **Deflation** – this occurs when the economy is affected by a decrease in demand.

At the same time it will cause prices to rise from P to P1, creating inflation, and because the prices are higher this will mean the country will sell fewer exports and buy more imports. The balance of payments will therefore be worse.

The government can also take demand out of the economy, e.g. by increasing income tax. This is called **deflation**. This will decrease output, Q to Q2, and reduce employment. It will also cause prices to fall, P to P2, and help to improve the balance of payments.

Table 2.5.3 Effects of a change in demand

	Inflation		Balance of Payments		Economic Growth		Unemployment	
Reflation	Higher	✗	Worse	✗	Increased	✔	Reduced	✔
Deflation	Lower	✔	Better	✔	Decreased	✗	Increased	✗

✗ *Shows a negative effect on the economy,* ✔ *shows a positive effect.*

Figure 2.5.6. How a change in supply will affect the economy

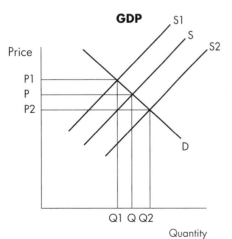

The government can also affect the economy by changing the conditions of supply. If the supply was decreased, this would cause prices to rise at the same time as reducing growth and causing more unemployment. This is not a very sensible action for a government to take but it does occur.

If supply was increased, which is the objective of **supply-side economics** (see below), then prices would come down, we would sell more exports, produce more goods and lower the level of unemployment. This is the best solution of all, but it is very difficult for governments to achieve.

Table 2.5.4 Effects of a change in supply

	Inflation		Balance of payments		Economic growth		Unemployment	
Supply decreased	Higher	✗	Worse	✗	Decreased	✗	Increased	✗
Supply increased	Lower	✔	Better	✔	Increased	✔	Reduced	✔

✗ Shows a negative effect on the economy, ✔ shows a positive effect.

Managing the trade cycle

Trade cycle – this shows the way that production and trade fluctuate over time.

Every decade the total amount that is produced in the UK rises, but it does not rise at a steady rate each year.

Some years it grows very fast and in other years it can actually fall. These fluctuations up and down do, however, follow a pattern and it is this up and down trend over time that is called the **trade** (or business) **cycle**. Figure 2.5.7 shows how the total production has grown in the UK from 1978 to 1998.

Figure 2.5.7 Percentage change in real GDP, UK 1978–1998

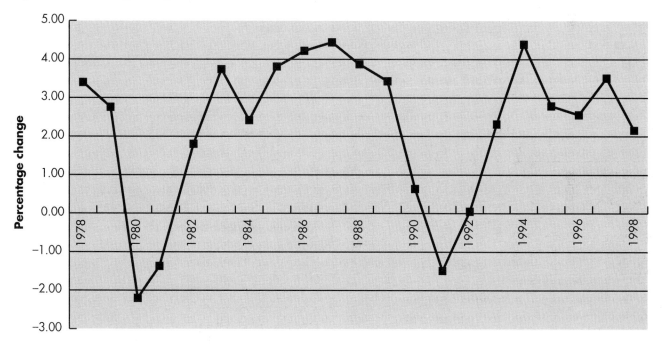

When growth is very high, in the **boom** period, there is a shortage of labour and raw materials to produce goods. As businesses compete against each other for scarce resources prices rise, the country experiences inflation and it is more difficult to sell our exports.

When growth is very low or negative (in **recession**) less labour is needed so there is unemployment and prices can be kept down. This helps export sales and discourages us from buying imports.

Figure 2.5.8 Negative effects of the trade cycle

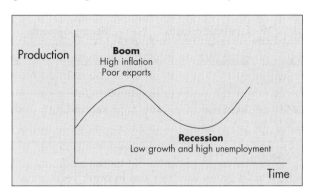

Figure 2.5.8 shows the negative effects of the trade cycle on the economy and business. The fluctuations also make it difficult for businesses to plan for the future and in recessions many weaker businesses have to close. The ideal growth rate would be a steady one of about 3 per cent to 4 per cent per year. This is shown in Figure 2.5.9, but to get to this position governments first need to remove excess demand during the boom period and pump in extra demand during the recession period. Typical measures for doing this are also shown on the graph.

Figure 2.5.9 Using government policies to affect the trade cycle

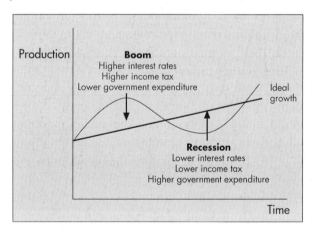

Government policy

Governments have various policies that they can use to control the economy. We will look at some of the most important ones below.

Fiscal policy

> **Fiscal policy** – the control of the economy through changing government revenue or government expenditure.

Fiscal policy refers to any measures that are used to control the economy, either through changing government revenue or through government expenditure. Generally, these will change the amount of demand in the economy but, as we will see below, they can affect the supply side as well.

Government revenue comes from:

- taxation
- the sale of state owned assets, such as the water and electricity industries
- charges on some of their provisions, e.g. entry charges for municipally owned swimming pools
- interest earned on monies that are in savings or have been lent, particularly by the councils.

The main source of revenue, however, is taxation. Figures 2.5.10 and 2.5.11 show the major sources of taxation in 1999 and the main areas of the economy where the government spent its revenue.

Figure 2.5.10 Types of taxation in £billion and percentage of total (1999)

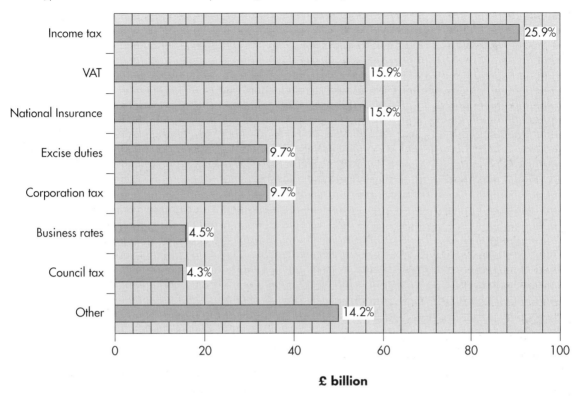

£ billion

Figure 2.5.11 UK government expenditure by sector in £billion and percentage of total (1999)

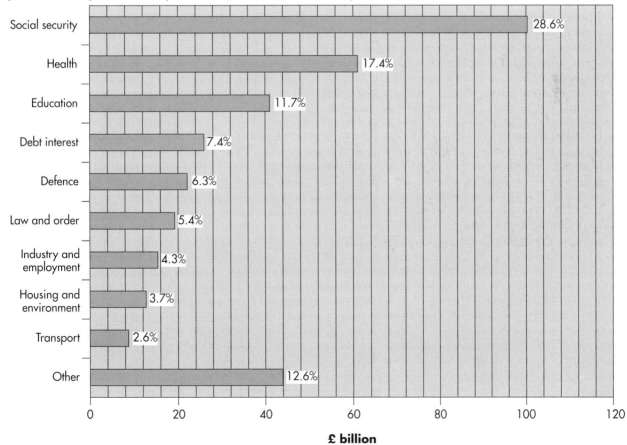

£ billion

When the government removes money from the economy through taxation, it takes away our ability to buy goods and services. Demand decreases and businesses have to lower their prices if they want to keep their customers. Demand will also decrease if the government decides to cut expenditure because that also affects people's incomes.

Figure 2.5.12

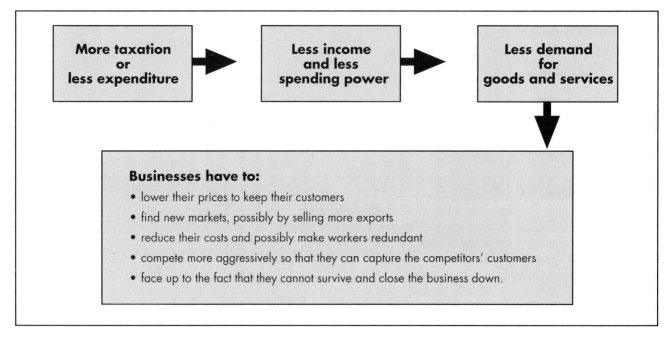

More taxation or less expenditure → **Less income and less spending power** → **Less demand for goods and services**

Businesses have to:

- lower their prices to keep their customers
- find new markets, possibly by selling more exports
- reduce their costs and possibly make workers redundant
- compete more aggressively so that they can capture the competitors' customers
- face up to the fact that they cannot survive and close the business down.

When the government lowers tax rates or increases expenditure, this will give people more income and therefore demand will increase. More goods and services will be needed and businesses will have to respond in order to maximise their revenues and profits.

Figure 2.5.13

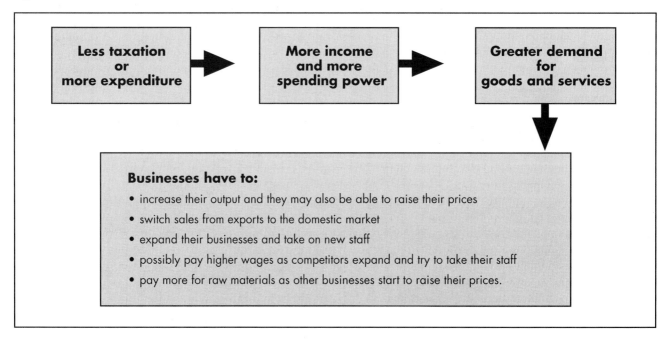

Less taxation or more expenditure → **More income and more spending power** → **Greater demand for goods and services**

Businesses have to:

- increase their output and they may also be able to raise their prices
- switch sales from exports to the domestic market
- expand their businesses and take on new staff
- possibly pay higher wages as competitors expand and try to take their staff
- pay more for raw materials as other businesses start to raise their prices.

Public sector borrowing requirement (PSBR)

Public sector borrowing requirement (PSBR) – the amount of money that the government must borrow to meet its expenditure if its revenue will not cover this.

When governments spend money they frequently cannot raise enough revenue through taxation, privatisation monies, charges, etc., and they therefore have to borrow money in order to meet the expenditure. This borrowing is called the **public sector borrowing requirement** (PSBR).

The PSBR is an important part of fiscal policy because changes in PSBR tell us whether or not the government is planning to **deflate** or **reflate** the economy. Each year the government produces a **Budget** in which it sets out its plans for expenditure and states how it intends to pay for this. The PSBR is a major part of this.

If the government intends to spend more than it is going to raise through taxation etc., it will need to borrow money. This is shown below as the PSBR rises from £10 billion to £15 billion. The government is even more in debt so this is called **budgeting for a deficit**.

	Government revenue £ billion	Government expenditure £ billion	PSBR £ billion
Before the budget	345	355	**10**
After the budget	355	370	**15**

If the government wanted to reduce demand in the country it would make the PSBR fall. This is called **budgeting for a surplus**.

	Government revenue £ billion	Government expenditure £ billion	PSBR £ billion
Before the budget	345	355	**10**
After the budget	355	360	**5**

Budgeting for a surplus affects the economy by taking out spending power and reducing demand. Budgeting for a deficit will put additional spending power into the economy and cause demand to increase.

Examples of specific fiscal changes

Main taxes and expenditure affect how much demand there is in the economy but when we look at individual industries or businesses it is the actual type of tax or expenditure that is important. Tobacco taxes affect the tobacco industry more than any other industry. An increase in teachers' pay affects the education industry more than any other industry.

Raising indirect taxes

Indirect tax – a tax that is paid by the producer and is a cost for the business.

For businesses, these **indirect taxes** are costs and therefore the taxes will decrease the supply (see Figure 2.2.18 on page 94).

The reaction of businesses will depend on how elastic the demand for the product is. The effects are shown in Figures 2.5.14 and 2.5.15 below. If the demand is inelastic the producers will pass the cost on to the customer. Prices will rise, P to P1, and they will lose only a few sales, Q to Q1. The customer will pay most of the additional tax.

If the demand for the product is elastic, businesses would be very foolish to try to pass the cost on by raising the price to P1. If they did, they would lose Q to Q1 sales. To try to minimise the effects of the tax on their sales they will put the price up only to P2, and lose only Q to Q2 sales.

Figure 2.5.14 Product with an inelastic demand

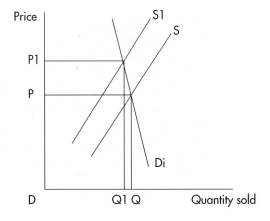

Figure 2.5.15 Product with an elastic demand

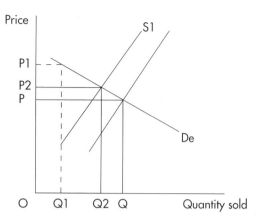

When businesses are faced with increases in indirect tax they will have to take one of the following actions:

- try to pass the cost on to the customer

- absorb the extra cost and reduce the level of their profits

- find other forms of production that do not have the tax burden on them, as most producers of cigarettes have done – Imperial Group also sell wines, food, packaging, and hotel services

- reduce the costs of production in order to compensate, e.g. cut wages or sack staff.

Lowering indirect taxes or giving subsidies

Indirect taxes can also be brought down. This would lower the costs to industry. The same effect would be achieved if the government gave subsidies to businesses by paying part of their costs. In this case the supply would increase, costs and prices would fall and businesses would sell more goods and services.

Monetary policy

Monetary policy – changes the economy by changing the amount of money that is available for people to spend.

Monetary policy affects the economy by changing the amount of money that people have to spend. It does this in two ways:

- changing the rate of interest

- controlling the ability of banks and other lenders to lend money.

Monetary policy is now controlled by the Bank of England. It decides what the interest rate will be and how much money banks can lend.

Interest rate controls

Interest is the charge that people, or businesses, have to pay if they borrow money. If interest rates are increased, people will have higher charges on their borrowing so they are less likely to borrow. This will reduce the monies that they have to spend and demand will decrease, D to D1 in Figure 2.5.16.

Figure 2.5.16 The effects of a rise in interest rates on Gross Domestic Product

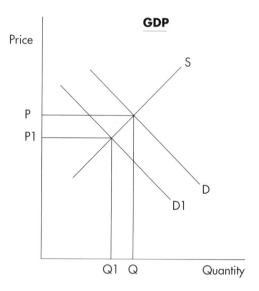

For businesses, an increase in interest rates will decrease the demand for their products. It will also affect their supply if they are borrowing money. Many businesses borrow money to buy plant, equipment, etc., but also sometimes simply to pay wages and buy raw materials. Any increase in interest rates for these businesses is an increase in costs, and this will decrease supply, S to S2, as shown in Figure 2.5.17.

If interest rates were lowered more people would be willing to borrow and this would increase demand. It would also lower the cost of borrowing for businesses and this would increase supply.

Figure 2.5.17 The effects of a rise in interest rates on businesses

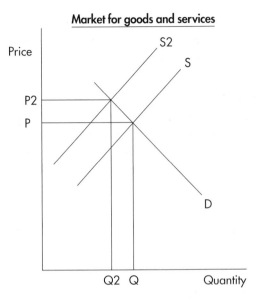

Market for goods and services

Controlling lending by banks and other financial institutions

The Bank of England can control how the banks lend money. It can make them change the amount of money that they have available to lend to individuals and to businesses. If the Bank of England reduces the banks' ability to lend money this will have the same effect as raising interest rates. If it allows banks to lend more money this will have the same effect as lowering interest rates.

Controlling exchange rates

When the value of the pound is high, foreigners need to use more of their currency to buy pounds. They will, therefore, be reluctant to buy our exports. At the same time, we can buy more of their currency when the pound is strong and this encourages us to buy more imports. If the pound is weak, foreigners will buy more of our exports and we will import less of their products.

The value of the pound will affect UK businesses and our economy. Therefore, through the Bank of England, the government tries to control the value of the pound so that British industry can prosper.

> **Hot money** – money that flows into or out of a country to take advantage of different rates of interest.

The main tool used for controlling the value of the pound is the interest rate. If interest rates are high this encourages foreigners to keep savings and make investments in the UK. Before they can do this, of course, they have to change their currency into pounds. This increases the demand for pounds so the pound rises in value. If the interest rates are low speculators will wish to save and invest elsewhere, but first they must sell their pounds, thereby increasing supply and causing the value of the pound to fall. This movement of money into and out of the country because of the interest rate is called **hot money**.

Figure 2.5.18 Effect on pound if interest rates are high

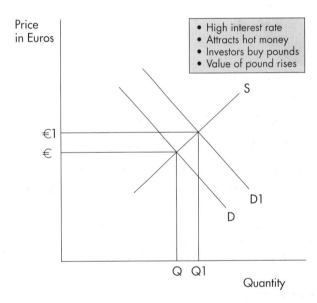

Pound on foreign exchange

- High interest rate
- Attracts hot money
- Investors buy pounds
- Value of pound rises

Figure 2.5.19 Effect on pound if interest rates are low

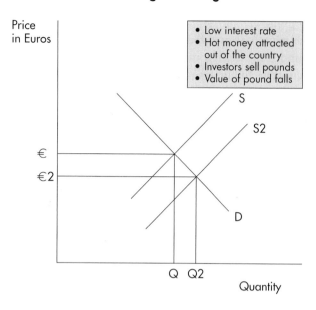

Pound on foreign exchange

Price in Euros

- Low interest rate
- Hot money attracted out of the country
- Investors sell pounds
- Value of pound falls

S

S2

€

€2

D

Q Q2

Quantity

Supply-side economics

The government can control the supply side of the economy in various ways, some of which are given below. Usually, we would expect these measures to increase supply, increase growth and employment, help to control inflation and improve the balance of payments (see Table 2.5.4 – page 145). There are, however, exceptions, as we will see with the minimum wage.

Labour controls

In the 1970s and early 1980s trade unions had a great deal of power in the UK and were able to demand higher wages on a regular basis. Often, businesses had no alternative but to pay them. Throughout the 1980s measures were brought in by the Conservative Government to curb the power of the unions. There were Employment Acts in 1980, 1982, 1988, 1989 and 1990, Trade Union Acts in 1984 and 1992, and the Trade Union Reform and Employment Rights Act in 1993.

Details of employment relations can be found at

www.dti.gov.uk/er/index.htm

These controls included:

- banning strikes that had not been properly voted on

- introducing secret ballots on strike action

- effectively banning the closed shop where workers could work only if they were members of the union

- banning action against an employer unless the workers were directly involved in the dispute

- making unions give a seven-day written notice before industrial action can take place

- giving the right to any citizen who might be affected by industrial action to sue the union if it has been in breach of the law.

The European Union has also affected the way that the labour market works in the UK (see page 173).

(see page 173)

The Employment Relations Act 1999

This Act goes some way to reverse the anti trade union legislation of the Conservative Government. The four main elements of the Act are:

- the setting up of procedures for the recognition of independent trade unions in organisations employing 21 or more workers where the majority of the workforce wants recognition

- making it illegal to discriminate against employees because they are members of trade unions

- parental leave with a guarantee that jobs will be kept open. This includes 18-week maternity leave for all women, three months' parental leave for mothers and fathers and emergency time off to care for dependants

- a widening of the range of cases of unfair dismissal where the employment tribunals can insist that employers take back dismissed employees, or pay compensation for not taking them back.

Wage controls

In the past the government has directly affected the level of wages by dictating to firms by how much wages and salaries will be allowed to rise. This was usually part of what was called **prices and incomes policies**, where the maximum price rise and wage rise allowed was set by government. In some extreme cases in the 1960s a rate of zero was set. These policies have not been used in the UK for a very long time, but what has now been introduced is a **minimum wage**.

Minimum wage – the minimum hourly wage that employers must pay to their employees.

The minimum wage was introduced in the UK on 1 April 1999. It stipulated that workers over the age of 22 must be paid at least £3.60 per hour and that workers aged between 18 and 21 must be paid at least £3.00 per hour. The rates are reviewed each year and adjusted if the government feels that this is appropriate.

From October 2000 the national minimum wage will be raised to £3.70 per hour for employees over 22 years of age and to £3.20 per hour for 18 to 21 year olds. This will benefit over 1.5 million workers.

For businesses already paying above the minimum rate there was no direct effect, although workers close to the minimum might expect wage rises if people in other firms were getting them. For businesses that were paying below the minimum wage there was an impact as shown on Figure 2.5.20.

Surveys carried out at the beginning of 2000 have found that the minimum wage has not, in fact, created extra unemployment. This is because businesses have either absorbed the extra cost out of their own profits, or passed the extra cost on to customers in higher prices. The increase in wages has also meant that low-paid workers have more income to spend and can afford the higher prices.

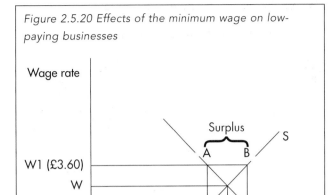

Figure 2.5.20 Effects of the minimum wage on low-paying businesses

At the new minimum wage of W1 there will be a surplus of labour, A to B. The higher wage will encourage more people to look for work Q to Qb, but will discourage employers from taking workers on. Employers will want only Qa workers. There will therefore be unemployment of Qa to Qb.

Regional policy

In the UK, as in all EU countries, there are significant differences in production and employment levels in different regions of the country. Where problems arise they do not naturally disappear and therefore the government steps in to provide assistance to areas with high unemployment. Figure 2.5.21 shows the differences in the rates of unemployment in different UK regions.

In order to help areas of the country that need assistance the country is divided into different categories. These **assisted areas** are currently being reviewed and the proposed new areas are shown on Figure 2.5.22. The assistance is provided through **Regional Selective Assistance** (RSA). This includes grants given to businesses to help to secure employment opportunities and increase regional competitiveness and prosperity.

Figure 2.5.21 Percentage of workforce unemployed

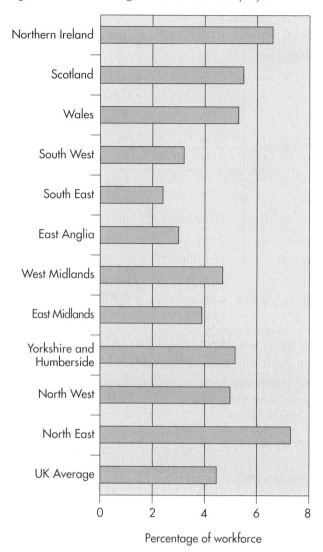

Figure 2.5.22

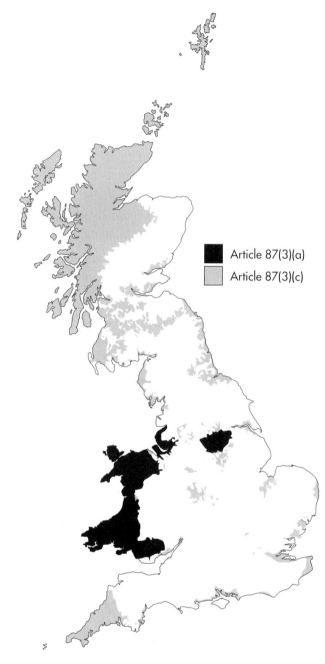

> **Assisted areas** are areas where regional aid may be granted under European Union law.

Tier 1: under Article 87(3)a the government is proposing four Tier 1 areas that would receive a high level of aid:

- Cornwall
- Merseyside
- South Yorkshire
- West Wales and the Valleys.

Tier 2: under Article 87(3)c the government has targeted Tier 2 areas where unemployment is a major problem. These areas have also been chosen as ones with good opportunities for job creation, investment and regeneration. These areas include the Highlands and Islands Enterprise Area.

Tier 3: assistance is also planned for Enterprise Grant Areas for businesses employing up to 250 people. Enterprise Grant Areas will include:

- local authority districts with high unemployment
- coalfield areas

- rural development areas
- areas designated by the newly devolved Welsh and Scottish Assemblies.

(See also regional aid from the European Union on page 175.)

Nationalisation, denationalisation and privatisation

Nationalised industries – industries that are taken into public (state) ownership through an Act of Parliament.

In the late 1940s many of the basic providers of raw materials and power for industry were taken into state ownership, including coal, iron and steel, electricity and gas. Transport industries were also nationalised, including railways, waterways and docks. Communications such as postal services and telecommunications were already in state ownership.

Denationalisation – the process of returning nationalised industries to the private sector.
Privatisation – the process of changing any state owned or run business into a privately owned or run business.

The main reason for nationalising these industries was that it was felt that they were so important for the economy that they should be run for the benefit of the country as a whole rather than simply for the benefit of private owners. Unfortunately, as large state owned monopolies they had no competition and little incentive to improve their efficiency, output or costs. In the 1980s it was decided that they should be put back into private ownership and made to compete. This is referred to as **privatisation** but it is also **denationalisation**.

Privatisation occurs when any state owned or state run business is put into private control. When schools contract out the cooking in the canteen, that is privatisation. When the government sold the state owned shares of British Leyland, the car company, that was privatisation. Denationalisation can only occur if the firm that is being put into private ownership was already a nationalised firm. Privatisation covers denationalisation as well.

The benefits of returning the state owned monopolies to the private sector were argued to be:

- The sale raised funds for the government to spend.
- Shares were sold below their market value so many people were encouraged to buy them. This increased share ownership in the private sector.
- The conditions on which many of the businesses were sold required that more competition should take place. Where it did take place this increased efficiency and reduced prices.
- Being able to make and keep profits acted as an incentive to managers and they worked harder to improve the businesses.

There have also been disadvantages with privatisation:

- Many of the people who bought the shares cheaply sold them as soon as they rose in price, so private share ownership did not increase very much.
- Before privatisation we all owned the businesses. Now less than 5 per cent of the country own them and benefit from the profits they are making.
- Many of the industries, such as water and the railways, simply moved from being state owned monopolies to being private monopolies and have needed regulators (see below) to control them.
- Frequently these businesses have reduced costs by cutting their workforce. This has caused unemployment and, in some cases, a drop in services.

The regulators

Although these large businesses are now in private ownership they are not given a completely free hand to do what they want. Regulators have been appointed to ensure that the companies do not ignore the duties that they had under nationalisation to provide other businesses and the public with a reasonable service.

The regulators, such as the Office of Telecommunications (OFTEL) and the Office of Gas and Electricity Markets (OFGEM – formerly OFGAS and OFFER) have tended to control the price that the privatised firms are allowed to charge, but they have also insisted that competition takes place. British Telecom, for example, must allow any competing telecommunications firm, such as Mercury or the cable companies, to connect to and use BT's lines.

Where the businesses taking over the nationalised industries agreed to specific conditions, the regulators are also responsible for seeing that these are met. When Railtrack was set up and the train operating companies (TOCs) bid for and won their franchises, they agreed that they would run the train services on time. If they have more than a set percentage of late trains, they are fined by the regulator.

CASE STUDY

Ofgem brings in measures to save £500 million costs of energy and reduce pollution

Ofgem is insisting that the providers of gas and electricity meet new guidelines that should reduce the need for gas and electricity and, at the same time, reduce the harmful pollution that the production of these energy sources can cause. The measure came into effect on 1 April 2000.

The main direct beneficiaries will be people on low incomes who have difficulty in meeting their fuel bills. Electricity and gas companies will be required to offer these people cut-price energy-saving support, such as help with the cost of loft insulation and discounts on energy-saving equipment such as low energy light bulbs and time switches on central heating.

The scheme will not be without cost. Funding for the scheme will come from an additional charge of £1.20 on all domestic electricity and gas bills, a cost of £75 million to householders around the country. At the same time the gas and electricity companies will lose £500 million worth of sales. Ofgem would argue that the social and environmental benefits are worth the price.

Further Study

The effects of government actions are all around us. When we shop more than 50 per cent of the goods and services we buy have taxes on them. The way in which shops sell to us is controlled by laws on health and safety, contracts and how goods can be described. When we work we are affected by income tax, national insurance contributions and laws that dictate the rights and responsibilities of employers and employees. When the Bank of England decides to raise interest rates it affects our mortgages and, because it also affects the value of the pound, it affects the price of our holidays abroad. Simply by reading newspapers regularly or watching the news on TV it is possible to understand why, and how, the government interferes in the economy and business.

Sources of information

All major government organisations now have a range of sources that should provide you with up-to-date information.

- Publications, many of which are provided free, can be ordered by post, telephone or e-mail. Do check first that they are being provided *free*.

- Websites exist for most of the major government organisations. These are regularly amended and should give you the latest details.

- Many of the statistical publications of government data now charge a fee. You can access free information by using the local library. Good libraries will have up-to-date copies of such publications as *Social Trends*, *Regional Trends*, the *Monthly Digest of Statistics*, and the *National Income (Blue Book)*.

Keeping up to date

Very few sources of information are completely up to date. Governments make decisions every day and these change the rules by which businesses and the general public have to live. You need to know what major changes are going on and how these affect business. You should:

- read a quality newspaper every day

- watch the main news programmes every day

- read weekly specialist publications such as *The Economist*.

Widening your knowledge of the range of government influences on industry

This chapter has looked at only a few of the ways in which governments influence business. There are a great many others and when you take your external examination for this unit you can use any examples that help to answer the question set. You should try to gain as wide as possible an understanding of how governments influence business, noting down any occasions you come across where this takes place.

Revision Questions

1 What is the main aim of the government in terms of:

   a) inflation

   b) unemployment

   c) economic growth

   d) balance of payments? (4 marks)

2 Outline **four** benefits and **four** problems with a high level of competition in a country. (8 marks)

3 Explain how anti-competitive business practices are controlled in the UK. (6 marks)

4 What are the main purposes of the following Acts of Parliament?

   a) Trade Descriptions Act 1968

   b) Sale of Goods Act 1979

   c) Food Safety Act 1990 (6 marks)

5 Taking one product you have studied explain how the law places controls on the product so that the environment is protected. (4 marks)

6 Explain the difference between internal and external costs and benefits and give examples from (a) a business producing chemicals **or** (b) farming. (6 marks)

7 a) Draw a supply and demand graph to show the difference between "deflation" and "reflation". (4 marks)

   b) Explain how deflation and reflation will affect:

      i) inflation

      ii) unemployment

      iii) economic growth

      iv) balance of payments. (8 marks)

8 If the government wanted to reduce the level of inflation in the UK, how could it use (i) monetary policy and (ii) fiscal policy to achieve this? (10 marks)

9 Draw a typical trade cycle and indicate how inflation and unemployment will change at different points on the cycle. (6 marks)

10 a) What is an indirect tax? (2 marks)

   b) Draw a graph to show how an increase in hydrocarbon tax will affect the price of petrol. (3 marks)

11 How will a rise in the interest rate affect businesses? (6 marks)

12 What are the **four** major categories of government expenditure? (4 marks)

13 Explain what happens to the economy when the government budgets for a deficit. (6 marks)

14 Explain what "hot money" is and how it is affected by changes in interest rates. (3 marks)

15 Give **four** examples of changes that the government have made to increase supply. (4 marks)

16 Explain how a rise in the value of the minimum wage to £4.50/hour would affect each of the following groups of workers:

   a) supermarket checkout staff.

   b) 16 year old paper boys.

   c) skilled computer operators (6 marks)

17 Name **two** parts of the UK, which receive Regional Selective Assistance and explain why this special treatment is offered. (6 marks)

18 a) Explain why privatisation might make businesses more competitive.

   b) Why do many nationalised industries still have regulators? (8 marks)

How Business is Affected by International Competition

In this chapter you will learn why international trade is important to countries and businesses and how the growing amount of international trade affects businesses. In particular, we will look at:

- the importance of international trade for the UK

- how businesses are set up to trade internationally and how they react to competition from abroad

- the changes that have been made to reduce the barriers to international trade

- the influence of the European Union on UK businesses and society.

The importance of international trade for the UK

UK imports – the purchase of goods or services by UK firms or individuals from businesses abroad.
UK exports – the sale of UK goods and services to individuals or businesses abroad.

Great Britain became wealthy and powerful because of its international trade. In the last century, India, Canada, Australia, parts of Africa, America and Asia were all included in the British Empire. The East India Docks Company and the Hudson Bay Company traded goods around the world. Today the UK still has special trading relations with the Commonwealth and now also with the European Union.

All nations have some level of international trade. They trade because this is beneficial to them. The main reasons why nations trade with other nations include:

- **The country may not have any internal source of a particular raw material.** The UK has no diamonds; France has no oil fields.

- **The country may have some raw materials but not enough to satisfy the demand for them.** The UK has tiny gold resources and needs to import gold to meet the demand from jewellers, dentists and the Bank of England. It is possible to ski in Scotland but the snow is not guaranteed and there are only a few runs, so keen skiers travel to the Alps, Pyrenees, or Appalachians.

- **It is cheaper to import products than to produce them at home.** The UK could produce enough bananas in heated greenhouses to meet UK demand but it would be very expensive. The West Indies can grow and transport bananas at a fraction of this cost.

- **Consumers want variety.** People want variety and they want to buy products that come from other countries. Today, designer labels are a major selling point and people do not want UK Levis or Japanese Rolls-Royces.

For the UK international trade is a major part of our economy. Many of our raw materials are imported and many firms rely upon sales abroad in order to survive and make a profit. Figure 2.6.1 shows how important our export markets are to us.

Because the UK is a relatively small nation with limited basic raw materials, we also need to import materials such as wood, iron ore, copper, tin and bauxite in order to produce many of our manufactured goods. We also wish to import many services, particularly tourism, because more and more people now take holidays abroad. Table 2.6.1 below shows the breakdown of our exports and imports of goods in terms of what is exported and imported.

Figure 2.6.1 UK imports and exports as a percentage of GDP

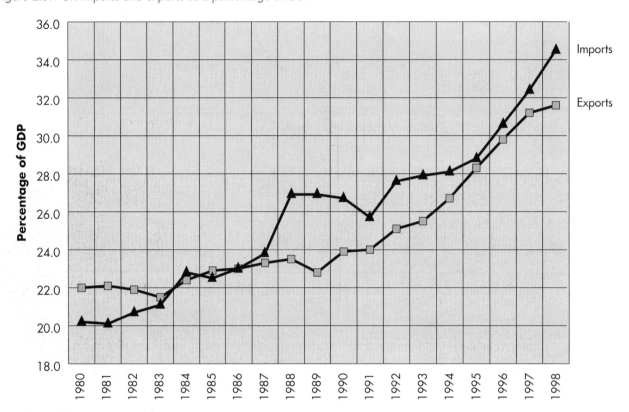

Table 2.6.1 UK major exports and imports by category, 1998 (percentage)

Category	Exports	Imports
Food and live animals	3.8	7.4
Beverages	1.9	1.3
Tobacco and tobacco products	0.7	0.3
Basic raw materials	1.5	3.3
Fuels	6.0	3.5
Chemicals and plastics	12.7	9.5
Manufactured goods	25.8	29.8
Machinery	33.2	29.0
Vehicles and transport equipment	13.0	14.7
Other	1.4	1.2

Our major imports and exports of goods are products that have been manufactured, such as cars, computers, machinery and equipment. Because people have different tastes and there is now a high level of competition throughout the world, many of these imports and exports are in the same categories. For example, we import cars such as Fiats, BMWs and Volvos, but we also export Nissans, MGs, and Land Rovers.

As well as knowing what kind of goods and services we import and export, it is important to know which countries we export to and which countries we receive our imports from. This is shown in Figure 2.6.2. The importance of the European Union is obvious and has increased considerably in recent years. In 1955 only 16 per cent of our exports went to current EU countries. By 1985 that figure had risen to 51 per cent and in 1998 it was 58 per cent. The main reason for this growth has been the fact that we have joined the EU and the EU has removed almost all of the barriers to trade between its member countries (see details of the EU on page 170).

Figure 2.6.2 UK imports and exports by origin and destination, 1998 (percentage)

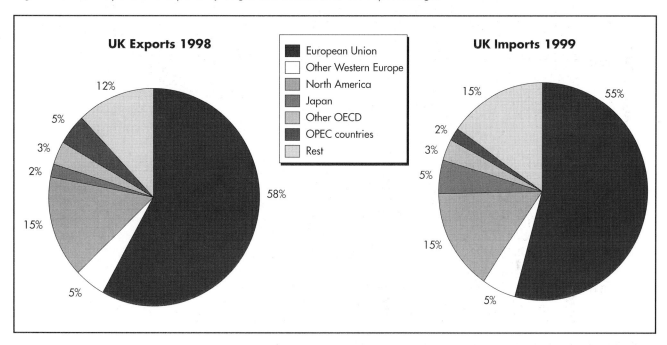

When most people think about imports and exports they tend to think about solid, tangible products such as cars, machines, grain, oil, fruit and vegetables. However, the sale of services is also a vital part of this trade. The UK remains a world centre for insurance and banking, for trade on the Stock Exchange and as a major tourist destination. We also make growing use of foreign services, particularly tourism, but now also international banks and the internet. The trade in goods is known as **visible** trade. The trade in services is known as **invisible** trade.

How businesses trade internationally

All businesses, even relatively small and localised businesses, need to recognise that more and more trade operates on a global basis. This will affect them whether or not they want it to and they need to react. All businesses will be involved in international trade to different extents and this is what we will examine in this section.

How local newsagents are affected by international trade

Many local newsagents, selling newspapers, tobacco products, sweets and canned drinks, may not think that they are part of international trade but they are. International trade will affect them for all of the following reasons:

- The paper for the newspapers and magazines is imported from Sweden, etc.

- The tobacco products they sell come from the West Indies, etc.

- They sell Coke and Pepsi owned by US companies.

- They may bank with HSBC (the Hong Kong & Shanghai Banking Corporation).

- They may keep their accounts on Excel, supplied by Microsoft of the USA.

Home-based businesses selling to the UK market

Even when firms do not want to compete internationally, they frequently find that they are forced to because international firms are competing with them. In the 1950s there were almost no international businesses competing in the takeaway food industry. In those days takeaway outlets mainly prepared and sold British foods such as fish and chips. In the 1960s and 1970s there was a rapid growth in Indian and Chinese takeaway outlets, but these were set up by people living in the UK and were therefore domestic British businesses.

In the 1980s and 1990s these takeaway and fast food restaurants continued to grow and produce more variety, with kebab houses, pizza parlours and burger bars. There has, however, been a major change in how they are run and owned. Many of the large chains of takeaway outlets and fast food restaurants are now international, such as Burger King, McDonald's, Pizza Hut, and TGI Fridays. Many of them are also franchises, with an international parent company with outlets all over the world.

In these industries the international competition is obvious, but when most individual firms are examined carefully an element of international competition will still be found. UK firms selling in the UK will find themselves in competition because:

- Foreign firms are selling their products here. UK potters selling their plates and mugs will be in competition with imported crockery from Europe, the USA and Hong Kong.

- Foreign firms are setting up production here. UK-based car-hire firms find themselves in competition with Budget, Hertz, and Avis.

- UK firms are selling to foreign tourists. If a tourist from Austria or Canada buys a cream tea in a Devon tea shop, this will be in competition with any other country that the tourist might have gone to.

International UK businesses

International business – a business that produces in one country and sell its products to a number of other countries.

Duval, leading UK supplier and international business

Duval Ltd was set up as a dry cleaning business in 1950, located in a small Hampshire town. In 1972 the business started selling machinery to other dry cleaning businesses. Duval now concentrates on manufacturing dry cleaning machinery and providing customers with training on their use and aftersales service.

Expansion has been rapid, with three moves to larger factories, and annual sales of over £7 million. Duval is now the largest supplier of dry cleaning machines in the UK, with over 4,000 machines operating, and is now also a leading supplier in the European market.

Some businesses produce goods and services in the UK and sell them to customers in other countries. These businesses are known as international businesses. The UK had about £250 billion worth of exports to other countries in 1999 (over 30 per cent of our gross domestic product), so it is clear that this international trade is very important to the UK.

International businesses include multinationals (see below), but there are many businesses that produce only in the UK yet still make most of their revenue and profits by selling abroad. Many of these companies are relatively small as really large companies such as British Petroleum (BP) and Imperial Chemicals Industry (ICI) tend to be multinational and produce in other countries as well. There are, however, well known UK producers who only produce goods here such as Rolls-Royce (cars), Wedgwood (pottery) and Black & Decker (tools).

Trading internationally has the following benefits:

- **bigger markets**: there are greater potential sales and profits to be made
- **expansion is easier**: this is particularly important if the home market is saturated
- **spreading the risk**: if one market is doing badly others will help the firm to survive
- **improving the corporate image**: international firms are often considered as being better than domestic firms.

There are, however, drawbacks to trading internationally:

- **added costs**: added costs come from transportation, the cost of changing currencies, added insurance, etc.
- **greater risks**: there can be greater risk selling abroad, as if customers prove unreliable and do not pay, it is then difficult to get the money back. The government does help through the Export Guarantee scheme
- **language barriers**: instructions, guarantees, etc. may have to be written in other languages. Language barriers may also make it more difficult to make the sales in the first place
- **rules and regulations**: many countries have laws about products and how they can be sold. The products may have to be altered before they can be sold in the other country.

Because the businesses have to export their products to other countries, they often use agents or distributors to help sell the products.

Agents – they act on behalf of the business and find customers in the other countries.
Distributors – independent, separate firms who buy the products from the exporting firm and then sell them to their own customers.

Multinational businesses

Multinational business – a business that produces in more than one country.

Some businesses take their international status a stage further. Instead of just exporting to other countries, they set up factories, retail outlets, distribution centres, etc., in other countries and start to produce abroad as well as at home. The businesses are known as **multinational firms**.

The headquarters will be in one country and other production units will be abroad. Ford and General Motors have their headquarters and main car production factories in the USA, but they also have plants in the UK and other EU countries. Sainsbury's headquarters are in the UK, as are most of its supermarkets, but it also has branches in France and other EU countries. HSBC (which now owns what used to be the Midland Bank) is centred in Hong Kong but has branches of its banks throughout the UK and many other countries. McDonald's (like many other businesses) has used the franchise process to makes its name a multinational one around the world.

Tesco plc expands its multinational base

As Tesco enters the new millennium it has established itself as the number one UK supermarket, with sales and profits now well ahead of its main rival, Sainsbury's. But Tesco is more than just a UK company, it is now an established, and growing, multinational company.

Tesco has expanded into Western Europe, with a major presence in Ireland, and has also opened up an extensive range of supermarkets and hypermarkets in Central Europe.

Further afield, Tesco now has stores in the Far East, in South Korea and Thailand, and on 22 March 2000 it announced plans to open up 20 hypermarkets in Taiwan.

As with international companies, there are benefits and drawbacks for multinationals. Many of these are the same (see above) but some are specific to multinationals.

Additional benefits to the multinational business:

- **reduced costs**: some of the costs will be reduced if the new business is being located where it used to export to, e.g. transport costs and the costs of changing currency

- **cheaper factors of production**: labour, land and raw materials may all be cheaper, which is why multinationals often tend to locate in developing countries.

- **escaping import controls**: many countries still have import controls, e.g. quotas and tariffs. If the business is located inside the country the products will be considered home produced and will therefore escape these controls

- **grants and subsidies**: many countries want major multinationals to set up there and are willing to offer grants, subsidies, special tax concessions, etc., in order to attract them.

Additional drawbacks to the multinational business:

- **difficult communications**: having branches all over the world makes it difficult to communicate and to gather senior branch staff together to make important decisions

- **unstable countries**: some countries are rather unstable politically and there is a risk in setting up there. Some firms have found their businesses taken over or destroyed with no compensation

- **recovering profits**: some countries make it difficult for the multinationals to get their profits back out, applying very high taxes and occasionally refusing to allow any profits to go out at all.

Multinationals also have a major impact on the countries where they are set up. Some very big multinationals are richer than the entire countries in which they are setting up. The impact of the multinational can be good or bad for the country.

Good points:

- They provide additional jobs.

- They usually provide training and improve the skills levels of the workforce.

- They inject money, through jobs, investments, etc., into the economy.

- There will be lower imports and there may be higher exports and this will improve the country's balance of payments.

Bad points:

- They can exploit labour and provide little more than basic training.

- All profits may be taken out of the country instead of being reinvested.

- If they are powerful they may produce goods without applying the health and safety controls that they would have to have in their own countries. This can lead to labour being injured or even killed and pollution of the factory and local communities.

- This may stop investment into domestic industries and make the country even more reliant on what foreign businesses and countries do.

International trade barriers

Trade barriers have existed almost since people began to trade. Even the ancient Greeks and Romans put taxes and other controls on imported products. Today, we still have major barriers to international trade, although we have also finally recognised that many of them actually make the world a poorer place to live.

Typical trade barriers include:

- tariffs

- quotas and voluntary export restraints

- subsidies

- legal restrictions, e.g. what safety features must be added to a car before it is allowed to be imported

- administrative controls that dictate how, when and where products can be imported.

Tariffs

Tariff – a tax placed on the import of a good or a service.

Tariffs act as a barrier to international trade because they put up the cost of the imported products and make it more difficult for the importers to compete with home produced products. The effect of a tariff is shown in Figure 2.6.3.

Figure 2.6.3 The effect of a tariff on an imported good and on domestic goods

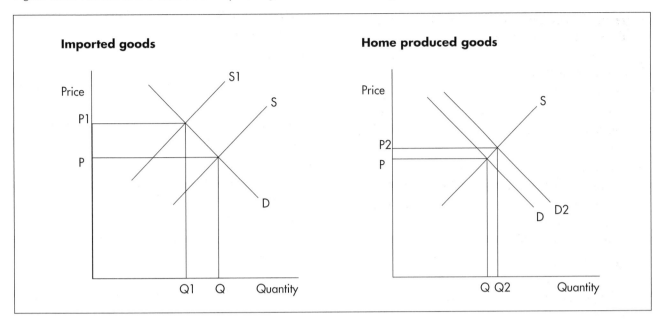

The tariff is like any other tax. It increases the costs for the importer and this causes the supply to decrease, S to S1. This causes the price to rise, P to P1, and therefore customers buy less of the product, Q to Q1.

Because the import is now more expensive, some customers will switch to buying alternative home produced products. This will increase demand, D to D2. Producers will be able to sell more goods, Q to Q2, and the price will be bid up from P to P2. This shift from imports to home produced goods is called **expenditure switching**.

In the UK we have tariffs on a wide range of goods that come from outside the EU, e.g. Japanese videos, American cars, Swiss chocolate and silk from Syria.

Quotas

Quota – a limit placed on the amount of a good or service that is allowed to be imported into a country.

A quota places a physical limit on the amount of a product that is allowed to be imported into a country. If the intention is to limit the number of imports, the quota will be set below the current level of imports. The effect of a quota is shown in Figure 2.6.4.

Figure 2.6.4 The effect of a quota on imported products

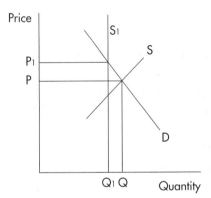

The quota will restrict the number of the product that can be imported, in this case to Q1. The supply curve, S1, will become vertical because, irrespective of how much demand might increase, no more is allowed to be supplied. This limit to the amount of imports allowed will cause the price to rise, P to P1.

As with the tariff, the price of the import has risen and the quantity has fallen. Customers will again switch to buying more of the home produced products.

Quotas artificially limit the import of goods and some producers may not be able to import goods even though they want to. This can lead to a black market, when goods are smuggled in. With goods such as soft and hard drugs the quota is set at zero with a complete ban.

When this happens and some people want the goods very much, suppliers will be prepared to take the risk of being caught and will smuggle drugs in.

Quotas are also placed on products such as foreign films, where these can only be shown if British-made films are also shown.

The General Agreement on Tariffs and Trade, GATT (see below) has put pressure on governments to remove all quotas. Some quotas still exist, but others have been replaced by what are called **voluntary export restraints**. These are really the same as quotas but in this case the business or country selling the goods agrees voluntarily to restrict how much it will export to the UK, i.e. it agrees to a self-imposed quota. In the 1990s, for example, the EU and the Japanese government agreed a voluntary restriction on the number of cars that Japan would import into the EU.

Subsidies

Tariffs are a tax on the import of goods and services, but countries can also create barriers by subsidising home produced goods so that they will be lower in price than imported goods. This also creates a barrier to trade. The effect of these subsidies is shown in Figure 2.6.5.

Figure 2.6.5. The effect of domestic subsidies on home produced and imported goods

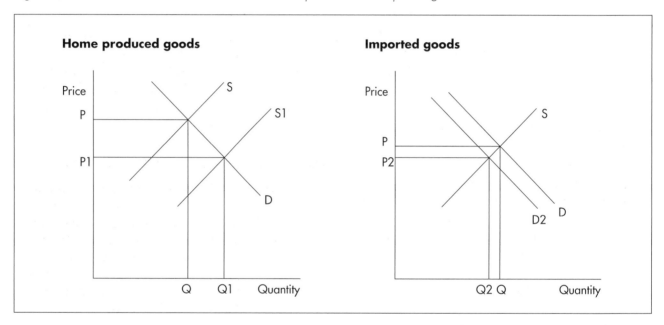

When the subsidy is put on home produced goods it will lower the costs of production and cause the supply to increase, S to S1. This will lower the price, P to P1, and encourage more people to buy the goods. They will, therefore, reduce their demand, D to D2, for imports and the importers will sell fewer goods, Q to Q2, and have to lower their prices, P to P2, in order to stay competitive.

In the EU and the UK subsidies are offered for a wide range of products. The Common Agricultural Policy (CAP) provides subsidies for a range of agricultural products. The Regional Policy of the UK and the EU provides grants, subsidies and reduced taxation levels for businesses that set up in certain parts of the country.

Legal restrictions and controls

Quotas and bans are created by legal restrictions, but we also place a great many other legal controls on goods and services that are imported or exported. It is, for example, illegal to sell military arms to Iraq and to many other countries where there are unstable or aggressive governments.

Many legal controls affect imports and exports purely by accident. These laws are part of controls that the country thinks are important and if other countries wish to export to them they must obey these rules. The following examples should show how wide these effects can be.

- UK law requires us to drive on the left-hand side of the road. Importers who want to compete with UK produced cars have to put the steering wheel on the right and fit the dashboard etc. the other way round. This increases costs.

- The UK has very tight controls on the safety of children's toys. UK manufacturers already meet these standards. Producers in other countries may need to change the way that they produce and check quality before they can sell in our country.

- The UK does not allow the use of growth hormones to increase the size and weight of cattle. As this is a fairly common practice in the USA, beef farmers in the USA cannot export their beef to the UK.

- Australia has laws that prohibit the importation of anything that might affect the natural environment. Goods therefore cannot be packaged in anything that has been alive, e.g. straw or wood chippings, and UK exporters must find other packaging materials.

- Most countries require instructions, guarantees, etc. to be written in the language of the country where they are being sold. Producers must therefore pay for new labels, translations, etc.

- In the USA producers are liable for almost any damage that the product might do to the customers. This is called **product liability**. If UK producers want to sell their products in the USA they need to be aware of this and take out suitable insurance.

Keeping Japanese tofu safe

The Japanese government has announced that from April 2001 all food products sold in Japan will have to state if they contain genetically modified (GM) ingredients.

This decision has been made after growing concerns that nearly 50 per cent of imported soyabeans and grain, mainly from the USA, may come from GM products. Japanese consumers have already started to boycott these products in favour of home produced products that are guaranteed GM free.

For producers of GM products this may well mean that they lose sales. If this policy is copied by other major importers of food products, it will either put GM producers out of business or force them to change the way that they produce their products.

Administrative controls

When goods are imported or c procedures need to be carried out dictated by the government and may trade. For example:

- In order to import alcoholic drinks into t importer will need a licence. If fewer licence issued, fewer alcoholic drinks are likely to be imported.

- In the EU most documents that were once needed to import and export goods have been abolished, but for many countries complicated documents still exist. These are time consuming and expensive to fill in, so many businesses find it easier not to trade with these countries.

- Many countries have very tight customs controls, where all goods are checked very carefully before anything is allowed in. This is time consuming and sometimes expensive. This makes it more difficult to compete with the home-produced goods that have none of these controls.

Actions to reduce trade barriers

In the 1920s and 1930s many countries tried to protect their own industries by increasing the barriers against competitive imports. This greatly damaged international trade and prevented competition and growth. After the Second World War it was agreed, by all the major economic nations of the world, that these barriers must be reduced and that a more competitive and dynamic environment for business and for countries must be created.

In 1947 the Bretton Woods Conference set up the General Agreement on Tariffs and Trade (GATT), signed by 23 founding members. The membership has now grown to 123 nations, which account for 90 per cent of world trade (by value). The primary objective of GATT was to reduce the level of tariffs, quotas and other barriers to international trade.

The barriers to trade are reduced through lengthy discussions between representatives from all the member countries. These discussions take years to complete and are referred to as **rounds**. The Kennedy Round, in the 1960s, reduced manufacturing tariffs by one half, on average, taking most of the tariffs down from 20 per to about 10 per cent. In the latest round, the ...guay Round, the member nations have agreed, for ... first time, to reduce tariffs on agricultural products ...nd to try to ensure international recognition of intellectual property rights such as patents and copyright.

In 1995, as a result of the Uruguay Round, the World Trade Organisation (WTO) was set up. Its role is to continue to expand the work of GATT. Member states have agreed to follow the regulations of the WTO and, where there is a dispute, to follow the rulings of the WTO.

As part of GATT the member nations agreed to follow the decisions of GATT and where disputes arose, the officials at GATT, and now the WTO, would decide who was in the wrong and what action should be taken. Part of the agreement was called the 'most favoured nations clause'. This stated that if one nation gave preferential treatment to another member nation, it must offer the same treatment to all of the member nations. If, for example, Canada offered to lower its tariffs to Australia, it must also lower them to the UK, Japan, Brazil and every other WTO member.

There are important exceptions to the GATT/WTO rules. These include:

- Preferential treatment, e.g. no tariffs and no quotas, is allowed inside official trading blocks. This is why the EU can still impose common external tariffs on non-EU countries.

- If imports might endanger a country's security or cause serious damage to its domestic production, it is allowed to put up barriers to protect itself.

- If a nation is 'dumping' its surplus products in another country, the country receiving the dumped products can use barriers to prevent the dumping.

- In developing countries it is difficult to build up new industries (**infant industries**) when developed countries with well established industries, economies of scale, high levels of advertising, etc., are competing with them. In this situation the WTO allows the developing countries to use barriers to protect their infant industries.

Going bananas?

- In July 1998 the EU created new import licensing rules that would have the effect of reducing the import of bananas from the USA and affect imports from Ecuador, Guatemala, Honduras and Mexico.

- In August 1998 these five countries asked the WTO to arrange for consultations between themselves and the EU.

- In November 1998 the United States announced that it would, in retaliation, place a 100 per cent tax on selected EU products.

A lengthy dispute about which panel of the WTO, if any, could judge the dispute and make decisions then took place. In the meantime the EU changed its policy on the import of bananas and created a licence process and quota allocation that applied to all non-EU nations equally.

The WTO ruled that the revised EU banana regime was 'secure, predictable and fair'.

Full details of the WTO can be found at **www.wto.org/**

Trading blocks

When countries feel that they have important trading relations with other countries they have sometimes formed trading blocks with agreed rules and benefits. These trading blocks can be of three types:

- a **free trade association**: this is an agreement between the member states to allow goods and services to be traded between the countries with no tariffs or quotas

- a **customs union**: this has the same free trade benefits as a free trade association but it also has **common external tariffs**. This means that any country that is outside the union will have to pay the same tariff, irrespective of which member country it is exporting to. The EU is a customs union. A Japanese car will have the same tariff if it is imported from Japan by France, Greece or the UK.

- a **common market**: in a common market the member states will trade as though they are in a single market. Not only will goods and services be allowed to trade free of barriers but all the factors of production will also be allowed to move freely. A full common market will have all the following features:

  i   no tariffs and no quotas between member states

  ii a common external tariff on products imported from non-member states (not all imports will have tariffs)

  iii free movement of labour, capital and businesses between the member states

  iv common tax levels for all member states

  v   a single currency.

Trading blocks clearly encourage more competition in the member states because there are fewer barriers to trade. This helps to keep prices down and offers customers more variety. At the same time, however, there is a danger that smaller businesses may be competed out of business. Because of this, most trading blocks have rules and regulations that protect small businesses and prevent large businesses from becoming monopolies and harming other businesses or the general public.

The **North American Free Trade Agreement (NAFTA)** was formed in 1993 because of fears of the growing economic power of the European Economic Community (now the EU). NAFTA provided a free trade agreement between the United States, Canada and Mexico, a population of just over 370 million people, a figure very close to the population of the EU.

While these trading blocks are good for the member states, they do make it more difficult for non-member states to trade. Where tariffs are placed on imports, exporters from non-member states will have to pay while businesses in the member states can trade without paying the tariff.

The European Union

Figure 2.6.6 The European Union in 2000

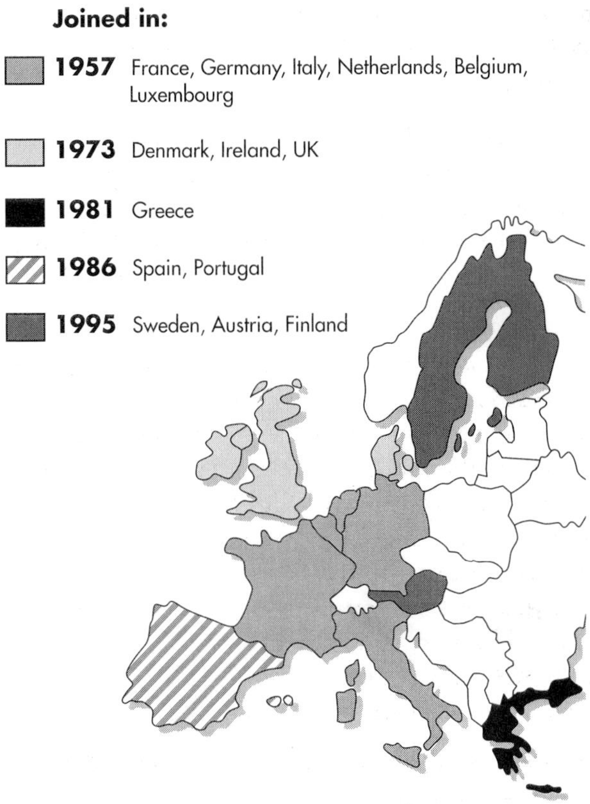

Joined in:

- **1957** France, Germany, Italy, Netherlands, Belgium, Luxembourg
- **1973** Denmark, Ireland, UK
- **1981** Greece
- **1986** Spain, Portugal
- **1995** Sweden, Austria, Finland

The European Union (EU) was formed as the European Economic Community (EEC) in 1957 by the Treaty of Rome. Its growth and development is shown in Figure 2.6.7. Initially, it was founded as a customs union but it now has many of the aspects of a common market, with free movement of the factors of production and a single currency in 11 of the 15 member states. There is also an agreement, under the Maastricht Treaty, to make taxes the same, but very little progress has actually been made on this.

The growth of the European Union has added new conditions for the member states, but the basic objectives have always been the same:

- the creation of a customs union with free trade between member states

- the creation of a common market for factors of production, and eventually a single currency

- the ultimate integration of the separate national economies into a single European economy

Figure 2.6.7 The development of the EU

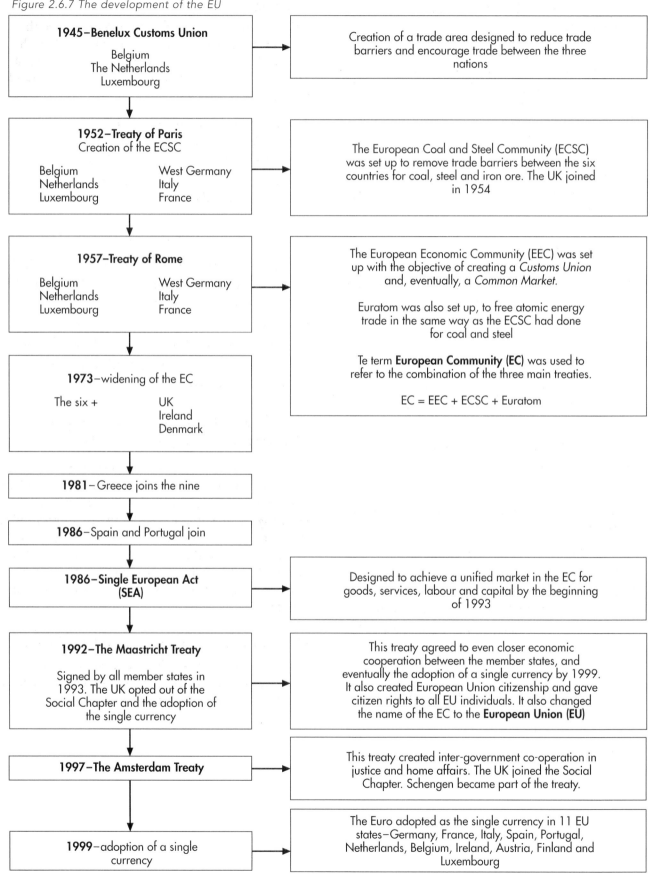

- significant integration of the member states toward political union.

The movement toward these final objectives has been achieved through three major agreements and a huge range of laws and regulations that have come from the four main institutions of the EU: the European Commission, the Council of Ministers, the European Parliament and the Court of Justice of the European Community. The major agreements laid down the framework of laws and conditions that govern the EU. The details of these laws have been developed mainly by the Commission.

The Treaty of Rome 1957

The Treaty of Rome created the basic objectives and philosophy of the EU – the belief that nations working together could achieve more than the nations working separately and for their own ends. The Treaty gives:

- the Community the right to make laws that apply to all member nations

- every individual the right to take any other individual, business or government to court if they break Community law.

The Treaty of Rome established the European Economic Community with the following specific objectives:

- to remove all tariffs and quotas on trade between member nations

- to create common external tariffs on agreed imports into any part of the Union

- to remove all barriers to the movement of people, services and capital between member nations

- to create a common policy for agriculture and for transport

- to monitor and control competition to make it fairer

- to create a European Social Fund to improve employment opportunities and raise workers' standard of living

- to create a European Investment Bank to support new developments in the Union.

The Single European Act 1986

This built on the Treaty of Rome and accelerated the move toward a completely free area of trade where the EU could act as a single marketplace with no artificial barriers to trade. It established the following rights and benefits:

- the right to free movement of goods and services so that EU citizens can buy goods and services from any part of the EU and pay only local rates of tax

- the right of EU citizens to work in any part of the EU with the same rights, protection and duties as nationals

- increased consumer protection

- improved health and safety controls in the workplace

- the right to set up a business in any EU country that an EU citizen or business wants to

- the movement towards European standards for products in terms of quality, labelling, safety, etc.

- allowing businesses from other EU countries to compete for government contracts (public procurement)

- closer levels of VAT and excise duties (e.g. on alcohol, tobacco and petrol) across the EU.

All of these objectives have now been met except the objective of unifying taxes on goods and services. The effect of the Single European Act has been to further encourage EU countries to trade with each other rather than with non-EU countries. As we saw on page 161, UK trade with the EU rose from 16 per cent to 58 per cent in the latter half of the twentieth century. Our major trading partners in the EU are shown in Figure 2.6.8 below.

The Treaty on European Union 1992 (Maastricht)

The Treaty on European Union created the concept of Union citizenship. We are all now not only UK citizens, but also EU citizens with clear rights.

Figure 2.6.8 – UK imports to and exports from other EU member states (1998)

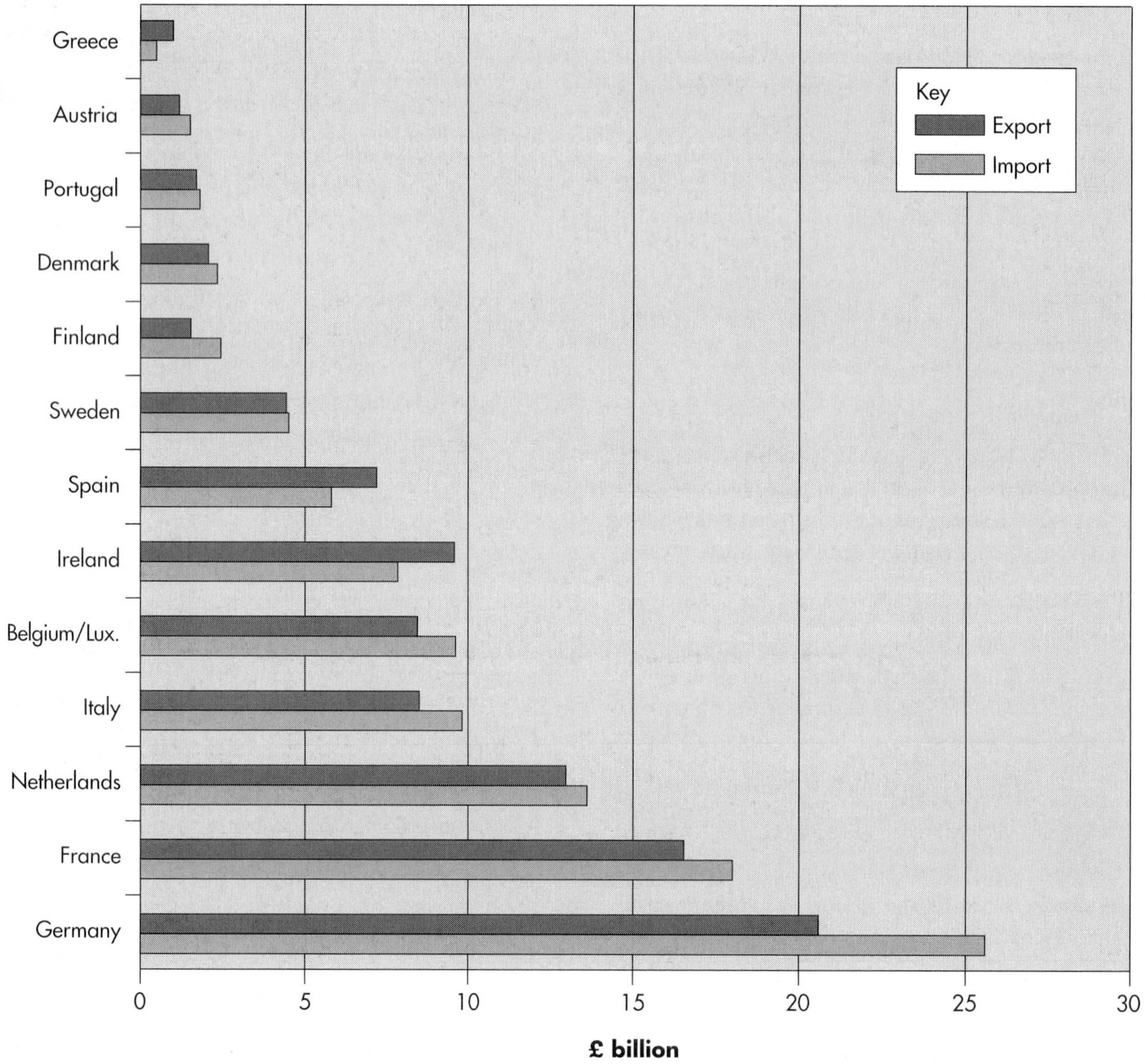

£ billion

European Union citizens' rights

EU citizens now have the following rights laid down in law:

- the **right to free movement** throughout the EU

- the **right to reside** in any EU country that they want to live in

- the **right to work** in any EU country where they want to work

- the **right to vote and stand as a candidate** in municipal and European Union elections in any EU country.

The main objectives of the Maastricht Treaty were to:

- create Union citizenship and the rights that go with this

- give the Union additional powers in terms of transport, communications, education and vocational training, consumer protection and health

- move towards and establish a single currency for the EU (see page 174)

- develop a common foreign and defence policy

- establish closer co-operation on legal matters, immigration policy and police forces

- to adopt the conditions laid down in the social charter to protect workers (see below).

The UK opted out of both the agreement to move towards a single currency by 1999 and the adoption of the social charter.

New laws and regulations are being added, mainly through the Commission, all the time. There are also periodic meetings of all the member states to decide on other major changes. These sometimes lead to new treaties and new rules.

The Amsterdam Treaty 1997

In this treaty the following major agreements were made:

- to create inter-governmental co-operation in justice and home affairs and create conditions to combat crime and create better links between police forces
- to create the Schengen accord as part of the treaty, and hence part of EU law. Special consideration was given to the UK, Ireland and Denmark who still do not follow the Schengen agreement

---

The Schengen Agreement

The Schengen Agreement, set up in 1995, gives citizens the right to move freely between the states which have signed the agreement (all EU states except the UK, Ireland and Denmark).

Citizens from Schengen countries display a green sticker on vehicle windows and can then drive across borders with no checks at all.

- for the UK to adopt the Social Chapter and end its opt-out of that part of the Maastricht Treaty
- to establish a charter of human rights, outlawing discrimination based on race, origin, religion, sexual orientation, age or disability. Parts of this will come into force in 2000.

How European legislation, rules and benefits affect businesses and individuals

The effect of EU laws and regulations on businesses is huge, and growing. It would be impossible to cover anything but a minute percentage of the total. Some

major influences were listed under the different treaties and agreements given above. Further examples are given below, but for a fuller picture of the range of new laws and regulations you will need to look at specialist textbooks, internet sites for the European Union, and government publications.

The Social Chapter

In May 1989 the European Commission approved the **Community Charter of Fundamental Social Rights of Workers.** This was initially known as the Social Charter but as it then became one of the chapters in the Maastricht Treaty it is now referred to as the **Social Chapter.** The main points of the Chapter were:

1 the right to work in the EU country of one's choice

2 the right to a fair wage. (This has led to the introduction of a minimum wage)

3 the right to continuing improvements in living and working conditions

4 the right to adequate social protection, generally through social security benefits

5 the right to belong to a professional organisation or a trade union, and the right to be represented in collective bargaining

6 the right to receive vocational training throughout one's working life

7 a guarantee that men and women will be treated equally in the workplace

8 a guarantee that workers will be consulted, provided with relevant information and be allowed to participate in decisions of firms, where appropriate

9 the right to satisfactory health protection and safe working conditions

10 a guarantee to protect children and adolescents, to include a minimum working age of 15 years, fair pay, and reasonable hours

11 a guarantee of a minimum decent standard of living for the elderly

12 a guarantee to bring about changes that will make it easier for disabled people to become part of the workforce.

Even in 1989 the UK had its own laws that already dealt with nearly all of these areas, so adopting the

Social Chapter in 1997 did not make a great deal of difference to UK businesses and workers. But what has made a difference is the additional regulations brought about by the principles of the Social Chapter.

Despite objections by the UK government, it has now been forced to introduce the Working Time directive. This limits the maximum number of hours an employee can be made to work to 48 hours per week.

Again, in March 2000, the UK government delayed the implementation of new laws to protect workers. In this case it tried to delay implementing equal rights for part-time workers. This would give them the same kinds of protection as full-time workers already receive. As before, the government will, eventually, be forced to pass these laws.

The Single European Currency

Of all the changes that have occurred because of the EU, this is perhaps the most dramatic. Eleven countries in the EU now have a single currency system. Until 2002 there will be no actual Euro notes and coins but these 11 countries already have a single currency and businesses can buy and sell using Euros or the national currencies. In reality, they are the same thing because francs, Deutschmarks, lire or pesetas will always exchange at a fixed rate against the Euro and at a fixed rate against each other.

The main internet site for details on the Euro is **http://europa.eu.int/euro/**

With the introduction of the Euro there have been very dramatic changes as to how business and economic controls work in the EU. These changes include:

- **no transaction costs:** for businesses in the countries that have a single currency there are no transaction costs for changing their money to another currency. This reduces costs and puts businesses in the UK, Denmark, Sweden and Greece at a disadvantage because they have to pay these costs

- **centralised monetary policy:** the single currency cannot work if individual countries have the ability to control their own money supplies and interest rates. A necessary part of a single currency is to give up national control of monetary policy and allow this to be controlled by a **European Central Bank**. Monetary policy for individual countries is impossible. The UK still runs its own monetary policy through the Bank of England

- **ease of comparing prices:** a single currency means that it is much easier to compare prices across EU countries and this is likely to make markets more competitive as everything will be priced in Euros. It is also easier to compare wages, profits, the levels of GDP, etc., because they are measured in one single currency

- **no exchange rate policy:** it is no longer possible to change the rate of exchange between countries to help control the economy. In the past some countries would allow the value of their currencies to fall when they had a negative balance of payments. This would encourage greater sales of exports, because they were now cheaper to foreigners. It would also reduce imports because these were now more expensive to individuals and businesses in the country. The effect was to improve the balance of payments. This cannot now be done and countries with a balance of payments deficit will have to cut back on expenditure and deflate their economies through increased taxes or less government expenditure

- **interest rates will be the same:** interest rates are dictated by the European Central Bank and are the same for all Euro countries. This will increase competition between banks and other lenders, and probably bring interest rates down

- **stability in payments for importers and exporters:** before the single currency an importer or exporter might make a contract to buy or sell goods with a price set in one of the currencies. Then, if the currency changed, the price would also change. This made it very difficult to plan costings for the future. A single currency removes this problem for importers and exporters within the Euro area.

The Euro will help to create stability, growth and jobs

The strong feeling amongst supporters of the Euro is that it will help to stabilise the economies of the countries that have joined. There will be no more speculations and currency fluctuations where the value of one nation's currency can rise or fall dramatically overnight or in the space of a week. The speculations of 1995 are thought to have caused a drop in economic growth in the EU of 2 per cent and a loss of more than 1.5 million jobs.

The EU member states conduct more than 70 per cent of trade internally and this may rise with the introduction of the single currency. The single currency will prevent speculators from buying and selling Euros purely to make personal gain. There is a common interest rate, which will reduce the impact of 'hot money'. The economies have a central monetary policy, which will help to ensure that all the countries have a similar economic trade cycle. Interest rates are no longer used to protect individual currencies and this should lead to lower interest rates and lower borrowing costs for business and for homeowners with mortgages. Investment will be encouraged and this will lead to higher growth and more jobs.

The EU structural funds

One of the objectives of EU policy is to support areas that have particular social and economic problems. This is mainly done through the four structural funds outlined below. To raise the money required to pay for this support the EU uses three sources of revenue.

- a percentage of each member country's VAT is paid to the Union

- a percentage of each member country's Gross National Product is paid to the Union

- tariffs are placed on the import of non-EU goods into the EU.

The funds that are raised from these sources of revenue are used to support specific objectives of the Union.

The objectives of the structural funds are set for a number of years. In the period 2000 to 2006 it is estimated that the funds will spend the equivalent of £161 billion.

The objectives for the 2000 to 2006 period have not been finally agreed at the time of writing this book but the main changes have been hinted at. The objectives will follow those of the 1995 to 1999 period and will most likely be:

Objective 1: to provide support to regions of the EU which have a per capita GDP of below 75 per cent of the EU average. In the UK, these regions are Northern Ireland, the Highlands and Islands of Scotland and Merseyside.

Objective 2: to help to redevelop regions or areas which have high unemployment levels due to industrial decline with funding for industrial, rural, urban and fishing areas. In the UK these areas are likely to include South Wales, North East England, West Cumbria, Furness, Greater Manchester, Lancashire, Cheshire and Plymouth.

Objective 3: to provide training and assistance to help the long-term unemployed, the young, the socially excluded and people affected by changes in industrial and productive systems. These measures will apply anywhere in the UK other than those covered by objectives 1 and 2.

These objectives will be met out of the four fund areas outlined below. Each fund can be used to support any of the three objectives.

The European Regional Development Fund (ERDF)

The ERDF provides funds to help to reduce unemployment and create and maintain jobs. Assistance is given to fund infrastructure projects such as transport links, but also to help businesses to set up and expand in areas of high unemployment. Funds are also available for education and training schemes for local businesses, research and development and investment into environmental projects.

Examples of aid provided by the ERDF and the ESF

- Improvements to the Greater Manchester motorway network.

- Improved insulation in houses in Glasgow to conserve energy.

- The provision of computer access for small and medium sized businesses at North Lincolnshire College so that they could test product designs on computers which, individually, they could not afford.

- The provision of training courses in Ballymena for the unemployed to ensure that they achieve appropriate NVQs at levels 1 to 4 and are then qualified for work.

The European Social Fund (ESF)

The ESF was set up in 1960 and provides funds for vocational training, retraining and job-creation schemes. It helps the long-term unemployed, young job-seekers and people excluded from the labour market. It helps to promote equal opportunities, and provides funds for equipping workers with new skills as industrial processes change.

The ESF will provide funds directly for training and retraining schemes, but it will also supply funds indirectly through improving teacher training or supporting changes to the curriculum. Funds are also available for improving the quality of research, science and technology services and providing a skilled workforce to deal with these new technologies.

Details about the ESF can be obtained from the Department of Employment EU Branch, European Social Fund Unit, Level 1, Grays Inn Road, London, WC1X 8HL (Tel: 020 7211 3000)

The European Agricultural Guidance and Guarantee Fund (EAGGF)

The EAGGF provides funds for the EU's Common Agricultural Policy (CAP). Through this it aims to support agriculture and to work towards changes that will make it more efficient. One branch provides funds to help to keep agricultural prices stable and, with this,

to stabilise farm incomes. The other sections provide support to help to modernise farming.

This support combines to help farmers in areas of poor farming, such as the Welsh Hills, but also encourages new young farmers, the creation of producer organisations to market farm produce and investment in the tourist sector, heritage and village protection.

The main benefits have been paid through providing farmers with a minimum guaranteed price for certain products such as grain, milk, wine and beef. This has lead to massive overproduction which has made large farms very wealthy but has done little for the small, low-production farms. As a result of growing 'mountains' and 'lakes' of surplus products that cost a great deal to store and frequently have to be sold off at a loss by the governments, the CAP is now being radically changed. This is also changing the role of the EAGGF.

Six new policy objectives have been created for the CAP for the new century:

- to improve the Union's competitiveness through lower prices

- to guarantee the safety and quality of food to consumers

- to ensure stable incomes and a fair standard of living for the agricultural community

- to make production methods environmentally friendly and to respect animal welfare

- to integrate environmental goals into its instruments

- to seek to create alternative income and employment opportunities for farmers and their families.

Source: European Commission

The Financial Instrument for Fisheries Guidance (FIFG)

Set up in 1994, the FIFG carries out a similar role for the fishing industry as the EAGGF does for agriculture. It regulates the amount of fishing that can be carried out in order to preserve stocks for the future. It also provides funds to develop fish farming, develop port facilities, promote fish products, and help people who earn their living from fishing to move into other forms of employment as the industry has declined.

> PESCA operated between 1994 and 1999 to help the fishing industry restructure as fish stock declined and market conditions changed. Measures provided by the fund included aid to find and develop new markets and to find alternative ways for fishing communities to earn income, e.g. through the development of tourism.

EU environment policies

Articles 2, 3 (k) and 130r of the Treaty of Rome established a clear aim in the Community to work towards better protection of the environment in the EU:

- to protect and improve the quality of the environment

- to protect the health of the population

- to ensure the careful and rational use of natural resources

- to promote levels of environmental control at an international level so that vulnerable regions will be better protected from inter-country pollution.

Many parts of the work of the structural funds listed above have an environmental element within them. The CAP, for example, tries to reduce the use of unnecessary fertilisers and pesticides and thereby protect rivers, etc. from pollution. In the 1990s there were very specific EU initiatives designed to protect the environment. These included:

- the introduction of a common environment tax on energy and CO_2 emissions. This was not actually passed but many individual countries have introduced their own taxes. In the UK we have increased taxes on hydrocarbons well above the rate of inflation

- the Altener programme, designed to encourage the use of alternative and renewable energy sources

- the SAVE programme, designed to encourage methods of saving energy, both in the home and in businesses

- the banning of CFC production by mid-1995 as a measure to protect the ozone layer

- the provision of funds for projects that help to improve the environment. The funds are distributed through the **LIFE Financial Instrument for the Environment**, set up in 1992

- loans from the European Investment Bank for the creation of waste disposal plants and sewage treatment plants.

With all of the initiatives that the EU has introduced, businesses are affected either directly or indirectly. Grants to help fishing communities build up tourism or craft industries will directly affect the fishing industry, but will also indirectly affect businesses that provide the new tourist area with postcards or the new craft industry with its clay, paint, wicker, etc. You should look back over all of the ways that the EU affects the Community and the member states and think how they will affect individual industries.

Further Study

To understand the impact of international trade on business you will need to know what controls governments place on international trade. These controls change fairly frequently and it is important that you are up to date. You should check the following sources to see how regulations, benefits, etc. are being changed.

Sources of information

1   UK government publications, e.g. from the Department of Trade and Industry, the Overseas Trade Board and the 'Pink Book' which records details of imports and exports.

2   A wide range of EU publications from the Commission and the Office for Official Publications, but also from the EU office in London and the European Information Centres around the UK. There are also a great many internet sites with information on laws, regulations, the role of different organisations, etc.

3   Major banks provide publications, mainly for businesses, that outline rules and regulations for businesses involved in international trade.

Finding details on international and multinational businesses

To find details of which businesses operate internationally and which are multinationals you should check:

1   annual reports, which will outline the main areas of trade

2   directories on companies, which are available in libraries

3   reports on new business ventures in newspapers, such as the *Financial Times*, and magazines such as *The Economist.*

You also need to have up-to-date examples of trade restrictions. These also change and you need to check press reports to find current examples. The press reports also outline current disputes and details on the WTO, new measures from the EU, etc.

Revision Questions

1 Explain, giving examples, the difference between a visible and an invisible export.

(4 marks)

2 Give **three** reasons why countries import products. For each reason give **three** examples of products that we import. (6 marks)

3 a) Explain the difference between an international business and a multinational business. (2 marks)

b) Give **three** benefits and **three** drawbacks of being a multinational business.

(6 marks)

4 How are multinational firms likely to affect national firms? (6 marks)

5 How do franchises help businesses to expand internationally? (4 marks)

6 For each of the following trade barriers give one example of a barrier that exists for imports into the UK.

i) quotas

ii) tariffs

iii) legal controls

(3 marks)

7 Draw a graph to show how a UK produced product will be affected by the imposition of a higher tariff on the import of a substitute.

(4 marks)

8 Explain why the imposition of a quota, or a total ban, can lead to a "black market" for an imported product. (4 marks)

9 What is the basic objective of GATT (WTO)?

(2 marks)

10 Explain what an "infant industry" is and why a country should be allowed to use this status as a reason for not following the basic agreements of GATT/WTO. (3 marks)

11 List the counties that joined the EU in:

i) 1973

ii) 1995

(4 marks)

12 What were the main agreements of the Single European Act? (4 marks)

13 What is the minimum allowed level of VAT in the EU? (1 mark)

14 Explain what the Schengen agreement is and why the UK does not want to be a full member of this agreement. (4 marks)

15 List **three** benefits and **three** drawbacks for the UK of joining the European single currency (euro). (6 marks)

16 List **two** objectives of each of the following EU institutions:

a) European Regional Development Fund.

b) European Social Fund.

c) European Agricultural Guidance and Guarantee Fund

(6 marks)

UNIT 2

End of Unit Revision Test

Questions 1 to 5 relate to the data given below.

Supermarket chess, but no checkmate!

With the start of the new millennium, competition in the supermarket industry is 'hotting up'. Wal Mart has laid down the challenge to the other supermarkets by lowering most of its prices and the other supermarkets have been forced to follow suit. They have also lowered their prices, but only to match those of Wal Mart.

In the spring of 2000, Safeway announced that it was going to scrap its ABC loyalty card following the results of a nationwide survey that concluded that these cards have little effect on shopping habits. The survey showed that the majority of shoppers are either loyal, so the card does not make them change supermarkets, or disloyal and will shop where the best deals are. This disloyal group tend to have all of the supermarkets' loyalty cards and shop where they want. Sainsbury's quickly followed Safeway's lead and announced that it would scrap its Reward Card.

For the smaller supermarket chains any additional competitive pressure is always a problem. As the competition intensified between the few oligopolistic giants, Somerfield found sales falling, but had limited ability to cut its own prices and costs. The John Lewis Partnership has stepped in to buy a selection of Somerfield branches and has now converted them to become branches of Waitrose, which John Lewis already owns.

---

1 Supermarkets provide both goods and services to consumers.

   a) Explain, giving examples, what goods and services are provided by the supermarkets *themselves*.   (4 marks)

   b) Explain why these products are "consumer products".   (2 marks)

2 The supermarket industry is an oligopoly.

   a) Explain what an oligopoly is.   (2 marks)

   b) Which parts of the case study above support the view that the supermarket industry is an oligopoly? Explain your answer.   (8 marks)

3 Supermarkets use non-price competition, such as loyalty cards, to attract customers. List two other forms of non-price competition used by supermarkets and explain how they are used to attract customers.   (4 marks)

4 a) How would you expect a rise in interest rates to affect the supermarket industry? Explain your answer.   (6 marks)

   b) Raising interest rates might be used to control the rate of inflation. Explain how the government achieves the same effect using fiscal policy.   (4 marks)

5 Supermarkets have very specific pricing policies because they are oligopolies. With reference to a business you have studied, explain how and why the business uses skimming.   (8 marks)

Questions 6 to 8 relate to the data given below.

> Growers of grapes in the famous Champagne region of France had to wait until June 2000 to find out if they could meet the demand for champagne for the year 2000. The growers are able to produce about 300 million bottles a year, but the millennium celebrations led to 330 million bottles being sold in 1999.

6 a) Draw a fully labelled supply and demand graph to show the effects of the millennium celebrations on the Champagne market.

(3 marks)

b) Explain why the changes you have shown on the graph have occurred. (3 marks)

7 Although champagne is considered by some people as the only suitable drink for really special occasions, many other people would be willing to buy substitutes from Australia, South Africa and the USA.

If the growers of grapes in the Champagne district has a poor harvest, how would that affect the following stakeholders of the growers?

i) The shareholders/owners.

ii) The suppliers.

(6 marks)

8 a) Explain why the existence of the single market and a common external tariff (CET) makes it easier for producers of champagne substitutes in Germany to sell their wines in the EU than for producers in the USA. (6 marks)

b) How do the rules and objectives of GATT (WTO) affect the trading positions of US growers trying to sell wine in the EU?

(4 marks)

9 a) Explain the difference between a merger and a take-over. (2 marks)

b) With reference to a business you have studied, explain how and why the government acts to prevent anti-competitive practices.

(8 marks)

10 a) What is an international company?

(2 marks)

b) What are the benefits for a multinational company of locating its production in different countries? (4 marks)

c) What disadvantages might there be for the country in which the multinational company is setting up its production?

(4 marks)

(Total marks: 80)

UNIT 3

Marketing

What is Marketing?

In this chapter, you will learn about marketing, what it means, and why it is a necessary function of a business organisation.

WHERE ARE YOU?

Introduction

It is very important that you understand precisely what **marketing** means. As you already know, business organisations consider marketing to be so important that many have marketing departments, and their marketing managers hold senior positions, on par with the managers of production and finance. However, quite often the term 'marketing' is misunderstood, and many people think that it is the same as 'advertising'.

Marketing

Marketing is the management process which identifies, anticipates and supplies customer requirements efficiently and profitably.

Source: CIM

The above definition has been formulated by the Chartered Institute of Marketing, and is widely used in the UK. Consider what it means. All businesses exist in order to provide customers and clients with goods or services. All businesses also strive to be efficient, in order to be profitable. As we all know, a business organisation which does not make a profit will, sooner or later, cease to exist. Every business therefore must try to ensure that it produces what the customers want. However, making the goods or providing the service is not enough. Several important questions must be answered first.

1 What should be produced? What do customers need? (This is another way of saying that customer requirements must be **identified**.)

Identify – to select by careful research and analysis.

2 How can future needs of customers be identified? (In other words, how can these needs be **anticipated**?)

Anticipate – be aware of what is likely to happen in the future, and to take steps to deal with the future situation.

3 Finally, once we know what customers need and what they might require in the future, what should be done to make sure that the products and services are there? (If a business fails to **supply** the goods or services, it cannot meet customer needs and will not be efficient or profitable.)

It is important to remember that in the modern marketplace many firms are competing for a share of sales. In order to survive, these firms try to stay one step ahead of their competitors. One of the ways to do this is to be ready with new or improved products before other firms. In order to be first, **anticipating** what people might want and be prepared to buy has become of prime importance.

Marketing therefore tries to answer the above questions. It is the link between production and sales. In today's world, the functions of marketing are very complex, and require an understanding not only of the principles of marketing, but of the ways in which correct and reliable conclusions can be reached.

In the past, when consumer choices of goods and services were very limited, the producer could concentrate on making sure that they were available, and then wait for the customers to come. In the present day, however, the customers, and potential customers, are the most important link in the production–sales–buyer chain.

This chain can be very long, with the manufacturers supplying wholesalers or overseas agents and never meeting the consumers. Combined with the much greater choice of goods and services available, this makes good communication with the consumers vital in today's world. The need to know, and often to anticipate, what the consumers want and need has led to the development of marketing as the complex business function it is today.

We must also remember that the world is constantly changing. There are still people living who have seen the invention of many of the things that are now in everyday use. Think of radio, television, CDs, mobile phones, to name just a few. As people's standard of living rises, their expectations rise with it. A business organisation must keep up with, if not always strive to be ahead of, the trends and fashions in the market.

When the motor car was first invented, it was regarded as an outlandish toy for the very rich, and nobody thought that it would become the most widely used form of transport for the masses. In the USA, when Ford cars were first being made on an assembly line, the Ford slogan advised people that they could buy a Ford car 'in any colour, as long as it is black'. In the year 2000, car manufacturers not only produce cars of different specifications, sizes, colours and price ranges in order to stay competitive, they must also be aware of changing social attitudes and political, legal and environmental issues, and research the feasibility of more efficient, environmentally friendly cars and fuels.

Marketing's main purpose is to ensure that the transaction between the seller and the buyer takes place. This applies to all goods and services which the providers wish to sell in order to make a profit. The consumer market and the industrial market have the same ultimate objective, but different marketing routes must be taken to achieve it. This is why marketing is a complicated and skilled area of business activity.

Industrial goods are those used to produce consumer goods. All machinery and equipment are in this category. Manufacturers of industrial goods sell to other manufacturers, not to the public, but they still have to market what they make.

What is marketing?

'Marketing is a social and managerial process by which individuals and groups obtain what they need and want through creating, offering and exchanging products of value with others.'

Philip Kotler, Professor of International Marketing, formulated this definition of marketing in 1997 at Northwestern University in Illinois, USA. Professor Kotler is one of the founders of modern marketing. In the 1960s Kotler and some others took marketing out of its backroom role as part of the sales department and put it into its modern and central role in terms of strategy and the integration of the other functions of management.

According to Kotler:

'... marketing is much more than just an isolated business function – it is the philosophy that guides the entire organisation. The goal of marketing is to create customer satisfaction profitably ...'

and:

'Real marketing is less about selling and more about knowing what to make.'

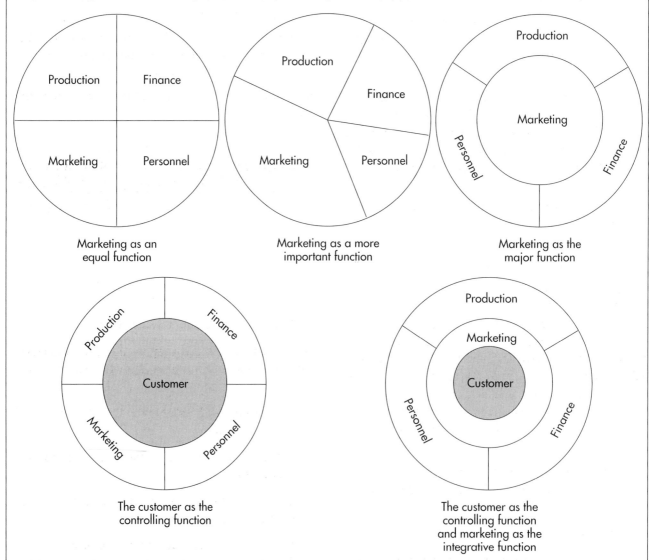

Marketing as an
equal function

Marketing as a more
important function

Marketing as the
major function

The customer as the
controlling function

The customer as the
controlling function
and marketing as the
integrative function

The above figures show the development of the marketing function from an equal function to an integrative function.

Kotler also introduced the concept of **customer delivered value** to explain why customers buy from one source rather than another. He argues that customers buy from the firm that offers the highest customer delivered value. This is defined as the difference between:

i **total customer value** – the bundle of benefits anticipated from the product, and

ii **total customer costs** – the bundle of costs incurred in evaluating, obtaining and using the product.

Market leadership is gained by maximising customer delivered value through improving and augmenting the product or price reductions, simplifying the order process or absorbing some of the buyer's risk, e.g. by offering a warranty.

Kotler also introduced the idea that marketing has a role in non-profit making organisations. Although novel at the time (1967), this idea is universally accepted today, especially in the field of education where schools, colleges and universities compete for students.

Source: Business Review, Nov. 1997

The main functions of the marketing department

In order to identify, anticipate and supply customer requirements, the marketing department has to carry out a number of distinct functions.

1 **Market research** – which includes not just collecting information by various methods, but recording and analysing it. Depending on facts that must be established, the researchers attempt to gather data on the economy, the competitors, the customers and the effectiveness of the strategies used by the organisation.

2 **Advertising** – this includes a number of other functions, such as promotions, publicity, sales literature and advertising itself.

3 **Planning** – deciding on the product mix that will ensure profitability.

4 **Sales** – forecasting and budgeting of sales, choosing appropriate distribution methods and outlets; monitoring the sales process.

Each of the above functions is complex and can be split into several activities.

> **Product mix** – the 'portfolio' or range of products that a company makes, or the range of services that it provides.

CASE STUDY

Twenty or so years ago, there were no computers in the office. Secretaries used manual, or perhaps electric, typewriters and corrected any errors with correction fluid. All accounts were done, and checked, manually. With the coming of the new office technology, all that has changed. Today, office workers, book-keepers and accountants are all expected to be computer-literate, but this 'office revolution' did not just evolve naturally.

When computers were introduced into the working environment, many other needs became apparent. For example:

- Workers had to be trained to use them.

- There was urgent need for more sophisticated software.

- Purpose-designed furniture was needed.

Many organisations anticipated the above and marketed their new products even before customers became aware of their needs. Thus:

- Colleges organised word-processing and computerised accounts courses.

- Companies such as Microsoft introduced continually updated software.

- Equipment ranging from computer stations to mouse pads began to appear in the shops.

All these show how manufacturers and providers of services can successfully anticipate customer requirements.

The marketing concept

The marketing concept, first formulated in the 1960s, is based on two principles:

1 All the activities of a business must be oriented towards the customer.

2 The main objective of a business is achieving **profitability** through sales.

> **Profitability** – the amount of money left over after all the costs have been deducted.

While everyone knew and understood the profit principle, the customer-oriented approach was still not fully appreciated by many businesses. Large businesses often suffered from a lack of communication with their customers, and a corresponding shortage of information about the customers' changing financial status, needs and tastes.

In a small business, there is usually no designated person in charge of marketing. The owner manager, or perhaps one of the partners or directors, takes care of what needs to be done. This is not to say that no marketing function is carried out. Those running a small business are usually more directly in touch with the people with whom they deal and are more likely to respond to wishes or complaints. A large organisation, divided into quite separate departments, is often in danger of losing touch with the most important people – the customers.

It is therefore vital that the marketing section of a business has clear and efficient lines of communication with its existing customers, as well as with all the other departments. It must also seek and obtain as much information as possible about its customers, its competitors and the trends in the economy as well as in its own industry and location.

CASE STUDY

Finding out about the competition

Elma has inherited £10,000 from her great uncle. She has recently completed her Vocational A Level Business, and has been looking for a job. Now she thinks that she would like to start her own business. Elma lives in a residential area, where many houses have been divided into flats for students and people working in the city. While at college, Elma often heard her fellow students complain about the lack of laundry facilities in the area. She has now decided to open a launderette, and is certain that there will be a great demand for such a service.

Elma's elder brother, however, was not so sure. 'Have you checked how many other launderettes there are nearby?' he said. 'And what facilities do they offer apart from

washing the clothes? And would enough people come to your launderette? You don't know whether they have their own washing machines!'

'But so many people at college said that they needed laundry facilities,' said Elma.

'True,' said her brother, 'but you are talking about a very small number of people. Before you decide to invest your money in such a business, you'd better find out if it is really needed, and whether you can really provide it.'

'Oh,' said Elma, feeling disheartened. 'How can I do that?'

'Well,' answered her wise brother, 'Better learn a bit about marketing ...'

We know that the function of marketing is very important to a business. It is also used in non-profit making organisations, such as charities, whose objective is to raise the greatest possible amounts of money for a particular cause. Oxfam, the Imperial Cancer Research Fund and other charities all have clear-cut marketing strategies but in this chapter we shall concentrate on marketing in business organisations. In this unit, you will learn how this function is carried out. Creating a **marketing strategy** does this.

> **Marketing strategy** – a company's plan of action relating to marketing its product/s in line with company policy.

In order to decide on a suitable marketing strategy, the management of a business must ask a number of questions, such as:

* what to produce?
* how much to produce?
* how to price the product?
* where to sell?
* who is likely to buy it?
* who are the main competitors?
* what is happening in the economic and political environment?

Various research methods are used to try and establish these facts. When the research is completed, the results are analysed and conclusions reached. The analysis of such findings will form the basis of the marketing strategy of the organisation, but the work of the marketing team does not end there. They are also in charge of sales promotion, including all advertising, and must monitor the progress of the strategy.

Finally, remember that marketing deals not only with new products, but with improving or changing existing products. Thus it can be said that the work of the marketing department is never done.

Figure 3.1.6

Marketing strategy

__Stephen Barnes__ considers the importance of an effective marketing strategy in a changing market environment

When a company is formed, it takes on a legal identity. The business becomes a legal 'person' able to own property and act in law. The analogy between a company and a person goes further. Business literature is full of references to the company as a kind of person: 'the company knows ...', 'the firm suspected ...', or 'it was an ethical organisation ...'.

A distinguishing feature of human beings is their ability to recognise the passage of time: to look back and learn, to look forward and plan. In the same way, companies use a kind of corporate intelligence to reflect on their experience and to set their aims and objectives.

If the future was always the same as the past, planning would be simple. But change is one of the few certainties in business. Planning is therefore complex and difficult. In fact, effective planning is a key factor in managing for business success.

What is a strategy in general and a marketing strategy in particular? A good starting-point is to distinguish between aims and objectives. An *aim* is a direction or intent. For example, an electronics firm might aim for 'profitable expansion in the UK'. This is a perfectly plausible direction in which to aim, but to make it happen some hard *objectives* need to be set. An example might be 'to gain a 25% market share within 2 years while holding margins above 10%'.

An objective is most likely to be fulfilled through a planned pathway of management action: this is called a *strategy*. As so often in the real world, the most direct route towards an objective may not be the best. A mix of strengths and weaknesses within the firm combined with threats and opportunities outside may suggest a strategy that is indirect yet more effective and more likely to succeed (see Figure 1). So the electronics firm might promote its brand at low prices in the first year to gain share and then rebuild margins on the strength of established loyalty.

Evolution or crisis

A marketing strategy may evolve or it may be forged in the heat of a crisis. Back in the early 1980s Woolworths lost its profitability because it offered cheap, low-quality merchandise when its customers wanted something better. Woolworths was purchased by the Kingfisher group (see pp. 4–6) and recovery followed as stores upgraded their range and the shopping environment was improved. Trouble surfaced again in the mid-1990s when Woolworths appeared unfocused in trying to match its products to the market. Competition was intensifying as more focused stores such as Our Price records, Toys 'R' Us and BhS nibbled into Woolworths' market. The result was another rethink and the rolling out of three new Woolworths fascias: Local, Heartland and City. Each has stock and a marketing mix adjusted to suit a different sales and competitive environment.

By contrast, Marks and Spencer is securely anchored a little above mid-market with highly competitive costs and above average quality. But the reputation of its St Michael brand is not the outcome of crisis. It has evolved in a long tradition and at no point has there ever been any complacency. The firm is a watchful guardian of customer satisfaction, yet its marketing strategy stresses innovation. M&S made early but highly successful entries into such diverse markets as sandwiches and personal finance.

SWOT analysis

The formation of a marketing strategy involves linking the firm's internal resources with the anticipated external environment. One simple approach is to carry out a SWOT analysis, where a group of managers identifies the firm's present strengths and weaknesses and its future opportunities and threats (see Figure 2). A SWOT analysis is useful in creating awareness of all the possible factors in a marketing strategy, but it does not reveal how those factors interact nor does it resolve them into a decision-making pathway.

The internal resources that really count are those that are special: what the company owns or can do that other firms don't own or can't do as well. These are the forces of competitive advantage — the qualities that enable a firm to sustain higher levels of profitability. John Kay (1993) splits these between:

- **distinctive competencies** — the special qualities within the firm e.g. BMW's reputation for quality, Glaxo-Wellcome's ability to innovate

technical knowledge; strong brands; distribution network	erratic supplies; down-market image; inexperienced salesforce
technological breakthrough; chance to enter US market; ending of a legal monopoly	me-too products from competitors; cheap imports; takeover bid

Figure 2 *SWOT analysis*

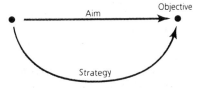

Figure 1   *Aims, objectives and strategy*

- **strategic assets** — any barriers to competition owned by the firm e.g. the franchise held by Carlton TV or the location of a large hotel in a small town.

Distinctive competencies exist as part of the firm and are special to its identity. They are hard to copy although they do not bar competition. *Strategic assets* are owned by the firm but *could* be transferred to any other firm. Thus they only block competition while they are owned by the firm in question.

Models and the marketing environment

Internal resources — however impressive — do not make a marketing strategy if they fail to address the marketing environment. A common way of tackling this problem is through the use of models. One of the best known comes from a pioneering study of business strategy by Igor Ansoff (1965) (see 'Management Gurus' in Vol. 5, No. 1 for a detailed discussion of Ansoff's work). He argued that a firm was really a portfolio of 'strategic areas' — products or product groupings, and that for each product group to follow its growth pathway, a distinctive competitive strategy is needed.

This field of analysis was taken forward by Michael Porter (1980, 1985). He pointed out that any firm in a profitable market will attract competitors whose efforts to gain market share will always erode returns. Protection from this depends on a sustainable source of competitive advantage. There are three possible routes:

(1) Cost leadership where a firm becomes the lowest cost producer, able to undercut its rivals yet maintain its profitability. In the furniture market, MFI pursues cost leadership.

(2) Differentiation where a firm makes its products distinctively different to those of competitors and is then able to charge a premium price. Maples with its stylish, up-market products, differentiates successfully.

(3) Focus where a firm targets only one segment of the market and then pursues cost leadership or differentiation. A local pine shop would follow this strategy.

One model that relates both the product portfolio and competitive pressures is the Boston matrix, so-called because it was developed in the 1970s by the Boston Consultancy Group. The idea is to assess the firm's product groups in terms of market growth potential and market share (see Figure 3). The circles represent the product groups with a size proportional to sales. Stars, such as Product A ('product' referring to a distinct business unit or a range of related products), are already successful and strongly profitable but need high continuing investment to sustain their progress. Problem children, such as Product B, have the potential for success but have not yet secured a high share. Cash cows, such as Product C, are at maturity stage in their product life cycle and generate an excellent net cash flow. This may be used to support stars and selected problem children. Finally, dogs, such as Product D, have poor prospects. They are usually sold or discontinued unless earning cash at low risk.

The Boston matrix helps managers to plan a balanced product portfolio which ideally might contain some clear stars, a few problem children and enough cash cows to finance marketing investment. It is a dynamic picture. The effect of the product life cycle is to exert on products a downward force in the matrix (see arrows in Figure 3) which it takes active marketing to counteract.

Product and price

Any marketing strategy needs to act on real markets where transactions with customers take place. This is achieved through the marketing mix where product and price are the two Ps that conceptually define the strategy. The *product* represents all the sources of satisfaction that consumers anticipate: this is the prospect that persuades them to part with money. It is also the source of production costs for the firm. *Price* is the sacrifice. It is the amount of money that consumers must offer to enjoy the product and carries an opportunity cost. This is the satisfaction to be gained from the next-best alternative — perhaps a rival brand or the product of an immediate competitor.

From here a strong and integrated marketing mix is needed to guide the brand or product proposition to its target market. The accuracy of this 'fit' between a product and its market has become increasingly important. Firms are generally getting much better at segmenting the market and customising their mix accordingly.

Market segmentation

A market has many dimensions. Often there is a range of criteria that could be used to segment a single market. Broadly these can be grouped by their focus on:

- consumers, e.g. age group, neighbourhood, lifestyle
- product, e.g. specification, type of use, usage rate
- price/income level, e.g. up or downmarket.

The choice of segmentation criteria is vital if the market is to be properly understood and the target segment well defined. The clothes retailer, Next (see Box 1), chose age group and price/income and has a very precise understanding of its market segment. This enables the company to get close to its customers, understanding their psychological and cultural needs and not just their patterns of purchase. Such knowledge helps the firm to build distinctive competencies in its segment and anticipate change.

The choice of market position depends not only on the firm's competitive advantage but also on the size, density and prospects of a given segment. A niche player such as Holland & Barrett health foods will want enough potential customers *within* its segment and, preferably, the prospect of the numbers growing. Surveying, analysing and monitoring segment change is an important part of formulating marketing strategy.

Conclusion

As market change quickens and market structures become more complex, the importance of a well-conceived marketing strategy is likely to increase. Firms will need highly sensitive antennae in the market and a capacity to respond flexibly and swiftly to fill strategic gaps. In 1989 Charles Handy described 'the Triple I Organisation' where adding value depended on Intelligence, Information and Ideas. Ten years on, its time has come.

References

Ansoff, H. I. (1965) *Corporate Strategy*, McGraw Hill (Penguin Revised Edition, 1988).

Handy, C. (1989) *The Age of Unreason*, Business Books.

Kay, J. (1993) *Foundation of Corporate Success*, MacMillan.

Porter, M. (1980) *Competitive Strategy*, Free Press.

Porter, M. (1985) *Competitive Advantage*, Free Press.

Stephen Barnes is co-Director of the Nuffield Economics and Business Studies A-level and the author of Essential Business Studies, *published by Collins Educational (2nd edn 1997).*

Source: Economics and Business Studies, February 1999

Revision Questions

1 What is the main objective of a business organisation? (1 mark)

2 What is likely to happen to a business which is not efficient? (1 mark)

3 Explain the meaning of the phrase 'identifying customer needs'. (2 marks)

4 Why is it important for a business to anticipate customer demand? (4 marks)

5 Why is good communication with consumers of greater importance today than it used to be a hundred years ago? (5 marks)

6 Explain the difference between the consumer market and the industrial market. (3 marks)

7 According to Kotler, people choose to buy from a source that offers the greatest customer delivered value. Explain what this means. (5 marks)

8 Today, marketing is used in non-profit making organisations. Name three such organisations, and give examples of their marketing. (5 marks)

9 What is market research, and what is its main purpose? (4 marks)

10 What is the product mix, and why is it important for a business to get it right? (4 marks)

11 Why is a large organisation often at risk of losing touch with its customers, and not realising what their needs are? (3 marks)

12 What is meant by 'trends in the economy'? Why is it important for a business to be aware of such trends? (4 marks)

13 Explain why 'the work of the marketing department is never done'. (2 marks)

14 List the functions of a marketing department. (3 marks)

15 With reference to the case study 'Finding out about the competition', suggest what Elma should do to find out if her idea is feasible if she decides to take her brother's advice. (8 marks)

CHAPTER 2

What is Market Research?

In this chapter you will learn about primary and secondary research, and the methods used in carrying out and analysing the results of such research. You will also learn how to interpret the results of market research, and how they can be used by business organisations to decide on their marketing strategies.

Introduction

As we know, the main objective of any business organisation is profitability. Finding out as much as possible about a potential market for its products helps business organisations to maximise their profitability. In simple terms, this means that a business which knows what products are likely to be bought, by whom, where, when and at what price, has a much greater chance of being successful. This information can be gathered through different methods of research.

Market research – systematic gathering, recording and analysing of data about problems relating to the marketing of goods and services.

Source: American Marketing Association

Data – known facts that can be used as a basis for making decisions.

Internal data

Many companies can gather a lot of important and relevant information about the market for their goods or services from their own records. If the details of individual customers and their transactions are collated and analysed, the company can find out about tastes, trends and volume of sales. An accurate picture of existing customers can be built up.

However, this kind of data is only available to businesses which supply goods or services to named customers, such as providers of registered services like gas, water or electricity. Other businesses might be able to check their sales to some, but not all, customers.

CASE STUDY

Why are we losing customers?

At Your Leisure Ltd is a mail order firm selling sports and leisurewear throughout the UK. It is located in the north of England, and has been doing well since it was established 15 years ago.

The firm has a database of customers, which is updated regularly. All customers on the database are included in the mailing list and receive information about new lines and special offers.

During the last trading year, the management of At Your Leisure Ltd has noticed that a number of customers have not sent in any new orders and, in addition, new lines have not been selling well.

Jack Hawks, the Managing Director, was very concerned, and asked his Marketing Manager, Javeed Gupta, what was going wrong.

Javeed carried out some research and came back with several possibilities.

First of all, he referred to the CRN (customer reference number) of all customers, and found that 40 per cent of those who had not placed repeat orders were people living in areas of high unemployment. He concluded that prices charged by At Your Leisure were too high for many people.

Secondly, the lack of success of the new lines could be attributed to the firm's marketing strategy of appealing to the middle aged, middle income group. Very few younger people were shopping with At Your Leisure.

Javeed was of the opinion that more market research should be carried out before reaching a decision on what to do in the future.

'Internal information,' said Javeed, 'is very useful, but it does not answer all questions about marketing our products.'

Primary research

Primary research collects items of information (known as data) for a specific purpose. There are three ways of gathering primary data:

- survey
- observation
- testing.

Survey

Survey is the most widely used method of primary data collection. Most people are familiar with door-to-door interviewers who come armed with questionnaires about people's spending preferences. These are known as **personal interviews**.

Some big business organisations have enough resources to carry out primary research, but most hire the services of specialist market survey agencies. If you have ever participated in this type of survey, you will know that the subject might vary from the type of ketchup you like with your chips to the kind of holidays you like to take.

The questionnaires have to be carefully structured to include all the information needed by the client. This includes the age, sex and occupation of the respondents, as well as where they live. The data collected is divided into **qualitative** and **quantitative** data.

> **Qualitative** data gives opinions, while **quantitative** data gives facts.

Some people, when asked about their personal details by the interviewer, do not understand why they should answer these questions, and sometimes they might think that it is an invasion of their privacy. Interviewers are therefore trained to ask personal questions as tactfully as possible, and often the answers required do not have to be precise. For instance, a person might not want to tell the researcher exactly how old he or she is, or to give his or her exact address. Few would object, however, to stating that they live in a particular area of a city, or that they belong to a particular age group, perhaps 25–40 or 41–54. Getting the questions right is most important.

Imagine that you have been asked to find out the kind of food that people like to eat. If you put the question to a large group of people, without first establishing how old they are, and where they live, the results would not show whether older people tend to like different types of food from those preferred by teenagers. Tastes in different parts of the country also tend to differ, so the preferences of people from Scotland might not be the same as those of Londoners.

Personal interviewing is a very good way of collecting data, but it needs careful preparation and planning, as well as supervision of interviewers, which makes it expensive. It is also important to choose a suitable **sample** of people to be interviewed.

Figure 3.2.1

> MARKET RESEARCH
> COMPANY
>
> Requires articulate and well spoken interviewers for Day, Evening or Weekend work - hours are flexible and rates of pay are excellent, paid weekly. Call now for an **immediate start** if you speak
>
> **English, Dutch, German, Italian, Flemish, Swedish, Danish, Finnish, Spanish or any Eastern European language.**
>
> Call Natalie on 0208 962 6201 between 10AM and 4PM - students welcome!

Sampling – asking relevant questions of a selected group of people.

Sampling

There are several types of samples, used in different situations. The reason why samples must be used when collecting information is that asking everyone in the population would not only be expensive, but take a very long time so that, by the time the results have been analysed, they would have become out of date.

In statistical terms, the total number of possible interviewees is known as the 'universe' or, more commonly, the 'population'. When planning interviews for primary research purposes, the first step is to decide how many out of the 'universe' need to be interviewed. These are known as the 'sampling frame'. Those who are actually interviewed are called the 'sample'.

It is most important to try and select the sample in such a way that it reflects the 'universe' and the 'sampling frame'.

A **population census** is an example of research which does not use sampling, but gathers information from every member of the population. This type of research is very expensive and very time consuming in terms of planning, preparation, execution and analysis. This is why population censuses are carried out only once every 10 years.

At the other end of the survey scale there are industrial producers who can identify, and research, all their existing and potential customers. Manufacturers of ocean-going liners and commercial aircraft fall into this category. Most businesses, however, must use only one of the sampling techniques and it is very important to choose the correct one.

Random sampling

When using this method, it is necessary to ensure that everyone has an equal chance of being included. This term is often used incorrectly for groups selected from a particular section of population, such as teachers or doctors, or people chosen from a telephone directory. A random sample must be chosen very precisely, and the researchers have to be given clear instructions on whom they can include when interviewing. The **electoral roll** can be used for this purpose, with the starting point decided at random (hence the name).

Quota sampling

In this method, the interviewer decides whom to interview in accordance with detailed instructions, such as:

- how many
- age
- sex
- occupation
- location of interview.

Strata sampling

This method is used in research which must include more responses from some levels, or strata, than from another. For example, a survey of traffic flow in a geographical area might stipulate that more urban dwellers than rural should be included.

Multi-stage sampling

In multi-stage sampling, costs are kept down by selecting different samples from the large to the small, instead of trying to select small units scattered over a large area. A random sample within a county is followed by a random sample in one of the towns, then by a sample in one area of the town, finally finishing with a number of households in that area.

Random sampling and quota sampling are the two most commonly used techniques.

Telephone interviews

The second type of primary research is through **telephone interviews**. It is easy to reach a large number of people on the telephone, but often those contacted refuse to answer any questions. There are several reasons for people's unwillingness to answer questions on the telephone. Often the researcher interrupts someone who is doing something important or watching television or even having a rest. A telephone conversation is much more impersonal than a face-to-face interview, and many people are unwilling even to listen to the reasons why they have been called. Even when somebody does agree to answer questions, a telephone interview is normally quite short and does not allow the interviewee to relax and answer fully.

Telephone interviews do have one advantage, however, in that many people can be reached within a short time, and the cost is considerably less than that of personal interviews in the street or at home.

Postal questionnaires

Postal questionnaires are another method of gathering information. They are cheap but not very efficient as the response rate is low and often many returned questionnaires are not properly completed, making them worthless.

Qualitative primary research also includes **panel discussions** and **focus groups**.

Panels are groups of people brought together to answer questions about a product or service, over a period of time. The idea behind panel discussions is that the same person's views often change and can, therefore, reflect new trends in economic status and fashions. The difficulty lies in keeping panel members together and interested enough to wish to participate.

Focus groups are groups of selected customers, and would-be customers, brought together to discuss their own feelings and attitudes towards a product or a service, or even a political party's policies. A focus group must be led by a trained and skilled market researcher who will ensure that the discussion does focus on the central question. Focus groups are very costly to organise and run.

Observation is a method of collecting information by looking at what people do, rather than asking them why they do it. A well established example of marketing use of conclusions reached by this method is the way in which large supermarkets lay out their merchandise. Everyday items are most often located towards the back of the store, with luxury goods and new lines being promoted on display near the entrance. This is done as a result of observing that shoppers are more likely to look at new products, or more expensive ones, if they have to pass them on the way to goods which they have come to buy as a matter of course.

New technology, in the form of EPOS (electronic point of sale), now allows stores to monitor how many items of each brand have been sold.

Experiment

Research by this method is a way of trying out new or improved goods by allowing customers to make their own choices, rather than by asking them what they think they are likely to buy in the future.

Such experiments are usually carried out in several closely monitored locations, and the results of the experiment are noted and analysed.

CASE STUDY

An unhappy customer

Mrs Talbot is a housewife with a husband and three children to look after. She usually shops for food and household goods once a week, at the local supermarket, and if she needs any additional items such as fresh bread, she goes to her corner shop.

Several times over the last couple of months Mrs Talbot returned from her weekly shopping trip very disgruntled.

'I don't know what they are up to,' she confided in her neighbour, Mrs Black. 'I've been shopping at this place for at least 10 years, and I was quite happy with what they had and where it was. Now, twice, I was stopped by a lady with a clipboard and a long list of questions that wasted my time, asking me silly things like "What kind of detergent do you buy?" And "Why?" and "How do you think the layout of the store could be improved to be more convenient and customer friendly?" What's the point of asking me that? I was quite happy with things as they were but yesterday I went in as usual and found that the sugar is where the jams used to be and I couldn't find pudding rice anywhere. A complete waste of time, if you ask me. I'm sure they will lose a lot of loyal customers like me if they go on this way, especially as they have now withdrawn some products which I like and replaced them with new ones!'

EXCUSE ME MADAM! COULD YOU SPARE AN HOUR OR TWO?

Stages of primary research

All the methods of primary research outlined above can be used by businesses to try and establish the potential market for new or improved products. The bigger the business, the more it can invest in research. This does not mean that the cost of research projects is not important to big organisations. Before embarking on such a project, several important decisions must be made, always bearing in mind two objectives:

- The financial return on the project must be greater than its cost.

- Responses to questionnaires etc. will only be as good as the questions asked.

The decisions to be taken are:

- What information is needed?

- Where is it going to be obtained and by which method?

- How important is the information to the future of the company?

- How much is to be spent on the research?

- When is the deadline for the results?

- Which 'market' is to be researched?

- What sampling technique should be used?

When the above questions are answered, preparations for the research can then be made. If using the survey technique, the next step is to create the questionnaire.

How to draft a questionnaire

A questionnaire must be:

- worded precisely

- easy to understand

- concise.

It should contain questions which will ensure that the answers will provide the specific data needed by the business.

It must record general details of the respondent and, if necessary, specific details relevant to the research.

Three types of question are used in a questionnaire:

1 **Yes/no questions** (known as **dichotomous**). These are easy to answer and to record by ticking the relevant box. A 'don't know' box is usually included.

2 **Open-ended questions**. The respondent is asked to give his/her own answer, which must be written down. These questions take more time to record.

3 **Multi-choice questions** allow the interviewee to choose one answer from a list of possible responses. Easy to ask, and to record, the disadvantage of the multi-choice question is that none of the listed answers might suit what the person interviewed wants to say.

There are also several rules on how questions should be phrased. These include:

1 The questions should be short and precise.

2 They should not be 'leading' questions. A leading question is one which suggests a particular answer, e.g.: 'You do like watching television, don't you?'

3 They should not be ambiguous – in other words, they should never have a possible double meaning.

4 Complicated questions should come towards the end of the interview when, hopefully, the respondent has become interested and is more willing to answer in depth.

5 Finally, questionnaires should not be too long.

Example of a questionnaire

Flyaway Ltd, a travel agency, decided to send the following questionnaire to all customers who had booked one of its holidays during the last 12 months. Flyaway Ltd wants to establish whether its customers were happy with the service, how they compared Flyaway with other travel agencies, and if there were areas in which improvements could be made.

Figure 3.2.2

Questionnaire

Flyaway Ltd.

It is our policy to provide all our customers with the best service possible. In order to achieve this, we need to know what you think about Flyaway Ltd. We should be grateful if you would kindly fill in this questionnaire and return it to us, and we assure you that all responses will be carefully considered.

Please let us have some details about yourself. Tick the appropriate box.

Sex: Female ☐   Male ☐

Age: under 25 ☐   25-35 ☐   36-45 ☐   46-55 ☐   56-65 ☐

over 65 ☐

1 How often do you use the services of a travel agency?

several times a year ☐
once a year ☐
occasionally ☐

2 What do you use a travel agency for?

business travel ☐
leisure travel ☐
both ☐

3 Do you use the services of other travel agencies?

yes ☐   no ☐

4 How many times have you used Flyaway Ltd.?

1 ☐   2-5 ☐   5+ ☐

5 On a scale of 0 to 10, how would you rate the following aspects of the service provided by Flyaway Ltd.?

a) efficiency and reliability ...
b) advice given   ...
c) information provided   ...
d) quality of accommodation ...
e) quality of package tours ...
f) courtesy of staff   ...
g) dealing with complaints ...

6 How would you rate the service provided by Flyaway Ltd. compared to that of other travel agencies?

better ☐   similar ☐   worse ☐

Please give details.

7 Do you intend to use Flyaway Ltd. again?

yes ☐   no ☐   maybe ☐

8 In your opinion, how can Flyaway Ltd. improve its services to customers?

Thank you very much for taking the time to answer our questionnaire.

CASE STUDY

Word of mouth is not enough

Rebus Ltd is a medium sized company manufacturing jigsaw puzzles for children and adults. The company was established in 1975 and is doing quite well. Recently, the Managing Director, Stan Newall, discovered that the quality of the puzzles could be improved, giving them a longer life, by using a new process that protects the surface of the puzzle. The process, however, is expensive, and prices would have to increase. Stan wants to know if people would be prepared to pay higher prices for better quality goods. He also wants to find out what people think about existing Rebus Ltd products compared to others, and whether they would welcome other designs. While people's views are being sought, it would also be useful, Stan thinks, to establish if enough people would buy other toys if Rebus Ltd decided to diversify.

The firm has not previously conducted any market research, relying on word of mouth, goodwill and a few advertisements. There is no marketing department at Rebus Ltd, so Stan decides to call in a specialist agency.

Analysing the results

When all the questionnaires have been collected, they must be carefully processed. This is a skilled job which needs to be undertaken by an experienced person who will read each questionnaire and reject those which are obviously not to be included. There might be some in which too many questions have remained unanswered or where the respondent was obviously not serious in his or her replies.

These days, the remaining questionnaires are normally analysed by computer, and there is a wide range of computer software for this purpose. The results are then presented in tabular form to the management of the business organisation which has commissioned the survey.

Some managers will need specialist help in order to understand clearly the significance of the results, particularly if they are not familiar with this kind of data.

Example

The table below shows the results of a survey carried out in a further education college. Sixty students were asked whether, in their opinion, work experience was a useful part of their course. This is what they said:

Was the work experience useful?	Number of students
Very useful	18
Useful in part	26
Not useful at all	16

While the table does give some information, the answers are not precise enough to be of much use to the staff who organise the students' work experience. There are several ways in which the data could be improved.

1 by providing the answers in the form of percentages.

Was the work experience useful?	% of students
Very useful	30
Useful in part	43
Not useful at all	27

Even more precise information would have been gathered if the student respondents to the survey had been divided into males and females, and the answers of the two groups tabulated separately.

The following results show clearly that the female students found their work experience much more useful than their male counterparts. Since a very large percentage of the male students thought the work

Was the work experience useful?	% of female students	% of male students
Very useful	34	7
Useful in part	40	30
Not useful at all	26	63

experience to have been a waste of time, those responsible would now have to analyse carefully the reasons for the male students' dissatisfaction.

Secondary research

The other method of gathering marketing data is secondary research, sometimes called desk research. As this name implies, secondary research means looking at various existing sources of data to find information that will be useful in marketing the products of the business.

There are many suitable sources of data and analysing them should be easier and cheaper than doing primary research from scratch. However, there are also disadvantages to this technique. Sometimes good

sources of the information required are difficult or even impossible to find. Great care must be taken to ensure that the figures are not only sound, but also up to date – this is why a large proportion of the data gathered in a population census is often of no use to business organisations, because the results are not published quickly enough.

Many statistics released by government offices contain valuable secondary data. Other sources are published by organisations as diverse as the UNO, Times Newspapers Ltd, and various financial institutions. As with primary research, secondary research is only worth doing if the findings are precisely recorded and analysed, so that helpful conclusions can be drawn.

Socio-economic groups

For the purposes of market research, people are often divided into easily identifiable groups. Today, such division into classes has become unacceptable to many, but market researchers still divide the population into groups based on occupation and earning levels because people's tastes and spending power are closely linked to their income and what they do for a living. The National

Readership Survey publishes such a breakdown into what are called **socio-economic groups**. (It is still widely used.)

Socio-economic groups

A – higher managerial, administrative or professional

B – intermediate managerial, administrative or professional

C1 – supervisory, clerical, junior administrative or professional

C2 – skilled manual workers

D – semi-skilled and unskilled manual workers

E – state pensioners, casual and lowest grade earners, the unemployed

---

- **A** – in this group we can include those who hold high executive positions in business – Sir Richard Branson is a good example – and others who have reached the top, or nearly the top, of their chosen professions. They would include the Chairman of Marks & Spencer and the Director General of the BBC, as well as university professors and well established medical consultants.

- **B** – this group includes managers of middle size companies, college and high school principals, solicitors, accountants and other professionals.

- **C1** – here you will find office managers, personal assistants and many first line managers and supervisors.

- **C2** – carpenters and joiners, qualified motor fitters and skilled bricklayers belong in this category.

- **D** – building site labourers, farm labourers, refuse collectors and a number of others are classified as belonging to this group.

- **E** – in addition to pensioners and the unemployed, in this category we find casual staff working in shops and stores and in catering establishments.

Members of socio-economic groups tend to share similar attitudes to such aspects of life as education, jobs and pay and expectations. As a generalisation, those belonging to the A and B groups are likely to read *The Times* or *The Guardian*, while members of C2 and D have been found to prefer tabloids such as *The Sun* or the *Mirror*. The same principle is applied to television channels – BBC is said to cater for the higher managerial and managerial groups, while the rest are more likely to switch to ITV. We must remember that this is only a generalisation and that many people enjoy reading or watching a variety of programmes.

Market segmentation

Some products are bought by almost everyone. These are often staples, like potatoes, bread, rice and pasta. Growers and processors of such products can be sure that they will be sold. This is not the case with most other products, however, particularly when there is a wide choice.

The poor peasants in the Middle Ages all wore very similar clothes, and had no problems in deciding what to select to wear as there were no shops offering a great variety of items, nor any money for such purchases. Today, even when going to buy such everyday things as shoes, we are faced with dozens of different materials, colours and styles in every shop. We can say, however, that different people are likely to choose different footwear. The businesswoman is likely to buy formal shoes to wear to work, while young people tend to go for new fashions, such as platform soles and branded trainers. The first decision that the manufacturer must make is whom to target as buyers for a particular good or range of goods.

To help in this process, the market has been divided into parts, called segments, each of which has its own characteristics. The manufacturer or provider of a service must decide whether to concentrate on a small, distinct group of people, or maybe two or three such groups. Market segmentation is the process of selecting the segments and then ensuring that the goods or services offered will meet the requirements of that group or groups. A large organisation often aims to satisfy the needs of several groups, tailoring its products to different tastes and price levels.

An example of market segmentation is the Saga organisation, which specialises in providing a number of services, from car and home insurance to holidays, for the over-fifties.

In recent years, several exclusive designer houses have targeted another segment of the fashion-buying public by introducing a cheaper, ready to wear label which still carries the famous name but is accessible to people in the middle range income groups.

CASE STUDY

Segmentation, targeting and positioning

RAC

In 1995 it was reported that the RAC's market share in the consumer breakdown service market had been squeezed between the market leader, AA, and an aggressive budget challenger, Green Flag. The marketers at RAC knew that they needed a determined effort to keep the company's existing customers as well as to attract new ones. In fact, RAC research showed that only 80 per cent of its members renewed their annual subscriptions for breakdown cover. To counter this trend, RAC commissioned a marketing agency, Lowe Direct, with the task of increasing the number of people renewing membership, the overall aim being to yield a large increase in profitability.

The STP strategy

The agency realised that it needed to revisit RAC's current database and segment it more carefully. This was to increase the organisation's awareness of customer needs and to enable it to communicate more effectively via direct marketing. The RAC used statistical software to identify those people less likely to renew their membership – these were the target segments.

The agency then considered the RAC's current market position and identified that the emphasis had been based on the car, i.e. vehicle-based membership. After further research, the RAC implemented a repositioning strategy which was more customer focused. The objective was to ensure mobility for its members in both their own and any other car in which they were travelling.

The RAC then launched a campaign to communicate with all its customers on a more individual basis. A renewal pack reflecting the new positioning was designed. Covering letters were tailored to the length of the customers' membership, how they joined, and how their breakdowns had been solved.

The result

The target of 86 per cent for the year 2000 had already been achieved in 1997, indicating the steady improvement during the three-year period since the repositioning campaign had been launched. Segmentation, targeting and positioning clearly worked for the RAC.

Source: Business Review, Feb. 1999

There are several different market segments.

- **Geographic** – if the producer knows that there is high demand for a product in a country, or a region of a country, he can concentrate on marketing the product in that particular geographical location.

- **Demographic** – by age or sex. As we have noted already, the tastes of young people differ from those of their parents and grandparents, and women tend to want different things from men. Car manufacturers like Fiat and Volkswagen have recently begun to target young women by screening a series of television advertisements not only showing young women drivers, but ascribing to the car qualities which would appeal to young females. People carriers, on the other hand, use scenarios showing the advantages of their roomy, safe vehicles for the whole family.

- **Ethnic group** – in a multicultural society like the UK, different ethnic groups often have different tastes in food, drink and cosmetics. One advantage of ethnic group segmentation is that the segment is easy to identify.

- **Psychological** – brand loyalty often means that people choose a particular product like perfume, cigarettes or beer. The image created by advertising, packaging and promoting the brand creates a response in a distinct segment of the population.

Once the decision of which segment to target has been made, the marketing of the product can begin in earnest. In order to make this decision, particularly when the business intends to launch a new product, market research is required.

Revision Questions

1 What is market research? (1 mark)

2 Why do business organisations use market research? (2 marks)

3 What is internal data, and why is it not available to all businesses? (3 marks)

4 What is a survey? (1 mark)

5 What is meant by 'sampling'? (1 mark)

6 Which two sampling methods are the most widely used? Explain briefly how each of them operates. (5 marks)

7 Name two sources of secondary research. (1 mark)

8 What are the most important characteristics of a good questionnaire? (3 marks)

9 What are 'leading' questions, and why should they not be used in a questionnaire? (3 marks)

10 Why should the results of a survey questionnaire be analysed by an experienced person? (1 mark)

11 Explain what is meant by 'socio-economic' groups. Why do many people object to categorising the population in this way? (3 marks)

12 Read carefully the list of people given below, and place each one in the correct socio-economic group:

i) Stan Newall, MD of Rebus Ltd

ii) your local postman

iii) the head teacher of a small primary school

iv) a telephone engineer

v) a part-time market researcher

vi) a high court judge

vii) an office junior

viii) a window cleaner

ix) a retired office worker

x) the owner of a small estate agency

xi) the Chairman of Tesco

xii) a middle manager in a manufacturing company. (12 marks)

13 Why is it necessary to divide potential buyers into segments? (3 marks)

14 Explain what is meant by the 'demographic' market segment. (2 marks)

15 Several large supermarket chains advertise their products on television, among them Asda, Sainsbury's and Safeway. Analyse the commercials of these three stores, and then answer the following questions:

i) Which market segment is each of the advertisements aimed at?

ii) Are the segments in each case the same, or different?
(Give reasons for your answer.)

iii) If the target segments are different, how is this shown in the commercials?

iv) What methods are used by each of the chains to reach their target segment? (12 marks)

In this chapter you will learn about the first two Ps of the marketing mix, **product** and **price**, and about the techniques that can be used so that the right choice of both is made.

Introduction

You now know the definition of marketing, and have learnt how, through research, a business is able to identify, and anticipate customer requirements.

CASE STUDY

Price must be right

A small Chinese restaurant, situated in a busy suburban parade, found its business dwindling because of competition from two other restaurants, one Indian and one Portuguese, both open during the same hours, and both offering mid-range food.

A survey of existing and potential customers (all local) showed that most were interested in a cheaper, self-service eating place, with longer opening hours and shorter waiting time, particularly at lunch time.

The owners also realised that many of the customers were bored with the restaurant's menu, which was never changed, unlike those in some of the other local eateries.

Mr Liu and Mr Chang came to the conclusion that if they were to stay in business, they would have to make some changes.

'Our prices are too high,' said Mr Liu.

'I don't know how the others can charge less and still make a profit,' said Mr Chang.

'We should change the menu, maybe once a month. Perhaps add some new dishes ...,' said Mr Liu.

'Some people think that the quality of our food could be improved,' added Mr Chang sadly.

'Perhaps it could be, but is it worth it with so many competitors in the same parade?' wondered Mr Liu.

Yen Liu, Mr Liu's nephew, a student of Business at a local college, had been listening to the conversation, and now felt that he had to speak.

'Of course, it's worth trying,' he said. 'We have just learned about this sort of problem at college. You should review a part of your marketing mix.'

'What's that?' asked Mr Liu suspiciously.

'Quite simple, really,' said Yen. 'You must look carefully at your product – that's the food you serve – and decide whether it can be changed or improved. However good the product, the price must also be right, so you will have to try and fix prices at a level that will not frighten your customers away.'

Mr Liu and Mr Chang became quite interested in what Yen was saying, and decided to try and follow his advice.

Marketing mix

In order to succeed in marketing a product, four conditions have to be met. These four are called the **marketing mix**, or the '4 Ps' for short. Look at the grid below:

PRODUCT	PRICE
PLACE	PROMOTION

Product – good or service sold by a business in order to make a profit.

A marketing strategy, or long-term plan, is based on these four key elements. If any of the four are wrong, the strategy is bound to fail. In this chapter we shall look closely at the first two: product and price.

Product

A product which does not satisfy customers will not succeed however much money is spent on promoting and advertising it. Have you ever bought anything because you thought you would like it, and then found it was not as good as you had been led to believe?

If that happened to you, would you buy the product again? It is quite certain that you would not, and the same goes for all other buyers. Here are some examples:

- an expensive jacket which comes unstitched after it is worn a few times
- a vacuum cleaner, advertised as silent and very efficient but in reality noisy and not powerful enough to lift the dust and dog hairs
- fish and chips from a new shop, tasting of nothing at all.

Activity

Working with a friend, conduct an informal survey among your friends and family members. Ask 20 people about their experiences of buying something which proved not to be as good as they expected.

You should:

1 find out why they bought the product in the first place

2 ask why they did not like it

3 find out if they would buy it again.

Present your findings in the form of a simple table.

Getting the product right is therefore of the greatest importance. It must be remembered, however, that in some circumstances people might not choose the best product, particularly if it is expensive and they can only afford a cheaper version. This is particularly true in times of recession and in less affluent areas of high unemployment. The rise in recent years of charity shops and cut-price stores illustrates this point – but even here people will buy at the most affordable charity shop or cut-price outlet.

The function of the marketing department is to liaise with production in order to ensure that the product is what the customers want.

This applies to both existing products and to new products which the company intends to introduce. The decision as to what to produce, for whom, where and at which price forms the basis of a company's product strategy, and must take into account the resources that the organisation can afford to invest in its products, the changing environment and competition.

Four main product marketing strategies can be used by a business organisation which wants to increase its business volume.

1 **Market penetration** – the business wants to increase its sales of existing products. It does not intend to look for new markets, or to change or extend its product range, so it must rely on more promotion and advertising.

2 **Market development** – here the company intends to sell its existing range of products in new markets, perhaps in a different geographical area or to a different customer group.

3 **Product development** – new products are to be offered in existing markets.

4 **Diversification** – new products are to be offered in new markets.

Diversification – the introduction of a range of new products into a company's product portfolio.

Whichever of these method is to be used, it must be remembered that customer requirements are changing all the time because a number of factors, and decisions made about products today may well prove to be out of date in a year's time. There are many reasons why customer requirements do not remain static. As global, national and local circumstances change, so does people's demand for goods and services.

- **Changes in income and expectations** – today in the UK we expect a certain standard of living. Many items which either did not exist, or were considered to be luxuries, out of reach of ordinary people, 50, 40 or 20 years ago are, today, to be found in most homes. These include TV sets, refrigerators, freezers, the telephone and, increasingly, the personal computer.

- **Changes in social habits and customs** – in the last half century the social structure of the UK has undergone great changes. The influx of people from other parts of the world, such as the Indian sub-continent, and more frequent travel abroad have changed traditional British attitudes towards food and drink. People have become much less rigid and traditional and are happier to accept new styles of clothing, new food and different ways of behaviour.

Great British traditions, such as the cooked breakfast and the roast Sunday lunch at which the whole family always sat down together, have been largely replaced by a continental-style light breakfast and ready made meals which can be popped in the microwave and eaten in front of the television set. These changes have brought about corresponding changes in demand.

Another factor affecting product changes in order to meet customer requirements is fashion. In the past, fashions were much more static, and were taken up only by the well to do. Today, everyone has access to information as to what is available in clothing, home decoration and so on, and manufacturers respond to what people want to buy.

Technological advances have brought to the market gadgets and devices that were not only non-existent 50 years ago, but which are continually changed and improved, thereby creating constant new demand. Black and white television sets, once the most amazing examples of technological progress, are now obsolete. People are no longer satisfied with their old colour sets, hence the demand for digital television and as many viewing channels as they can get.

IT EVEN DOES THE HOUSEWORK, YOU KNOW

CASE STUDY

Bernard Matthews

Creating a market

In 1950, Bernard Matthews bought 20 turkey eggs and an old incubator – a total investment of £2.50. Today, Bernard Matthews plc is a multinational company with a turnover in excess of £400m, employing over 6,000 people worldwide.

Although the company was a market leader in the frozen turkey and other poultry products, its position increasingly came under threat from competition during the early 1990s. In 1992 Bernard Matthews plc's turnover dipped after a period of steady growth. Further examination of the data might suggest that the mature stage of the product life cycle had been reached and that some sort of extension strategy was needed. Faced with such a situation, a firm can adopt a number of strategies. Firstly, it has to decide whether to persevere in the same market or to try to enter a new one; developing a new product or staying with the existing one.

Bernard Matthews plc decided to consolidate within its present market and develop its product portfolio, specifically prepacked sliced meats. It was hoped that this strategy of product development would spread the product base and provide a more secure business. The capital investment required would be substantial, the market was already dominated by supermarkets' own label products and there were very few poultry products available.

Product development

The company already had a number of strengths on which to build, i.e. a strong brand identity and an easily recognisable brand name and it was hoped that consumer loyalty would remain strong.

The company is unusual in that it is one of the **fully vertically integrated** firms in the UK, controlling all the production processes from the breeding and rearing to the end product.

Initial market research was not hopeful. Mintel, the independent market research agency, investigated the sliced meats market in 1989 and decided that it was stagnant. However, it did highlight the importance that the consumers in the market placed on quality. This was seized upon by Bernard Matthews plc.

It was discovered that customers were specifically looking for:

- good visual appearance
- quality (with a higher price taken to indicate higher quality)
- packaging (the more the meat is visible, the better the product is perceived to be).

Total quality management was introduced to ensure the highest quality at every stage of production. Highly automated systems were used to produce the highest possible specifications. One of the results was a shelf life of 21 days, a significant increase on that of some competitors.

Three new factories were opened, two in Norfolk and one in Hungary, at a total capital cost of £20.5m. This was a considerable risk, but it has been proved to have been worth taking.

At the same time, and probably due to some health scares, the demand for prepacked, as opposed to loose cooked meats, increased considerably, making it easier for Bernard Matthews plc to achieve its objectives.

Since 1992, when ham dominated the market, other cooked meats have gained in popularity, and wafer thin sliced cooked meats have been introduced. The market has been growing steadily and the company has come to dominate it. In 1997 Bernard Matthews plc produced 49 per cent of all sliced cooked poultry sales, with its nearest rival, a supermarket own brand, providing just 13 per cent.

Conclusion

Profit in business is often considered to be a reward for taking a risk. Sometimes firms take risks even when the initial prospects do not look encouraging – they believe strongly in their product and the firm's strengths and capabilities. The Bernard Matthews experience emphasises the value of a strong brand when used prudently. The brand name enabled Bernard Matthews plc to 'umbrella' product category development and develop its portfolio profitably.

Source: Times 100

> **Life cycle** – the period of existence from the beginning (birth), through growth and maturity to the end (death).

Product life cycle

Because of the dynamic nature of the market for products, it is now accepted that new ones appear and replace old ones. Each product is said to have a limited life which goes through a number of changes during its existence. As with human life, the life expectancy of a product varies, but the concept of the product life cycle is of major importance to business organisations, and particularly to the marketing function.

The life cycle has five stages:

1 **Development**
   This stage includes market research, planning and designing the product, manufacturing and promotion and advertising. You will notice that during the development stage the curve does not rise steeply. This is due to the high costs incurred, and the slowness of sales when the product is first introduced.

Figure 3.3.1

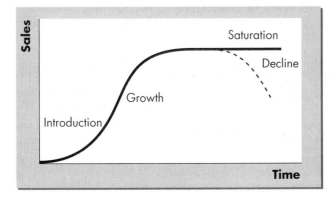

2 **Growth**
   If all goes well, volume of sales increases during this stage. The product becomes known, and more and more people buy it.

3 **Maturity**
   Initial demand is now satisfied. Competitors enter the market. There is a reduction in the increase of sales, and a corresponding drop in profits.

4 **Saturation**

> **Saturation** – 'filling to the brim' – in other words, there is no room for any more.

   In this situation, customers have as much of the product as they want. This leads to a decrease in sales, and in profits.

5 **Decline**
   When this stage is reached, sales drop sharply, and it becomes very difficult to make a reasonable profit.

The concept of the product life cycle is useful, but it must be remembered that, like many other concepts, it does not apply to all products, and even when it does the length of the various stages can vary greatly.

Because every product has a life cycle (in some cases, a very long one), businesses must realise that there is a danger in relying on one particular product. For this reason, companies are continually researching the market, watching consumer trends, and developing new products or improving existing ones.

CASE STUDY

Keep in touch: give a dog a phone

Dogs may soon be able to keep in touch with absent owners by mobile phones designed for animal use.

Japanese engineers are working on a system that allows a dog or cat to hear the reassuring sound of his or her owner's voice without pressing buttons. The system can also be used to keep track of a pet, sparing many an owner the anxiety of searching for a missing animal.

At least two rival Japanese companies are developing 'pet mobiles'. The reason is simple: NTT DoCoMo, the cellular phone offshoot of telecoms giant NTT, has seen the future, and it looks saturated – 43 million Japanese, one in three of the population, are already mobile phone subscribers. Only the US has more.

Competition for the new market share is ferocious. Operators reckon that at the present rate they will have signed up every non-infant Japanese, apart from a handful of eccentric holdouts, by the third year of the new millennium.

Phone operators are working on lightweight electronic devices that will fit on a collar. NTT DoCoMo will base its gadget on a low-cost system. Using it, a centre could report the position of a lost dog by faxing a map of its location to an owner.

NTT DoCoMo said there were some 'technical problems' to be ironed out.

Mineko Ikehashi, a banker, said: 'Most dogs recognise simple messages, such as *chotto matte ne* (just wait a little longer) or *mo sugu* (just a tick) and hearing the voice of their owner down a phone line would certainly break the monotony of being left alone.' She said she had often dreamt of a phone system that allowed her to comfort Mako, her mongrel bitch, when she expected to be late home.

The Times, 27 October 1999

CASE STUDY

Has washing clothes gone out of fashion?

Trevington is a small market town in the Midlands. It has a high street with a range of shops, a restaurant, a supermarket, a bank and several pubs. Many people from neighbouring towns and villages come to Trevington every Wednesday which is market day. After buying or selling at the market, they usually visit the shops, all of which are busy on Wednesday.

For many years, nothing much changed in Trevington but in 1990 a new agricultural college opened two miles out of town. The student intake came from all over the country and many of them looked for accommodation in the town. The businesses in Trevington were very happy with this turn of events.

John Smiles, a Trevington resident, was particularly pleased. He had been thinking about a new business venture, and decided to open a launderette in the high street. He spoke to his bank manager, talked to a number of the newcomers and came to the conclusion that the agricultural students lodging in the town would welcome such a facility, especially as there was no other launderette in Trevington.

John's launderette opened in early 1992. To begin with, business was slow but it built up gradually. The launderette was efficient, the prices reasonable, and John provided a service wash for those who did not have the time to stay and do their own. After two years, another launderette opened a few hundred yards down the high street, and both did well until a year or so ago.

For reasons which John finds difficult to understand, business has become very slow. Some regular customers remain, but others have stopped coming. Although he is still making a living, John's profits have become much less and, instead of thinking of expansion, as he had been, he is now worried about the future of his business.

Activity

1   Some everyday products have been around a long time, like Heinz baked beans, or Marmite. Others appear and disappear within a short period of time. Try to find 10 food products which have been on the market for at least 10 years. Why are they still in demand? Ask someone who shops for food regularly for his or her opinion.

2   In 1999, Heinz announced that it would no longer produce its traditional salad cream. The reasons for this decision were a much lower demand, and the popularity of new, more exotic salad dressings, such as mayonnaise and olive oil.

Shortly afterwards, newspapers reported an outcry from customers, many of whom protested against Heinz's decision, and demanded that it should continue to sell its salad cream.

How should Heinz react to this protest? What should its marketing department do?

In an ideal market situation, a company should stagger the introduction of new products so that it has only one in the costly development stage, or nearing the end of its cycle, at any one time. A manufacturer of a whole range or 'portfolio' of products must continually review all its products, and decide which ones to keep, which to improve and which, perhaps, to discontinue. This process is illustrated by the Boston Matrix, which allows products to be divided into four distinct groups.

STAR	CASH COW
PROBLEM CHILD	DOG

MILKING THE CASH COW

1 Star – this category of products has a large share of a growth market and brings in high profits for the company.

2 Problem child – these products are not generating expected profits, but could turn into stars with more investment and better marketing.

3 Cash cow – well established products. Profits made by cash cows enable the organisation to support the problem children, and help the stars to become well established.

4 Dog – products which are failing, for any reason, and which might well have to be discontinued.

The principles of product life cycle apply not only to consumer goods but also to industrial goods and to all kinds of goods, from consumer durables to industrial durables.

Price

Price – the amount of money for which a good or service is bought or sold.

The above definition of price is quite correct, but does not take into account the different meaning of price to the seller and to the buyer. The seller is interested in the proportion of price that is his profit; the buyer wants to know the cost of buying a product.

You will know that the laws of supply and demand state that when price rises, demand falls, and vice versa. It is also true, however, that quite often the reverse is true. The so-called 'luxury' goods often sell more when the price is raised because customers are convinced that the higher price more exactly reflects high quality.

There are also cases of products being priced too low, leading buyers to think that their quality must be suspect. At the beginning of the 'price war' between supermarkets, several of them introduced a very cheap, white sliced loaf. The price of this bread was between 17p and 21p, as compared to other white sliced loaves selling for between 49p and about 75p. The result should have been a drastic drop in demand for the more expensive bread, as the ingredients of the cheap loaf were the same. This did not happen, and customers continued buying the dearer loaves, believing that good quality bread could not possibly be sold at 17p!

It is very important, therefore, to ensure that the pricing of products is right. It should:

- include an acceptable profit margin
- not be positioned too low
- not be too high (if it is, customers will look for substitutes).

Pricing strategies

When deciding how to price its products, a company must first decide on a pricing strategy. The founder of Tesco stores, Sir Jack Cohen, had a very simple one: 'Pile'em high, and sell'em cheap.' In other words, he realised that a low profit margin can turn into large profits provided that the volume of sales is large enough.

Today pricing strategies are much more complex, but are still based on the first objective of any business, which is to maximise profits. There are also other objectives which might have to be met, such as:

- achieving targets set for returns on investment
- maintaining or improving share of the market
- matching competition
- undercutting competition.

When deciding on a pricing policy, companies must also take into consideration several other factors.

1 **Product-related** – when dealing with a new product, choice must be made between skimming and penetration techniques (see below). A product of high quality, with a glamorous image, can be priced higher than a similar product which is new to the market.

2 **Promotion-related** – if little is spent in promoting a basic product, the price is likely to be low.

3 **Distribution-related** – if a product is to be sold through a large network of wholesalers and retailers, special offers and prices must be offered to them.

4 **Outside factors** – competition, costs of production, the situation in the economy and interest rates will all affect decisions on pricing strategies.

Several different pricing techniques can be adopted.

Skimming technique

This means setting the price rather high, and is often used for new products. There are several reasons for using this method, e.g. the need to recoup high investment very quickly. In the case of new products, no competitors are likely to engage in a price war. The skimming technique is a short-term one, and allows the price to be lowered later, which is likely to please the customers.

Its success depends on low elasticity of demand for the product – in other words, little risk of customers responding unfavourably to a price that is high.

Cost-plus pricing

Very many companies use this very simple technique. It involves adding a profit margin to the cost of a unit. It is much easier to do this than to try and set a price on the basis of information about such variables as future revenue. The mark-up is usually worked out as a percentage of the cost.

Cost-plus pricing is popular but it has a disadvantage. Organisations using it as the sole technique of pricing tend to look only at their own products, not at the customers' tastes and requirements, or their competitors' prices.

Penetration pricing

This pricing technique is used in situations where new products are introduced into an elastic market. When a quick return is required because of high development costs, the products are priced low to encourage buyers to try them. Once the buying public accepts the products, prices can be increased gradually. Penetration pricing is particularly suitable for products which are produced in large quantities and at low unit costs. Once the product has penetrated the market, sales should increase and, with the sales, so should the profits.

Competition based pricing

This technique is used when the product is very similar to other products and when competition is very strong. In the short term, price is set without regard to costs or profit margins, the objective being to keep in line with, or to undercut, the competitors. While this might achieve the aim of maintaining a share of the market, lowering prices in this way can be dangerous for the organisation.

Sometimes an organisation wishes to establish itself as 'better' than its competitors. It will then set its price higher than the competitors, in the hope that customers will believe that its product is superior because it costs more.

If there is little or no competition in the market, the producer can, in theory, set a price at any level. In reality, this cannot be done, as setting the price too high will lead to customers looking for substitute products.

In addition to the above, companies must also be aware of the difference between price and value. If price is the cost of a product to the customer, how can the producer provide that customer with greater value?

Guarantees, warranties, aftersales service and service contracts are all ways in which the customer is given additional value for the price he or she pays.

It is also useful to know that, in addition to the main pricing techniques, companies sometimes set prices for reasons specifically relevant to the market or the product itself.

1 **Essential product pricing** – in many cases, if the customer purchases one product, he or she must then buy other products as well. Quite often, the product itself might be priced low, but the accessories or ancillary products are the ones with a high mark-up. Many goods that we buy today need ancillary products, e.g. videotapes for use with a VCR, or software for a computer.

2 **Pricing according to the customer group** is a method of charging different prices to different groups. Cheap haircuts for pensioners and discounts for students are good examples of this.

CASE STUDY

Is the price right?

Ghazala and Omi are two friends who are about to set up their own business. Ghazala has completed a course in jewellery making and is confident that her original, modern designs will sell well to the young segment of the market. Omi, whose qualifications include Vocational A Level Business, is going to look after the accounts and the marketing.

Everything is set for the opening. Ghazala has prepared a range of rings, necklaces and earrings in silver, enamel and crystal. They have acquired suitable premises, a shop in the high street with workshop space in the rear. The equipment has been bought, and they have already taken on a shop assistant and two experienced production workers. All that remains to be done is to price the products and then print the publicity material. Unfortunately, Omi and Ghazala cannot agree.

'Let's price them high,' says Ghazala. 'These are beautiful objects, not just cheap trash. I'm sure people will look at them and buy, even if we make them expensive.'

'You're wrong,' says Omi. 'We can't yet compete with the well established jewellery lines that everyone knows. If we do what you suggest, we shall price ourselves out of the market. We should look carefully at the prices that others charge, and try to undercut them.'

Ghazala is not convinced. 'If we do that,' she says, 'we might not even make a profit at all!'

'I know you're a very good designer,' says Omi, 'but your knowledge of marketing is non-existent! I'm not suggesting prices so low that there'll be no profit. All I'm saying is this: we must work out our costs very precisely, decide on the profit margin we must add, and then work out how many items we will have to sell at those prices to break even. We might even find that it will be better to sell more items with a low profit margin than just a few with a huge mark-up.'

Unless their difference of opinion is resolved soon, the business may never get off the ground!

Revision Questions

1 How can a good product be defined?   (1 mark)

2 What is likely to be the result if the price of a product is set too high?   (1 mark)

3 List and explain the factors which cause demand for goods and services to change.   (6 marks)

4 What is meant by diversification, and why do businesses decide to diversify?   (4 marks)

5 Refer to the Bernard Matthews case study (page 209) and explain:

   i) how the company succeeded in developing a successful product

   ii) what 'vertical integration' is, and what the advantages are to a company such as Bernard Matthews of being vertically integrated

   iii) what risks were involved in the company's strategy.   (9 marks)

6 What is the likely effect on a company's sales of saturation point being reached?   (3 marks)

7 The 'cash cow' product group in the Boston Matrix is the safest source of income. Why do businesses with well established 'cash cows' often decide to introduce 'problem children' into their product portfolio?   (4 marks)

8 When offered similar products at different prices, customers do not always go for the cheapest. Explain why.   (2 marks)

9 What is the skimming pricing technique, and in what circumstances is it likely to be used?   (2 marks)

10 What are the advantages and the disadvantages of cost-plus pricing?   (3 marks)

11 In penetration pricing, the products are priced low. What is the aim of such pricing?   (2 marks)

12 Why are digital boxes being offered free to customers by digital television providers?   (3 marks)

13 How can a supplier add greater value to a product? Give two examples of added value that might tempt the customer to buy from a particular supplier.   (4 marks)

14 Many restaurants and pubs offer low price drinks during the so-called 'happy hour'. What is the reason for doing this?   (2 marks)

15 In the case study 'Is the price right?' (page 215) the two partners cannot agree on a pricing policy. Which one of them is right, in your opinion, and why?   (5 marks)

CHAPTER 4

Place and Promotion

KEY TERMS:

promotion

chain of distribution

factor

broker

place

brand

agent

In this chapter you will learn about the final two components of the marketing mix – **place** and **promotion**, which are external to the company.

Introduction

Once the product, or range of products, has been decided, the marketing department must decide on where to make it available, and how the public at large can be informed about it, and persuaded to buy it. These are very complex operations, as the choice both of place and of promotion techniques is wide. Making the right choices is necessary for the process to be successful, and can be achieved only if market research has been thoroughly carried out.

Place

Place – in the marketing mix, place means any location where goods can be bought and sold; such locations include shops, stores, markets and showrooms, as well as 'placing' the products through mail order, telephone sales and, nowadays, the internet.

The third of the four Ps of the marketing mix is of no less importance than the first two, but, together with promotion, it concerns activities outside the business organisation. If the decisions about the product and the pricing are correct, but the decisions where to sell the product are not, the marketing strategy will fail.

In simple terms, products must be made easily available to the customers, but the right 'place' for one product might not be suitable for another.

In the past, when local industry made goods and then sold them in neighbouring areas, the problem of finding the correct place did not arise. Modern companies often manufacture goods in one location and then sell them to customers scattered all around the country, and often also abroad.

Activity

Visit your local supermarket, and look at 20 products displayed on the shelves. Make a note of:

- place of origin
- name of manufacturer and the address.

Make a list of your findings, and answer the following questions:

1 How many of the products were made/grown locally?

2 How many were made/grown abroad?

3 If abroad, list the countries of origin.

You will probably find that many imported goods are also grown or manufactured in the UK; e.g. we import tomatoes from Holland and strawberries from France and the USA. Why do you think we bring in foreign goods which we can produce ourselves?

There still exist situations where the manufacturer must deal directly with the customer, but in the great majority of cases such direct contact is not necessary. If a girl who is getting married wants to have a dress made especially for her, she must be able to visit and talk directly to the dressmaker. On the other hand, if, like most brides-to-be, she wants to buy a ready made wedding dress, there is no need for her to meet the dressmaker. What she does need is to be able to see a wide selection of bridal wear without having to go very far from home.

Since, as we have said, most large manufacturers do not have to meet their customers personally, the problem that they must solve is how to get their product to the customer. The way of doing this is through the distribution chain. (See also p. 393.)

> **Chain of distribution** – all the business organisations involved in ensuring that products reach the consumer.

The chain of distribution, also sometimes called the channels of distribution, offers several choices or routes.

1 **manufacturer to customer** (as mentioned above, this route is used by a minority of organisations)

2 **manufacturer to wholesaler** or **trade supplier** (wholesalers sell the goods on, usually in conveniently smaller quantities, to retailers, while trade suppliers provide goods for business use)

3 **retailers** sell to the customer, having first bought the goods in bulk from the wholesalers. Retailers are the people who have direct contact with the customers, and often supply not just the goods but advice, aftersales service and sometimes servicing

4 **customers** or **industrial** and **commercial users** – these are the people for whom the goods were made, and the whole chain exists to ensure that they can obtain the goods with the minimum of trouble.

Although many goods go through various stages of distribution, quite often one or more stages are missed out. The direct route from manufacturer to customer has already been mentioned. Some manufacturers sell directly to the retailers. Such is the case with expensive Swiss watches, such as Omega, Longines or Rolex. There are two reasons for a manufacturer to take this route. First, it allows him to control the retailing outlet; secondly, in the case of expensive luxury goods there is no bulk buying and no need for large storage space, so this part of the wholesaler's service is not needed.

Function of the middleman

The middlemen are the businesses which link the manufacturer with the customer.

1   **The wholesaler** – buys goods from the manufacturer in bulk, and sells them on to the retailer. Wholesalers must have large storage facilities and be able to purchase large quantities of goods at any one time. An interesting development of the function of the wholesaler in recent years has been the introduction by some of them of selling directly to the public. The wholesalers who supply individual customers provide goods that are cheaper than in shops, but usually stipulate the minimum quantity that can be bought, e.g. 12 tins of baked beans. The Booker Group is an example of a wholesaler to the catering trade. Its main customers are owners of restaurants, shops and institutions such as schools and hospitals. Like other wholesalers, Booker does not provide aftersales service.

2   **Retailers** – the next, and final, link to the customer. Retailing outlets can be large stores, such as Harrods or Selfridges in London or Kendal's in Manchester, multiple outlets, such as Marks & Spencer or Dolcis Shoes, or small high street or corner shops. Retailers try to provide convenient and pleasant surroundings for shoppers, and also offer advice, and, in some cases, servicing and maintenance, particularly when selling electrical and electronic goods, cars and so on.

3   **Agents and brokers** – this link in the distribution chain differs from the others in that those involved help to arrange the transactions between the producer and the customer for a fee, but do not buy or sell on their own behalf.

Agent – someone who acts on behalf of another in business transactions.

Broker – an agent who buys products for someone else.

While very many manufacturers use independent businesses as links to their customers, today a number of large business organisations have their own channels of distribution. This, as you know, is called vertical integration, and allows the manufacturer to control the route from the factory to the buyer. Very frequently, we, as buyers, are not aware of this.

Different types of retailing outlets

There are several types of retailing outlets, each organised in a different way, although their function is basically the same.

- **Multiple stores** (or **chain stores**) have many outlets in different locations, selling the same range of goods, and under the strict control of the parent organisation. It has been said that, nowadays, wherever you go in the UK, all high streets look the same. While this is not strictly so, it is true that in most shopping centres we are likely to find a branch of BHS, Marks & Spencer, Woolworth's and perhaps The Sock Shop or Body Shop.

- **Department stores** are often defined as 'many shops' under one roof. Each department carries its own specialised range of goods. Sometimes floor space is rented out to independent retailers.

- **Supermarkets** and **hypermarkets** are self-service stores. Supermarkets have been with us for quite a long time. The definition of a supermarket is a store with a floor area of over 4000 square feet. Supermarkets offer a wide choice and lower prices than in a small shop because of the supermarket's ability to buy a wide range of goods in large quantities. The decline in small independent shops has largely been caused by the advent of supermarkets.

    The trend to one-stop large-scale stores has been further developed with the coming of hypermarkets which are stores with a floor area of over 25,000 square feet. Hypermarkets are so large that they have to be located out of town, and many people cannot get to them easily unless a good transport service is provided.

- **Franchises** – a franchise is an independent retailer (the franchisee) who distributes goods made by the franchiser. In return for the franchisee's investment, he receives assistance in marketing and promoting the business. Spud-U-Like, Wimpy, Kwik Print and Hertz are just some examples of successful franchise operations. This type of selling 'place' has advantages for the manufacturer as well as for the retailer.

CASE STUDY

Marketing on the internet

Marketing is an expensive business. But when all a company has to do to reach a global audience is to set up a website, it is not surprising that many have jumped at the chance of advertising on the Internet, writes Biz/ed on the Net's Catherine Sladen.

However, for students of GNVQ and Vocational A Level Business, this is not necessarily good news. Unfortunately for the student searching for quality marketing information, such as brand strategies or marketing approaches, offerings tend to be partisan and insubstantial. None the less, there are some sites that are worth visiting.

One of the best sites for students is the Marketing Council site. This organisation claims to exist 'to help British business increase wealth creation and competitiveness through marketing'. The site has plenty of background information, including an account of 'Marketing Redefined', and context details. More usefully, it has created a library section with case studies covering wellknown companies such as Sony, British Airways, Glaxo and GKN. These can be printed off for use in the classroom.

There are on-line versions of magazines on marketing and advertising. *Marketing Week* is a weekly, UK based magazine and its Internet version contains regularly updated reviews of company marketing sites. At the time of writing, these included: Levi Strauss, Virgin Radio, Pepsi, Disney and Abbey National.

There is the European Society for Opinion and Market Research (ESOMAR) site. The organisation's main objective is to advance the understanding and application of marketing research in Europe. The site contains some interesting documents, including the International Code of Marketing and Social Research Practice; guidelines on maintaining the distinctions between marketing research and direct marketing, and an Internet position paper on market research and the Internet.

Obtaining marketing information on specific companies is not as easy as it sounds. Of the dozen or so company web sites I looked at, none provided clear policy, An alternative strategy is to make use of Biz/ed's company facts section. Here, a range of companies provide details of their marketing strategies, covering branding strategies, product launches, changes in marketing approaches, marketing campaigns, customer profiles and sales strategies. Companies include: Amway, The Body Shop, BMW, BP and Unilever.

Source: Business Review, April 1998

Direct marketing

Many goods are sold by this method. It is extensively used by manufacturers of industrial products, who employ sales personnel to call on business buyers. Other manufacturers sell goods directly to the public by a variety of means:

- **door-to-door** – Avon cosmetics is perhaps the best example

- **selling to people at home** (organising parties in private homes, with the hostess receiving a gift or a discount) – this method was introduced by Tupperware, makers of plastic household containers

- **mail order selling** – mail order firms produce and distribute catalogues of their goods, which can be bought by filling in an order form. Many large mail order companies, such as Universal, sell a variety of goods, ranging from clothing to household goods to electrical and electronic appliances. They also offer the facility of buying on credit, and will readily exchange unsuitable goods. Some manufacturers of one type of merchandise, e.g. knitwear, also use this method. Buying by mail order is simple and is popular with people who might not be able to get to the shops easily because they live far away from towns or are unable to leave home for some reason. There is also the advantage for the customer of conducting the whole transaction by post, and being able to try the products at home. On the other hand, the inevitable delays caused by having to order and receive the goods through the post can be a disadvantage.

- **The internet** is now being increasingly used as a direct marketing method, and is likely to increase in volume.

Physical distribution

Whichever method of deciding on the 'place' is chosen, there remains the problem of making sure that the products reach the customer. In the case of direct selling through mail order, postal services are used. This is much simpler than getting products through the various links of the normal distribution chain.

Before products can be moved, they must be suitably packaged and stored in the company's warehouse, which must be large enough and suitable for the purpose.

If the goods are to be moved to the wholesaler or the retailer, it is necessary to decide how this is to be done. When transporting goods by road, some companies use their own fleet of vehicles, while others use the services of independent haulage companies. Rail can also be used, but the goods must be brought to the station and arrangements made for their collection at the destination point.

Exported goods can be sent by ship, ship and then train, or by air. Air transport is quickest but it is also the most expensive, and is unsuitable for very heavy goods. If the products to be transported are perishable, like many foods or flowers, air cargo is the preferable form of transport when selling abroad. When sent by road, this type of goods requires special vehicles, either refrigerated or kept at certain temperatures.

As there are so many places where a company can sell its products, the choice can sometimes be very difficult, and requires the marketing department to formulate a very careful strategy.

The **logistics**, or management, of physical distribution involves all the functions necessary to store the products and then move them on. Its aim is to make sure that the goods are available to customers when and where they are needed. Which channels of distribution to use is a management strategic decision that can only be made if the marketing specialists provide the board of directors with sufficient information.

The logistics mix consists of the following components:

- facilities, such as where and how many warehouses and plants there are
- communication systems required. This includes forecasting demand, and using an efficient system of ordering and invoicing
- packaging of goods and combining them into batches
- transport decisions
- information and advice for middlemen and also for customers.

Correct decisions regarding the logistics mix ensure efficiency and are of vital importance.

CASE STUDY

Weak link in the chain

The Yannis family runs a small newsagents and confectionery shop in a residential area. They provide a newspaper delivery service for their customers, and have done so for the last five years. The newspapers are delivered to the shop at 6 a.m., and Mr Yannis's team of paper boys and girls makes sure that all customers have their newspapers before 7.45 a.m. on weekdays, and by 8.30 a.m. on Sundays.

Several weeks ago the wholesaler's delivery to Mr Yannis's shop on Sunday was two hours late, causing the house-to-house delivery to be very late too. Several irate customers complained to Mr Yannis who called the wholesaler. He was told that there had been a problem with the vans and that the situation would not happen again.

Unfortunately, every Sunday since, the newspapers have not arrived on time. Last Sunday, the van did not come until 9.30 a.m., by which time the boys and girls had gone home, and Mr Yannis had to use his own car to deliver the papers, with the help of his wife and sons.

Several customers have now cancelled their orders, not just for the Sunday papers but for the dailies as well.

There are other aspects of 'place' in the marketing mix. The physical environment of the outlet is an important consideration. For example, manufacturers of expensive luxury goods, such as watches or jewellery, will not allow them to be placed in outlets with a reputation for cheap products. On the other hand, a manufacturer of inexpensive but popular goods will want them to be made available to the widest possible section of the public but will be quite prepared for the place of sale to be a 'no frills' one. Producers of industrial goods have to ensure that prospective customers can see the equipment in a place where it is not only displayed, but its uses can be demonstrated – sometimes the 'place' will be on the buyer's premises. Providers of leisure facilities such as leisure centres have to provide an environment that is in keeping with the level of facilities offered.

CASE STUDY

AMWAY

Leader in direct selling

Amway was founded in Michigan, USA, in 1959. It manufactures a wide range of cleaning products, and has become one of the largest direct selling companies in the world. It now sells more than 400 products, employs 13,000 people, and operates in over 70 countries. Its products range from household cleaners, laundry products, toiletries, cosmetics and housewares to food supplements and vitamins. It also markets products of other manufacturers, including Kenwood, Aiwa, Philips, Black & Decker and Pierre Cardin.

The company mission statement declares that:

'Through the partnering of Distributors, Employees and the Founding Families, and the support of quality products and service, we offer all people the opportunity to achieve their goals through the Amway Sales and Marketing Plan.'

There are 2.5 million independent Amway distributors worldwide. In the UK alone there are 37,000. Each is self-employed. The company assists them in setting up on their own, and offers help and advice whenever needed. The distributors sell person-to-person, and earn their income through retail profit on the goods they sell. There are also individual bonuses from Amway based on volume of sales.

Source: Times 100

Promotion

Promotion, the last of the 4 Ps, is as important as the other three and, like them, requires careful research, planning and execution.

> **Promotion** – the marketing activity which aims to inform and influence the customer.

When the first 3Ps of the marketing mix have been satisfactorily dealt with, there still remains one problem. It is not enough to have the right product, to have established the correct price, and to have decided where to sell it, if you do not have the means of telling people about it.

In an economy such as the UK, the problem of promotion is now much more complicated than it was in the past. Imagine that when you go shopping for food you find only 20 different products. If this were so, everybody would know the products being sold. Today, there are thousands of products and no individual can know them all. This is the first problem. The second is even more difficult. Now imagine that there is only one brand, or model, of everything that you might want to buy. In this situation, a person needing a washing machine, a mobile phone or a pair of jeans would not be faced with the decision of which washing machine, phone or jeans to buy. This situation still occurs in some developing countries, but in the UK shoppers are faced with a very difficult choice.

Activity

With a friend, visit a local store and gather as much information as you can about an appliance, such as a dishwasher, microwave oven, camcorder or VCR. If possible, obtain manufacturers' leaflets. Draw up a table, comparing all the available models of your chosen product, under the following headings:

1 name of model

2 name of manufacturer

3 price

4 size/appearance

5 functions

6 special features.

When you have completed the table, you should be able to recommend the model which you think is the best buy. You must give reasons for your answer, and also explain how this product differs from the others.

Promotion strategy and techniques vary considerably. When trying to launch a new product, it is essential not only to inform people of its existence, but also to persuade people to try it. This alone can be difficult if the new product is to compete with others already on the market. Persuasion is also necessary if customers are being asked to switch from something well tried and tested to a new item.

Promotion is not limited to new products. Companies wishing to maintain or increase their existing market share often promote an established product which has been improved in some way. Such improvement can be of the product itself, its packaging or general appearance. This is known as changing the product's image, and requires careful promotion.

Promotional mix

You are already familiar with the term 'mix' in connection with products, and with marketing itself. In each case, it refers to a number of methods and techniques which can be used to achieve a business aim. Not all of these will be suitable in every case of marketing a product. Even when the same methods are used, their relative value might be different.

Promotional mix, therefore, is the list of techniques used to promote a product. The manufacturer or provider of a service must decide on a suitable promotional strategy. As in all functions of marketing, communication between the seller and the buyer is of paramount importance.

Positioning

Every product should be placed in the correct position if it is to succeed in attracting those who are likely to buy it. This poses several problems. A different approach must be taken if aiming at young people rather than older age groups, and vice versa. Existing products sometimes need repositioning. If a product is a well established one, its appeal might be limited to older customers, with the young avoiding what they consider to be an old-fashioned image. If this is the case, a new image must be created. Repackaging, or linking the product with contemporary activities or well known popular celebrities can do this.

Products which have been so repositioned include Oxo, Guinness, and Heinz tomato ketchup.

If you watch TV commercials over a period of time, you will see how existing products come to be advertised in a different way.

For example, TV advertisements by providers of life insurance for the elderly use mature actors to promote their policies, while car manufacturers such as Fiat and Volkswagen create an image of sporty, fast vehicles which fit in well with the lifestyle of young people.

Branding

Branding is often thought to be just the name of a product. This is true as, without the name, buyers could not distinguish between different products in the same range. When buying soft fizzy drinks we remember such names as Fanta, Orangina or Tizer. Branding, however, goes further than naming the product. It includes logos, design of container or packaging, choice of colours and often a catchphrase or slogan. B&Q, for example, uses the slogan: 'You can do it, if you B&Q it'. Branding is useful in several ways:

- buyers tend to identify and remember the product
- new products under an existing brand name have a good start
- advertising and other forms of promotion are linked more easily.

When communicated to the customer, brand names aim not only to tempt him or her to buy a product or a service, but also, in the long run, to generate customer loyalty. Hence the claims and promises that so often form part of the brand image.

- -

CASE STUDY

Virgin Atlantic

The brand is everything!

'Virgin isn't a company. It's a brand name. If you like, it's a lot of companies that use a very strong brand name and it works in a completely different way to any other British company.' (Will Whitehorn, Virgin's corporate affairs director)

Sir Richard Branson's business group is unorthodox. It does not own assets, leases everything from aircraft to the televisions on the backs of seats, and puts everything out to tender. The management structure is 'a unique combination of a very flat non-pivotal structure, and an enlightened dictatorship which gives people room to work creatively. When we go into a business, it's because we want to, because we think we can do it differently, with flair, and have fun,' says Whitehorn.

Branson was led to this unorthodox business strategy by necessity. In 1986, in response to a powerful bull market, Branson took Virgin into the stock market. When the London exchange crashed in October 1987, the company's share price fell precipitately. In 1988, he resolved to quit the stock market.

However, Branson considered that he owed a moral debt to his shareholders. Consequently, he had to raise £200,000 quickly to buy back publicly held shares at the original asking price. His strategy was to separate various businesses within the group and either sell them off or set up joint partnerships.

'The net result is that we have built a brand and an image that is very, very different to most British companies, and that's great for us,' said Whitehorn. 'The word Virgin can be appropriate for almost anything you can think of. People expect quality from Virgin, something a little bit different. This isn't just my opinion. Last year, *PR Week* carried out a piece of research on the Virgin name globally and Branson, the individual who is at the heart of the game. The general perception was that Virgin was about high quality, low prices, innovation and fun.'

Source: Business Education Today, May/June 1996

- -

Own brands

When shopping in a supermarket, we often see a choice of branded goods and goods sold under the supermarket's own name. These are known as 'own brands', are sold at a lower price and aim to provide value for money. Next time you are in a supermarket, look at the displays of coffee or baked beans. You will see the shop's own brand on the same shelf as branded items. It is interesting to note that, although many people do buy own brands, the more expensive branded items, like Heinz baked beans for example, still sell very well. It is likely that brand loyalty, the image projected, the feeling that we know who has actually made the product, and also the higher price are all factors which influence the customers' choice. This is only true, however, when the customers can afford to pay more for the same product.

Activity

i   Make a list of products and services advertised on television on one particular evening.

ii Analyse the adverts under the following headings:

- new product/service

- well established product/service

- the market segment at which the advert aims

- use made of visual aids such as logo

- claims made for the product

- any catchphrases or slogans.

Put the advertisements in your list in order of effectiveness, and explain your reasons.

Sometimes brands become identified with external aspects of the good or service. The Body Shop, for instance, is closely linked with the values which form its mission, e.g. no testing on animals. This ensures the customer loyalty of a large section of buyers of cosmetics and toiletries.

CASE STUDY

Boots the Chemist

No 7 The relaunch of a brand

When a new product is launched that is subtly different from existing brands, and the new arrival is successful, this often leads to hectic activity as competitors introduce rival versions. Marketing involves managing the effects of change and competition. An organisation cannot stand still in a changing environment. It needs to determine how these changes affect consumer wants and needs and then develop objectives and strategies to address these changes.

No business can survive for long without responding to a changing marketplace. This is what Boots had to do.

The No 7 brand was launched in 1935 as Boots's own cosmetic brand, as women everywhere were striving to copy glamorous, famous women like Greta Garbo and Marlene Dietrich. The market for cosmetics was thriving, and demand was rising.

The original range contained seven basic products for beauty care (hence its name). It was presented in classic art deco packaging, using a scripted 'Number Seven' logo.

Since 1935, the brand has been relaunched several times, in line with changing demand. In the 1950s, cosmetics became more sophisticated, with lustre being added to several preparations. During the 1960s pale lipsticks and heavy black eye make-up were 'in', popularised by many singers like Dusty Springfield. By the 1970s the emphasis had shifted to skin care, due to an increased interest in healthy eating and living. By the 1980s the range of cosmetics had increased to meet all tastes. Products now offer state-of-the-art technology combined with the latest scientific developments and natural ingredients from all over the globe. Marketing specifically for particular age groups and socio-economic groups had arrived by the 1990s.

In the huge cosmetics market of 1995 the Boots brand held a 13 per cent share of the UK skincare market, and a 16 per cent share of the colour cosmetics market.

The market for cosmetics is divided into three sectors:

- teenage/budget market, aimed at fashion-conscious young women and including brands such as 17, Rimmel, Outdoor Girl and L'Oreal

- mid-market, for those who require premium products at an affordable price. Brands include Revlon, Max Factor, Almay and Sensiq

- premium market – expensive products, such as the Estée Lauder brand, for customers prepared to pay higher prices for what is perceived as greater value.

Before 1995, the mid-market was relatively static, while the other two were growing. No 7, positioned in the mid-market, did not have a strong brand identity and was often confused with 17. Although it was widely used, it had a large number of older customers and was biased towards the 31- to 45-year-old woman.

The driving force behind the 1995 relaunch was to move the brand from the mid-market to the premium market. The objective of the relaunch was to encourage lapsed users to buy again, and to generate new customers.

No 7 now offers an innovative and exciting range of products with many new colours and advanced scientific skincare, and is packaged in stylish and classic design.

Now No 7 products are:

- not tested on animals

- hypo-allergenic and less likely to cause allergy

- dermatologically tested on human volunteers

- non-comedogenic (non-pore blocking)

- mostly fragrance free.

Relaunch strategy

Before the relaunch No 7 products were perceived as being good quality but drab and old-fashioned. The relaunched product radically altered this image, as they were now of the highest quality and at value for money prices.

1 Two thirds of the colour relaunch products were new, allowing every possible innovation to be incorporated.

2 To ensure that the Boots No 7 range was equal to the premium brands, an extensive level of benchmarking with existing products took place.

3 All new No 7 products were tested on at least 100 volunteers. The best existing competitors' products were tested against the new No 7 formula. The products were presented anonymously, in the same packaging, and the volunteers were asked to fill in an extensive questionnaire as to how each performed in relation to the other. No 7 products were accepted for launch only if they outperformed the competitors.

4 Packaging generates one of the strongest messages to the customers. Previously, the packaging, dating from 1991, was grey, lacked visual appeal and had now become outdated. For the move into the premium market, it had to be redesigned. It had to stand out, be modern and distinctive. The design chosen featured classical shapes and lines. The compact had a gold clasp and its dark colour was seen as timeless and premium.

5 Advertising on television was a new venture for Boots. The central character in the scenarios was shown as confident, independent and enjoying life to the full. The endline of the advert, 'be extraordinary, not ordinary,' was meant to indicate that women could reach any level of extraordinariness either by changing their daily routine or by being totally outrageous. Clear branding was emphasised by using the new pack shots at the end of the commercials. The advertising was successful in projecting the aims of the relaunch to make No 7 premium and accessible by being more upmarket, more interesting, more exciting and more relevant and contemporary.

In addition to the TV ads, there was a press campaign and advertisements were placed in popular women's monthly magazines including *Vogue*, *Elle* and *Cosmopolitan*. They reached 60 per cent of the target market of females from the socio-economic groups BC1, aged between 20 and 35. A press launch was held in October 1994.

6 Merchandising of the new No 7 range included providing all counter sites with a dedicated consultant, whereas before some self-selection stores had no consultants and others had to rely on sales assistants.

7 A new sales counter was designed to display all the products and colours. Premium products are normally displayed at counters with testers, and are sold from under the counter. This was impractical for Boots stores because of the large numbers of customers, so some self-selection was important. About 1200 stores were fitted with the new counters overnight!

8 The No 7 range was relaunched on 22 February 1995, with the products featuring in window displays of every store.

As a result of the relaunch, the claimed usage by the target market increased by 7 per cent to 40 per cent. The relaunch changed the brand's personality which is now perceived as more seductive, independent and individual.

Advertising

We are all familiar with advertising on television, in the press, on hoardings, billboards, etc. We are surrounded by advertising and accept it as part of life. We also tend to think that advertising is very expensive but this is not always so. It is true that the advertising budget of large firms, such as Asda or Carlsberg, runs into millions of pounds, but smaller organisations on a tight advertising budget can also communicate effectively with their target segment.

ONE POUND A MONTH FOR ACCESS TO RAC BREAKDOWN SUPPORT.

AND NO SPIN.

- £1 A MONTH ACCESS FEE
- ONLY £49 FOR A CALLOUT

0870 733 7222

www.redrac.com

RE**D**

THE NEW PAY-AND-GO SERVICE FROM RAC

Advertising is a major part of promoting a product, and has been used for a number of years, but it is still difficult to say with any certainty what it can achieve, and how. An advertising strategy should set objectives and there are now methods of analysing and measuring the effectiveness of an advertising campaign.

As long ago as 1925, E. K. Strong formulated the AIDA model for advertising. It is based on the idea that before a customer decides to buy a good or service, he or she goes through four distinct stages of consciousness (although the customer is not aware of this!).

Following on from AIDA, Lavidge and Steiner formulated the **hierarchy of effects** model, which takes the stages of response to advertising further.

AIDA model

Attention must be attracted

Interest must be maintained

Desire must be aroused

Action must be taken

Hierarchy of effects

awareness

knowledge

liking

preference

conviction

purchase

Many promotional activities can be used to make sure that the various stages of the hierarchy are experienced.

- Advertisements, logos, slogans, catchphrases and jingles all help to make the customer aware of what is available on the market. Sometimes the viewer or reader consciously watches or reads; at other times he or she might not even realise that new ideas for shopping are being introduced. This is particularly true of advertising on television. There are very few people who would admit that they actually watch the commercials, but most retain some of the information shown in the breaks during their favourite programmes. Perhaps, once or twice, you have seen a huge balloon hovering overhead. If so, you must have noticed that it was advertising a product. Stunts like this cost a lot of money, but they are eye catching and certainly help to increase **awareness**.

- If the potential customer is to gain **knowledge** of a product, factual information, perhaps with photographs or pictures, is necessary.

- If the promoted product has a certain image, it will create a **liking**. Nike trainers and Giorgio Armani clothes are examples of this. If you like to wear well known brands, or are impressed by glamour, you are sure to like them.

- The next step, **preference**, is more difficult. It is not enough that the potential customer likes the product, he or she must be persuaded to like it more than other, similar products.

- **Conviction** comes when the viewer or reader becomes sure that the price, quality and image of the product are all just right for him or her.

- The final stage of the hierarchy is **purchase**. If the first five succeed, purchase is the logical outcome.

Both of the above models are really communication networks, and they emphasise the need for good, clear and efficient lines of communication in the marketing process. In the same way that different forms of written communication are used in business situations, different advertising and promotion communications are required to make sure that the customer will, in the end, make the all important decision to purchase.

Advertising objectives

In line with the steps to be taken to reach and persuade customers, advertising has different objectives at each stage of the process.

1 Creating awareness is the first step. In television advertising quite often the viewers are told briefly to look out for a new programme which 'will be coming shortly', or exhorted to be sure and see a new advertisement for an exciting product.

2 Only after awareness has been created is it worth providing more specific information.

3 At this stage, people are urged to find out more about the product. An advertisement may give details of how and where such additional information can be obtained. Travel firms and insurance companies often do this by asking those interested to write or phone for details or, increasingly, to 'visit our website'.

4 When a large organisation markets a range of different products under a corporate name, advertising that name is also of importance – this type of advertising is often used by organisations such as ICI.

5 Firms dealing in industrial products may have a problem in reaching the people who make the decisions to buy. This requires specific advertising in trade journals that must be informative and comprehensive. Visits and demonstrations are often a part of the advertising package.

6 When people are already interested in a product but have not yet reached the 'desire' stage, advertising sets out to create such desire, often by making comparisons between the product in question and other, similar products of competitors, or by appealing to people's aspirations.

7 Advertising can also make dealing with the middleman easier. The wholesaler or the retailer will be happier to take on a well advertised and promoted product, in the belief that it is likely to sell better.

Where to advertise

An important part of the promotion strategy is where and how to advertise. Decisions about this are based on the company's advertising budget, the targeted segment, the type of product and the aim of the advertisement.

In addition to television advertising, which has already been mentioned, there are many other choices:

- national newspapers

- local newspapers

- 'free' newspapers

- special interest magazines like *Woman's Own*, *Which Car?* and *Homes and Gardens*

- professional magazines

- commercial and business magazines

- directories like *Yellow Pages* and *Thomson's*

- commercial radio – many stations are local and advertise local companies and their products

- advertising in cinemas – often aimed at the younger age groups as these now form the majority of those visiting cinemas

- advertisements on buses, taxis and underground trains

- hoardings, posters and neon signs which are aimed at passers by

- other advertising media – air balloons, airships, banners, video tapes (used by travel companies), post office videotapes etc.

- internet – now a growing means of reaching potential buyers.

It is important to realise that advertising is under the strict control of the Advertising Standards Authority, so companies must be aware of, and obey, some clear rules.

Advertisements must not show prejudice of any kind, or offend anyone. The clothing manufacturer Benetton was ordered to withdraw its advertisement showing a newly born baby after a deluge of complaints from the public.

Another constraint is the need to ensure that the claims made for the product in any advertising or publicity campaign are not false or misleading. A well known brand of household bleach used to claim that it 'killed all germs'. This statement had to be changed to the less absolute 'kills 90 per cent of all known germs', as the original statement could not be substantiated.

Sales promotion

This term is often confused with advertising but, although the two are closely linked, they have different objectives. Advertising aims to inform and give reasons to buy, while sales promotion is intended to give the customer additional reasons for choosing the product, in other words, to provide an *incentive* to buy.

Sales promotions

- trial offers (usually of a new product)
- special offers
- trading stamps (which can be exchanged for goods or cash)
- coupons (also exchangeable, and widely used by cigarette companies)
- free samples (available in stores, or delivered house-to-house)
- store loyalty cards, now widely used, such as Sainsbury's Reward card or Boots' Advantage card
- free gifts
- in-store demonstrations
- in-store tastings of food or wine
- trade-in allowances for goods ranging from cars to washing machines
- competitions.

Plus

- discount or commission for retailers
- special credit terms and trade-ins for industrial goods customers.

Anyone who goes shopping regularly will have seen at least one or two ways in which such incentives are provided. The list of these is quite long.

Parents of young children might choose a cereal pack containing a small toy in preference to one without. Instant coffee drinkers are likely to buy a brand which offers a free jar in exchange for 20 coupons from jars previously bought.

Incentives, when well planned, and organised, can be very successful. Sometimes, however, things do go wrong. Several years ago, Hoover offered free air tickets to anyone who paid over a certain sum for a Hoover product. This offer was taken up by so many buyers that Hoover was unable to satisfy the demand.

Exhibitions

As a method of promoting products and services, exhibitions can be very useful, and are widely used by producers of industrial products and consumer durables, as well as of such services as travel and gardening. Many, although not all, exhibitions have trained staff in attendance, and would-be buyers can obtain advice and have any questions answered on the spot by experts. There are also mobile exhibitions and roadshows, which have the advantage of being able to reach people in different locations.

The Ideal Homes Exhibition in London and the Motor Show in Birmingham are examples of well-established, annual exhibitions which are well attended by exhibitors and the public.

International trade fairs are important for companies exporting their products abroad. British producers participate in many such fairs, e.g. in Hanover and Leipzig in Germany and Poznan in Poland.

Sponsorship

This form of promotion has grown in recent years, and is now widely used by many companies. In return for financial support of an activity such as a sporting event, the company's name and logo are displayed on the recipient's clothing, headed paper or publicity material and often get shown or mentioned in the media.

Individual tennis players, for instance, are often subsidised by manufacturers of tennis racquets or shoes. Football clubs are sponsored by business organisations.

The London Marathon is sponsored by ADT. Sponsorship does not have to be nationwide. Local businesses often sponsor local organisations and ventures, such as school projects.

It is difficult to measure the effectiveness of sponsorship, and the decision to sponsor might sometimes prove to be ill advised. Imagine a sponsorship contract for a successful football club which then suffers a setback and loses a number of games in a row.

Public relations

As the name implies, this term relates to the communication between the company and the public. Its objective is to create a positive image of the company and its products and maintain this, adjusting, if necessary, to changing external factors such as the activities of competitors, the economic situation and government pressure.

Large companies usually have a dedicated PR section in their marketing department, while others use the services of independent PR companies.

PR activities include:

- media relations – ensuring that the coverage of the company and its activities is continual and positive. This is done through press releases and PR conferences, to which representatives of the press, radio and TV are invited

- product publicity

- monitoring interest in the company and its product, and advising the management of any new development

- monitoring new legal developments and government decisions which may have consequences for the company, and lobbying those responsible.

The 4Ps are the framework for marketing any product or service. This framework is, as you have seen, quite complex, and only a skilled team can ensure that the marketing strategy fulfils all its requirements. This explains why the term 'marketing' means all the functions of getting the product or service from the provider to the customer, and why using it as a synonym for 'selling' is incorrect.

Revision Questions

1 Explain why, in the marketing mix, the meaning of 'place' is not limited to shops and stores only. (2 marks)

2 What is meant by place and promotion being the two Ps external to the company? (2 marks)

3 Give three examples of situations in which, even today, the customer must meet the manufacturer or provider of a service. (3 marks)

4 Why is the middleman an important link in the chain of distribution? (2 marks)

5 What is a multiple outlet? Give two examples. (3 marks)

6 Travel agents and estate agents are examples of businesses acting as go-betweens for sellers and buyers. How do the agents earn money for themselves? (3 marks)

7 What are the advantages of franchises for the franchisees? (3 marks)

8 Why is mail order selling so popular? (2 marks)

9 If you have access to the internet, make a list of six types of products which you can buy there. What are the advantages of buying and selling on the internet? (6 marks)

10 Why are the producers of cut flowers likely to use air freight if exporting abroad, while manufacturers of washing machines never send their goods by air? (5 marks)

11 Why is promotion an important part of marketing today? (2 marks)

12 Why is it sometimes necessary to reposition well established products, such as Oxo or Guinness? (4 marks)

13 Explain why a brand name is considered to be a vital part of the promotion process. (4 marks)

14 The relaunch of Boots No 7 range proved to be successful. Why did it succeed? If Boots had not relaunched it, what might have been the result for the product? (10 marks)

15 List five slogans, logos or jingles that, in your opinion, are effective in attracting people to the products which they advertise, and explain why. (12 marks)

16 Which of the sales promotions listed on page 231 do you think are most attractive to:

- mothers of small children

- pensioners

- people who like to take part in activities

- housewives?

Give reasons for your answers. (10 marks)

17 Write a press release (not more than 200 words) about a new ice cream which is being launched. (12 marks)

Marketing Strategy

In this chapter you will learn how the principles and techniques which you have learned about in previous chapters are used to create an overall long-term plan, or strategy, for the marketing of a product. You will also learn about shorter-term marketing plans, and their component plans, sometimes called sub-plans.

Introduction

The decision to introduce a new product or service, or to improve and 'rejuvenate' an existing one (see the Boots No 7 case study on page 227), are **strategic** decisions, not **incremental** ones. An incremental decision is taken on the spur of the moment, in response to something that has happened and needs dealing with. Incremental decisions are operational ones. Strategic decisions are based on a number of factors. The 'vision' or long-term objectives of the company dictate strategic decisions.

Long-term objectives are not the same for all businesses or for one business at different times. A company may want to:

- maintain its market share

- increase its market share

- do better than its competitors

- change its image (see Boots case study again)

- diversify

- expand its market base from local to national or international.

It is also wrong to assume that every business organisation always wants to grow. Some have no intention of doing so, and others might decide against growth on the basis of their own financial situation or the economic and political situation in the country. Whatever it is that a company wants to achieve, it is the job of senior management to formulate a strategy aimed at achieving it. The **operational plans** are then tailored to fit in with the strategic objectives, and are carried out by the relevant department of the company.

It is worth remembering that large business organisations benefit from **economies of scale** and can often afford to take greater risks when investing in new products, improving existing ones, or trying to break into a new market.

Economies of scale – these are the advantages of size, and include the ability to buy in bulk, often at reduced prices, to store large quantities of parts, materials and finished products, and to be flexible in response to changing levels of demand.

Operational plans – based on objectives laid down in strategic plans, these show exactly what must be done and by whom to turn the strategic theory into practice.

It should also be remembered that a business does not operate in a vacuum. It must be aware of the needs and wants of customers and potential customers. It must also work within the constraints of the legal system and, increasingly, take into consideration the changing social and ethical values in the marketplace. In recent years, public opinion has turned against the use of animal furs in the clothing industry. This has led clothing manufacturers to substitute fake fur for the real thing. This reflects the realisation that sales would suffer if it was not done, as well as humanitarian concern for animal welfare.

The same is true of the cosmetics industry, and the rising demand for products not tested on animals. The best known organisation to sell exclusively cosmetics not tested on animals is the very successful Body Shop. Anita Roddick, its founder, also travels widely in search of new supplies, and has become known for her support of industries in some of the poorest countries of the world.

Marketing strategy

The whole marketing process comes together for the purpose of creating a marketing strategy.

Depending on the objectives of the company, different strategies can be adopted.

New product strategy

This strategy is based on the prospects of profits on investment being at least equal to the current rate of return on capital. Sometimes, however, a company might decide on new product development just to stay in business.

New markets strategy

This strategy aims at increasing sales, but sometimes it is very difficult to enter a new market. If the increased volume of sales will allow the company to gain the benefits of economies of scale, the prospects of increased profitability are greater.

Existing markets penetration

A company might decide to try for increased volume of sales in a market in which it sells already. If an existing market is expanding, this can be achieved without too great a financial investment by persuading new users to buy. In a saturated market, extra sales can come about only through increasing the market share. (A good example of this is Bernard Matthews, see case study on page 209).

Adjusting prices

This method is used when trying to increase gross

profits without the loss of sales revenue. Here the product might be repositioned or changed.

Cost reduction

This strategy for reducing the **profit gap** tries to achieve it through using the factors of production more efficiently, and reducing distribution and research costs.

> **Profit gap** – difference between forecast profits and achieved profits.

Diversification

Diversification is a long-term objective and requires considerable investment. It involves new products and new markets, and carries high risks, but can bring about great increase in profitability. A firm might diversify horizontally, into related products, or move into the production of unrelated products. Virgin Atlantic (see case study on page 225) is one of the best examples of success through diversification.

Vertical integration

The strategy of vertical integration aims at acquiring manufacturing units at different stages of production, e.g. a bakery chain acquiring a flour mill. One of the greatest strength of Bernard Matthews plc is that it is a vertically integrated company and thus can control fully all the stages of production.

A company must take a number of factors into consideration even before it begins to formulate its strategic, or corporate, plan.

1   The economic, political and social trends in this country, and perhaps even abroad. In recent years tobacco products manufacturers have faced great difficulties in marketing their products because of the well established links of smoking with cancer and heart disease, while British beef has suffered a serious setback both in the UK and abroad because of BSE.

2   Its own position in the market. Here the SWOT analysis is useful.

3   Products and services which are the most likely to succeed, given the company's strength.

The next step is to set realistic targets and work out strategies needed to achieve them.

When the above are in place, detailed operational plans must be prepared for all parts of the organisation. Often, additional **sub-plans** are also needed.

> **Sub-plan** – a detailed plan dealing with operational aspects of one part of the overall plan.

CASE STUDY

TENCEL

A new product

The British-based international chemical group Courtaulds introduced Tencel in 1992. Tencel is the first new man made fibre to be marketed for 30 years.

Tencel is a Courtaulds brand name for a fibre generally known as lyocell, produced via a revolutionary solvent spun cellulose-based technology. It offers unique properties to the world of fashion. It is strong enough to be suitable for the creation of denim. It can be spun, woven and knitted.

It produces vibrant colours when dyed and is now being used to make fabrics new to the fashion industry.

Tencel's versatility and strength make it suitable for blending with other materials.

Courtaulds decided to market Tencel as a result of research into the feasibility of producing a new high quality and performance fibre, which could be made by an environment friendly process. The research commenced in 1978, and was mainly carried out in the company's plants in Coventry and in Grimsby.

After exhaustive market research, Tencel was first introduced in Japan. Courtaulds now sell Tencel in 31 countries worldwide, including USA, Europe, South America and some Asian Pacific countries.

Source: Times 100

SWOT analysis

Before deciding on a marketing strategy, it is essential for the company to assess as accurately as possible its current position in the market, and to examine all future possibilities. This is often done on the basis of the **SWOT analysis**.

STRENGTHS	WEAKNESSES
OPPORTUNITIES	THREATS

SWOT, as you can see, is the acronym made up from the initial letters of its four elements.

The SWOT grid can be used for the strategy of the whole company, but also to formulate strategies for individual goods or services.

CASE STUDY

Tarminster College

Looking for new opportunities

Tarminster College was established as a technical college in 1954. It served the local community, and many companies sent their trainees and apprentices on day-release courses at the college.

In the 1970s and 1980s, some of the businesses moved away, while others were forced to cut costs and stopped sending students to the college. However, every year there were many enquiries about courses in business studies and computer studies. Gradually, the college menu of courses changed, and with it, the profile of the average student. Many more women were enrolling on courses, and the numbers of mature students also increased. The next strategic decision to be made came when GNVQ courses were introduced. At first they were regarded with suspicion by many of the lecturers, and even senior managers were not sure about this new route to professional and academic success.

It soon became apparent, however, that if the downward trend in student numbers was to be halted and reversed, something had to be done.

The marketing department was asked to investigate and report to the management and the Board of Governors.

The investigation was carried out in accordance with the SWOT principles. Here are the results:

1 Strengths

- good reputation in the region
- experienced and enthusiastic staff
- excellent facilities for teaching and learning, including computer rooms and a well equipped library.

2 Weaknesses

- little understanding of the concept of the GNVQ programme
- few staff with experience outside teaching
- little staff training.

3 Opportunities

- meeting growing demand for GNVQ courses
- offering an alternative route to higher education
- the possibility of attracting students who might otherwise stay on at school and study for A level examinations
- the possibility of gradually changing the staff profile
- ensuring that the college does not lose out by not taking up new programmes.

5 Threats

- competition from local schools which also intend to offer GNVQ programmes
- competition from other colleges, some of which already have GNVQ courses.

The management must take a long and careful look at the organisation, helped by the SWOT analysis principle. Depending on the type or types of goods or services to be offered, the strategy might be planned for two, three, five or even 10 years ahead. A manufacturer of aircraft components or defence systems, for example, will look at a strategy that will take the organisation through at least a decade. This timespan is much shorter for producers of consumer goods or providers of services.

To decide on a strategy, it is necessary to:

- decide the objectives
- research the market
- decide on the product mix, or individual product
- allocate budgets
- decide the market segment/s to be targeted
- decide on place and promotion
- investigate any possible external constraints.

By definition, the company's strategic plan is comprehensive and lays down the vision for the future of the organisation as a whole. In line with the overall strategy, separate strategic plans are made by different parts of the company. Thus, the marketing department will formulate a strategic plan of the activities to be undertaken within the overall plan.

The marketing plan

This is usually composed of several different plans, each dealing with one aspect of the marketing process. So we are likely to finish with a:

- product mix plan
- research plan
- pricing plan
- distribution plan
- sales plan
- promotion plan
- advertising plan
- (in some cases only) regional plans.

In a large organisation, different members or teams from the marketing department will work on these sub-plans. In a smaller one, one team might be in charge of producing all the plans. In either case, there must be close co-operation between the planners, and all the plans must fit together.

CASE STUDY

Marketing Plan
of
Very Best Wishes plc
(manufacturer of greeting cards, wrapping paper, boxes and novelties)

1 Corporate strategy – to increase market share by introducing new lines, e.g. greeting cards for Sikh, Hindu, Jewish and Muslim holidays

2 Market research – to establish market opportunities and the probability of profitability

3 Deciding on details of new products

4 Deciding on budget for the venture

5 Fixing price

6 Establishing precise market opportunities

7 Formulating promotion policy

8 Implementation

9 Monitoring

Budgets

In marketing planning, budgets are of great importance. In simple terms, the revenue generated by marketing must be much greater than its cost. Normal accounting principles apply here.

Imagine that you have decided to supplement your income by providing a car washing service in the neighbourhood. You are quite certain that there is a demand for such a service. You are quite capable of cleaning cars really well. You have also found out that some friends of yours, living in another part of town, have been washing cars successfully for over a year. They have been helpful and have told you that, on average, you can charge £4 to wash a car and £7 if you also do valeting of the interior.

You, therefore, have:

- the product
- the price
- the place

and all you need is promotion. You decide to have some leaflets printed, and will deliver them door to door in your chosen area. The leaflets will cost £200. You have also worked out that the cost of cleaning materials and of your time will be £1 per car. You hope to make a profit on your investment within one month.

Here are some possible outcomes at the end of your first month of operations:

Outcome 1	14 cars washed	£42
	2 cars valeted	£12
		Total: £54
Outcome 2	31 cars washed	£93
	18 cars valeted	£108
		Total: £201
Outcome 3	40 cars washed	£120
	18 cars valeted	£108
		Total: £228

You can see that the first example shows a loss, the second just about breaks even, and it is only in the third that a real profit is made.

> **Break-even** point – a situation in which income just covers costs.

In a business organisation, costs are not only larger but also much more complicated, and correct forecasting, and later monitoring, of the allocated budget is essential.

When marketing a new product, in the first stage of the process the costs always exceed any revenue. It is important to try and forecast the cash flow for each stage of the marketing operation, so that the process does not run out of funds.

Forecasting

> **Forecasting** – this simply means predicting the future. In this context, forecasting is trying to calculate as accurately as possible costs and revenue for the next financial period.

In marketing terms, the forecasting function tries to establish what is going to happen if and when a product is introduced, or a decision to extend the sales of a new product is implemented.

Knowledge of the company's products, familiarity with its customers and clients through sales personnel, and the results of market research are all important when trying to forecast future events, such as volume of sales and profitability. It must, however, be remembered that in a constantly changing world, external influences and events can render even the most careful forecast invalid. Minimum wage legislation, recently implemented in the UK, has meant that a number of firms will now have to pay their workers more – this means that their forecasts of the cost of wages have now had to be revised. Many companies make their forecasts based on the cost of imported materials. A rise in the prices charged by their overseas suppliers will render their forecasts invalid.

Businesses are constrained not only by legislation but by the standards set by the government in order to protect the public. The Trades Description Act, for instance, makes it illegal for a company to misinform the public about the quality of products and services. A nylon shirt must not be described as silk and manufacturers of plastic footwear must not state that the shoes are made of leather. The Advertising Standards Authority and the Code of Advertising Practice Committee act as watchdogs to ensure that material used in advertising and publicity is based on fact, and does not upset or offend.

The above item demonstrates clearly how careful a company must be when advertising its products or

---

Misleading Asda

Complaints that Asda misled customers over price cuts have been upheld by the Advertising Standards Authority. A 'rollback' promotion apparently implied that cuts on 2400 lines were permanent, but some were not.

Source: The Times, 8 December 1999

---

policies. As the complaint against Asda has been upheld by the ASA, the series of commercials based on the price rollback will have to be withdrawn. This will cost the company money, and will not improve its public image.

Constructing realistic marketing strategies, and then developing operational marketing plans which will turn the vision into a reality is, as you have learned, a very complex process. While not a science in the strict sense – there are too many uncertainties in the business world – marketing is the means by which a company always tries to identify, anticipate and supply customers' requirements.

The question 'How successful is marketing in achieving its objectives?' is often asked. While it is impossible to answer it precisely, the growth of its importance in the last decades proves its worth to business organisations.

Revision Questions

1   How does a strategic plan differ from an operational plan? (5 marks)

2   Why might a company want to change the image of its product? Give three examples. (5 marks)

3   Some business organisations do not want to expand. Explain why this may be so. (3 marks)

4   Why is it often very difficult for a company to enter a new market? (2 marks)

5   Why is diversification very expensive? (2 marks)

6   Explain what is meant by the profit gap, and why companies want to reduce it. (4 marks)

7   With reference to the Tencel case study (page 236), explain why the new fibre was successfully marketed. (5 marks)

8   Why is it important for all marketing sub-plans to fit together? (3 marks)

9   If the costs of running your own small business are £1200 per week, how many items priced at £2.50 must you sell to break even? (4 marks)

10   Why is forecasting never certain? (2 marks)

11   In a SWOT analysis, what might be the 'threats'? (2 marks)

UNIT 3

End of Unit Assignment

You have now learned a lot about marketing, its aims and its importance to business organisations. This assignment will give you the opportunity to put the theory into practice. You must read all the instructions carefully, and not forget to carry out the tasks in the given chronological order. All the tasks are based on the case study.

CASE STUDY

Well Pet plc

Well Pet plc is a large manufacturer of a wide range of pet foods, toys and accessories, including dog and cat beds, shampoos, worming tablets and toys.

The company employs about 300 people. Its main factory is situated in the Midlands, and it also has two smaller factories in Wales. There is a Well Pet supermarket in London, selling all its own brand products.

Well Pet plc has a dynamic and energetic Board of Directors, headed by the Chairman, Bob Wright. The company has its own R&D department which has, in recent years, been responsible for some major improvements in the quality of a number of food products.

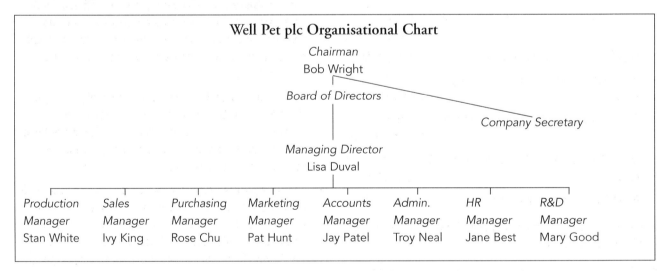

Well Pet plc Organisational Chart

Chairman
Bob Wright

Board of Directors

Company Secretary

Managing Director
Lisa Duval

| *Production* *Manager* Stan White | *Sales* *Manager* Ivy King | *Purchasing* *Manager* Rose Chu | *Marketing* *Manager* Pat Hunt | *Accounts* *Manager* Jay Patel | *Admin.* *Manager* Troy Neal | *HR* *Manager* Jane Best | *R&D* *Manager* Mary Good |

The company's mission statement reads:

> Well Pet plc is committed to supplying its customers and their pets with the highest quality products available at reasonable prices, and to providing advice, information and comprehensive aftersales service.

The organisation is aware of keen competition from other, sometimes larger, firms in the same field. Although sales figures for the last financial period have been good, Bob Wright and the Board of Directors are keen to increase the company's share of the market. This, they feel, could be done in one of several ways:

- improving an existing product
- introducing a new product or range of products for existing target groups
- targeting a new section of the pet market
- launching a marketing campaign aimed at raising the company's profile.

Currently, the company's best selling products are:

- Good Boy – canned dog food in the lower price range
  (42p per tin)
- Good Cat – competitively priced canned cat food
  (55p per tin)
- Veggie Pet – meatless dog food   (75p per tin)
- Good Rest – moderately priced range of dog and cat fleece-lined beds   (from £8 to £16)
- Good Bites – dog biscuits sold in 5lb packs only
  (£4.15 per pack)
- Clean Pet – insecticidal shampoo, suitable for dogs and cats   (£1.18 ea.)
- Good Chew – rabbit food mix   (95p per lb).

However, some of the lines produced by Well Pet plc have not been doing so well.

- Xtra Good Dog – an expensive, top of the range dog food, sold in small vacuum packs   (89p each)
- a range of traditional toiletries for pets, including deodorant sprays, combs and brushes, and a cheaper pet shampoo
- budgie and canary food mixes   (69p per lb)
- the whole range of products aimed at owners of pet fish.

The overall strategy of Well Pet plc, over the next two years, looks to establish how its market share can be increased, but no decisions have been made as yet about the operational plan.

Although the company prides itself on a good communication system and a democratic management style, distinct differences of opinion between the departmental managers have arisen regarding the way forward.

Here are some of their views:

- Stan White, head of Production, sees no need to change any of the products, or introduce new ones. This would be too costly, and Stan thinks that the best solution would be to spend more on advertising and publicity of the existing product mix.

- Accounts Manager, Jay Patel, is concerned with the inability of the company to increase profitability in recent years. This, in his view, combined with rising production and distribution costs, is likely to lead to a marked decrease in profits. Jay thinks that the company must pay more attention to what competitors are doing, and is all for introducing a new product range.

- Ivy King, Sales Manager, is also concerned with the rather static level of sales. She is adamant that the company's sales force is very good and efficient, but considers that the products are run-of-the mill, not very well presented and, although the quality is good, do not compare well with similar products of other manufacturers.

- In the opinion of Rose Chu, the Purchasing Manager, the most important aspect of the matter is the constantly rising cost of raw materials. Therefore Rose is in favour of coming up with cheaper, downmarket versions of existing products.

- The only positive response came from the head of R&D, Mary Good. She has reported that her department has already evolved a new, improved formula for the Veggie Pet, and is nearly ready with recipes for a range of specialised foods for kittens and puppies, older pets, and those suffering from various gastric disorders. Mary thinks Well Pet plc should not be afraid of targeting new segments of the market but says that her staff are disillusioned because none of their new products has been utilised in the last three years.

- Pat Hunt, head of Marketing, agreed with Mary in principle, but emphasised that further research into the market must be carried out before a final decision is taken. Whatever the outcome of the research, Pat is certain that the Well Pet brand needs rejuvenating, and has urged management to authorise an additional budget for new packaging, advertising and publicity.

Lisa Duval agrees with Pat Hunt and has authorised the head of Marketing to organise a comprehensive research programme without delay. The MD wants to know:

1 Should the company try to strengthen its market position by improving the best selling existing products? If so, which ones, and how can they and their image be revamped? Should any of the slow sellers be dropped from the portfolio? If so, which?

2 Should Well Pet introduce a new product range aimed at its existing market? If this were the answer, what would the new products be?

3 Should a new segment be targeted, e.g. exotic pets and/or farm animals?

4 Should the company diversify and begin manufacturing products such as aquaria, rabbit hutches and dog crates?

5 What steps could be taken to lift the rather staid image of the company and make the brand a household name?

Pat has four weeks in which to carry out the research, analyse the results, and present a report to Lisa. After one of the options has been chosen, Pat's department will have to formulate a marketing strategy and a marketing plan. As Well Pet plc does not have its own market research section, Pat will use the services of a specialist agency, Find Out Ltd.

• •

You are a trainee with Find Out Ltd. Your line manager, Chris O'Mullen, is very pleased with your progress and has decided to hand the brief from Well Pet plc to you, although he will advise you and supervise what you do. Here are your tasks:

Task 1

1 Draft a questionnaire that can be used to find out:

- the importance to pet owners of quality of pet foods

- the importance of price

- the demand for pet accessories

- the interest in new foods for a particular segment – e.g. older or infirm animals

- the most popular brands now available

- the importance of high quality packaging and external appearance

- responsiveness to advertising and publicity.

You should decide what type of questions are most suitable in this case, and be able to justify your choice of format. Remember that the questions must be clear and unambiguous, there must be no leading questions, and the questionnaire should not be too long.

You have to find at least 30 pet owners willing to answer your questionnaire. You must decide what type of sampling to use, and explain why.

When you have conducted this research, use a computer software package to analyse the results and present them in tabular form. You should now be able to tell your boss whether there is likely to be a market for new products, and what motivates buyers of pet products.

You should present your findings to Chris O'Mullen with a short factual memo. This should contain a summary and conclusions drawn from the sample interviewed.

2 Identify the major suppliers of pet products in the UK. Find out (in a good library or from the internet and from material produced by the various companies themselves), as much as you can about each of them. You should include the following:

- size of company

- when established

- legal status

- main products

- most successful products

- segment of market targeted

- financial performance in the last two years.

(*Which?* magazine and company annual reports will help you in this task.)

3 Now visit at least three supermarkets and make a list of pet food brands, types of animal food and accessories that are available in each.

Draw a table comparing products and prices of the competitors with those of Well Pet plc.

Task 2

Before Well Pet plc can decide on its operational plan, it is necessary to analyse its position in the market. Using SWOT analysis, draw up a detailed summary of its strengths and weaknesses. What, in view of the results of your research, are the best opportunities for Well Pet? Are there any threats?

Present your conclusions in the format of an informal report to your line manager.

You now have a clear idea about the steps that Well Pet should take to try and increase its market share. Decide whether it is going to be:

a   relaunch of an existing product

b   the launch of a new product.

It is now your responsibility to create a marketing strategy for either a) or b).

In either case, you must:

• name and define the product

• explain your reasons for choosing the product

• with reference to marketing strategies, explain the sub-plans which will have to be drawn up to launch, or relaunch, the product most effectively and efficiently

• explain how the product will meet identified customer needs, and why you think that the decision anticipates demand

• indicate how new product strategy, or existing markets penetration strategy, will be used to achieve the objectives

• decide if any price adjustment will be necessary

• give details of the types of advertising and any publicity which will be used as part of your marketing strategy

• suggest ways in which the Well Pet brand will be strengthened as a result.

NB:

When choosing a new product, or an existing product which could be improved, you can use any of the products mentioned in the case study. However, if you wish you may choose a product that has not been listed but which, in your opinion, would be the most likely to sell well to pet owners in this country.

The marketing strategy must be presented in the form of a formal report to Chris O'Mullen. The report should include all relevant details, refer to marketing principles and explain your choices.

Task 3

Now that your research and marketing plan have been completed, you have been asked to make a presentation to the management of Well Pet plc.

You should prepare a series of bullet point notes from which you will speak. The presentation should take 10–15 minutes, and it is essential that you use visual aids (flip charts, OHP transparencies and handouts) to make the presentation easier to follow and more interesting.

At the end of the presentation, Lisa Duval and her team will ask you questions about your findings, conclusions and marketing strategy. It is very important that you are able to answer these questions.

UNIT 4

Human Resources

CHAPTER 1

Human Resource Planning

KEY TERMS:

specialist staff	competition	recruitment and selection
key roles	labour turnover	succession planning
local skills base	internal/external labour market	supply
demand	stability index	wastage rates
absence rates	trends	organisation and department levels
age breakdown	retirement	young recruits
retention levels	training needs analysis	cascading
specialist courses	continuity	targeted training

In this chapter you will learn why people are such a key resource to different types of businesses selling goods or services, government departments meeting community needs or charities working to relieve hardship.

Introduction

All businesses require the assistance of staff to carry out the daily activities related to the nature of the organisation. In a small business, such as a sole trader or a partnership, the owners are likely to perform many of the functions themselves and employ only a few additional staff to spread the workload.

A medium to large sized organisation needs many employees to cover a wide range of specialised tasks. This may necessitate a search in the local environment for people with the right skills. It may also bring the organisation into competition with similar businesses who will try to attract the best workers by offering enhanced benefits and higher salaries.

Examples of different skill requirements for particular jobs are shown in Table 4.1.1.

These people are all important members of staff to their specific organisation and fulfil a key role in its operation. The organisation would not be successful without them and even if it does use a considerable amount of sophisticated technology, human beings are responsible for setting the equipment up correctly, pressing the right buttons and repairing it if it malfunctions.

Table 4.1.1

Shop Assistant	School Teacher	Fund Raiser
communication	communication	communication
managing people	managing people	managing people
listening	team working	tact and discretion
accuracy	planning	planning
till operation	preparation	co-ordination
handling money	record keeping	gaining donations
problem solving	subject knowledge	attracting sponsorship
basic maths	meeting standards	negotiation

Once inside the organisation, staff perform various duties in connection with their role and the organisation expects their work to be of a satisfactory standard, completed within a timescale and to be cost effective. Training may be provided to help employees improve their levels of efficiency and this may be rewarded with promotion or a bonus in recognition of their efforts.

None of this would occur if the employer had not selected potential workers in a careful way. The skills required to carry out a particular job can be identified and matched against the abilities of people looking for work. If the employer takes on staff who are unsuitable, it can cause a number of problems, e.g.:

- poor productivity levels
- bad feeling among other staff
- dissatisfaction with the job
- high levels of absenteeism
- customer complaints
- dismissal or resignation
- the search for a replacement.

Local employment trends

Within a local community many small businesses are set up to serve the needs of each other and private customers and to support larger organisations with specialist assistance. A self-employed painter and decorator will search for work in private households as well as refurbishing the premises of other businesses. They will be employed for a short time on a specific contract, providing a service, and will prepare a quotation for this work. This will be based on the number of hours that the painter and decorator has calculated it will take him or her to complete the work. If difficulties arise during the contracted hours and it takes longer to finish the task than originally estimated, the price agreed is unlikely to be increased and the painter and decorator could even make a loss if the job runs into serious problems.

A self-employed worker has to provide a good standard of service to the customer otherwise no further contracts will be given and no recommendations will be received. The customer has employed the painter and decorator for a fixed contract to provide a service and

has no obligations to make statutory deductions from the fee paid, such as income tax and national insurance. These are the responsibility of the sole trader.

It has become common practice for larger organisations to employ many part-time staff to cover certain duties within its operation. These people supplement the work of the full-time staff and allow the business to open for longer hours than is normal for the working day in an office environment. For example, many Tesco and Sainsbury supermarket branches open from 8 a.m.–10 p.m. Monday to Saturday and 10 a.m.–4 p.m. on Sunday; some designated stores remain open 24 hours a day. This requires the assistance of many employees – both full-time and part-time.

Other types of business, e.g. clothing shops, have identified that certain days of the week or periods within a 24-hour span, are slack and there is not enough work to keep full-time staff occupied. The business reserves the right to keep fewer staff employed at these periods and to bring in additional workers at the busiest times each week, such as Friday and Saturday and at sale times.

This mix of staff has to be carefully planned and managed and accurate records need to be maintained so that the workers can be paid at an agreed rate for the hours worked. Both parties to a contract of employment must fulfil their obligations in a fair and reasonable manner (see Table 4.1.2).

If an employer expects staff to carry out their duties correctly, then careful selection is needed to find people capable of completing these tasks properly. The majority of medium to large businesses will study the surrounding environment to see if it is suitable to open a branch or build a factory or a new office complex. Features such as accessibility by road and local bus and train transport services will be investigated. This is not just to see if sufficient customers will be attracted to the facility but, more importantly, to find out if enough skilled staff will be available to fill the jobs on offer. It is no good setting up a highly technical operation, such as making TV sets and computers, if the skill base of the local residents is more suited to manual work. A sophisticated training programme will need to be developed to convert the existing abilities to the current level needed by the organisation and this is additional expenditure that a company may not want to invest.

Table 4.1.2

Employee must:	Employer must:
• carry out the duties allocated in an efficient way and to an acceptable standard • comply with any rules and regulations applicable to that specific job, e.g. health & safety	• outline the tasks and responsibilities required by the job • pay the employee at the agreed timescale • provide suitable resources and equipment for the worker to carry out the duties satisfactorily and safely

Careful analysis of the local labour market will be carried out. This will include:

- skill mix of local people available for work
- breakdown of male/female numbers in age bands
- travel to work distances and transport facilities
- competitor organisations in a similar business operation
- local rates of pay and benefits
- surrounding education provision.

An example of such details researched in the Horsham area of West Sussex, which has one of the lowest unemployment rates in the UK, shows that this mix fits 1.1 per cent of the working population.

An extract of data available to local business operations in the Horsham area is shown on page 299. Considerable assistance is given to new firms wanting to set up businesses in a particular locality and your own region will have similar information which can be used as the basis for your unit assignment.

Activity

Research similar data in your own locality.

This information can be obtained from your local library, who keep a 'reference only' copy of similar documents, or you may obtain a copy of your own local council plan from your local council offices. Many councils also place this information on the worldwide web because it is public knowledge.

Compare your own local data with the Horsham material on page 299; discuss the difference.

Local skills shortages

Once you have located similar information to the above, it will show the potential **supply** of labour available to a business and help that business to match their current **demands** in an effective way.

Employers are obliged to consider the supply-demand factor before recruiting staff because it can affect their approach to recruitment and the rewards they will agree to offer (see Table 4.1.3).

Table 4.1.3

Supply and Demand

If supply exceeds demand:

- plenty of candidates available
- wages will be lower
- benefits reduced
- low level recruitment campaign
- staff attracted easily
- careful selection methods used

Demand and Supply

If demand exceeds supply:

- few applicants available
- higher wages offered
- benefits increased
- recruitment campaign targeted at specific candidates
- more lengthy interview/ selection process
- discussion of career progression

This means that recruitment policies and human resources staff aim to assess the expectations of people wanting to join the organisation and adopt suitable methods of attraction, application and selection of new employees.

Some vacancies can be filled from the **internal labour market** by training and promoting staff to a higher post once they have proved themselves. Each year several members of staff will voluntarily leave an organisation for a variety of reasons, e.g. family commitments, moving to a new location, retirement or change of career. Not all of these vacancies will be refilled and it is likely that only a small number can be met from the internal labour market.

This leaves the business with a shortfall in its requirements and it is this factor that prompts the human resource department to recruit new staff from the **external labour market**. Before doing this a full assessment will be made of the current external climate. This can change on a regular basis and must be constantly monitored to keep up to date. Some reasons why this external climate changes regularly are:

- established firms close down, putting more people back on the job market
- new firms open, taking people out of the skills base in the locality
- new housing developments are completed which bring in new residents and potential employees.

Labour turnover

In addition to continually monitoring the external labour market, organisations need to establish how useful their existing employees are to the business. If this assessment shows that there are problems in keeping staff levels up in some departments, changes need to be made to improve the environment, e.g. working hours, nature of duties, less autocratic management or an improved recruitment method. If the assessment shows that there is no need to fill a vacancy because the role can be broken up and re-allocated among existing staff, then the job will disappear from the departmental requirements.

Organisations tend to record staffing levels and the length of time people stay in that position. This is known as the **Stability Index** and gives an indication of the number of staff who have been with the firm for over a year. It is calculated as follows:

Stability rate (%)

$$\frac{\text{Number of employees with service of 1 year or more}}{\text{Number of employees employed a year ago}} \times 100$$

If we use this calculation and apply it to a company selling goods by mail order which had a total of 3250 staff 1 year ago:

e.g. $\dfrac{2500}{3250} \times 100$ $\qquad$ $\dfrac{43}{72} \times 100$

$= 76.9\%$ $\qquad\qquad$ $= 59.7\%$
organisation level $\qquad$ despatch department level

This figure can be calculated as a total organisation rate and also by departmental analysis. In the above examples, two different percentages have been noted, showing that there may be a problem in one particular department.

However, a single figure such as this is of little consequence and needs to be recorded on an annual or monthly basis over several years. If this happens, a **trend** will be noted and decisions can be made to stem the flow of leavers, if that is what has been recorded. An example of such data is shown in Table 4.1.4.

Table 4.1.4

Area	1995	1996	1997	1998	1999	Notes
Organisation	88.6	87.8	86.2	85.8	76.9	Steady pattern until this year
Despatch Department	70.4	69.0	68.3	72.1	59.7	Recent problems indicated

The trend shown is reasonably consistent for the organisation but a problem seems to have developed in the despatch department during the last year. A study of the external labour market could show that a new firm in the same line of business has recently opened and some of the staff have been attracted by a different working environment. Decisions can now be made to counteract this problem in an attempt to retain existing staff. It is expensive to replace experienced staff and also causes unrest among the remaining staff because they have to do more work while the new employee is being trained up to standard.

A second analysis may concentrate on the **wastage rate** experienced by the same firm. This uses the number of leavers during the year as the basis for the calculation.

This is sometimes known as the **turnover analysis** and is calculated as follows.

$$\text{Turnover rate (\%)} = \frac{\text{Number leaving in 1 year}}{\text{Average number of employees in same period}} \times 100$$

e.g. **Organisation**

$$\frac{1140}{3248} \times 100$$

$$= 35\%$$

Despatch Department

$$\frac{34}{70} \times 100$$

$$= 49\%$$

Table 4.1.5

Area	1995	1996	1997	1998	1999	Notes
Organisation	20	21	22	23	35	Consistent until 1999
Despatch Department	35	36	37	33	49	Unacceptable for 1999

Although the trend for the organisation has been within acceptable limits between 1995–98, the 1999 figure clearly shows that a problem exists. This will also be confirmed by the increased recruitment costs necessary to replace these essential staff. The organisation figure does not show which department has contributed most to this increase and a second analysis by department is required to confirm the highest turnover figures and whether more than one employee has been recruited and left to fill one particular vacancy.

As you can see, the figures have provided different results for both calculations and an organisation does not rely on one set of statistics to show the current position of its labour force. Each set of statistics shows a specific trend and this is the significant figure on which to base decisions. The manager of the despatch department in this example may have been arguing for changes to be made in his department for three years. Little attention has been paid to his request until now when the calculations linked with recruitment costs clearly show that there is a problem. At last the manager has some hard evidence to prove his argument and this is more likely to make senior management take action.

Sickness and absence rates

In addition to labour turnover figures, departmental managers will be asked to record sickness and absence rates. These are important to determine the difference between an employee who is genuinely sick and unable to perform his/her duties and an employee who deliberately takes time off without a genuine reason. Both of these courses of action by a member of staff mean that the manager may have to re-allocate work in order to meet deadlines and customer delivery dates. Sometimes extra staff may have to be employed at short notice or overtime authorised and this increases the wage bill for that department. An explanation will have to be given for exceeding the budget and if this occurs on a regular basis, it will be a great cause of concern to senior management.

Genuine sickness is unavoidable in any organisation and most can cope with small amounts from time to time. Many organisations have a system in place to record the hours/days sickness for each employee. There are three main reasons for this:

- The total number of days must not exceed those allocated under the terms of the contract and can occur in small batches during the year, e.g. flu, migraine, stomach upset.

- Long-term illness, such as a broken leg or a serious operation, may require the work to be covered by a temporary replacement.

- Sickness pay will be calculated according to government regulations and a doctor's certificate may be needed if the absence carries on for a long time.

An employer should be notified in total confidence if an employee is subject to a recurring health problem such as epilepsy. Special arrangements can be made to deal with situations of this nature and in general it will not affect the employee's ability to perform his/her duties. In some circumstances, e.g. the broken leg mentioned above, the employer can make arrangements for the employee to carry out lighter duties on return to work until the limb is sufficiently mended for the employee to return to normal duties.

A simple form is generally used to record the sickness period and this will be sent to the human resource department to be added to the employee's personal file. A spreadsheet may be used if a central recording system is in operation and this allows access by several sections of the firm, each of whom need this data for further actions. These are likely to be:

- the human resource department

- the departmental manager

- the wages/salaries department.

An example of such a form is given on the following page:

Figure 4.1.1

SICKNESS AND ABSENCE RECORD

DEPARTMENT   Despatch   WEEK BEGINNING   8 May

TOTAL HOURS PER EMPLOYEE   39

Name	Mon	Tues	Wed	Thurs	Fri	Sat	Total
Anna Bryant				0.5	1	0.5	2.0
Yvette Oluwi			1				1.0
Kevin Sinclair		1	1	0.5			2.5

Notes: Full day   8.30 am – 5.30 pm   =   1 (minus 1 hr lunch)

Half day   8.30 am – 12.30 pm   =   0.5

Department Manager   *A Bradley*   *(signature)*

Date   *13 May*

Staff absences can be calculated using the formula:

Absence rate (%)

$$\frac{\text{Number of employee hours lost in period}}{\text{Total possible employee hours in period}} \times 100$$

Based on this formula, the total possible employee hours in 1 week is
72 staff $\times$ 39 hours = 2808 therefore the calculation will be:

$$\frac{39}{2808} \times 100 = 1.4\%$$

This is equivalent to one person's total weekly output hours for this department. But if this was multiplied by, say, 12 departments across the firm, it would amount to 468 lost output hours. However, the despatch department would be able to calculate that a total of 48

days would be lost in a year (48 working weeks) if the pattern was repeated each week – this is more than two months' work for one employee.

If an organisation wants to gain more accurate information about the nature of the absence, the form may be more detailed and show the difference between genuine sickness, authorised absences and unauthorised absences, e.g.:

Table 4.1.6

Name	**Monday** Sickness	Authorised Absence	Unauthorised Absence
Anna Bryant			
Yvette Oluwi			
Kevin Sinclair			

This breakdown is more useful to an organisation because it can distinguish between the different types of absence and build up a picture of the reliability of members of staff. It will be much easier to spot a trend in connection with unauthorised absences and action can then be taken to discipline individual employees, e.g. carrying out a personal return interview with the member of staff concerned. This shows that the organisation has noticed that the number of unauthorised absences is excessive and could make the employee think about their commitment to their colleagues and the company.

Authorised absences can be accounted for by such activities as:

- staff attending training days away from the workplace
- meetings with clients
- staffing exhibitions
- attendance at conferences.

On these occasions staff are actually working but just not on the firm's premises.

Other reasons for authorised absences may be pregnancy and parental leave.

Activity

Using the case study material for Smoothmove Ltd. at the end of this chapter, calculate the:

- stability index
- turnover analysis
- absence rates.

Give brief comments on the position identified by each of these statistics.

Age, skills and training

These three areas are closely linked and form another part of the recording procedures carried out by human resource staff. Of particular importance is the **age breakdown** of the current workforce and this is generally watched very carefully.

It is more useful for an organisation to have a workforce that contains a good spread of age bands. This would indicate a depth of experience and therefore consistency in the standards of work produced. More mature employees tend to have a strong sense of loyalty to the firm but may cause a problem if they all retire at the same time.

At the other end of the scale, if the organisation only has young staff who do not stay very long there will be no one experienced enough to train the new starters or take on the role of supervisor or manager. A good mix is best and a constant check is likely to be made to ensure that this is retained.

A recent analysis of the Despatch Department has produced the following data:

Figure 4.1.2

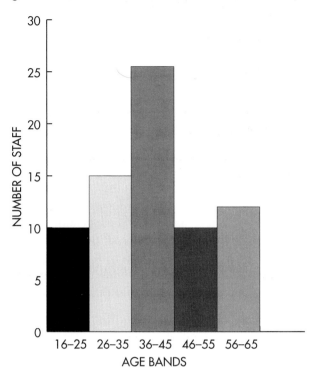

This indicates that 12 staff are getting close to retirement and the organisation will lose their skills and abilities if it does not plan to train up staff to take on their responsibilities. A further breakdown will be needed showing their jobs and levels of authority. An analysis may even be made of the male/female numbers in each age range.

If some of these people occupy key roles, then **succession planning** will need to be implemented so that the organisation does not leave itself in a vulnerable position (see page 259).

Figure 4.1.2 shows that the largest number of employees is in the 36–45 age bracket and there could be potential supervisors and section managers among this group of people. The data also shows that only 10 of the 72 staff are in the 16–25 age range. Here it could be noted that more people in this age range should be targeted in the next recruitment drive. Further evidence may be provided by compiling an age breakdown of the 34 staff who have left the Despatch Department in the last year to see if it is the younger group who mostly make up this contingent.

This type of evidence will lend a powerful argument to the Despatch Department manager, who has been arguing for three years to be allowed to carry out changes to improve working conditions. It could indicate that the current recruitment programme is ineffective because the wrong calibre of candidate is being attracted – short-term fill-in jobs rather than long-term commitment to a job role.

Training

This feature also highlights a key difference in the type of skills and abilities offered by employees in various age bands. This can be matched with the amount of technology currently used or planned for future installation. Additional equipment could mean that two important steps need to be considered:

- a reduction in the number of staff in that department
- training needs analysis of current staff to be able to use new equipment effectively.

Some facts are already known:

Younger staff

- learn to use technology in an educational environment
- often have home computers and good skill levels
- are willing to try new activities.

Mature staff

- have loyalty to the organisation but limited access to technology
- can perform some tasks once shown
- may be reluctant or afraid to increase skill levels.

These facts present the employer with several more important decisions to make:

- Which jobs will now be redundant once the new technology has been installed?
- How long will it take to train staff to use it effectively?
- Which people/age ranges will need to be dismissed? This is crucial because a fair method must be adopted and the organisation does not want to leave itself with staff in one predominant age band for the reasons mentioned previously.
- What type of skills/abilities will be central to the new job roles?

A full analysis will be completed on all the above areas to assist in the decision making process. An example of a skills analysis is given in Table 4.1.7.

The despatch department manager will compile two sets of data – one showing the current skill areas and one showing the requirements associated with the new technology. This will help him or her to identify the people who will require training to adjust to the new technology but it will also indicate the jobs that will no longer be available within the department.

Training courses can be arranged in almost any skill area needed by a firm, e.g. computer software use, telephone techniques or customer service. Some of these can be carried out internally by the human resource department staff but others may require the services of external trainers. Specialist organisations offer training in their related areas, e.g. health and safety specialists can provide a range of courses from first aid, manual handling of goods and emergency evacuation procedures. Other organisations will discuss the company's requirements and devise suitable courses to meet their needs.

In this instance, it is likely that the firm installing the new technology will provide adequate training for staff to be able to use the facilities efficiently. This will be followed up by a HELP service (by telephone or internet) to resolve any difficulties staff experience once they are using the equipment and its operational programs.

Some training may be provided by the organisation on a **cascading** basis. This means that some staff in each department will attend a specific training course and then return to their department to put the new skill into practice. Once they feel competent, it is then their role to train several other people within the department who will, in turn, pass on the new skill to other staff. Figure 4.1.3 shows how it might work.

Table 4.1.7 Skills analysis of jobs in the despatch department

Job Role	Communication			Manual			Customer Service		
	Written	Verbal	IT	Lifting	Moving	Delivering	Telephone	Writing	Face to face
Administrator	✓	✓	✓				✓	✓	✓
Driver	✓	✓		✓					
Packer		✓	✓	✓	✓	✓			
Routing Co-ordinator	✓	✓	✓				✓	✓	✓

Figure 4.1.3 Training on a cascading basis

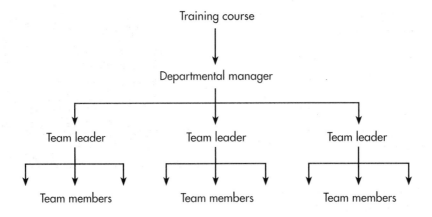

This is quite a cost effective method of training but has one particular disadvantage in that misunderstandings from the original receiver of the training can be passed on to the other members of staff. If an organisation embarks on this pattern of training it would be advisable for a monitoring system to be set up to check the accuracy of lower levels of staff otherwise bad habits can affect the outcome of employee actions.

Succession planning

This is an important aspect of human resource planning and there are several reasons for including it in the development outline of an organisation.

First, there is the issue of continuity of performance from the department as well as the organisation itself. Any reduction in performance of key staff will affect the quality of goods/services produced and, ultimately, the reputation of the firm will suffer. Once damaged in this way, it is difficult to recoup customer loyalty and so attention must be paid to this part of the planning operation.

Secondly, if an organisation suddenly lost several key staff (resignation, retirement or death), it would cause considerable damage to the internal functions of a particular department. These people would take away with them important and essential knowledge about the current position of a project, the thinking behind the new design, the ability to set up and operate software systems and an efficient level of work. This would leave a definite gap in the departmental provision.

Thirdly, when authorised absences from work are being taken (holiday or attendance at conferences etc.) the department must have someone in place who can continue the work of the original member of staff or make decisions in an informed manner.

The above points are some of the main reasons why succession planning is carried out by the human resource department. It means that **key roles** in each department will be identified, e.g. the despatch department manager and the routing co-ordinator. If either of these employees is absent, the work of the department must still continue.

Obviously the department manager is important because of the daily decision making role he performs. A second person must be able to step into this role

when he is away and he or she would not be able to fulfil the duties required to run it efficiently if training and assistance had not been given. It is not practical to leave all decision making tasks until the original post-holder returns – some decisions may be of a critical nature.

In similar circumstances, the role of routing co-ordinator cannot be left unfilled if the employee is absent because it would cause chaos if all the company vehicles were sent in the wrong direction with the wrong loads. This is a particularly crucial job and the post-holder will have local knowledge about one-way systems, parking restrictions, access to motorways, journey times, etc. It would be an expensive operation if all the delivery vehicles took twice as long to complete their rounds.

Both of these key roles will have a nominated second person who will gradually be trained to perform all the tasks carried out by the original occupant. This may take a long time and the intention is *not* to replace the first person but to make sure the department will cope when he or she is not working. It also seeks to aid the promotion prospects of the second person being trained and raises motivation levels. This person will be able to step into the role when needed with the least reduction in service to the customer.

This is an essential **survival** technique used by many medium to large-scale organisations and is one of the main features of the manpower plan devised by the human resource department.

Activity

Identify three more jobs that are likely to be carried out in the despatch department and compile a skills analysis for these roles.

Select one of these jobs and discuss in groups why you consider this to be a key role. What arguments will you put forward to the human resource department for adding it to the Succession Planning programme.

CASE STUDY

Smoothmove Ltd is a small family-run firm carrying out household and business removals. It was set up in Brighton 10 years ago, using two removal vans, but continued to grow slowly each year until larger premises were purchased five years ago. Now expansion is again planned and they are looking for a site on a small business park on the outskirts of Horsham in a good position with easy access to the road network in West Sussex and also motorway routes. The current structure is:

Ian Fairchild (father)	Managing Director and Fleet Operations
Douglas Fairchild (son)	Finance and Marketing
Cathryn Fairchild (daughter)	Administration and Human Resources

Full-time staff work 40 hrs per week (5 × 8 hr days) agreed on weekly basis according to removal schedules.

Part-time staff work 20 hours per week.

Casual drivers/Removers work as needed – 1 / 2 / 3 days per week.

Table 4.1.8

No. of full-time staff	Age bands	Years' service	Left during year
5	56–64	5	0
3	46–55	4	0
7	36–45	3	1
8	26–35	2	0
10	16–25	1	2

No. of part-time staff	Age bands	Years' service	Left during year
2	56–64	5	0
3	46–55	4	0
15	36–45	3	5
7	26–35	2	4
2	16–25	1	0

Staff roles

Table 4.1.9

Permanent Jobs	Number	Sickness/Days
Directors	3	9
Chief accountant	1	5
Clerk	1	12
Recruitment officer	1	4
Marketing co-ordinator	1	3
Telephonist/receptionist	2	12
Estimator	1	5
Depot managers	2	10
Routing co-ordinator	1	6
Drivers	6	18
Removers	12	48
Maintenance engineers	2	6
Total	33	
Part-time staff		
Assistant accountants	2	4
Clerks	3	9
Assistant personnel clerks	2	8
Assistant depot administrators	4	8
Casual drivers	4	–
Casual removers	14	–
Total	29	

Activity

1   Work in small groups.

Look at the Horsham Strategic Plan on page 299 and consider the data relating to business parks and the motorway network. Prepare a 5–10 minute presentation to the directors of Smoothmove Ltd, giving reasons for your recommended choice of business park to site their new depot.

Show how the local employment base would provide new recruits for any additional jobs created and also replacements for those staff not wanting to move when the firm relocates.

2   Calculate and comment upon:

- the stability index
- the turnover rate
- the absence rate.

3   Identify any key training areas that should be planned for if the firm installs a new computer system and updated loading equipment in the new depot.

Recruitment and Selection

KEY TERMS:

growth

recruitment documents

contracts

job description

criteria

restructuring

selection procedures

equal opportunities

application form

tests

cost effectiveness

interviewing techniques

legislation

induction

In this chapter you will learn why people are recruited or dismissed and some of the main reasons that contribute to the decision making process of business organisations in relation to the employment of staff.

Introduction

As discussed in Chapter 1 of this unit, people are a key resource in any organisation but the decision to hire or dismiss staff is generally driven by more acute factors. The easiest of these to understand is when a business has reached its maximum operating capacity in terms of physical and human resources. If forecasts show that customers will maintain their demand for products at peak capacity, expansion of the current facilities will be considered.

This type of **growth** is not a new phenomenon and many organisations have found themselves in this position. The logical step is to search for larger premises within the existing locality. Here consideration will be given to any special funding arrangements by the local council or development zones being promoted by central government departments. If these are not available in the present location, then a search further afield will be made. The final decision in this case will be determined by a comparison of the additional costs that will be incurred as a result of the expansion plans and the benefits that will be gained over a reasonable period of time.

Expansion of a firm's activities ultimately means either an increase in the number of employees to meet the higher demand *or* a complete change in job roles in several departments gained by installing more effective technology. Recruiting the right type of employee to help the organisation meet its new targets is one of the main contributory factors that will determine the location of the business.

Here the market information given in Chapter 1 will be used to assess the potential availability of the right type of employee. Take the example of our mail order company which currently works 5.5 days a week. Expansion plans may include setting up an order and delivery service 7 days a week. In this case, more staff will be needed to cope with the additional hours:

* telephone order clerks

* packers

* drivers.

The firm will carry out an investigation to see if the demand is there and whether or not sufficient business will be generated to cover the increased operating costs. Only then will a search for the new staff begin and constant monitoring of the situation will ensure it remains **cost effective**.

A more frequent occurrence in the present economic climate is the **restructuring** of organisations to reduce the size and scalar chain. This may be instigated by a merger or take-over bid by a rival competitor, which will inevitably lead to duplication of jobs between the two units. After a study of both operating procedures and locations that serve the customers, it is usual to announce that some jobs will be redundant and therefore staff must be dismissed.

The merger between Royal Insurance and Sun Alliance in the Horsham district is one such example and has led to many staff losing their jobs in various parts of the UK. Other insurance companies have followed this example and some staff have found themselves without work as a result of the reduction in the number of jobs available. On 2 November 1999, Prudential said it was closing *all* 103 branches with a loss of 840 sales operation staff, and was axing 400 support staff jobs plus other associated jobs. These jobs are located in the service sector and illustrate the point that it is not just manufacturing units that are being closed down.

The increased use of computer technology has helped staff raise their levels of efficiency and similar organisations, such as banks, are currently:

- reducing the number of branches
- reducing the number of counter staff
- increasing 24-hour telephone banking services.

A constant activity that pushes many organisations to take this course of action is the monitoring of the external climate. Essential analysis of a fast moving business climate prompts senior management to react in order to survive. If this means a reduction in the size of the company and the ultimate loss of jobs for residents of a community, it is a crucial decision that will be made.

On 15 June 2000, the clothing retailer C & A dramatically announced that it was going to close its whole UK operation. The decision to cease trading means that 3000 staff will lose their jobs. But a reduction in the competition could aid the survival rate of firms like Marks & Spencer.

• •

CASE STUDY

MARKS
&
SPENCER

Marks & Spencer

Difficulties have been experienced recently by this major high street organisation and it has lost its market position.
On 2 November 1999, Marks & Spencer announced a 43 per cent drop in profits. This has caused the Board of Directors to make important decisions that affect many employees across the country:

- fewer staff are now employed in the branches

- the graduate recruitment programme has been reduced, particularly for middle line managers

- increased use of surveillance technology to help counteract theft

- two large contracts with traditional UK manufacturers, providing clothes for this giant operation, have been cancelled and thousands of employees across the country will lose their jobs

- more items are being manufactured abroad, taking jobs and finance out of the country.

• •

This is a classic example of the plight of several companies if they are to stay viable in a competitive economy. Marks & Spencer is just one of the many firms having to consider taking such a drastic step because the cost of labour abroad is considerably cheaper than in the UK. A further example of work going abroad is the printing of books and magazines. At the present time it is cheaper to send the written material to another country to be typeset and printed and then import it back into the UK for sale.

Cost effectiveness means looking at all the operating costs and performance levels of staff necessary to produce goods at a low price in order to attract sufficient customers. Unfortunately, this also has a knock-on effect for suppliers to these organisations, and their staff, who rely on continuous support from major retail outlets.

CASE STUDY

Ellington Colliery, Northumberland

On 1 November 1999, the owner of RJB Mining announced the closure of the last deep mine in Northumberland. The workers were given this news at the beginning of the early shift. The owners said it was not cost effective for the colliery to remain open.

This means a loss of 400 jobs in the area and a further blow to the families of these workers who have been supported by the mine for many years. It is particularly painful news to be received just before Christmas. The workers say there is still a large quantity of coal to be mined in this colliery and that the owners have declined to invest in new technology to help them extract it in an efficient manner.

The owners said it would cost £8 million to extract £3 million worth of coal, despite the fact that there is a market for it in the locality. The decision was made that it was not cost effective to invest in new technology and the only course of action was to close the mine.

The above examples show a range of jobs across a variety of professions in manufacturing and manual work that have been lost in recent years. This means that lost jobs have not been concentrated in one sector but are being lost across all three industrial sectors in the UK. Changes like this cause a dramatic alteration in the **nature** of the jobs on offer. The roles staff were originally trained to do are no longer available and people have to be willing to be retrained in order to stay in work. Adaptability is a modern ingredient for a potential worker and one that some traditional professions find it hard to adapt to.

Several factors have contributed to the position organisations find themselves in:

- higher wage levels for all types of job
- increased benefits, e.g. holidays, sick pay, maternity/paternity leave, pension scheme, expense accounts
- more legal requirements imposed on employers, e.g. working time directive, fair and equal treatment, disability provisions, health & safety needs
- greater expectations of potential employees
- trade union influence to improve the working conditions of members.

All of these have to be accounted for in the price of the products offered to customers. If wages are high in a company, the board of directors is almost forced into considering a reduction in the number of staff taken on. This also accounts for the increased practice of target setting and performance measurement to determine which members of staff are providing a cost effective contribution to the operation. We have already looked at some ways of recording this in Chapter 1, with the calculation of absence rates and days of lost production. These are non-recoverable costs and reduce profit levels earned by conscientious employees.

Another key factor that leads a board of directors to follow this path is a re-investigation of the nature of the business itself. If it was originally set up a long time ago, the chances are that its current operations have moved on from the initial objectives. A completely new mission statement may have to be written, identifying the focal point of its present business activities and this can often lead to a change of direction in order to remain competitive in a fluctuating marketplace.

Redefining the business objectives will lead to an analysis of existing job roles and what must be done to change these to meet the revised functions within the organisation. This will match up with the supply-demand factors discussed in Chapter 1 and provides a new outline model of where the organisation now stands.

The company will begin to put appropriate plans into operation to deal with each of these three factors. The aim will be to end up with a workforce that is committed to the objectives of the organisation, is willing to give a high quality of performance in job roles and will be flexible enough to deal with any further changes needed to remain competitive.

In return for such loyalty, the firm will provide good working conditions, treat workers fairly and with equality and will offer opportunities for advancement. For both sides of this equation to work harmoniously, there has to be a strong desire to be part of a successful operation. The procedure is likely to start with the selection of the right employee in the first instance.

Activity

Investigate employment activities in your own locality and analyse recent movements in different occupations. Look at companies that have:

• reduced their operations and shed workers

• increased their activities and created jobs.

Compare the nature of both of these factors and note the variation in the type of work available in your own 'travel to work' area.

Recruitment

Successful organisations pay attention to accurate methods of selection and this helps to avoid them being swamped by unsuitable applicants each time a job is advertised. The whole process can be very time consuming and expensive unless it is carried out systematically.

The main steps in the process can be identified as:

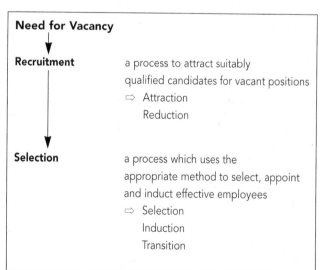

Each year people will voluntarily leave a firm and this number cannot be accurately predicted. The human resource manager will look at an historical analysis of the last three years and estimate that similar numbers will leave again this year. To some extent this will give a reasonable assessment of the number of resignations likely to take place but it will not indicate the specific jobs that will be left vacant. In addition, the economic climate also affects these numbers.

• In times of affluence, people move around the job market freely, attracted by a new challenge or different benefits.

• In times of recession, people stay in jobs in order to maintain their lifestyle and level of income.

In either case, the wrong calibre of candidate may be attracted if the advertisement is not worded effectively and application documents are not prepared that sort out the most suitable candidates. The starting point will be to ask the question: 'Does this vacancy need to be filled?' and if the answer is 'Yes', the process can proceed. Sometimes an analysis of current requirements will produce a 'No' response and the job will be lost from the departmental allocation.

It will be the departmental manager's job to prepare a **job description** of the role to be filled. This is because they will know about the tasks to be covered by the person occupying the job and can advise the human resource department of these requirements. This will be matched with job grade, salary band and benefits to agree a package that is similar to other market rates in the locality. This detail will assist the human resource department to write a suitable advertisement, giving accurate information about the job requirements and the candidate abilities that are needed to match these. Additional detail may include hours of work, rate of pay, benefits and contact point. It is now common practice *not* to quote salary levels because this commits an organisation to pay the stated sum rather than take advantage of current market forces.

The three job categories mentioned at the beginning of Chapter 1 have been used to extract advertisements from the local newspaper in the Horsham area.

These are typical layout designs and show that various organisations are keen to attract specific candidates who are likely to fit into the existing working environment and team operations. These organisations have chosen to advertise their vacancies in an individual manner rather than through an agency. This allows them to display the corporate image and logo associated with the organisation and indicates that:

- good standards are important in all areas of company operations

- candidates with similar viewpoints and commitment are likely to be attracted.

TRAVEL RETAIL

GATWICK AIRPORT NORTH TERMINAL

WH S

Sales Assistants

Come aboard WHSmith Travel Retail for a fast, fun journey to the future of retailing. Most rail and air travellers are in a hurry, but others have time to browse, so we've designed our stores to suit both.

There are 'Read of the Week' novels, 'Hot off the Press' magazines and guides to relevant holiday destinations. All these exciting products make our airport and station stores the most buzzing places to shop and work – as you'll find out, if you join us in any of these roles at Gatwick Airport:

Sales Assistants
If you know how to treat customers in a hurry or just browsing, you have the makings of a great Sales Assistant. We'll provide you with all the training you need to build on your people skills. We'll also keep you busy – serving customers, working on the tills and taking deliveries – so you'll never be bored.

Full-time
Full-time hours are Monday - Friday 5am-2pm, 6am-3pm, 8am-5pm or 9am-6pm or 11am-8pm.

Weekends
Hours are 6am-3pm, 9am-6pm or 11am-8pm Saturday or Sunday.

Nights
Full-time hours are 6pm-6am shift.

Part-time hours are 6pm-12pm midnight shift. All shift positions are 3 days on 3 days off.

For an application form, please telephone 01293 502880 and ask for Mike.

183166

Enjoy your journey.

Activity

Search for a variety of advertisements in your own local newspapers.

- Select advertisements representing three different types of work offered locally.

- Study their content and comment on whether or not they have given appropriate information and are likely to attract the right candidates.

- Note the use of corporate detail and state how this will affect the quality of applicant.

- Analyse the effectiveness of your advertisements in terms of visual impact, quality of information and anticipated level of response.

INGFIELD MANOR SCHOOL

Team Member

Ingfield Manor is a day and weekly boarding school for primary aged children with cerebral palsy. It has a unique place in the development of Conductive Education in this country and has close links with the Peto Institute in Budapest. Ofsted have described the work of the school as outstanding. A person is required to be responsible as a member of the team involved in all aspects of education and care of a group of children (initially working with 4-6 year olds). Applicants should have a relevant child related qualification (e.g NNEB) and be experienced in working with children. Salary in the range £9492 to £13206 depending on experience. Single accommodation may be available. The post is temporary initially up to 14th April 2000, with a planned extension to February 2001.

For further information, job description and application form please contact:

Mrs Beryl Marshall, Administrative Assistant
Ingfield Manor School, Five Oaks
Billingshurst, West Sussex RH14 9AX
Tel: 01403 782294, Fax: 01403 785066

Closing date for return of completed application forms will be Friday 29th October 1999.

Scope (formerly The Spastics Society) is the UK's largest charity working with disabled people. We are committed to equal opportunities.

SCOPE

Working towards
Conductive Education

FARLINGTON SCHOOL

Strood Park, Horsham, West Sussex RH12 3PN

Tel. 01403 254967 Fax. 01403 272258

(GSA Independent Day and Boarding School)
400 girls, 4-18years

REQUIRED FOR FEBRUARY 2000 DRAMA TEACHER TO COVER MATERNITY LEAVE

There may be the opportunity of a part-time Drama post at the end of maternity leave period.
Candidates should have experience in teaching Drama from Year 7 to GCSE and A level.

Applicants should telephone the school as soon as possible for further information.

Companies may choose to advertise their vacancies in other ways to ensure a good range of applications is received. Some of the outlets available are shown in the table below.

The collection of data from all available sources will be part of the recruitment process and firms will want to know the source that is providing best quality of candidates for a given vacancy. Cost effectiveness is always studied in relation to recruitment and firms will want to continue to use the source that produces the

best response. This is *not* measured in numbers but by the calibre of candidates and whether or not they really match the job criteria and are not simply responding to a corporate image which they feel will give them higher benefits than other firms in the locality. Two or three methods may be used on each occasion a vacancy needs to be filled, and the combination selected will relate to the type of job and level of appointment within the firm.

Table 4.2.1 Recruitment methods

Recruitment method	Reasons for use
internal noticeboard	to allow promotion of current employees
specialist publications	to attract professional and highly skilled staff
regional/national newspapers	to attract new talent from outside the locality
TV, radio and the internet	to gain applicants from a wider source
waiting lists	to reduce costs and sort out potential candidates from interested people
employment agencies	to use their facilities and assist internal HR staff
schools, colleges and universities	to attract specific employees at different levels who already possess particular skills
recruitment fairs	to target interested people from other fields of work and talented people in the same field, both seeking new challenges
job centres	to gain staff who are genuinely seeking work

The **job description** written by the departmental manager will give a brief outline of the main tasks covered by the role. It may also state responsibility levels so that the holder will know where they fit into the scalar chain. An example of the general format for a job description is given on the next page.

Larger organisations will add much more detail about specific requirements, particularly in relation to the nature of the business activity carried out by each department. Additional facts may be added to indicate the personal abilities required of the candidate. These will be listed under two headings – essential and desirable – and will help potential applicants to decide whether or not they meet these criteria. If the applicant decides to return a completed application form, a covering letter should provide convincing statements relating to these points. Similar detail has been added at the end of the job description below. As well as being useful to the candidate, this is used by the human resource department to select a shortlist from the applicants who closely match the firm's requirements. Once all the applications have been received, they will be sorted into categories according to how well they have responded to the details sent out.

Many organisations have had to redesign their application forms to take account of recent legislation about equal opportunities. In some cases this has meant removing details such as age, marital status, gender, race and family commitments. The main purpose of an application form is to provide information about a candidate's suitability for the job. This must be judged on the basis of qualifications, skills and abilities and previous experience. No other data should be allowed to influence the final decision. An example of a basic application form is given on page 271.

Most application forms follow a similar pattern and identify key points of interest about the applicant. This enables the interview panel to ask the same questions of all candidates. It is then easier to match the answers for all shortlisted candidates against a defined person specification and allows the candidates to see that a fair interview has been carried out. Any organisation concerned with its corporate image will want to be seen to give equal opportunities to each person shortlisted and for there to be no controversy about the fairness of the interview procedure.

Equal opportunity has a much higher profile in the current employment market and most organisations will want to meet their obligations to this employment condition. A separate detachable form is usually sent out with application details and this will be used as part of the monitoring process to ensure that applicants from different backgrounds are being given the opportunity to join the company's staff.

XYZ Company

Job Description

Job title	*Part-time sales adviser*
Reporting to	*Branch manager*
Location	*Horsham branch*
Hours of work	*Up to 10 hours per week, by arrangement*

Purpose of post
To assist the Branch Manager to achieve a successful level of sales and meet customer needs.

Key duties
- *To assist and advise customers in the selection of equipment.*
- *To demonstrate the equipment and answer any questions from customers.*
- *To organise the packing, despatch and delivery of equipment.*
- *To advise customers about the variety of payment methods.*
- *To use and keep up-to-date current stock control systems.*
- *To arrange for faulty equipment to be repaired or replaced.*
- *To notify Head Office of any outstanding problems.*
- *To maintain the company image at all times.*
- *To carry out any other duties assigned by the Branch Manager.*

Person specification

Essential: GCE/GCSE Maths and English
Good communication skills
Smart, clean and businesslike appearance
Calm and polite manner
Ability to meet targets

Desirable: Technical skills
Decision making skills

XYZ Company

Application Form

Post applied for:

Surname: **Mr/Mrs/Miss/Ms** (delete as appropriate)

First names:

Address:

Postcode: **Daytime telephone number:**

EDUCATION AND TRAINING
(Include all places of education and qualifications gained since age 11.)

Place of education   **Dates**   **Qualifications**

PREVIOUS EXPERIENCE

Name of   **Position held**   **Dates**   **Main duties**
employer

OTHER INFORMATION
Hobbies and interests:

State of health:

REFERENCES

Should we contact you before applying for references?   **Yes/No**

Date available to start work:

Signature: **Date:**

Once it has recruited the employees it needs, the organisation will continue to monitor the background details of its staff. An annual graph may be produced showing the number of staff employed in each category. This will be compared to the previous two years to see if there has been a decrease or increase in people from different backgrounds. This information will also help to complete the statistical returns sent to various government departments to assist them to produce sets of data for publication which show the categories of staff employed in different parts of the country.

Similar statistics will be compiled showing the number of registered disabled staff employed by an organisation. This is another area that has attracted recent publicity because of the new legislation which aims to make recruitment procedures fairer for disabled people. In addition, attention has been drawn to the need to modify the working environment to help disabled employees complete their tasks easily and maintain the same standards as other employees. This could also cover better accessibility to and from buildings, between departments and equipment such as the photocopier and fax machine.

EQUAL OPPORTUNITY MONITORING

The following information will be used for monitoring purposes only.

Gender: Male ....   Female ....

Marital Status: Married   ....   Single ....

                Other (please specify) ....

Ethnic Origin: White   ....

                Black African ....   Black Caribbean ....

                Black Other (please specify) ....

                Pakistani   ....   Chinese   ....

                Bangladeshi ....   Indian   ....

                Asian Other (please specify) ....

                Other (please specify) ....

Please detach and return this form with your application.

The new laws not only refer to better conditions for staff but also to customer facilities to allow disabled people the chance to travel and move freely into all buildings and amenities enjoyed by the rest of the community. Many employers have included this aspect of their provisions as an important part of their equal opportunity policies and recognition of this fact is always appreciated.

The extract from the local newspaper in the Horsham area provides a good example of such a policy. Gatwick Airport is in the 'travel to work' area surrounding Horsham and is a key source of employment for many residents. Equal opportunities are practised by the many firms operating at the terminals and they pride themselves on their application of equal opportunities by covering both features of background and disability where possible.

Airport in top award

FOR the second year running, Gatwick Airport has won an EASE award for providing services and facilities for disabled people.

Developed by the Queen Elizabeth's Foundation for Disabled People, EASE stands for Ease of Access, Service and Employment. The awards are now in their third year.

Gatwick pipped Glasgow and Manchester to the winning post in the airports category of Getting Around. BAA Gatwick policy manager Steve Pidgeon collected the award from Nicholas Witchell and Heather Mills at the London Hilton hotel.

Debby Bond, general manager of Gatwick's South Terminal, said: ''We are delighted to win this prestigious award for the second year running, particularly as we were voted for by disabled passengers.

''It's a credit to all the thousands of staff from all airport companies, who work together to ensure that all our passengers have a smooth and trouble-free journey through the airport.''

Of the 30 million passengers who travel through Gatwick each year, about 350,000 use Gatwick's special needs facilities.

Source: Horsham Advertiser

Activity

Search for evidence of a range of equal opportunities policies being implemented by companies in your own area.

- Select articles from newspapers describing good practice.

- Collect examples from family and friends who are working in organisations adopting good equal opportunities policies.

- Discuss these factors in relation to the above points and also against the legal requirements on pages 280–1.

Interview procedure

The interview procedure can be considerably improved by careful planning of all stages. One of the issues to resolve is the **type of interview** to carry out. This will depend upon the number and category of employees the organisation is seeking to recruit. Several formats can be applied:

One-to-one

This tends to be less formal but may lead to a biased decision.

Panel

Between two and six people may form a panel and each person will ask questions according to their specialism within the organisation; one may be an observer to ensure a fair process has been carried out.

Group

Where a large number of applicants want to join an organisation, these are reduced during a group interview which concentrates on selecting candidates on the basis of sociability, self-confidence and competitiveness, e.g.

graduates being selected for potential management roles, or cabin air staff at airports.

In addition to the interview process, candidates may have to sit different **tests** which highlight certain skills required by the organisation. These can be assessed using:

Psychometric tests

These are based on the psychological characteristics of individuals. Specific questions are written to focus on key characteristics and should be interpreted very carefully by trained psychologists. Five areas are covered by these types of test:

- attainment
- general intelligence
- specific cognitive ability
- trainability
- personality questionnaires e.g. Myers Briggs Type Indicator, Cattell 16 Personality Factors, Saville & Holdsworth Occupational Personality.

Assessment centres

These combine several types of test to give a multi-dimensional evaluation of potential candidates. This is extremely expensive but aims to provide an excellent match between vacant jobs and shortlisted candidates. It is frequently used for high level management positions because of the costs involved but focuses on job analysis and the principal competencies needed to carry it out. An appointment at this level places the employee in a critical and often high profile role so the investment in the selection procedure is felt to be justified once the right person has been found.

The results of any of these testing procedures will not be used alone but as part of the whole selection process. It is unwise to rely on one method alone because behavioural characteristics will prevail once a person becomes an employee. Fitting into the corporate culture is an exceedingly important part of the employee's functions and relates back to the points about corporate image and objectives mentioned at the beginning of this chapter.

Good technique applied by interviewing panels starts by meeting before the candidates arrive and deciding on the type of **questions** to ask. These can be put in either closed, open or problem solving style:

- **closed** questions can be asked to assess the candidate's ability to carry out a specific job.

- **open** questions allow the candidate to develop certain points and expand on information suggested by the interviewer.

- **problem solving** – a problem that may arise in the working environment is described and the candidate's reaction is assessed in relation to decision making and initiative.

Generally, it is possible to use a combination of all three styles but the chairperson will start by introducing the members of the interviewing panel, each of whom will ask specific types of question. The interview will be structured into four sections controlled by the chairperson (see Table 4.2.2).

To assist the panel in their assessment of each candidate, an interview rating form will be used. This may be devised using one of the recognised methods that identify good practice and are part of a systematic procedure. This type of checklist will be linked to the person specification outlined at the foot of the job description on page 270. Each of the characteristics will be rated in relation to a particular job vacancy and will help the interview panel to pitch their questions in the right direction.

The two main classification systems used are the Munro Fraser 5 point plan (Figure 4.2.3) or the Rodgers 7 point plan (Figure 4.2.4). These two methods have been used for many years by medium to large organisations and can be adapted for use against any job description.

Table 4.2.2 Interview structure

Section	Areas covered
Introduction	• welcome • introduce panel members • supply basic information about job
Middle	• combination of closed, open and problem solving questions
End	• offer candidate the opportunity to ask questions • summarise main points covered • inform candidate how and when the result will be given
Afterwards	• record assessment grades • review key points and compare notes • make decision – select new employee • notify all candidates including unsuccessful ones

Figure 4.2.3 Munro Fraser 5 Point Plan (1958)

The 'Pentagonal Peg' allows different emphasis to be put on these qualities as required. In the hypothetical job profile below, qualifications and experience and emotional adjustment are the most important qualities.

Impact on other people

Those whose jobs involve regular contact with others, e.g. salespeople, receptionists, supervisors and teachers, need a good appearance, good manners and communication skills. Socially isolated jobs (e.g. long distance lorry driving) require a different type of person.

Qualifications and experience

These refer to the minimum skill and educational levels necessary for a job, plus the formal qualifications and documented work experience.

Intelligence

Some jobs require quick thinking, mental agility and the ability to interpret complicated issues.

Motivation

Repetitive, production line work can be boring so financial rewards are probably the major motivating factor.

Other jobs present opportunities for creativity and self-development and would be more appropriate for people with drive, enthusiasm, self-direction and personal ambition.

Emotional adjustment

Jobs which contain elements of stress should not be attempted by timid workers. Dealing with irate customers or coping with belligerent operatives, unsympathetic colleagues or unpleasant working conditions needs workers who are adaptable and self-assertive.

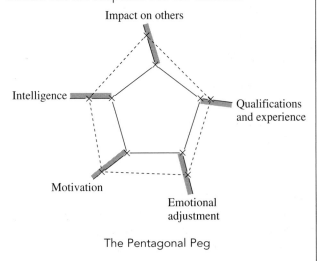

The Pentagonal Peg

Figure 4.2.4 Alec Rodgers 7 Point Plan (1952) for use by the National Institute of Industrial Psychology

Characteristics	Above Average	Satis	Below Average
1			
2			
3			
4			
5			
6			
7			

Rodgers 7 Point Plan

1 Physical makeup

2 Attainments

3 General intelligence

4 Special aptitudes

5 Interests

6 Disposition

7 Circumstances

Although both of the above methods have been used extensively in selection processes, the influence of equal opportunities has allowed another set of criteria to enter the frame. The 6 Factor Formula offered by Pilbeam attaches more importance to the issue of flexibility,

called for in ever increasing quantities by the modern employer. It concentrates on the abilities of candidates to perform current tasks as well as looking to the future when changes may need to be implemented in the working environment. The method covers:

Figure 4.2.5 Pilbeam 6 Factor Formula

Factor – where relevant and measurable	High 3 points	Medium 2 points	Low 1 point
Skills, knowledge and competencies			
Personality characteristics			
Level of experience			
Certificated qualifications			
Physical characteristics			
Development potential			
Overall rating and recommendation			

Whatever method of recording interview results is used, these will be assessed at the end of the interview schedule. In most cases, this will produce a positive result for one candidate but disappointment for others. Many organisations offer a feedback session to unsuccessful candidates to help them improve their interview technique or prompt them to gain more qualifications and experience. Sometimes the panel will decide that no suitable candidate has emerged to meet the person specification and the job will be re-advertised.

Once a decision has been reached, a letter of congratulation can be sent to the successful candidate asking if he or she is prepared to accept the appointment. The unsuccessful candidates will also be contacted to thank them for attending and wish them 'good luck' for future applications. This goodwill gesture is all part of the corporate image created by an

organisation and it is useful to maintain such a diplomatic relationship because the company may want to employ some of these people at some time in the future.

The human resource department now takes on the role of preparing a formal letter of appointment and a **contract** which the new employee will be asked to sign and return as their acceptance of the new appointment. Both of these should clearly reflect the job and points discussed during the interview so that the new member of staff knows exactly what the job will entail. Depending on the complexity of the job, the content of a contract will change to match these requirements but most contracts follow a standard pattern.

An example of a letter of appointment and a contract are given below for the position of Customer Services Agent at Gatwick Airport.

Figure 4.2.6 Letter of appointment

BM Handling Services

BM Handling Services
Room 639 Norfolk House
Gatwick Airport
West Sussex RH6 0NP

Ms Kirstie McAllister
4 Kingsfold Mews
Ashington Lane
Horsham
West Sussex
RH12 6PN

Tel + 44 (0)1293 502429
Fax + 44 (0)1293 502428

11 March 1999

Dear Ms McAllister,

Further to your interview, I am pleased to offer you the position of Part Time Customer
Service Agent, commencing 12 April 1999.

Your starting salary will be that of Band F Training Level 2, equivalent to £4.86 per
hour. After successful completion of two months your salary will rise to that of Band F
Training Level 3, equivalent to £5.12 per hour. After six months service, providing you
are deemed competent in the position of Customer Services Agent, you will rise to
Band F full grade - £5.40 per hour. In addition to the above you will also receive a
Shift Pay Premium according to the shifts that you work. Whilst based at Gatwick
Airport you will also receive an additional LGW Weighting payment of £1,000 per
annum full-time (paid pro rata).

If you are accepting this offer of employment, please complete the slip below and return
it to: Andy Williamson, Room 639, Norfolk House, Gatwick Airport, West Sussex,
RH6 0NP within 5 working days. In the event that we do not receive your signed
acceptance we will assume that you have turned down this offer.

As soon as we have received your acceptance, a Contract of Employment will be sent
out to you along with joining and training instructions.

Finally, may I take this opportunity to welcome you to British Midland and if you have
any queries at all please do not hesitate to contact Andy Williamson on 01293 502429.

Yours sincerely

pp

Val Eglesfield

The contract of employment is a legal document and
will be referred to if a serious dispute arises between the
employer and the employee which cannot be resolved
internally. However, it also covers two different aspects
– express and implied conditions.

Express terms

These terms cover the written details itemised in the
contract itself and place obligations on both parties.

Implied terms

These terms cover the additional factors or expectations
of both parties:

- The employer will provide suitable work, pay
  salary at agreed intervals, ensure a safe working
  environment, not ask staff to carry out any unlawful
  tasks and expect a good standard of work.

- The employee will carry out tasks to a satisfactory
  standard, attend work regularly, follow health and

safety procedures and not damage property
belonging to the employer.

A contract is an agreement between two parties – the
employer has work available and the employee provides
the skills to complete the task satisfactorily. Under these
circumstances, a potential employee should read the
document carefully and ask for clarification or
amendment of the wording of any statements they do
not agree with before signing it. A misunderstanding of
any area could lead to the disciplinary process being
invoked if the employer finds an employee has broken
any of these conditions. Similarly, an employee can sue
an employer if it does not meet its obligations, e.g. not
paying staff at the agreed interval or asking them to
carry out work that is illegal.

The Employment Rights Act 1996 covers the right of
employees to receive a written statement giving the
main terms and conditions of employment within two
months of starting work, if they work for more than
eight hours a week and for a period of more than one
month. The points to be covered in a written particulars
of employment document include:

- names of the employer and employee

- the date the employment started

- the date when continuous employment began

- place of work, or the required place of work, and the
  employer's address

- if non-permanent work, the expected length, or the
  end date if fixed term

- the particulars of collective agreements directly
  affecting individual terms and conditions

- rate of pay, method of calculation and payment
  interval

- hours of work and normal working hours

- holiday entitlement and holiday pay

- arrangements for sickness and sick pay

- pension arrangements

- length of notice periods, on both sides

- job title or brief description of the job

- disciplinary and grievance – rules, arrangements and
  procedures.

Figure 4.2.7 Contract of employment

BRITISH MIDLAND

TERMS AND CONDITIONS OF EMPLOYMENT

WITH BRITISH MIDLAND AIRWAYS LTD

Defined in accordance with the Employment Protection (Consolidation) act 1978, as amended, relating to:-

FULL NAME	: Ms Kirstie Mc Allister
JOB TITLE	: Part Time Customer Service Agent
DATE OF JOINING	: 26th April 1999

Employment with a previous employer does not count as part of your period of continuous employment with this Company

SALARY

Your starting salary is as per the attached letter, payable monthly by credit transfer to your bank account.

PLACE OF WORK

Your place of employment is London Heathrow Airport but the Company has the contractual right to require you to work at any location within or outside the United Kingdom at which the company operates or intends to operate.

HOURS

Your normal working hours are a minimum of 20 hours per week, and to a pattern agreed by management. Any additional hours worked will be paid at plain time rate up to 37.5 hours.

Where you are required to work additional hours over 37.5, overtime may be payable at the appropriate rate. Alternatively, at Management discretion, time off in lieu may be given.

ANNUAL LEAVE

Your annual leave entitlement is accrued at pro rata the full time rate. This leave is in addition to pro rata eight public holidays per annum.

Leave not taken cannot be carried to the following year and no payment will be made in respect of untaken leave, except for untaken leave at termination of employment. The Company reserves the right to deduct from final pay such monies as may have been paid in respect of leave taken in excess of entitlement.

Leave must be taken at such times as are agreed with your immediate Supervisor.

On transfer to full time status, your service for the purpose of leave calculation will count from your date of joining.

During the first six months of employment, leave in excess of accrued entitlement will only be possible with the Company's special agreement.

SICKNESS AND ABSENCE

You are required to advise your immediate supervisor within two hours of your normal starting time if you are unwell and unable to work.

SICK PAY SCHEME

Length of service	Period of "Normal Pay"
1 to 13 weeks	no pay
13 weeks to 36 months	13 weeks
3 to 6 years	26 weeks
Over 6 years	52 weeks

NOTICE

You are entitled to receive and required to give the following notice in writing to terminate your employment with the company.

Continuous Employment	Period of Notice Given by Company	Given by Employee
Less than one year	Four weeks	Four weeks
One to Two years	Four weeks	Four weeks
Two to Four years	Four weeks	Four weeks
Four to Twelve years	One week for each year of service	Four weeks

| After twelve years | Twelve weeks | Four weeks |

At the company's option payment may be made in lieu of notice.

You are also reminded that you would be in breach of contract if you were to leave the company without giving the requisite period of notice. Legal remedies would be pursued for any such breach.

CONFIDENTIALITY

You must not divulge or communicate to any person confidential information of the Company which you may receive or obtain whilst in the service of the Company. This restriction will continue to apply after the termination of your employment without limit in time but shall cease to apply if the information or knowledge passes into the public domain.

UNIFORM

The uniform provided by the Company should be regarded as on loan and you are required to wear it whenever you are on duty. You are responsible for its upkeep, maintenance and cleanliness. Replacement items will be supplied in accordance with the Company policy.

You will be charged for any replacement which is due to neglect or to wilful damage. All uniform items must be returned to the issuing officer on termination of employment.

DISCIPLINARY AND GRIEVANCE PROCEDURES

Details of the procedure can be obtained from your manager.

PROBATIONARY PERIOD

Your appointment is subject to a three month probationary period. You will be given formal notification of satisfactory completion of this period.

PROTECTION OF PROPERTY

The company seeks the co-operation of all staff in taking a preventative approach to the protection of both company property and the property of employees. Improper possession of property is a disciplinary offence.

Staff, if so requested by a designated official, are required to disclose the contents of any parcel, package, bag or motor vehicle being taken on or off British Midland premises or premises used by British Midland.

COMPANY IDENTITY CARD

You are required to carry your Company Identity Card at all times and produce it for inspection when requested.

AVIATION SECURITY AND IDENTITY CARDS

When entering or in an airport restricted area the appropriate airport pass must be worn visibly (unless a dispensation has been granted).

It is a company requirement that you wear your company identity card visibly at all times entering or on British Midland premises or premises used by British Midland.

Disciplinary action will be taken against any employee who fails to display the appropriate identity car/pass or loses or misuses any identity card or pass.

CONCESSIONARY TRAVEL

The reduce rate travel scheme operated by the company is not a contractual entitlement. It is a concession which may be withdrawn or amended at any time without notice. Applications for reduced rate travel should be made in accordance with the company's reduced rate travel scheme prevailing from time to time.

Signed ....

Print name (Andrew Williamson)

On behalf of British Midland Airways Ltd.

Dated 29 March, 1999

I confirm that I have read the statement of terms and conditions of employment relating to my appointment with British Midland Airways Ltd and accept the offer on these terms and conditions.

Signed ....

Dated   day of   1999

In addition, employers need to bear in mind that employees are entitled to see the information held on them in both manual and computerised formats and this will include interview notes. This right has been granted under the 1996 Data Protection Directive which came into force in October 1998.

If a successful candidate accepts a job offer, referees will be contacted to confirm the statements given in the application material. The new employer will be looking for notes that corroborate good attendance records and satisfactory standards of performance.

Employers recognise the need to help new employees settle into their role in a harmonious way. An **induction course** can be set up, which follows a general pattern, but considerable research has been carried out to show that the induction process should be extended beyond this initial programme to avoid the 'induction crisis' period.

Jobs which involve a wide range of skills will need more extensive training and this can include information technology and the different systems used in the new organisation. A planned series of activities over a 6–12 month period will allow the new recruit to gain knowledge and confidence, both of which will improve his or her levels of productivity.

If an employer presents the new employee with unrealistic goals, this will be a major contributory factor in causing the person to change his/her mind and leave. Furthermore, if a job has been falsely described, the new employee will soon find out it is below his/her expectations and will leave. The first two to three months of employment are crucial in establishing a good working relationship between the two parties. Showing an interest in the new employee's progress and the stages of settling in by the management can ease the burden of coping with a new environment and procedures as well as getting to know other colleagues.

The main function of an induction course is to present the new employee with enough information to help the settling in process. The key points to include in an induction course are:

- a brief description of organisational objectives and values

- a summary of departmental structure and where the job fits in

- main rules and regulations including health and safety

- identifying any training needs

- planning a systematic review of progress.

Often too much information is given and the new employee will be swamped with irrelevant detail that could be gained slowly over a period of time and when the extra detail is useful. This would eliminate some of the pressure placed on new employees and help them to become valuable members of staff.

Legislation

Equal Pay Act 1970

This Act covers the equal pay value for the same work performed by men and women. It was amended by the Equal Value Regulations 1983 which implies that the contract of employment should contain a clause on equality of rights. These statutes have been influenced by the Treaty of Rome (Article 119) which requires the UK to apply the principle that men and women should receive equal pay for equal work. It indicates that jobs should be rated using a job evaluation scheme which focuses on the content, tasks and abilities needed to carry out the role rather than the gender of the person carrying out the job itself. Employees claiming unfair treatment can take their case to a tribunal and the Equal Opportunities Commission can be asked to give advice. Successful claims will be awarded back pay up to two years but substantial investigations will be made to determine the success or failure of such claims.

Rehabilitation of Offenders Act 1974

This act aims to help people who have served prison sentences to have a reasonable chance of securing employment following a period of rehabilitation. Depending on the severity of the crime and sentence, applicants do not have to declare 'spent' convictions to potential employers. These can range between six months to 10 years after completion of the sentence but there are several exemptions, where high levels of trust are concerned because of working with vulnerable members of the community, e.g. in:

- the legal profession

- the medical profession

- jobs involving the care and control of young people

- work in social services.

Sex Discrimination Act 1975

This act covers the basic premise that it is unlawful in employment to discriminate on the basis of sex or marital status. Sometimes, in exceptional cases, the sex of the candidate may be a genuine occupational qualification, such as:

- the authenticity of a drama role where a specified sex is essential
- the job is to be given to a couple and requires one of each sex
- the job brings the employee into personal contact with people who would object to the presence of someone of the opposite sex.

The Equal Opportunities Commission was set up to oversee the terms of reference for this Act, which include:

- the promotion of the equal treatment of men and women at work
- the role of monitoring the operation of this legislation
- the drafting of recommendations for improvements to the legislation for presentation to government
- the prosecution of any case that is considered a blatant breach of the legislation.

Race Relations Act 1976

Following the pattern of the Sex Discrimination Act, this act makes it unlawful to discriminate in employment on the grounds of race, colour, nationality or ethnic origin. However, certain jobs do require a person from a particular racial or ethnic group to be recruited, such as:

- the modelling of specific clothes from a particular ethnic community
- the provision of welfare services to a particular ethnic community when these can be better provided by a person from this specific racial group.

This Act established the Commission for Racial Equality, with the main aim of promoting equal opportunities for minority racial groups as well as the monitoring of the operation of the Act.

Disability Discrimination Act 1995

This Act grants statutory rights to people with disabilities and gives limited protection to them. It describes disability as 'a physical and mental impairment which has a substantial and long-term adverse affect on a person's ability to carry out normal daily activities'. It refers to people who currently have a disability and people who have had such an occurrence. The main areas covered are:

- a physical difficulty affecting mobility
- an impairment of the senses, e.g. sight and hearing
- mental impairment, e.g. learning capabilities
- recognised mental illness.

The Act also covers severe disfigurements and progressive medical conditions such as HIV/AIDS and MS. The definitions go much further than employers had previously considered. People in wheelchairs were once nearly always treated less favourably and many objected to this, stating that although their limbs might not work as well as other people's their brains certainly do.

This legislation requires employers to adjust the working environment to help the disabled employee cope with his or her duties by:

- altering furniture, facilities and premises
- changing tasks and activities
- accepting absences from work for treatment
- providing training and supervision.

Employers with fewer than 20 staff are not covered by this Act but the National Disability Council advises the government on anti-discriminatory cases and suggests improvements.

Activity A

In addition to the laws described above, work in small groups to research legislation that has been passed in the last two years, particularly any laws that affect employment conditions, e.g. the Working Time Directive.

Many of the latest laws are directly linked to our membership of the EU and reflect the fact that we need to bring our employment practices closer to those of our EU partners. The aim is to have the freedom to live and work in any of these countries and know their working conditions will be similar.

Outline the implications the new laws will have for both parties to the employment contract, e.g. employer and employee. Summarise the changes in working practices that will be needed by employers to meet their new obligations.

Present your findings to the rest of the class as a networking activity.

Activity B

Using the case study material at the end of Chapter 1 (page 260) relating to Smoothmove, complete the following tasks.

1   The managing director has identified that because of a planned increase in business, additional staff must be recruited. These are:

- 2 full-time drivers
- 1 estimator
- 1 maintenance engineer.

2   Choose one of these positions and write a job description for the role.

3   Draft an appropriate advertisement to be printed in the local newspaper (bear in mind that company image is important).

4   Give brief notes on the legal obligations of employers in the recruitment process.

5   Design an interview rating form using one of the person specification models described in this chapter. Give examples of each type of question (closed, open and problem solving) for use by members of the interview panel for your chosen job.

6   Write the letter confirming the appointment of a candidate and attach a suitable contract of employment.

7   Outline an induction course and suggest any training needs the employer should provide for the new member of staff.

Performance Management

In this chapter you will learn about the factors that affect the performance of staff and how they can be rewarded for their contribution to the success of an organisation. Also given consideration is the area of motivation and ways in which employers can encourage their staff to maintain interest in their work.

provide the family with a home and sufficient food to follow a healthy diet, and afford luxuries such as holidays, cars and regular entertainment.

An employee is given an award for her work

Introduction

All members of staff take a keen interest in the methods used by an organisation to reward them for loyalty and hard work. It is generally recognised that the majority of people go to work for a range of reasons but predominant among these is the need to earn a living wage. To an employee, this means being able to pay bills on time,

affect operating costs. Other features that organisations will monitor are the quality of work being produced and the efficiency levels within departments. These are important from the point of view that customers will not return to a company for repeat purchases if staff are inefficient, because too many complaints and uncompleted tasks will push up costs to an exorbitant figure.

In some cases, poor performance will lead to dismissal but if inefficiency is allowed to continue unchecked, staff will lose interest, motivation will be reduced and there will be no incentive to produce good quality products. Employers will be unable to reward staff under these conditions because profits will be insufficient to cover high wage costs plus benefits. It is in no one's interest to allow this to happen and companies strive to avoid this scenario by ensuring staff are fully aware that their efforts are appreciated and therefore continually measured.

It is obviously easier to measure performance when a specific product is being made or sold, but it is much more difficult to set targets for a service environment. This has to be done, however, and so the number of telephone calls answered or letters replied to will be recorded on a daily basis. By monitoring progress in this way, departmental managers can assess the efficiency of staff and determine which ones are meeting the terms of their contract and contributing to company success.

Performance management

In the quest for efficiency, a comprehensive process of performance measurement will be central to the fair distribution of rewards. A number of stages will be set up and part of the recruitment procedure will be to gain staff with a high level of commitment to the aims and objectives of the organisation. These will be determined by the senior management team and will reflect the nature of the business activity carried out by the firm. From this, a **mission statement** will be identified and all staff will be encouraged to meet and exceed the levels of service described by it. Mission statements from some well known organisations are given below and signify the importance these firms place on the image created by such statements:

In today's modern world, a living wage has been gained through many years of negotiation by trade unions and other pressure groups. This has been aided by our membership of the EU and the passing of legislation on the minimum wage (currently £3.70 per hour). A normal salary package covers a good level of remuneration plus other benefits, such as paid holidays, sick pay, a pension scheme and an annual bonus. Senior management attract additional benefits such as a company car, expense account and profit sharing scheme. Employers are conscious of the fact that the overall remuneration package for each employee adds up to an exceedingly high proportion of any money earned from the sale of goods or services. Because customers demand ever increasing standards of performance plus lower prices, this always places pressure on organisations to search for reductions in operating costs.

The best way to achieve 'value for money' is to monitor the performance levels of staff and aim to reduce wasteful activities. In Chapter 1, the calculation for turnover of staff, the stability index and absence rates were discussed and these are three essential factors that

British Telecom	School	The National Trust
– to be the most successful world-wide communications group	– we will provide an extensive range of educational experiences to enable students to reach their full potential	– to promote the permanent preservation for the benefit of the nation of lands and tenements (including buildings) of beauty or historic interest

These definitions give a summary of the values and beliefs that support the cultural climate within the organisational structure. From this framework, the human resource manager will set up strategies to assist departmental managers to measure their staff performance levels. Each department will identify its own aims and objectives to contribute to the overall effectiveness of the company. The departmental objectives will be directly linked to the activity carried out within it and will then be cascaded down to each member of staff. In some cases, this will be at team level where several employees will be expected to make a contribution. Training may be provided to assist individual and team members to achieve their goals.

Departmental meetings and team meetings are likely to take place to agree such goals and to keep staff informed about progress towards achieving these. Co-operation by staff results in a higher degree of success than unwilling workers who are not prepared to play an equal part in their attainment. This will lead to extra work being done by some members of the team who take a pride in achievement and could lead to the unhelpful member of staff losing a bonus or potential increased responsibility level.

If employees are to meet their targets, these targets must be realistic and achievable and the organisation must provide suitable resources to enable them to complete tasks satisfactorily. Staff can easily complete tasks they are competent in performing but, to aid motivation, new tasks can be added to the existing skills and an allowance must be made when this occurs. A method of creating fair individual or team goals will be used by the human resource department and this could be done by

the SMART model:

Specific   use clear language to describe exactly what is required

Measurable   identify numerical targets and outputs which can be counted and assessed

Agreed   agree these with the employee so that they take responsibility for their own output

Realistic   set targets that are attainable for each individual, according to their skills and competencies

Time-related state specific dates when targets must be achieved and will be measured.

By discussing these objectives with each employee, the departmental manager will be able to make small adjustments to match individual employee capabilities. The aim is to keep motivation levels high so that staff feel able to concentrate their energies on achieving their particular targets. If these are unrealistic, this will lead to demoralised staff who know they will not be able to meet the targets and this will lead to unnecessary absences, placing the employee in an even worse situation. Examples of realistic targets to fit the three scenarios used at the beginning of each chapter are:

- **Salesperson** to achieve £5,000 sales per week and to minimise complaints by providing advice to enable customers to select the correct product for their needs.

- **Teacher** to achieve grade C or above for 60 per cent of GCSE candidates.

- **Fund raiser** to achieve £2,000 worth of donations each week and one new sponsor per month to allow the charity to continue its work with disadvantaged people.

Part of the monitoring process will be to see how close staff have come to meeting their targets and analysing the reasons for non-achievement. This can be done more frequently for staff who are falling behind the set target figures and it will be up to the departmental manager to give encouragement and assistance to the slower members of staff. Confrontation helps no one and will inevitably lead to resignations and poor performance levels for that particular department.

Activity

1   In small groups, select one job role from Smoothmove and prepare a set of objectives for that employee, using the SMART model as your guide.

2   Clearly indicate numerical targets and timescales when these will be measured.

3   Compare your group notes with other teams and produce a good example of SMART objectives.

If an organisation is directed by a mission statement, part of the procedure to meet its requirements will be the **performance appraisal system**. Most medium to large companies use different methods of appraisal for each level in the hierarchy. This is because the higher up employees are in the organisation, the closer it brings them to strategic targets and, ultimately, into immediate contact with the corporate objectives. The more complicated a system is the more time consuming it is – but if results are important, then this is time well spent!

Several models are available, as shown opposite.

Whichever method is used for each category of staff, it requires a positive approach from all participants. Employees dislike direct criticism of their performance at any level and the human resource department must introduce and operate such schemes with openness and honesty. If the scheme is run in too strict a way, this will limit the response of staff who will see it only as a method of not rewarding them if targets are not achieved. This is counter-productive and will cause considerable unrest amongst all parts of the hierarchy.

Human beings are not faultless and situations do occur during the period identified for measurement, e.g. six or 12 months, which will affect the intended targets. Employees would ask for understanding and tolerance of such occurrences and if a manager is continually monitoring progress this factor will be noted for discussion. In addition, human beings like to be congratulated for a job well done, use of initiative or the creation of a new idea. This is also part of the manager's role and shows staff that their efforts have been noticed and are appreciated.

A combination of these **feedback** mechanisms will be extremely valuable in strengthening the manager-employee relationship. Regular feedback is essential because it stimulates personal development, while specific feedback acts as a motivator by adding new responsibilities to work that can become mundane once it has been repeated for long periods without change. Many appraisal schemes are linked to the annual reward system and success can be recognised by pay increases, promotion, a higher job grade or other benefits, e.g. bonus.

However, managers may find themselves with the unenviable task of discussing poor performance with some staff. The main aim here will be to gain a change in attitude or standards of behaviour. Most of this can be remedied by training in the skill that is weak, making the employee see how relevant their job is to the rest of the team or, in a minority of cases, taking disciplinary action or even redeployment to another department. These actions will be agreed between the two parties and recorded as the outcome of the appraisal.

Training courses

The appraisal interview is a good source of finding out where employees require help. If a member of staff has not been able to achieve set targets, it could be due to a lack of skills. This is easy to remedy by giving training and there are many methods available, depending on the nature of the ability to be improved, e.g.

- limited use of IT software, communication skills and teambuilding can all be improved through in-house courses

- management abilities and accountancy can be improved by attending external courses.

Specific abilities related to job content can be assisted by 'on the job' instruction, e.g. sales representatives, or coaching/shadowing a particular supervisor/manager.

Scheme

Application

Top down

- The immediate line manager carries out the appraisal of individual employees.
- An impartial 'grandparent' appraiser can be involved to act as arbiter by reading the notes and ratings awarded and amending them, if necessary.

Self-appraisal

- This is becoming a more frequently used method because it involves the employee reflecting on his/her own performance.
- This would then be discussed against the manager's rating and agreement reached on the way forward.

Peer appraisal

- This method uses peers and colleagues to assess the performance levels of staff, e.g. managers.
- It may be carried out using an assessment questionnaire.

Upward appraisal

- This concentrates on management style and the effectiveness of managers and staff reporting to the manager will complete rating documents.
- These will be analysed and discussed with a view to improving features such as communication patterns or team responsibilities.

360° Appraisal

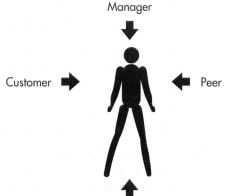

- This multi-rater method uses assessments from all angles and aims to gain a much wider view of employee performance.
- It seeks to raise standards and effectiveness within departments.

Many organisations bring in outside consultants to set up company-specific courses if their own provisions are not adequate. Some staff will be encouraged to join college courses which will be attended after work or an allowance of one afternoon/one evening will be given.

One of the most important aspects of training that companies must provide is related to health and safety. Careful operation of all equipment and machinery is a legal requirement and all firms need trained first aiders to assist injured staff. It must be stressed that staff should never attempt to fix malfunctioning equipment such as computers and it is part of a manager's role to remind staff of this fact.

Employees can do a lot to help themselves and many companies actively pursue personal development training. This is a competence-based activity and starts with the recognition and awareness by employees of their own shortcomings. It is much easier to change a person's attitude, behaviour and performance levels if they are actively engaged in the process. Sometimes a counselling or mentoring system will be set up to give assistance, depending on the severity of the problem, and this will be carried out by an employee in another department so that unbiased help is given. Managers themselves will be encouraged to participate in self-development and it is in the organisation's interests to provide a suitable climate for this to happen.

The aim of training is **to permanently change a person's ability by improving their skills**. Training needs can be identified on three levels:

- Organisation – If the firm is changing its requirements, new training will be needed to bring employees up to full knowledge.

- Department – Specific abilities may be needed to carry out tasks and new staff need help in mastering these techniques.

- Individual – Particular weaknesses can be noted for improvement and potential management candidates can be developed.

If gaps are found in any of these areas, training can be arranged to allow everyone to move forward. Once a training course is finished, the progress of the attendees will be monitored to see if they are applying the new skills satisfactorily. Encouragement and extra help are advisable at this stage, otherwise the value of the training received can be lost if the employees do not fully understand what they have just learnt. Being offered training is a method of motivation in itself and staff should take advantage of this additional facility.

Theories of motivation

The ability to motivate employees is central to the role of a supervisor and manager. This is needed both for individual members of staff and, more frequently, for teams in the current working environment where team activities play an important part in departmental operations. The ability to motivate people comes from a greater awareness and understanding of individual behaviour patterns. It is also aided or hindered by the style of management used within an organisation as well as the structural parameters designed by senior management.

The notion of motivation has been developed over a century of business practice and this has been studied by many theorists in an attempt to discover the perfect solution to keeping staff motivated. There is no such thing as a perfect solution, of course, because managers are dealing with human beings, each of whom has a completely unique personality. This means that one solution would not suit all employees and so the skill of a good manager is to use a variety of techniques to motivate all kinds of staff.

The senior management of an organisation will assist managers in their duties by providing a series of benefits and rewards for consistent levels of motivation for two reasons:

- to allow the manager discretion in the treatment of staff at different levels

- to encourage high standards from staff who will be rewarded for their efforts.

In addition, it is recognised that not all employees are willing workers and a series of disciplinary procedures will be agreed for those employees who fail to respond to the encouragement given by management.

In the smaller, leaner organisation of today, there is no room for employees who do not put in maximum effort. If one person lets the team down, then the whole team's rewards will be affected and dissatisfaction will spread quickly. If the company has flattened the organisational structure, fewer opportunities for promotion are available to offer as a reward to hard-working staff. This makes the manager's job all the more difficult since maintaining high levels of motivation are crucial to achieving targets and customer satisfaction.

The ideas of several major theorists have contributed to the change in approach taken towards people as **human resources** within a business. Theories develop as a result of the weaknesses pinpointed in existing ideas. These are then incorporated into new theories and used as guidance mechanisms for senior management to establish good practice within their operations.

Many theories have been established within the last 100 years and it is not possible to consider each one of these. What is important in the study of motivation are the key names that have influenced today's approach. Four major theories have remained at the forefront of motivational techniques and each one is linked to a different style of management. They are:

- Frederick Winslow Taylor
- Douglas McGregor
- Abraham Maslow
- Frederick Herzberg.

Frederick Winslow Taylor (1856–1915)

This was one of the first theories to be recognised and used by management to reinforce employee behaviour patterns. In the first instance, Taylor was a superintendent at the engineering firm of Midvale Steel Company, who looked at ways to improve efficiency levels. In 1898 he joined the Bethlehem Steel Company to improve work methods. His aim was to increase the productivity of pig iron workers and he studied the actions taken to perform certain tasks until he devised a system to improve completion rates.

Taylor used a stop-watch to time how long it took to carry out the different parts of a job. From this he calculated the optimum number of actions an employee could complete in a normal working day. This established a target setting system so that work was measured per individual and productivity rates could be calculated more accurately. If staff exceeded their quota, they were rewarded with a bonus, which was considered to be the first step in motivational procedures. Mass production techniques were developed from this idea.

Analysis

- The premise here is that people *only* go to work for money and if you can offer a way of increasing this, then that is motivation enough.

- This approach established the phrase 'managers have the right to manage' because the assumption was made that managers know best how to perform tasks and staff would willingly accept orders without question.

- This links with the **autocratic** style of management which still operates in many businesses today.

- What was useful from this theory was the idea that:

  a) There should be careful selection of staff on the basis of their abilities.

  b) Tasks can be broken down into small components.

  c) Training will develop skill levels and improve efficiency.

  d) Targets can be set so that staff know what they have to achieve.

  e) Rewarding staff with financial incentives aids motivation.

All of these points apply today in many companies, particularly where a very flat operation exists and each person must play a part to ensure the survival of the business.

If it is applied to Smoothmove, improvements in productivity rates could be gained. For example, it is usual to penalise furniture removers/drivers if they damage customer property or company vehicles during the removal process by deducting money from their wages. This demotivates staff and does not encourage long-term service.

The board could discuss a different approach and provide training to lift and pack items carefully, plus providing helpful resources, e.g. special trolleys, to make the job easier. A bonus every three months for accident-free work may help staff retention rates as well as reducing breakages. Installing a routing system to help drivers and warn them of any major road problems will reduce the need to reach destinations quickly. Provision of mobile phones would keep everyone in touch with the situation and relieve the need to find telephone boxes to maintain contact with head office. Lastly, target setting could be investigated to see if targets are realistic or unachievable and therefore demotivating staff.

Much has been learnt from this initial attempt to improve motivation but in theories that developed from Taylor's ideas it has become clear that this process was actually performance management rather than employee motivation. Criticisms of the approach state that employees are human beings *not* robots that can be programmed to obey orders. Also, the point that small, repetitive tasks lead to boredom and high levels of absenteeism, despite bonus payments for achieving targets, has been cited as a weakness.

Douglas McGregor (1906–64)

McGregor took a different view from Taylor and attempted to look further than the right of managers to manage. His views centred on the point that managers do make assumptions about their staff and this allowed him to develop the Theory X and Theory Y approach. In considering these two dimensions, it may be worth noting that there is a direct link between these and the general behaviour patterns of most employees. There is a clear separation of motivation levels in staff who do not want to be working in a particular organisation and those who have a high level of commitment. It is relatively easy for managers to note these factors and this awareness allows the managers to use different strategies for dealing with these staff.

The two dimensions identified by McGregor are:

Theory X	Theory Y
• The average person is lazy and has an inbuilt dislike of work.	• Work is a natural activity and can be enjoyable.
• Most people have to be persuaded, controlled, directed and threatened with punishment to achieve goals.	• People will willingly apply their skills if committed to organisational objectives.
• Security of environment is important.	• Their commitment should be recognised and rewarded.
• The average person will avoid any form of responsibility and needs good supervision to carry out work satisfactorily.	• Personal development is very important and additional responsibility will be welcome.

Analysis

- Theory X links with Taylor's view that workers need to be coerced to work well.

- A system of rules and regulations can be set up which staff will comply with once they are known.

- Management must pay attention to encouraging staff because they will put only minimum effort into their activities and work must be constantly checked.

- Motivation here is gained outside the working environment and the job is a means to an end.

- Theory Y matches Maslow's levels 3, 4 and 5 because staff have a strong sense of worth and are keen to do a good job.

- Motivation here is required by continual recognition of effort plus involvement in policy decisions.

- The challenge for management here is to keep finding new and interesting work to retain enthusiasm.

Without doubt, the structure of an organisation and the style of management used can encourage both aspects of McGregor's view. If the hierarchy and rules are too rigid, a **job centred** approach has been created and employees are likely to react accordingly. In contrast, if a more flexible system is in place, it will encourage employees to participate and put forward ideas they know will be considered. This **employee centred** approach is the preferred style of the majority of workers and higher levels of motivation are generally recorded in this type of organisation.

If this theory is applied to Smoothmove, it may be that rules are too rigidly enforced, particularly for the drivers/removers. At present, it is a small business and this generally leads to autocratic systems. Now that the firm is expanding, it can afford to look at its current style of management and change the atmosphere by building teams and consulting the workers on key aspects of business performance. Their increased commitment could be rewarded with a small profit sharing scheme and greater involvement in the decision making process. Gaining the respect of employees takes considerable effort but it will be noticed that staff are happier and more inclined to put in maximum effort.

Abraham Maslow (1908–70)

In an attempt to eliminate the weaknesses seen in Taylor's theory, other ideas were considered that attempted to remedy these faults. The best known of these was proposed by Maslow. Studies of poor performance indicated that many other factors contributed to the variation in motivation levels.

Maslow suggested that central to these was the concept that people need to be valued as individuals. Each one has needs and wants and these vary according to personality. Motivation is directly related to these twin characteristics and wise employers will benefit more by meeting the needs and wants of their staff because this reduces conflict.

Maslow's model has been widely used over the years and is still relevant today since people still have the same driving emotions, although they expect them to be met in different ways. The Maslow pyramid can be described as giving a series of stages through which people pass during their lifetime. The pace at which they progress through each stage will vary for a number of reasons but mainly because no two people seek the same thing at the same time. Briefly, the five stages are as shown in Figure 4.3.1.

These can be applied across all parts of a person's life – personal, social and job related. Here the definitions will be linked to the working environment to see how employers can raise motivation levels.

Analysis

- These features give guidance on issues that contribute to motivation at work.

- If basic resources are not provided, performance will be affected immediately.

- There is a difference between short-term and long-term tactics.

- It is very difficult for employers to meet the needs and wants of every individual and they tend to pitch facilities at a general level. This may leave a small number of dissatisfied people at both the top and bottom of the scale.

Before applying the factors in the working environment, it is essential that a distinction is made between **needs** and **wants**:

- **Needs** – features that *must* be met before any level of activity can be carried out well.

- **Wants** – individually driven *desires* for material rewards which add to personal prestige.

From this description, it is quite clear that employers can provide resources to meet the job related **needs** of employees. What is more difficult to achieve is the range of **wants** demanded by many staff. Many employers consider this to be a step too far and feel it is beyond their responsibility to meet these requirements in the majority of cases.

Figure 4.3.1 Maslow's Hierarchy of Needs

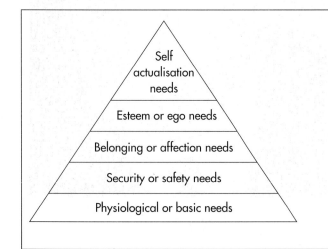

- becoming everything you are capable of becoming

- self-respect = confidence, independence, and achievement
- a sense of belonging, friendship and social activities
- secure environment, protection from danger, predictability and routine
- satisfaction of hunger, thirst, oxygen, sleep, warmth and stimulation, e.g. activity variation

Table 4.3.1 Distinction between needs and wants

Needs	Wants
achievement of special talents, interesting and varied work	personal goals achieved, e.g. owner of business, challenging activities
good at job, appreciated by management, status recognised	high role in company, in charge of many staff, prestige
working with colleagues, part of departmental/ social activities	harmonious team working, sports and social club/ benefits
secure job on a permanent basis, routine tasks, safe environment	important role in organisation, long-term contract, highly rewarded
comfortable resources, e.g. heat/light, drinks/snacks, up-to-date equipment	more luxurious furniture, own office, sophisticated equipment

Nearly all businesses apply these characteristics in their operations but the fact that it is impossible to meet everyone's needs and wants inevitably leads to some movement of staff out of one working environment into another. New situations often appeal to dissatisfied workers and it will take a little while for them to settle down, only to discover the same factors are present in the new working environment as in the recently left establishment. This fact is in total agreement with Maslow's theory which states '**People are always wanting something**' and stresses the point that they are rarely satisfied with what they already have but want other exciting experiences, many of which are beyond their reach.

Using Smoothmove as an example, the basic needs of employees can be met by providing suitable resources to carry out the different jobs effectively, e.g. computers for administrative staff and a comfortable office environment; well-maintained vehicles for drivers and suitable accommodation for overnight stops. Security of employment is better for full-time staff than for part-time or temporary staff but both rely on the continuity of the business for this aspect. Because it is a small company, few opportunities exist for more challenging work but a wider range of tasks could be given to most staff to create variety in their work and allow use of initiative.

Frederick Herzberg (1923–91)

This theory has had an impact on current thinking, mainly because Herzberg died only 10 years ago. Herzberg formed his views after studying 203 accountants/engineers in Pittsburgh and attempting to discover what made them happy in the working environment. The result of his investigations threw new light on the way in which employees perceive their daily routines.

One of the most important findings from his analysis was confirmation that people go to work for many reasons, but not just for monetary reward. He did reinforce Maslow's view that a basic wage is needed to support individual lifestyles but he separated the factors already regarded as motivational issues into two sections.

Motivators	Hygiene Factors
Achievement	Company policy and administration
Recognition	Supervision
Nature of the work	Salary
Responsibility	Interpersonal relations, e.g. supervisor
Growth and advancement	Working conditions

Analysis

- The analysis indicated that although money was important, it was not necessarily the first priority for many people.

- Being in a collective environment with their colleagues was a secondary issue, particularly if equality of opportunity was available.

- A belief in the value of the work undertaken was crucial to gain maximum performance.

- The need for recognition of efforts and participation in decision making were considered important motivators.

- The style of management adopted within an organisation affects general behaviour patterns.

However, it was noted as a critical point that if management changed only one factor to try and improve motivation, it would have a short-term effect before staff once more became dissatisfied. This draws attention to the points that are carefully discussed during the annual salary negotiations with trade unions, when a series of measures will be agreed upon for the next 12–24 months, e.g. reduction in working hours, better shift patterns, more frequent breaks, increase in pay and setting up a consultation committee.

Organisations do not have to be pushed into such deals by trade unions alone, but can decide to apply a combination of similar factors to increase motivation, possibly under the guidance of the human resource manager. In addition, Herzberg is credited with creating the concept of job enrichment programmes. These can be carried out in one of four ways:

Job Design

Job Rotation
moves people from one task to another and adds variety

Job Enlargement
increases the scope of work in a **horizontal** manner by adding tasks that take longer to accomplish

Job Enrichment
increases responsibility and involvement at the decision making stage by **vertical** integration of planning, operation and control of work in a complete project

Autonomous Work Groups
informal groups are given greater responsibility for choosing methods of meeting goals. This uses group decision making skills and reduces supervision

---

This wide range of job design techniques is much in evidence today across a range of business operations. Organisations have benefited from these suggestions by altering the way work is allocated and supervised and a century of theoretical ideas has seen a change from a fully autocratic style of management to wider use of democratic and participative methods of working. Many employees appreciate the difference in approach but it is not possible to please all staff and, without movement across business activities, companies would not reap the rewards of new ideas entering their environment.

Using Smoothmove as an example, several areas could be implemented to improve motivation among the staff. More flexible working hours could be allowed to match family commitments and staff could be given responsibility for arranging this themselves. As long as essential services are covered at critical times which meet customer needs, a variation in working hours could be set up for office staff and drivers/removers. A less autocratic style of management could see employees consulted more and their ideas used to improve weaknesses they know exist because they are the people who operate the systems. In this case, Smoothmove could be disputing Taylor's view that 'managers have the right to manage' by involving the staff more and creating a happier working environment, thus operating a participative management style. The result should be better standards of work, less absenteeism, fewer errors and more satisfied workers.

Activity

Divide the class into four groups. Allocate one theorist to each group:

- Taylor
- McGregor
- Maslow
- Herzberg

The group members are to adopt the character they are representing.

Select a business from your area and prepare a presentation to the board explaining how your newly developed theory will raise motivation levels for their staff. Use visual aids to help define the nature of your technique and role play your famous theorist to try and persuade the organiation to use your strategy.

Vote for the most authentic performance after the presentations have been made.

Flexibility

As a new millennium dawns, organisations are bracing themselves to cope with whatever the competitive environment brings them. Recent activities have seen the merging of many well known companies, producing extensive business empires with operations across the world. All of these giant corporations require staff to carry out major functions. These are made easier by the multitude of computerised technology gadgets available to perform mundane tasks at breakneck speed!

This working revolution requires employees with acute skills, extensive abilities to work as an individual as well as being a good team player, problem solving capabilities and the acceptance that a long-term full-time job is likely to be a thing of the past. Many organisations already operate in a flexible style and this will probably increase.

Flexibility requires a business to employ a few specialist staff as core employees plus a small number of supporting roles. At busy times, additional staff will be hired, but only for short periods until a particular project is completed. This asks a lot from workers who will not be able to rely upon a regular income from one main source but will have to search for other work if they are to maintain a basic lifestyle. Certainly, this will relieve the boredom factor of repeating certain tasks but it will take away the pleasure of working with colleagues on a regular basis. Both of these factors match the two lower levels of Maslow's hierarchy and leave people in a vulnerable position – the secure working environment will no longer exist.

If organisations are calling for your services on a part-time basis, they will expect high quality work on each occasion. This puts the onus firmly in the hands of individuals to provide excellent standards and removes the need to set up a system of benefits to reward staff for good work. This can be summarised as follows:

Employer	Employee
• employ staff as and when needed	• carry out a range of tasks/jobs for several organisations
• reduce costs/resources required	• responsible for a quality service
• remain competitive	

The dawn of flexibility prompts us to speculate on the dramatic changes that have taken place in the treatment of workers during the last century. This factor was discussed in a recent TV programme which sought to identify the requirements of a modern employee.

CASE STUDY

The Money Programme   12 December 1999

Representatives from prominent organisations were invited to discuss the working environment of the future. The key points noted included:

- the removal of hierarchies from organisational structures

- a significant increase in self-employment with many people working from home linked to the company via IT facilities

- flexibility being formed through a small core of specialists supported by myriad people able to do several jobs

- a decline in low manufacturing units (manual skills) to be replaced by high manufacturing units (computerised equipment)

- a need to develop new ways of doing things that do not use up natural resources to the point of extinction.

The conclusion of this programme was that the working environment was moving swiftly away from the pattern of working known to many; therefore people must be aware that they will be required to prepare themselves to cope with a different environment.

Summary

Finally, these issues had already been noted by Tom Peters in his latest book *Liberation Management*, the publicity for which states:

> Tom Peters revolutionised management thinking with *In Search of Excellence* and then *Thriving on Chaos*. Now, in his new book *Liberation Management*, he argues that hierarchies are dead, companies must perpetually renew by destroying themselves and that in the nanosecond nineties effective companies are structured in small units, geared to agility and matching solutions to customers' needs.
>
> His message will frighten and disturb some, excite and challenge many more. Here is an opportunity for business leaders and managers to re-focus on an agenda for prospering in an unprecedentedly competitive marketplace.

This examination of the theories of motivation has covered distinct differences and has indeed led us to the same conclusion. The first ideas of Taylor were adopted by Henry Ford to increase motivation in his workforce by the installation of mass production techniques. From here, the theories moved through the human relations approach to the team building and job enrichment programmes until our final destination, the flexible workforce. This is highlighted by the invention of information technology and by the mastermind Bill Gates who has revolutionised the working environment and changed the patterns of work for everyone forever.

It remains to be seen what the next development is likely to be. The only certainty is that whatever the size of the organisation or the nature of its business, *people* will always be needed to operate and manage the key functions that interact with customers.

Activity

Refer back to the documents you prepared for the job selected at the end of Chapter 2 (page 282).

Use the same job role to complete the following tasks:

1   The Senior Management Team has decided that as the company is taking on more staff, it is time to set up a proper Appraisal Scheme. Decide which method would be appropriate for the job role chosen and set out suitable SMART objectives and a rating form.

2   Outline the periods for monitoring progress by the new employee and indicate any gaps you think will be identified in his/her current skills and abilities where training should be arranged.

3   Briefly describe the factors relating to motivation that will apply to this employee and analyse the points from the theoretical models that can be used to improve his/her levels of commitment and performance.

4   Discuss your expectations of a workplace situation and attempt to design what you believe will be the environment of the future and how employees will be required to change their approach to working life.

UNIT 4

End of Unit Assignment

Although it is possible to use the three sections of Smoothmove plus the course activities as an end of unit assignment, a further example of such material is now offered. What follows is an extract of data from the Horsham Strategic Plan and it has already been noted that similar information will be available in your own region.

This data contains statistics about the local job market, skills mix, types of firms operating in the locality, infrastructure and transport patterns to help potential employees find a suitable job. Using the course specifications as an outline, select the data that relates to a business organisation and employment situation in your area. Prepare a folder which will contain all the necessary documentation, statistical evidence, analysis and comments about how this business attracts, selects, trains and motivates staff. Concentrate on several key jobs within that locality because it is not possible to cover all types of work. Include notes on relevant legislation and equal opportunities policies and try to include practical examples of some areas, e.g. taped recordings of interviews with managers or employees, or photographs of actual procedures taking place.

Conclude by comparing your own portfolio with those of your colleagues and provide a summary of improvements to your work, if you have noticed any omissions or changes in the method of presentation of evidence, or if you see a better way of setting this out.

1. INTRODUCTION

1.1 In April 1991 the Council published its first Economic Development Strategy under the powers introduced by the Local Government and Housing Act 1989. In publishing the document the Council undertook to review the Strategy on a regular basis, in consultation with all those interested in the local economy. This has taken place and the Council is currently embarking on a further review to cover the next two year period.

1.2 Since 1991 the Council has developed many fruitful partnerships with other organisations and local businesses to help stimulate the local economy. This is an ongoing process and hopefully this new draft Strategy will build on what has already been achieved in partnership with others.

Purpose of this Document

1.3 The purpose of this draft Strategy is to draw together all the Council's current economic development activities. The Strategy is intended to be compatible with other strategies and policies affecting the District, particularly those in the Horsham District Local Plan and the Council's document entitled "The Wider Vision" recently published.

1.4 There are three main reasons for preparing this draft Strategy:-

(i) to identify the role of the District Council in local economic development and explain the full range of initiatives carried out by the Council;

(ii) to provide a means of prioritising the Council's actions during the coming years as set out in the Action Plan, which is reviewed each year.

(iii) to form the basis for consultation with the business community and representative organisations in order to ensure that future activity is targeted effectively.

1.5 The draft Strategy examines the key issues relating to the local economic and employment situation and the problems which need to be addressed. It then considers the role of the District Council in economic development in partnership with others. Finally, it sets out its Action Plan for the year 1999 / 2000.

Horsham District - Major Communication Links

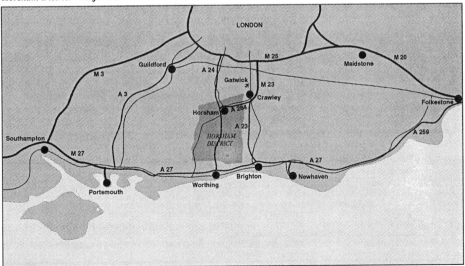

2. THE ECONOMY OF HORSHAM DISTRICT

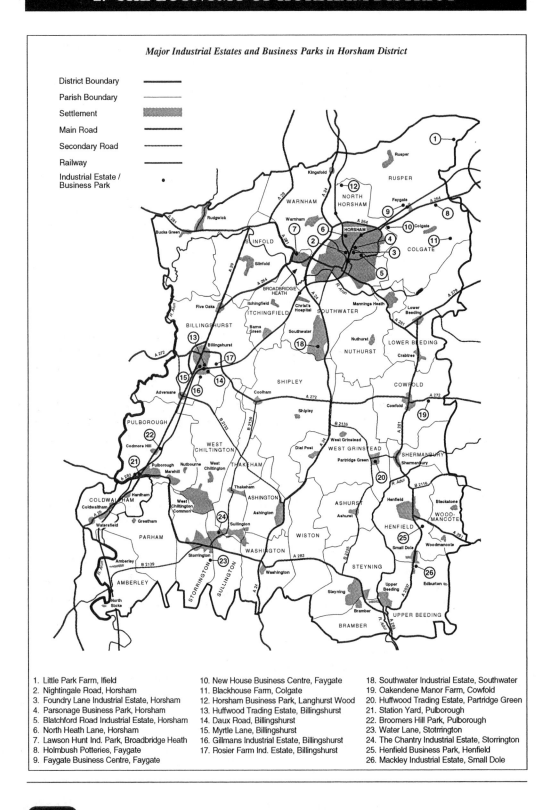

Major Industrial Estates and Business Parks in Horsham District

District Boundary
Parish Boundary
Settlement
Main Road
Secondary Road
Railway
Industrial Estate /
Business Park

1. Little Park Farm, Ifield
2. Nightingale Road, Horsham
3. Foundry Lane Industrial Estate, Horsham
4. Parsonage Business Park, Horsham
5. Blatchford Road Industrial Estate, Horsham
6. North Heath Lane, Horsham
7. Lawson Hunt Ind. Park, Broadbridge Heath
8. Holmbush Potteries, Faygate
9. Faygate Business Centre, Faygate
10. New House Business Centre, Faygate
11. Blackhouse Farm, Colgate
12. Horsham Business Park, Langhurst Wood
13. Huffwood Trading Estate, Billingshurst
14. Daux Road, Billingshurst
15. Myrtle Lane, Billingshurst
16. Gillmans Industrial Estate, Billingshurst
17. Rosier Farm Ind. Estate, Billingshurst
18. Southwater Industrial Estate, Southwater
19. Oakendene Manor Farm, Cowfold
20. Huffwood Trading Estate, Partridge Green
21. Station Yard, Pulborough
22. Broomers Hill Park, Pulborough
23. Water Lane, Stotrrington
24. The Chantry Industrial Estate, Storrington
25. Henfield Business Park, Henfield
26. Mackley Industrial Estate, Small Dole

2. THE ECONOMY OF HORSHAM DISTRICT

Introduction

2.1 Horsham District's economy is fortunate to benefit from both the administrative, industrial and commercial hub of Horsham town in the north of the District and a diverse rural economy based in growing settlements such as Billingshurst and Southwater and villages in the south such as Ashington, Pulborough, Storrington, Henfield and Steyning.

2.2 Following the period of recession of the early 1990s the economy has steadily improved with unemployment falling consistently to new lows. As a result of this buoyant economy, the business community has remained confident and continues to thrive. The main areas of industry in the District are business and financial services, advanced engineering, pharmaceuticals and electronics. In addition a number of companies have located their operation centres and Headquarters in the District.

2.3 Drawing from its strong position as a prime location for business with the added attraction of natural assets such as the Sussex Downs close by, the District has benefited greatly from overseas investors.

2.4 The following analysis represents a brief overview of the state of the local economy and acts as a basis for the development of the Economic Development Strategy and subsequent annual Action Plans.

Pattern of Employment

2.5 Horsham District is clearly not a single "local labour market" in its own right. It is normally considered as part of "Central Sussex", which comprises the three Districts of Crawley, Horsham and Mid-Sussex, and even this area is not self-contained. The southern parts of the District fall into the local labour markets of Brighton and Worthing, whilst the Central Sussex local labour market extends into Surrey.

2.6 The Horsham economy is dominated by businesses within the service sector with almost 43% of the workforce working within this sector in 1996. This is influenced largely by the presence of companies such as Royal & Sun Alliance. Within the services sector around 21% of the workforce work specifically within the financial and business sector. By comparison only around 16% work in manufacturing and 20% in wholesale / retail distribution.

Numbers of people employed in Horsham District by Industrial sector, 1991 - 1996

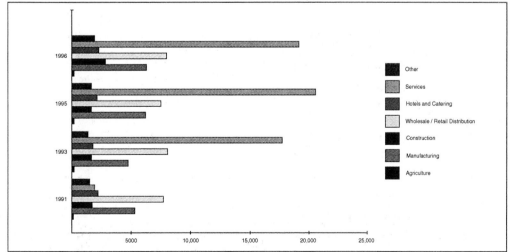

Source: Census of Employment / Annual Employment Survey, West Sussex County Council

Horsham District Council Economic Development Strategy : July 1999

2. THE ECONOMY OF HORSHAM DISTRICT

2.7 While the services sector has seen continued growth in recent years, the manufacturing sector has also started to experience growth in the proportion of the workforce working in that sector. Between 1991 and 1996 there was a 3% increase in the proportion of the workforce working in manufacturing.

Unemployment

2.8 Unemployment in both Central Sussex and Horsham District remains well below the rates found elsewhere in Sussex, as well as the regional and national average.

Comparative Unemployment Rates, 1996-98

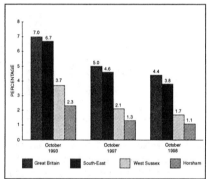

Source: Unemployment Statistics, West Sussex County Council, 1998

2.9 In recent years unemployment has set a trend which seems set to continue. In January 1996 unemployment in Horsham stood at 3.6% and has steadily fallen to 1.1% in October 1998. This figure is well below the national, regional and county averages and reflects the sound quality and the high demand for the workforce. With such a low unemployment rate, there could be a labour shortage. However, Labour Market Trends of 1997 have shown that in the Crawley Travel to Work Area (within which the north of Horsham District falls), the workforce makes-up only 71% of the total population of working age (compared to a national and regional average of 79%), therefore leaving 29% of the population who may be eligible for work.

2.10 Differences within the county continue to exist between Coastal and Central Sussex with 62% of the county's unemployed residing in Coastal Sussex. In addition the duration of unemployment is generally lower in Central Sussex.

2.11 Despite possible skills shortages in parts of the District, Horsham has historically had low rates of unfilled job vacancies in comparison to proportions experienced in West Sussex and the South East. This trend seems set to continue. In January 1999, of the total number of vacancies, 35% in the District were unfilled in comparison to 42% in Central Sussex, 37% across the County, and 44% in the South East.

Population

2.12 Between 1981 and 1991 the resident population of Horsham District grew by some 8.7% to a total of 108,560. In 1997 the population was estimated at 121,120, a more dramatic growth of 11.6% in only 6 years. Recent projections suggest that the population could increase to 122,400 by 2001. The District has a relatively young population profile with approximately 61% of the population being aged 16 to retirement age in 1991. This proportion is unlikely to have changed much since 1991 although it seems set to increase slightly.

2.13 The increase in population seems set to continue primarily because of a possible increase in the number of houses which are to be built as suggested in the draft Regional Planning Guidance for the South-East and by the Secretary of State for the Environment, Transport and the Regions. In December 1997, the latter issued a Direction to West Sussex County Council stating that 12,800 extra dwellings should be allocated across the County between 1994 and 2011 in addition to the 37,900 already allocated by the West Sussex Structure Plan Third Review. As a result of the Secretary of State's decision being upheld, Horsham District could face a further allocation of

2. THE ECONOMY OF HORSHAM DISTRICT

around 5,000 extra houses in the period up to 2011. Applying the District's average number of people per household (2.4) to this figure means that the population could increase by a further 12,000 in the period to 2011. In addition to the current projected figure of 127,210 for 2011, this could mean a total population of 139,210 by 2011.

2.14 A combination of the relative youthfulness of the local population, the current numbers unemployed and the projected increase in the resident population and workforce indicates the need to guide economic development in the District.

Workforce Trends

2.15 In 1991, the workforce in West Sussex was estimated at 346,200 of which 43.3% was female. In the county as a whole the workforce is expected to increase by 9.7% between 1991 and 2001, three times more the rate of growth expected nationally. This growth is expected to be greatest in Central Sussex and throughout the county the growth rate is higher for the female workforce than for males, as is the case nationally.

2.16 Due to the situation of the possible increase in the population in the District in the period to 2011 the number of people making-up the workforce is likely to increase substantially above the District figure of 64,800 in 2011.

Company Performance and Characteristics

2.17 The number of businesses in the District has steadily increased since 1994 with latest figures suggesting that there were 4,510 VAT registered companies in 1996. A business generally becomes VAT registered when it has a turnover of £45,000 (the threshold for registration in November 1993). Other companies not VAT registered will include those which trade mainly in exempt or zero-rated goods and services.

Number of VAT Registered Businesses in Horsham District, 1993-96

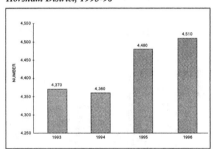

Source: NOMIS, West Sussex County Council

2.18 A large proportion of businesses in the District continue to be the small businesses with 120 being newly VAT registered in 1995 and a further 30 in 1996. There will be a significant further number of smaller businesses not VAT registered which could take the total number of businesses in the District in excess of 5,000.

Workforce Trends in West Sussex, 1991 - 2011

District	1991	1996	2001	2006	2011	Total Change 1991-2011	Total % Change 1991-2011
West Sussex	346,200	351,800	368,300	376,300	380,000	34,000	9.8
Adur	28,100	27,200	27,700	27,900	28,000	-100	-0.4
Arun	57,200	59,100	62,600	64,400	64,700	7,500	13.2
Chichester	47,800	47,900	50,900	51,500	51,600	3,800	8.0
Crawley	48,300	49,100	51,900	54,400	56,100	7,800	16.2
Mid Sussex	64,200	64,900	66,800	67,000	66,800	2,600	4.1
Worthing	44,100	44,200	46,500	47,600	48,000	3,900	8.8
Horsham	*56,500*	*59,400*	*62,000*	*63,600*	*64,800*	*8,300*	*14.7*

Source: West Sussex County Council, August 1996

2. THE ECONOMY OF HORSHAM DISTRICT

2.19 In 1998 the Council started a Business Care Programme which monitors the economic stability of large local businesses. Some businesses are concerned about skills shortages as a potential problem in some sectors.

2.20 The key sectors of business in the District are pharmaceuticals, electronics, advanced engineering and financial services. The major companies in the District (and their area of business) include:

* Allied Domecq (Spirits and Wines) UK Ltd. (Spirits and Wines);
* Applied Implant Technology Ltd. (Semiconductors);
* BASF Printing Systems Ltd. (Printing Systems);
* Caradon Trend Ltd. (Building Management Systems);
* Chesswood Produce Ltd. (Mushrooms);
* Covance Ltd. (Pharmaceuticals);
* Disctronics UK Ltd. (Compact Disc Technology);
* Ericsson Transport and Cable Networks (Communications);
* Novartis Pharmaceuticals UK Ltd. (Pharmaceuticals);
* Paula Rosa Kitchens (Kitchens);
* Royal & Sun Alliance (Financial Services);
* RSPCA (Animal Welfare); and
* Silvertech International (Oil Rig Safety Systems).

2.21 All of these companies employ over or near to 200 staff. Some of these are the headquarters of UK firms. Some companies will be less vulnerable to possible consolidation or rationalisation than those companies based here which are a regional division or national headquarters of a worldwide organisation.

2.22 The District continues to attract key companies to locate or re-locate here and the well-established companies continue to invest in the area. The success of the District as a prime location in the county for

businesses is reflected in the level of foreign inward investment in the District, approximately 20% of all foreign inward investment companies in West Sussex are located within Horsham District. This confidence in the local economy and location of the District has also been recognised by companies which have been established here for some time. For example, the RSPCA have chosen to expand their headquarters on a new site in Southwater; Novartis Pharmaceuticals UK Ltd. have chosen to remain in Horsham and invest heavily in their future here; and Silvertech International have decided to accommodate their expansion plans by moving to Broadlands Business Park near Horsham. Following the merger of Royal with Sun Alliance, the company has now committed to retain a major presence in Horsham.

2.23 Although there are positive signs that inward investment is continuing across the District, a potential problem may also be emerging. Continued investment could mean that in the near future demand may exceed supply. In 1997, research conducted by Sussex Enterprise confirmed this fact for both the Crawley and Worthing Travel to Work Areas which cover the north and south of the District respectively. Net employment generation has started to show signs of

2. THE ECONOMY OF HORSHAM DISTRICT

slowing and the historical low investment in industrial property in comparison to the UK average is continuing. In 1998 the forecast Gross Domestic Product (GDP) per capita for Sussex was £10,141, less than the GDP for the South-East, £11,193, and the UK, £10,643.

Conclusions

2.24 The local economy in the District remains buoyant with a broad range of company sizes but with significant proportion of work being undertaken in a few key industrial sectors. While these clusters of industry can be beneficial to the location of other companies within these key sectors, the lack of diversification of industry in the area in addition to the continuing low unemployment rates could lead to "overheating" of the local economy. Economic recovery in the District since the recession of the early 1990s has been steady and continuous although continued investment by commercial businesses may be slowing due to constraints in the availability of commercial sites. With the population growing at a greater rate than previously thought and with the possibility of the District population reaching close to 140,000 by 2011, there is now additional importance in addressing the provision of land and premises for businesses and of job opportunities to minimise the net outward migration of the workforce.

10. PROGRAMME FOR ACTION

ACTION 3 - PROVISION AND DEVELOPMENT OF QUALITY / TRAINED LABOUR FORCE		
NEW AND EXISTING PROGRAMMES	TARGET	PARTNERS
(a) Support Business Workshops - for smaller businesses	To increase opportunities for training and advice to businesses.	Business Link Sussex.
(b) Provide play schemes during holiday periods - to assist employees with children.	Maintain summer play schemes at 4 weeks and maintain Easter play schemes at 9 days.	Parish Councils.
(c) Securing provision of social and low-cost housing directly or through its planning policies	To provide affordable housing for employees in the District.	Housing Associations.
(d) Provide free accommodation for the Prince's Trust Volunteers projects.	To assist young people in developing work and project skills.	Prince's Trust.
(e) Provide funding support to West Sussex Tourism Initiative aiming to improve the quality and skills of those employed in tourism.	To explore the opportunities for delivering "Welcome to West Sussex" courses to Travel and Tourism GCSE and GNVQ students.	Sussex Enterprise, West Sussex County Council and Wakeford Hotels.
(f) Financially support TRAC Initiative aiming to raise shop assistant standards in Horsham town centre.	To run a further competition in 2000 / 2001.	Chamber of Commerce, Sussex Enterprise and Norwich Union.
(g) "Time out" initiative implementing after school club and summer club schemes to provide facilities for children of working parents.	To increase provision and extend the scheme to areas other than Horsham.	Sussex Enterprise.
(h) Use of a Mobile Technology Vehicle, in rural areas, to make available training in computers.	Help young unemployed people find work.	Brinsbury College.
(i) The creation of greater opportunities at Southwater Business Resource Centre for the disadvantaged.	To train and support people to achieve full-time work.	Southwater Business Resource Centre and Links.
(j) Development of the Horsham District Business Education Partnership.	To secure funding and arrange programmes to support businesses by appointment of a facilitator.	West Sussex County Council, HADIA, Southwater Business Resource Centre and Sussex Enterprise.
(k) Support "Young Enterprise" in assisting schools involved in forming companies.	To remain a Board Member and encourage all local schools to take part.	Board of Young Enterprise.

Horsham District Council Economic Development Strategy : July 1999

- 21 -

UNIT 5

Finance

Recording Financial Information

In this chapter you will learn how to complete the business documents used when businesses buy or sell goods or services.

Completing Business Documents

In order to help you to understand which documents are completed and in which order, imagine that a retail shop, which we will call 'Office Shop', is going to buy some goods from a supplier which we will call 'Universal Office Supplies Ltd'.

Seller:	Universal Office Supplies Ltd
Buyer:	Office Shop Ltd

Products Requirement

Suppose Office Shop Ltd wants to buy from Universal Office Supplies Ltd the following goods:

2 computer monitors
4 computer keyboards

How does Office Shop Ltd let Universal Office Supplies Ltd know that it wants this computer equipment?

It could telephone, but Universal Office Supplies Ltd might not copy the message down properly and this might result in Office Shop getting the wrong goods. To make sure that mistakes are less likely, Office Shop fills in a document called a **purchase order**.

The Purchase Order

Purchase order – completed by a customer and sent to a supplier to request the supply of goods or services.

The purchase order (see Figure 5.1.1) shows:

- the type of goods wanted
- the number of goods wanted
- the address to which the goods should be sent
- the date when the goods are wanted
- the price of the goods
- the reference or catalogue numbers of the goods wanted.

Note that the purchase order has the name of Office Shop on the top. This lets Universal Office Supplies know who is ordering the goods so that it knows who to send them to. Office Shop also puts a special number (12540) on the purchase order so that both Office Shop and Universal Office Supplies can refer to the order easily when they need to. This is called the **purchase order number**. This is useful because Office Shop may have sent more than one purchase order to Universal Office Supplies and without a purchase order number, Office Shop and Universal Office Supplies might get the orders mixed up.

If Universal Office Supplies wants to do business with Office Shop and has the goods in stock, it will arrange for the goods to be sent to Office Shop. Universal Office Supplies now fills out a **sales invoice**.

Figure 5.1.1 Purchase order

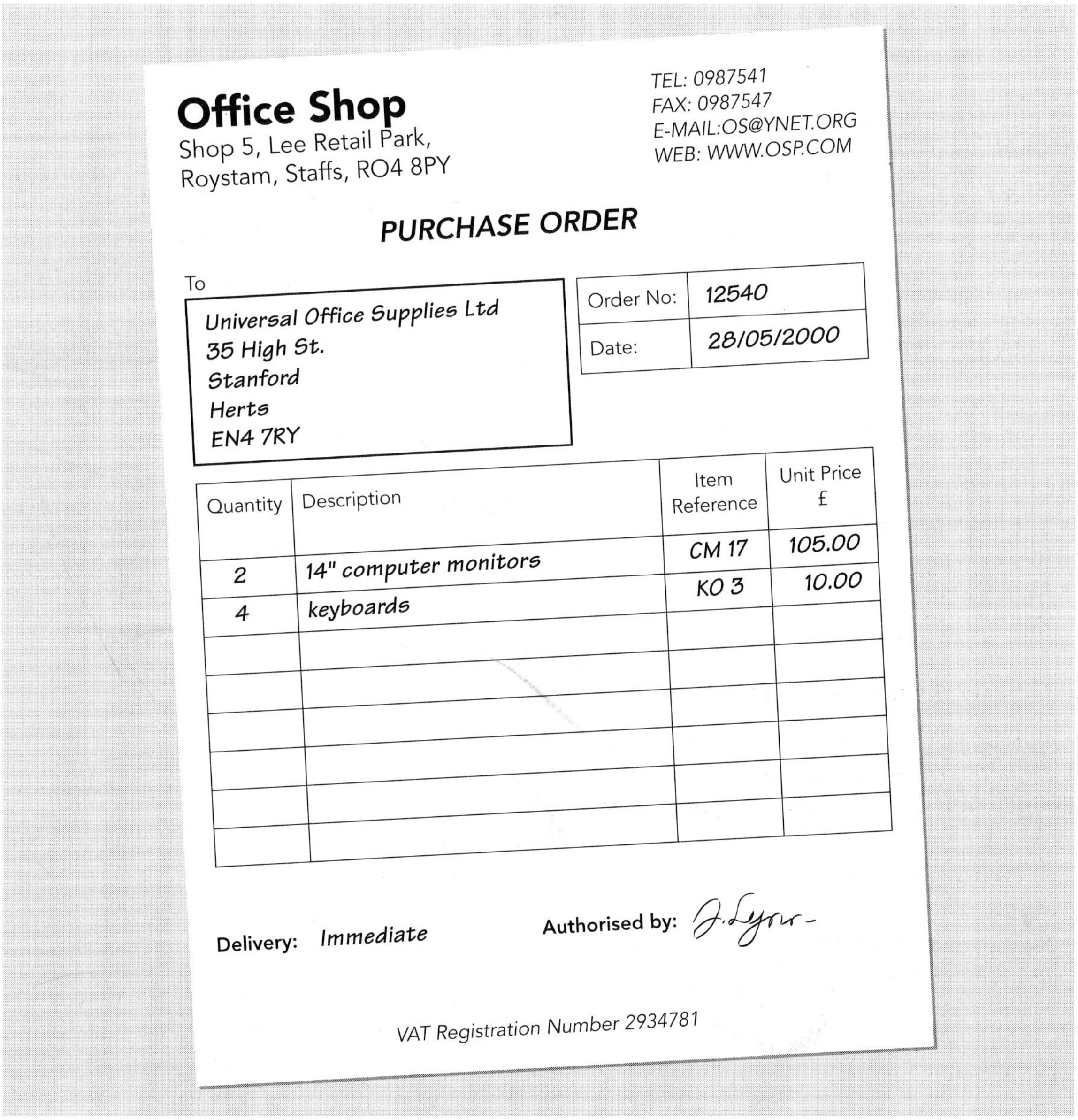

Office Shop
Shop 5, Lee Retail Park,
Roystam, Staffs, RO4 8PY

TEL: 0987541
FAX: 0987547
E-MAIL:OS@YNET.ORG
WEB: WWW.OSP.COM

PURCHASE ORDER

To

Universal Office Supplies Ltd
35 High St.
Stanford
Herts
EN4 7RY

| Order No: | 12540 |
| Date: | 28/05/2000 |

Quantity	Description	Item Reference	Unit Price £
2	14" computer monitors	CM 17	105.00
4	keyboards	KO 3	10.00

Delivery: *Immediate*   **Authorised by:** *J. Lynn*

VAT Registration Number 2934781

The Sales Invoice

Sales invoice – completed by a supplier and sent to a customer to indicate goods or services sold and the amount to be paid.

The sales invoice (see Figure 5.1.2) shows:

- the description of the goods being sold
- the number of goods being sold
- the address to which the invoice should be sent
- the address to which the goods should be sent
- the price of the goods
- any discounts that Universal Office Supplies is offering to Office Shop
- the amount of VAT to pay on the goods being sold
- the total amount that Office Shop has to pay to Universal Office Supplies
- the reference or catalogue numbers of the goods being sold.

Figure 5.1.2 Sales invoice

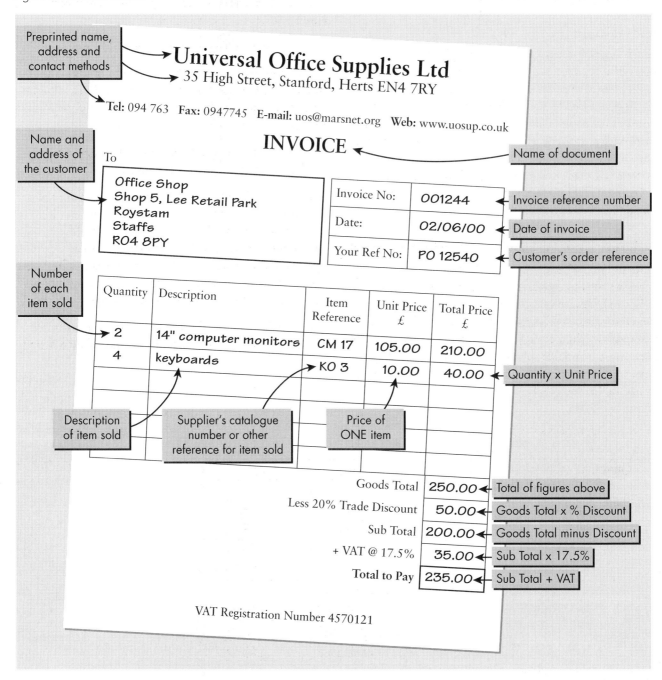

Note that the invoice also has a special number (001244) on it called the **invoice number** so that both Office Shop and Universal Office Supplies can refer to the invoice easily if there are any problems or queries.

Universal Office Supplies keeps one copy for itself so that it can update its own records and knows how much

Office Shop owes. Another copy is posted to Office Shop so that Office Shop knows how much money it needs to pay Universal Office Supplies for the computer equipment.

Calculating discounts

Trade discount

This is offered to customers who are given **unconditional** reductions in the prices of goods sold to them, according to an agreement. This means that they will be given the discount whatever happens. Effectively, these customers are charged less than other non-discount customer for the same goods. These customers are usually 'trade' customers, who may be retailers buying goods in order to sell them on to members of the public, or those ordering large quantities. A typical trade discount may be 25 per cent of the value of the goods.

Cash discount (also known as settlement discount)

Some students think that a cash discount is given if a customer pays for goods or services by cash (i.e. notes and coins). This is not the case. A cash discount is offered to customers as an incentive to pay the invoice promptly within a given period of time, as stated on the sales invoice. For example, the following phrase may appear on the sales invoice: Cash discount is calculated on subtotal before VAT.

> Terms: 2% may be deducted if payment is received within 14 days of the Invoice date

In this case, customers taking advantage of the cash discount by paying an invoice within 14 days can pay by cash, cheque, credit card or any other method – it does not have to be in notes and coins

If the invoice **is not paid** within the discount period, the final amount shown on the invoice must be paid.

If the invoice **is paid** within the discount period, the discount amount may be deducted from the invoice. This amount is given as a percentage value. (It is important to note that the cash discount percentage is applied to the 'value of the goods or services'. This is the amount shown on the invoice before the addition of VAT and not the 'final total' of the invoice.)

An example of an invoice prepared for a customer receiving both trade and cash discounts is shown below:

Figure 5.1.2a Invoice showing cash discount

Quantity	Description	Unit Price	Total
		£	£
10		18.34	183.40
8		11.04	88.32
1		30.11	30.11
			301.83
	less 20% trade discount		60.37
	subtotal		241.46
	+ VAT @ 17.5%		40.98
	Total Due		282.44

Cash discount 3% for payment within 14 days of invoice date

	Calculation	Result	
Actual cash discount	£241.46 × 3%	£7.24	= cash discount
Subtotal less cash discount	£241.46 – £7.24	£234.22	VAT is calculated on this
VAT	£234.22 × 17.5%	£40.98	= VAT (rounded DOWN to nearest penny)

If invoice is paid within 14 days:
deduct £7.24 cash discount = £282.44 – £7.24.
Amount payable = £275.20.

If invoice is not paid within 14 days:
amount payable is the amount shown on the invoice
= £282.44.

VAT and cash discounts

An unusual feature of cash discounts is the way that the VAT on the invoice is calculated.

> VAT is always calculated on the discounted price, whether or not the discount is taken.

This is an agreed procedure with Customs & Excise (who are responsible for the administration of the VAT system). This is to avoid the recalculation of VAT and the reissue of invoices to customers who do not take the cash discount.

VAT calculations

VAT entries are unusual in that VAT is always rounded *down* to the nearest penny. For example:

> VAT of £16.769 would be entered as:
>
> VAT of £16.765 would be entered as: } £16.76
>
> VAT of £16.764 would be entered as:

The Delivery Note

> **Delivery note** – completed by a supplier and sent with goods (not services) to show goods being delivered to a customer.

A delivery note (see Figure 5.1.3) can:

* be posted to the customer
* travel with the goods.

The delivery note shows all the same details that would appear on the invoice but any details relating to the price of the goods or the amount to pay are blanked out.

When the goods arrive Office Shop will use the delivery note to check that it matches the contents of the packages.

If the delivery note travels with the goods, the person delivering the goods will ask the person who receives the goods to sign the delivery note as evidence that they have been delivered. If the goods described on the delivery note do not match the contents of the packages, then Office Shop should write on the delivery note the differences or details of any damaged goods before signing it.

One copy of the delivery note is left with the customer and the second copy is taken back to the supplier's office as proof that the goods were delivered.

When the computer equipment is delivered the customer will complete a goods received note.

Figure 5.1.3 Delivery note

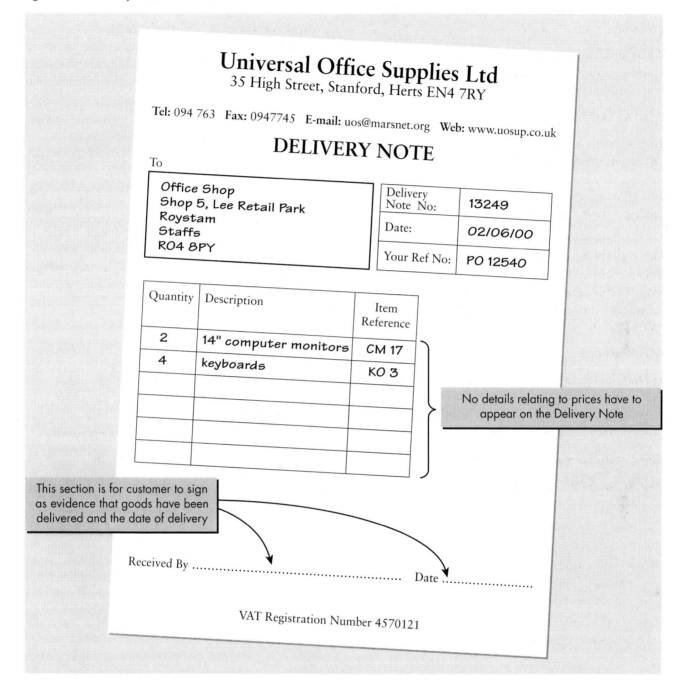

The Goods Received Note

Goods received note – completed by a customer to record goods (not services) received and their condition.

This is an internal document, which means that it stays on the customer's premises. It is not sent to the supplier.

The goods received note (see Figure 5.1.4) shows:

- the quantity and type of all the goods that have been received (even those that were not ordered!)

- if any goods were received in a damaged condition.

Office Shop will pay only for goods it can use so it will return to Universal Office Supplies any damaged goods. If Universal Office Supplies agrees that some goods are damaged it will post to Office Shop a **credit note**.

Figure 5.1.4 Goods received note

Office Shop   GOODS RECEIVED NOTE

Name and Address of Supplier

Universal Office Supplies Ltd 35 High St. Stanford Herts EN4 7RY	G.R.N. Number: **23344** Delivery Note Number: **13249** Purchase Order No **12540**

Quantity	Description	Item Reference	Condition of Goods
2	14" computer monitors	CM 17	satisfactory
4	keyboards	KO 3	2 damaged

Received by: *R. Binks*   Date: *4th June 2000*

The Credit Note

Credit note – sent by a supplier to a customer to reduce the amount owed by the customer.

The credit note (see Figure 5.1.5) shows the same details as shown on an invoice (for the returned goods only) and all the calculations are worked out in the same way – discount is still **subtracted** and VAT is still **added**.

The two main differences are:

- it has the words 'credit note' printed on it
- it reduces the amount owed by the customer, whereas an invoice increases the amount owed by the customer.

It may also contain an entry which explains why the credit note is being sent.

Note that the credit note also has a special number (CN117) on it called the **credit note number** so that both Office Shop and Universal Office Supplies can

Figure 5.1.5 Credit note

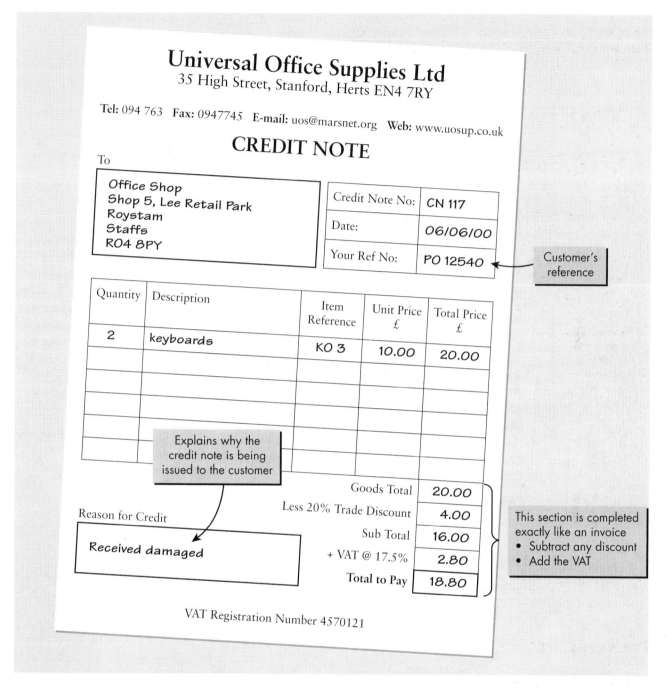

Universal Office Supplies Ltd
35 High Street, Stanford, Herts EN4 7RY

Tel: 094 763   Fax: 0947745   E-mail: uos@marsnet.org   Web: www.uosup.co.uk

CREDIT NOTE

To

Office Shop Shop 5, Lee Retail Park Roystam Staffs RO4 8PY		

Credit Note No:	CN 117
Date:	06/06/00
Your Ref No:	PO 12540

Customer's reference

Quantity	Description	Item Reference	Unit Price £	Total Price £
2	keyboards	KO 3	10.00	20.00

Explains why the credit note is being issued to the customer

Goods Total	20.00
Less 20% Trade Discount	4.00
Sub Total	16.00
+ VAT @ 17.5%	2.80
Total to Pay	18.80

This section is completed exactly like an invoice
• Subtract any discount
• Add the VAT

Reason for Credit

Received damaged

VAT Registration Number 4570121

refer to the credit note easily if there are any problems or queries.

Universal Office Supplies keeps one copy for itself so that it can record how much less Office Shop owes, and sends one copy to Office Shop. Office Shop can now update its own records to show that it owes Universal Office Supplies less than it did before receipt of the credit note.

Note: A credit note is not the same as a refund of money. The supplier does not send money to the customer when a credit note is issued. The credit note allows the customer to pay a lower amount by reducing the overall amount that is owed to the supplier.

When customers pay invoices they will often send with the payment a remittance advice slip.

The Remittance Advice Slip

Remittance advice slip – sent to a supplier with payment to indicate which invoices are being paid.

When Office Shop pays any invoices it encloses a cheque for the correct amount and a remittance advice slip.

The remittance advice slip (see Figure 5.1.6) shows:

- which invoices are being paid off
- any credit notes being used to reduce the amount owed.

Office Shop does not need to send a remittance advice slip but it helps Universal Office Supplies to match up the amount on the cheque with the invoices being paid off. This is particularly helpful if the cheque is paying off more than one invoice. A common payment method is by **cheque**.

Figure 5.1.6 Remittance advice slip

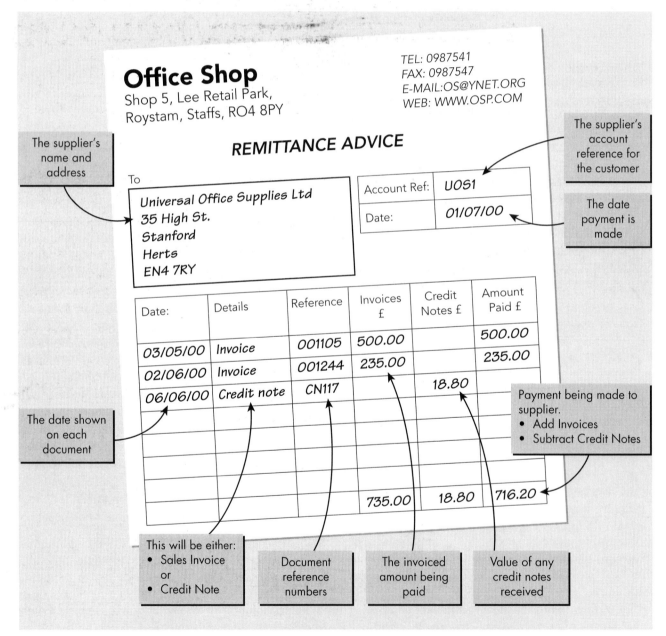

The Cheque

Cheque – a manual method of payment which allows money to be transferred from the customer's bank account to the supplier's bank account.

Rather than paying off invoices by sending notes and coins through the post, Office Shop can write out a cheque for the required amount. This cheque is posted to Universal Office Supplies which pays it into its bank. The cheque then passes through a system called 'clearing' which usually takes three days.

Figure 5.1.7 Cheque

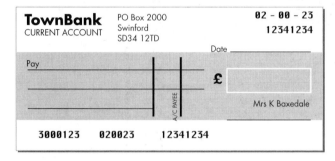

The Cheque Clearing System

This is a system run by all the banks to arrange for the transfer of money from one bank account to another. Once Universal Office Supplies' bank has received the cheque it arranges for the amount stated on the cheque to be transferred from Office Shop's bank account into Universal Office Supplies' bank account.

Paying off invoices by cheque is safer than sending money as thieves are less likely to steal cheques. It is also easier and more convenient than having to keep lots of different notes and coins.

At the end of every month Universal Office Supplies sends out to its **credit customers** a **statement of account**.

The Statement of Account

Statement of account – sent to credit customers to show them the transactions which have affected their account and to encourage them to pay their invoices within the agreed credit period.

If Office Shop regularly buys goods from Universal Office Supplies it will probably have a credit account. This means that Office Shop does not have to pay for the computer equipment immediately but can pay after an agreed period of time. The usual credit terms are 30 days. In other words, the customer is expected to pay the invoice amount not more than 30 days after it was sent. Some customers may get 60 or even 90 days' credit.

The statement of account (see Figure 5.1.8) shows:

- the amount owed by the customer at the beginning of the month (based on previous months' transactions)

- any transactions during the month which increased the amount owed, e.g. issue of a sales invoice

- any transactions during the month which reduced the amount owed, e.g. issue of a credit note or receipt of money from the customer

- the amount owed by the customer at the end of the month.

Figure 5.1.8 Statement of account

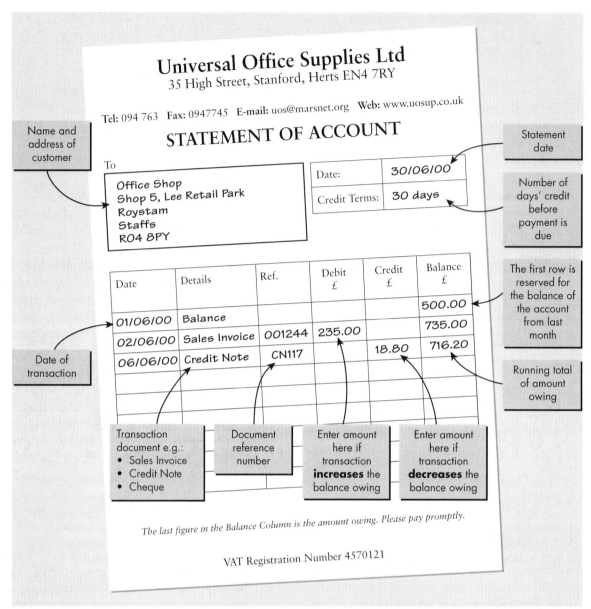

The Receipt

Receipt – given to 'cash customers' as evidence that a payment has been made.

A **receipt** (see Figure 5.1.9) is not usually given to 'credit customers' as the invoice acts as proof of the transaction. Customers who pay for goods or services immediately (cash customers) will not receive an invoice, however, and these customers often request a receipt to prove that a transaction has taken place.

Note that 'cash customers' can pay by cash, cheque, debit card or credit card – not just by cash.

Figure 5.1.9 Receipt

Universal Office Supplies Ltd
35 High Street, Stanford, Herts EN4 7RY

Tel: 094 763   Fax: 0947745   E-mail: uos@marsnet.org   Web: www.uosup.co.uk

RECEIPT

Customer

R. Pato		
	Receipt No:	**457**
	Date:	02/08/00

	£
5 staplers @ £2.00 each	10.00
6 packs staples @ £0.40 per pack	2.40
Sub-total	12.40
VAT	2.17
TOTAL	14.57

VAT Registration Number 4570121

The Petty Cash Voucher

Petty cash voucher – completed when a small payment in notes or coins is required.

A petty cash voucher (see Figure 5.1.10) is an internal document. This means that it is completed for use within a business by employees of that business. It is not sent to any other businesses. It is usually used for making small payments to employees of the business who have bought items for use in the business with their own money and want to be paid back. Payments are usually made for such things as:

- taxi, bus or train fares incurred on business
- stamps for business letters
- tea and coffee for staff refreshments.

A 'float' of notes and coins, known as the 'imprest' amount, is kept in a lockable petty cash box. A petty cash payment is made by taking out notes and coins and replacing them with a completed petty cash voucher for the same amount. This allows the cashier to check for theft or errors since the value of the vouchers in the box plus the value of the notes and coins should always add up to the imprest amount. Every week the imprest amount is topped up to its original level by replacing these completed vouchers with the equivalent value of notes and coins.

Figure 5.1.10 Petty cash voucher

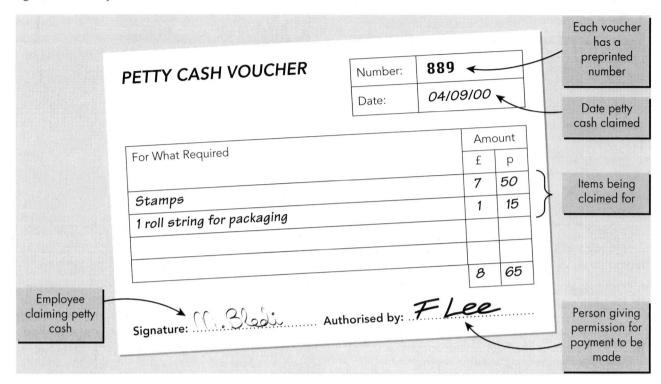

Checking the petty cash

In these examples assume that a weekly imprest (float) amount has been set at £100.

Figure 5.1.11 Petty cash

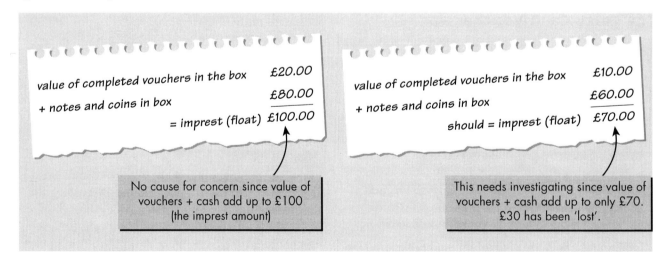

Checking Documents Before Paying Invoices

To make sure that only goods which have been ordered and received are paid for, the customer needs to check the three documents used in the transaction:

• Purchase Order

• Sales Invoice

• Goods Received Note

Table 5.1.1 Checking the transaction details

Question:	Check the:	With the:
Have we received the goods we ordered?	Purchase order	Goods received note
Have we been charged the agreed price?	Purchase order	Sales invoice

Office Shop checks that the quantity and description of the goods shown on the invoice it received from Universal Office Supplies are the same as on the purchase order and the goods received note.

It also checks that the prices and amounts shown on the purchase order match those on the invoice.

If it didn't check these three documents together it might pay for goods that it didn't order or that it hadn't received. It might also pay too much or too little for the goods.

Figure 5.1.12 Cross-checking the documents

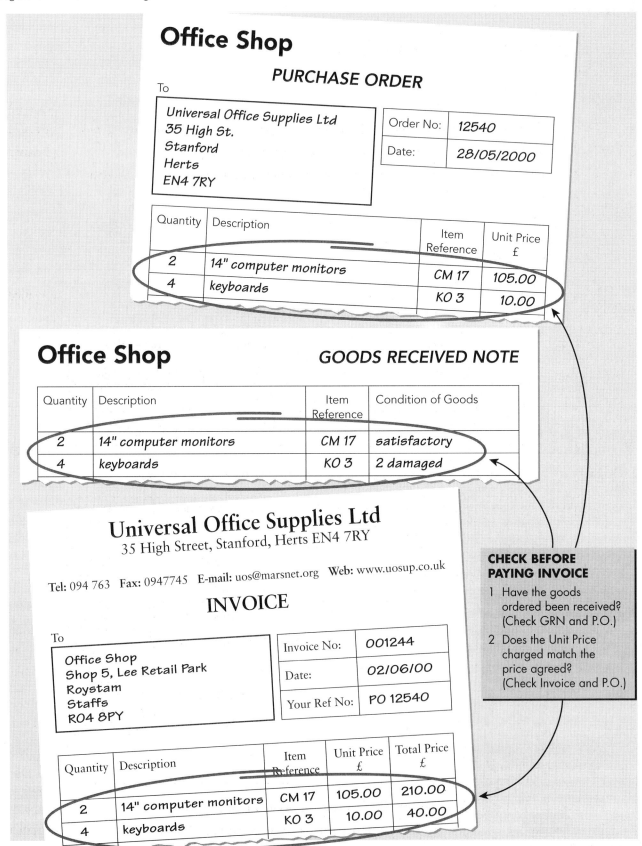

Office Shop

PURCHASE ORDER

To

Universal Office Supplies Ltd
35 High St.
Stanford
Herts
EN4 7RY

| Order No: | 12540 |
| Date: | 28/05/2000 |

Quantity	Description	Item Reference	Unit Price £
2	14" computer monitors	CM 17	105.00
4	keyboards	KO 3	10.00

Office Shop

GOODS RECEIVED NOTE

Quantity	Description	Item Reference	Condition of Goods
2	14" computer monitors	CM 17	satisfactory
4	keyboards	KO 3	2 damaged

Universal Office Supplies Ltd

35 High Street, Stanford, Herts EN4 7RY

Tel: 094 763 Fax: 0947745 E-mail: uos@marsnet.org Web: www.uosup.co.uk

INVOICE

To

Office Shop
Shop 5, Lee Retail Park
Roystam
Staffs
RO4 8PY

Invoice No:	001244
Date:	02/06/00
Your Ref No:	PO 12540

Quantity	Description	Item Reference	Unit Price £	Total Price £
2	14" computer monitors	CM 17	105.00	210.00
4	keyboards	KO 3	10.00	40.00

CHECK BEFORE PAYING INVOICE

1 Have the goods ordered been received? (Check GRN and P.O.)

2 Does the Unit Price charged match the price agreed? (Check Invoice and P.O.)

Revision Questions

1 When are the following documents used:

i) purchase order
ii) delivery note
iii) remittance advice slip? (3 marks)

2 What document would a supplier send to a customer if the customer returned unwanted goods? (1 mark)

3 What checks should a customer make before paying an invoice from a supplier? (1 mark)

4 Put the following documents in the order in which they would be completed for a transaction:

a) cheque
b) purchase order
c) invoice
d) statement of account
e) delivery note
f) remittance advice slip. (3 marks)

5 Complete the following invoice extensions by filling in the grey boxes.

Quantity	Description	Price per Item	Total Price
2	disc boxes	£3.00	
3	scanners	£52.54	
5	printer cartridges	£62.18	

(1 mark)

6 **(a)** Copy out and complete the following invoice section by filling in the grey boxes.

Quantity	Description	Catalogue Ref.	Price per Item	Total Price
6	mouse mats	mm 3	4.50	27.00
4	screen guards	sg	3.21	12.84
2	printers	p5	320.18	640.36
			Goods Total	
			less 20% trade discount	
			Sub total	
			+VAT @ 17.5%	
			Total to Pay	
Cash Discount 1.5% for payment within 14 days of invoice date				

(b) How much should the customer pay if payment is made within 14 days?

(c) How much should the customer pay if payment is not made within 14 days? (6 marks)

7 Two screen guards priced at £3.21 each have been returned to the supplier because they were the wrong size. Complete the credit note that would be sent to the customer, assuming that the customer was originally given 20 per cent trade discount on the purchase. (4 marks)

8 Copy out and complete the statement extract from the information given below:
Balance of the account on 1st May 2000: £1000.00 (3 marks)

Invoices sent to customer:			Cheques received from customer:			Credit notes issued to customer:		
Date	Invoice No.	Amount	Date	Cheque No.	Amount	Date	Credit Note No.	Amount
3/5/00	12457	250.00	11/5/00	564	800.00	18/5/00	cn2864	20.00
25/5/00	12884	50.00	28/5/00	578	100.00			

Statement of Account (extract)

Date	Details	Ref.	Debit	Credit	Balance

9 Why do suppliers check references of customers before offering them credit facilities? (1 mark)

Recording Transactions

In this chapter you will learn how to enter transactions into an accounting system using books of original entry and ledgers. You will also gain a basic understanding of the double entry bookkeeping system

Introduction

Documents about transactions between buyers and sellers of goods or services need to be entered into an accounting system so that users can access information easily without having to handle lots of original documents.

These documents are

- invoices received from credit suppliers (purchases invoices)
- invoices sent to credit customers (sales invoices)
- credit notes sent to customers
- credit notes received from suppliers
- receipts of money from customers (e.g. cheques)
- payments sent to suppliers (e.g. cheques).

Once these documents have been recorded into the accounting system they can be filed. In most cases they need not be referred to again.

Entering documents

Books of original entry

Books of original entry – these provide a means of transferring information from documents into the accounting record system.

Books of original entry comprise:

- the four day books
- the cash book.

The day books

For credit transactions there will be four day books – one to record each document.

Day book	Document to be recorded
Sales day book	Sales invoice (sent to customers)
Purchases day book	Purchases invoice (received from suppliers)
Sales returns day book	Credit note (sent to customers)
Purchases returns day book	Credit note (received from suppliers)

Alternative names for day books

Some of the day books have alternative names as follows:

Common name	Alternative name 1	Alternative name 2
Sales day book	Sales book	Sales journal
Purchases day book	Purchases book	Purchases journal
Sales returns day book	Returns in day book	Returns in journal
Purchases returns day book	Returns out day book	Returns out journal

Day book format

All the day books share the same layout.

Figure 5.2.1a

.... Day Book   Page: ....

Date	Reference	Name of Account	Total £
	Invoice or credit note number	Values are transferred from the invoice or credit note into this column	

*Figure 5.2.1b This day book records **sales invoices** sent to customers.*

...*Sales*... Day Book   Page: *SDB 67*

Date	Reference	Name of Account	Total £
02/06/00	0004578	J Wills & Co	117.50
02/06/00	0004579	G Georgiou	235.00
02/06/00	0004580	Ahmed Bros	470.00
03/06/00	0004581	G Georgiou	117.50

Sales Invoice Number

*Figure 5.2.1c This day book records **credit notes** sent to customers.*

Sales Returns Day Book   Page: SRDB 23

Date	Reference	Name of Account	Total £
02/07/00	CN00232	J Patel & Co	25.14
02/07/00	CN00233	G Georgiou	35.00
02/07/00	CN00234	Farr and Lee	16.57

Credit Note Number

The cash book

The cash book layout allows both receipts of money from customers and payments to suppliers of money to be recorded.

Figure 5.2.2

Cash Book

Receipts   **Payments**

Date	Details	Amount £	Amount p	Date	Details	Amount £	Amount p
04/07/00	M Lee	28	65	05/07/00	Brant Ltd	458	58
06/07/00	G Georgiou	470	00				

Values of Cheques Received are entered into this column

Values of Cheques Paid are entered into this column

The double-entry bookkeeping system

A system of recording accounting transactions is used which requires that each transaction recorded in a day book is transferred (posted) to two different accounts in the ledgers. One account will be debited and the other account will be credited. This is why the system is called double entry. By making two entries in this way, bookkeepers and accountants can check that entries have been made correctly, since the total of all the debit entries should be the same as the total of all the credit entries. This check is carried out periodically, by preparing a trial balance.

Credit and debit

The terms credit and debit have a special meaning when applied to accounting.

Debit the account – make an entry in the *left hand side* of the account.

Credit the account – make an entry in the *right hand side* of the account.

In handwritten accounting this account is called a 'T' account, because it looks like the letter T – it has a debit side and a credit side.

Figure 5.2.3

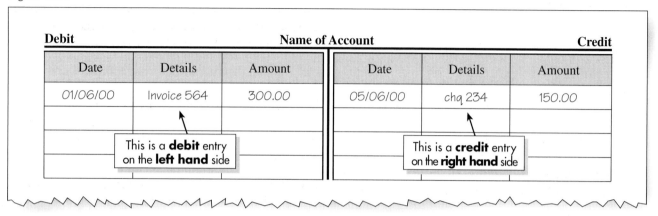

Debit					Name of Account			Credit
Date	Details	Amount		Date	Details	Amount
01/06/00	Invoice 564	300.00		05/06/00	chq 234	150.00

This is a **debit** entry on the **left hand** side

This is a **credit** entry on the **right hand** side

(The cash book is a special case – refer to the section on the cash book on page 327 to see how entries in the cash book are dealt with.)

Figure 5.2.4 Flow chart for recording entries – books of original entry – day books (VAT ignored)

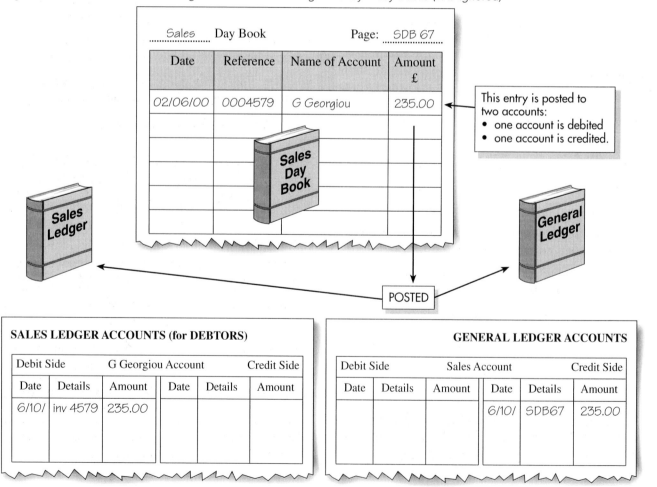

Sales Day Book   Page: *SDB 67*

Date	Reference	Name of Account	Amount £
02/06/00	0004579	G Georgiou	235.00

This entry is posted to two accounts:
• one account is debited
• one account is credited.

Sales Ledger

Sales Day Book

General Ledger

POSTED

SALES LEDGER ACCOUNTS (for DEBTORS)

Debit Side		G Georgiou Account		Credit Side	
Date	Details	Amount	Date	Details	Amount
6/10/	inv 4579	235.00			

GENERAL LEDGER ACCOUNTS

Debit Side		Sales Account		Credit Side	
Date	Details	Amount	Date	Details	Amount
			6/10/	SDB67	235.00

In practice, the general ledger receives daybook totals rather than individual entries.

The ledgers

The sales ledger (personal ledger)

This book is used to record all transactions affecting credit customers (debtors).

Sales ledger – a book which contains all the personal accounts of the customers to whom goods are sold on credit.

Because transactions are listed in the day books in date order only, it is difficult to find specific information relating to an individual customer's transactions because it is mixed up with all the other customers' transactions.

To overcome this problem an account or page is set up for each customer. All these accounts are kept together in a book called a sales ledger. These accounts are usually listed alphabetically to make it easier to find a specific customer

The main reason for keeping detailed records of transactions with customers is that a business needs to know how much each customer owes and when payment is due.

Any transaction which affects the amount that a customer owes must be recorded in the personal account of that customer.

Common transactions recorded in a customer's account:

- goods are sold to a customer (document sales invoice) – the customer now owes more

- a credit note is sent to a customer (document credit note) – the customer now owes less

- the customer sends a payment for goods (document cheque) – the customer now owes less.

The purchases ledger (personal ledger)

This book is used to record all transactions affecting credit suppliers.

Purchases ledger – a book which contains all the personal accounts of the suppliers from whom goods are bought on credit.

Because transactions are listed in the day books in date order only, it is difficult to find specific information relating to an individual supplier's transactions because it is mixed up with all the other suppliers' transactions.

To overcome this problem an account is set up for each supplier. All these accounts are kept together in a book called a purchases ledger. These accounts are usually listed alphabetically to make it easier to find a specific supplier.

The main reason for keeping detailed records of transactions with suppliers is that a business needs to know how much is owed to each supplier and when payment is due.

Any transaction which affects the amount that is owed to a supplier must be recorded in the personal account of that supplier.

Common transactions recorded in a supplier's account are:

- goods are purchased from a supplier (document purchases invoice) – the supplier is now owed more

- a credit note is received from a supplier (document credit note) – less is now owed to that supplier

- a payment to the supplier for goods purchased (document cheque) – less is now owed to that supplier.

General ledger (also known as nominal ledger)

General ledger – a book which contains all the other accounts not appearing in the sales ledger, purchases ledger, or cash book.

This ledger houses accounts such as:

Account name:	To record the:
Sales account	Value of goods sold to customers
Purchases account	Value of goods purchased from suppliers
Sales returns account	Value of goods returned by customers
Purchases returns account	Value of goods returned to suppliers

Figure 5.2.5 Flow chart for recording entries – books of origianal entry – cash book

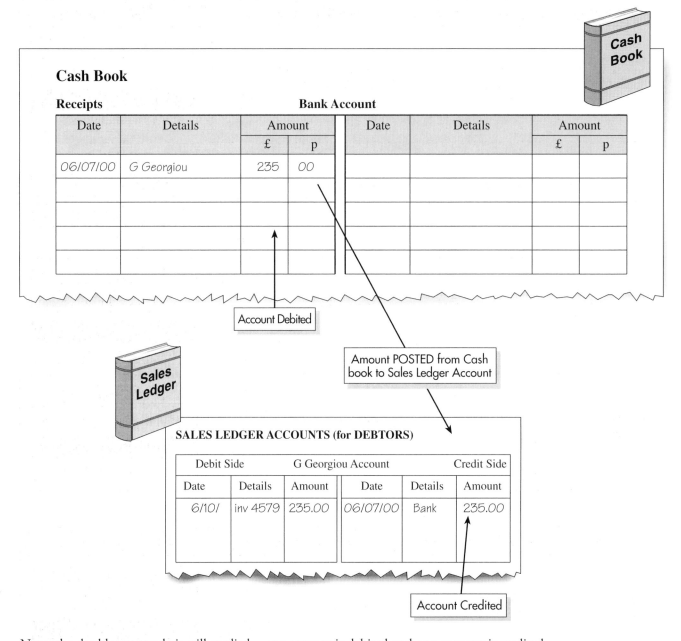

Note: the double entry rule is still applied – one account is debited and one account is credited.

The cash book has two functions. It operates both as a book of orginal entry and as an account. This means that only one further entry is required to complete the double entry. No entry is made in the general ledger when money is received from debtors or paid out to creditors.

Note: the cash book is for all receipts and payments – not just cash.

Figure 5.2.6 Entering credit transactions (summary) – the day books

Transaction	Source document	Book of original entry	Double entry posting
Goods **Sold** to a customer	**Sales** Invoice (sent)	**Sales** Day Book — Posted	General Ledger Entry (**Sales** Account) / Sales Ledger Entry (Customers Account)
Goods **Purchased** from a supplier	**Purchases** Invoice (received)	**Purchases** Day Book — Posted	General Ledger Entry (**Purchases** Account) / Purchases Ledger Entry (Suppliers Account)
Goods **Returned** from a customer	Credit Note (sent)	**Sales Returns** Day Book — Posted	General Ledger Entry (**Sales Returns** Account) / Sales Ledger Entry (Customers Account)
Goods **Returned** to a supplier	Credit Note (received)	**Purchases Returns** Day Book — Posted	General Ledger Entry (**Purchases Returns** Account) / Purchases Ledger Entry (Suppliers Account)

Figure 5.2.7 Entering payment and receipt transactions – the cash book

Transaction	Source document	Book of original entry	Double entry posting
Customer pays for goods	Cheque (received)	Cash book — Posted	General Ledger Entry (Not Entered) / Sales Ledger Entry (**Customers** Account)
Supplier is paid for goods	Cheque (sent)	Cash book — Posted	General Ledger Entry (Not Entered) / Purchases Ledger Entry (**Suppliers** Account)

Note: when a cheque relating to debtors or creditors is received or paid the entry is not posted to the general ledger. This is because the cash book itself is acting as an account as well as a book of original entry.

Revision Questions

1   In which day book would a sales invoice sent to a customer be recorded?   (1 mark)

2   In which book of original entry would a cheque received from a customer be recorded?   (1 mark)

3   Why is an individual account kept for:

a) every supplier?
b) every customer?   (2 marks)

4   Why is the general ledger not entered when recording cheque from debtors?   (1 mark)

5   Give one alternative name for the purchases returns day book.   (1 mark)

6   What document is entered in the sales returns day book, and who is the document sent to?   (1 mark)

7   Trace the accounting flow for the following transactions by entering information on the dotted lines:

a) In the accounts of Alpha Ltd, for an invoice sent from Alpha Ltd to Bravo Ltd.

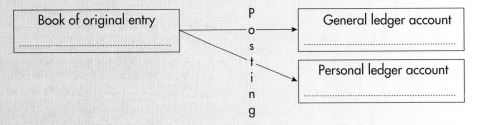

b) In the accounts of Alpha Ltd, for a cheque received from Bravo Ltd.

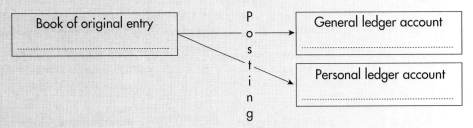

(3 marks)

Preparing Final Accounts

In this chapter you will learn how to distinguish between different types of accounts. You will also learn how to use a trial balance to construct final accounts and make adjustments to record depreciation.

Introduction

The term final accounts is usually used to describe:

- trading account
- profit & loss account
- balance sheet.

The trial balance

Trial balance – A list of all the debit balances and all the credit balances from all the individual accounts of the business.

The trial balance is drawn up by copying the balances from the 'T' accounts appearing in the cash book, sales ledger, purchases ledger and general ledger. Trial balances are prepared regularly, usually at the end of each month

A simple trial balance for a small sole trader may look like this:

Business 1 Trial Balance as on 31 December 1999		
Name of Account	Debit Balance	Credit Balance
	£	£
Capital		20 000
Drawings	25 000	
Bank	10 000	
Sales		60 000
Purchases	30 000	
Motor vehicles	8 000	
Rent & Rates	5 000	
Heating & Lighting	2 000	
	80 000	80 000

The trial balance has two functions:

- If the credit and debit columns of the trial balance are the same, it proves that debit entries and credit entries were matched when the bookkeeper posted entries into the accounting system. (**NB:** however, that doesn't mean that all the accounts are correct. Some errors cannot be detected by preparing a trial balance.)

- It is the source of the information used to prepare the trading and profit & loss accounts and balance sheet.

Figure 5.3.1 To show the transfer of a T account to the Trial Balance

Cash Book

Debit	Receipts			Bank Account	Payments		Credit

Date	Details	Amount		Date	Details	Amount	
		£	p			£	p
01/12/99	Balance brought down	8000	00	05/12/99	Brant Ltd	100	00
06/12/99	G Georgiou	1400	00	18/12/99	Insurance	300	00
23/12/99	Cash Sales	1000	00	31/12/99	Balance carried down	10000	00
		10400	00			10400	00
01/01/00	Balance brought down	10000	00				

A debit side balance is entered in the trial balance in the debit balances column

Business 1
Trial Balance as on 31st December 1999

Name of Account	Debit Balances £	Credit Balances £
Capital		20 000
Drawings	25 000	
Bank	10 000	
Sales		60 000
Purchases	20 000	
Motor vehicles	18 000	
Rent & Rates	5 000	
Heating & Lighting	2 000	
Totals	80 000	80 000

If the records have been entered according to the rule of double entry, the debit balances and credit balances totals of the Trial Balance should be the same.

Final accounts are prepared by transferring information from the accounts shown in the trial balance. In order to transfer items correctly you need to distinguish between the different classes of accounts according to the definitions given below.

Profit & loss account section

Expenses – day-to-day costs of running a business; *or* items used up in order to make a profit (sometimes a loss).

Examples:

- wages and salaries
- insurance premiums
- business rates
- stationery
- telephone bills
- bank charges
- motor repairs
- printing costs
- heating and lighting bills
- rent
- advertising
- postage

Revenues – sources which generate an income (opposite of an expense account).

Examples:

- rent received
- bank interest received

Balance sheet section

Fixed assets – items bought for use in the business; *and* not bought to be resold; *and* lasting longer than one year.

Examples:

- machinery
- equipment
- fixtures and fittings
- land
- motor vehicles
- buildings

Current assets – items bought to be resold for profit; *or* cash or items held for conversion into cash; *or* customers who owe money (debtors).

Examples:

- stock
- bank
- debtors
- cash

Current liabilities – amounts owed, payable within one year.

Examples:

- creditors
- bank overdraft

Long-term liabilities – amounts owed, payable over more than one year.

Examples:

- 5-year bank loan
- long-term loan
- mortgage

The balance sheet of a sole trader has a 'financed by' section to show the owner the effect the year's transactions have had on the capital.

Capital (at start of year) – owner's stake in the business at the start of year.

This figure can be obtained from the trial balance and must not be confused with stock at beginning of the year. (This confusion sometimes occurs because they share the same date.)

+ Net Profit – owner's stake in the business is increased by the amount of profit made during the year.

If a loss is made then the loss would be subtracted from the capital.

– Drawings – any amounts withdrawn by owner(s) during the year.

Sole traders will usually draw money from their businesses in order to pay themselves a salary. These 'drawings' are not recorded as an expense – they merely reduce the stake of the owner in the business. If a sole trader employs people, the employees' wages or salaries are recorded separately as expenses in the 'wages' or 'salaries' account.

= Capital at end of year – owner's stake in the business at the end of the year.

The Trading Account (gross profit calculated)

The trading account is prepared in order to determine the gross profit. The gross profit is the difference between the cost of goods sold and the selling price of those goods. It is important because the gross profit is a useful indicator of business performance.

Trading account – a final account to show the calculation of the gross profit.

	£	£
Sales		800
Opening Stock	40	
+ Purchases	350	
	390	
– Closing Stock	90	
Cost of Goods Sold		300
Gross Profit		500

Note

In accounting, the term 'purchases account' refers only to the purchase of stock – a current asset. Purchases of fixed assets are recorded in the accounts relating to those fixed assets.

For example, the purchase of a delivery van will be recorded in the 'motor vehicles' account, not the 'purchases' account.

The Profit and Loss Account (Net Profit or Loss calculated)

Profit and loss account – a final account to show the calculation of the net profit or net loss.

Expenses

All the expenses of the business for the year are shown in the profit and loss account. Expenses are **subtracted** from the gross profit.

Revenues

If the business has any revenue accounts these will also be shown in the profit and loss account. Revenues are **added** to the gross profit before the subtraction of the expenses.

Expenses only

Gross Profit		500
Wages	60	
Advertising	30	
Rent	10	
		100
Net Profit		400

Expenses and Revenues

Gross Profit		500
Bank Interest Received		50
		550
Wages	60	
Advertising	30	
Rent	10	
		100
Net Profit		450

Balance sheet – a final statement which lists all the **assets** and all the **liabilities** of the business on a specified date in time.

This document is a 'snapshot' or 'photograph' of the business *on one day* at the end of the financial year. It shows the overall financial position, how much a business is worth and the owner's personal 'stake' in the business.

Business 1 is a sole trader whose financial year ends on 31 December each year. The full set of final accounts, derived from the trial balance, is shown in Figure 5.3.2.

Figure 5.3.2

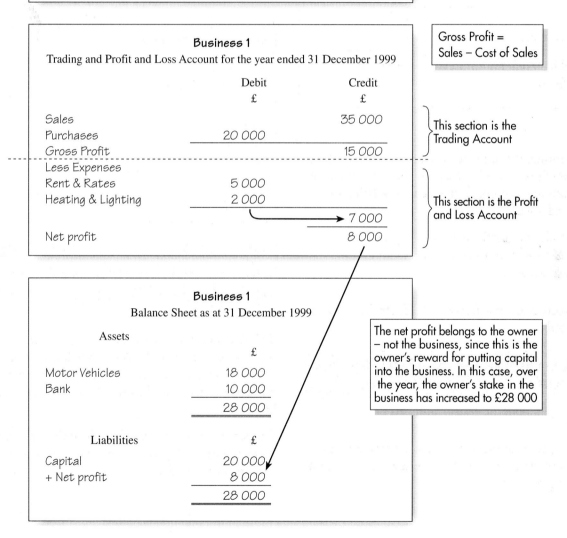

Business 1
Trial Balance as on 31 December 1999

Name of Account	Debit Balances £	Credit Balances £
Capital		20 000
Bank	10 000	
Sales		35 000
Purchases	20 000	
Motor vehicles	18 000	
Rent & Rates	5 000	
Heating & Lighting	2 000	
	55 000	55 000

Business 1
Trading and Profit and Loss Account for the year ended 31 December 1999

	Debit £	Credit £
Sales		35 000
Purchases	20 000	
Gross Profit		15 000
Less Expenses		
Rent & Rates	5 000	
Heating & Lighting	2 000	
		7 000
Net profit		8 000

Gross Profit = Sales – Cost of Sales

This section is the Trading Account

This section is the Profit and Loss Account

Business 1
Balance Sheet as at 31 December 1999

Assets	£
Motor Vehicles	18 000
Bank	10 000
	28 000

Liabilities	£
Capital	20 000
+ Net profit	8 000
	28 000

The net profit belongs to the owner – not the business, since this is the owner's reward for putting capital into the business. In this case, over the year, the owner's stake in the business has increased to £28 000

In this simple example the fixed assets of the business have been shown at their purchase price. In reality, fixed assets lose value over time and will not be worth the same every year. The final accounts have to be adjusted to show the effects of this depreciation.

> **Depreciation** – the reduction in value of a fixed asset during its lifetime.

All fixed assets lose value as a result of the following:

- physical deterioration: machinery and equipment wear out.
- obsolescence: machinery and equipment become outdated and uneconomic.
- depletion: mines run out of coal, or other minerals.
- the passage of time: leases, patents and copyrights expire.

Depreciation must be allocated to each accounting period which benefits from the use of that asset.

As a result, fixed assets should be shown at their adjusted reduced values. The amount of yearly depreciation is an expense item.

Depreciation of fixed assets is an expense which will appear in the profit and loss account

The depreciation expenses over the lifetime of an asset will be reflected in its net book value shown in the balance sheet.

CASE STUDY

Business 2 started trading on 1 January 1997 and has been operating for three years. The accounts for 1997 and 1998 have already been prepared and this example will show how final accounts for 1999 will be constructed to show the adjustments necessary to account for depreciation over the three years from 1997–99 inclusive.

Calculating depreciation per year

Straight line method of depreciation

This method allocates the same amount of depreciation in every year of the asset's life and is given by the formula:

$$\text{Yearly depreciation expense} = \frac{\text{Fixed asset at cost}}{\text{No. of years expected life}}$$

Business 2 bought a motor vehicle at £18,000 on 1 January 1997.

It was expected to last for five years and then be scrapped.

By applying the formula the depreciation for each of the five years can be worked out:

$$\text{Yearly depreciation expense} = \frac{£18,000}{5 \text{ years}} = £3600 \text{ per year.}$$

Alternatively, the depreciation can be worked out using a percentage, as given by the formula:

Yearly depreciation expense = fixed asset at cost × ?%

Yearly depreciation expense = £18,000 × 20% = £3600 per year (*Percentage rate to be used = 100% ÷ 5 years = 20%*)

Either way, the depreciation for each year = £3600.

Entering depreciation in the final accounts

Adjustments have to be made in:

a) the profit and loss account (because depreciation is an expense)

b) the balance sheet (because the value of the fixed assets will have to be reduced).

Entry in the profit and loss account

Depreciation for the year (1999 only)

Depreciation is an expense like rent, insurance wages, etc.

At the end of every financial year the depreciation *for that year only* (1999) needs to be calculated and entered in the profit and loss account as calculated above.

Motor vehicle depreciation expense for 1999 = £3600

Entry in the balance sheet

The balance sheet is supposed to give a 'true and fair' picture of the state of a business. Since fixed assets lose value over the years through the effects of depreciation, it would not be 'true and fair' to enter the fixed assets into the balance sheet at their original purchase cost. In order to show fixed assets at their current value, therefore, it is necessary to subtract from the original cost not just the depreciation expense for 1999 but all the depreciation which has taken place so far during the lifetime of that asset. This is the combined depreciation for each of the years 1997, 1998 and 1999.

Provision for depreciation (this account is shown in the trial balance)

A running total of all the *previous* years' depreciation (but not yet the current year of 1999) is found in an account called the 'provision for depreciation' account.

| Provision for depreciation = | £3600 + £3600 = £7200 |
| (for years 1997 + 1998 only) | (1997) + (1998) |

Since the depreciation for 1999 has also been calculated, it is now possible to calculate the total accumulated depreciation for *all* the years of the asset's life. This is known in the balance sheet as the 'depreciation to date'.

Depreciation to date (this is a column heading in the balance sheet)

This is the total amount by which the motor vehicle has depreciated since it was first bought.

It can be calculated as follows:

Figure 5.3.3

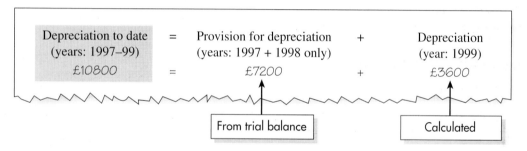

These entries, which account for depreciation, can now be seen in the full set of final accounts of Business 2, prepared at the end of the financial year 1999.

Net book value – the current value of a fixed asset

Net book value (this is a column heading in the balance sheet)

This is the latest adjusted value of the fixed asset after deducting the total depreciation for all the years.

It is shown in the balance sheet as follows:

Figure 5.3.4

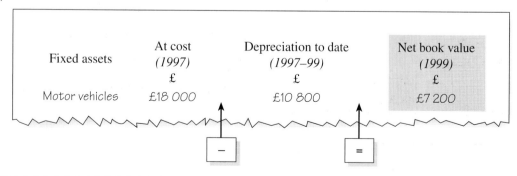

Figure 5.3.5

Business 2
Trial Balance as on 31st December 1999

Name of Account	Debit Balances £	Credit Balances £
Capital		20 000
Drawings	9000	
Motor vehicles at cost	18 000	
Motor vehicle – provision for depreciation		7200
Fixtures & Fittings at cost	7000	
Fixtures & Fittings – provision for depreciation		2800
Stock at 1st January 1999	200	
Bank	15 000	
Cash	1000	
Sales		44 300
Debtors	800	
Purchases	17 000	
Creditors		1700
Long-term loan		3000
Insurance	4000	
Rent & Rates	5000	
Heating & Lighting	2000	
Total	79 000	79 000

Owner's stake in the business at the beginning of the year → Capital

Amounts withdrawn by the owner for personal use → Drawings

Original purchase price of motor vehicle → Motor vehicles at cost

Total of all previous years' depreciation for motor vehicles **as at beginning of year** → Motor vehicle – provision for depreciation

Opening Stock held at the begining of the financial year → Stock at 1st January 1999

Total invoices sent to customers → Sales

Amounts owed by customers → Debtors

Total invoices received from supplies → Purchases

Amounts owed to suppliers → Creditors

A loan of more than one year → Long-term loan

Notes:
1. The stock at the end of the financial year (Closing Stock) has been valued at £300.
2. Fixed assets are to be depreciated at 20% per annum – based on the original cost.

Calculation of Depreciation of Fixed Assets

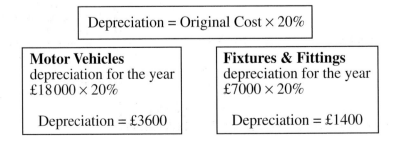

Depreciation = Original Cost × 20%

Motor Vehicles
depreciation for the year
£18 000 × 20%

Depreciation = £3600

Fixtures & Fittings
depreciation for the year
£7000 × 20%

Depreciation = £1400

Figure 5.3.6

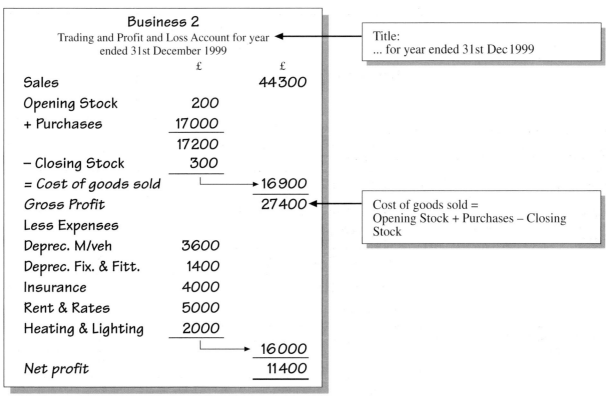

Business 2
Trading and Profit and Loss Account for year
ended 31st December 1999

	£	£
Sales		44300
Opening Stock	200	
+ Purchases	17000	
	17200	
– Closing Stock	300	
= Cost of goods sold		16900
Gross Profit		27400
Less Expenses		
Deprec. M/veh	3600	
Deprec. Fix. & Fitt.	1400	
Insurance	4000	
Rent & Rates	5000	
Heating & Lighting	2000	
		16000
Net profit		11400

Title:
... for year ended 31st Dec 1999

Cost of goods sold =
Opening Stock + Purchases – Closing
Stock

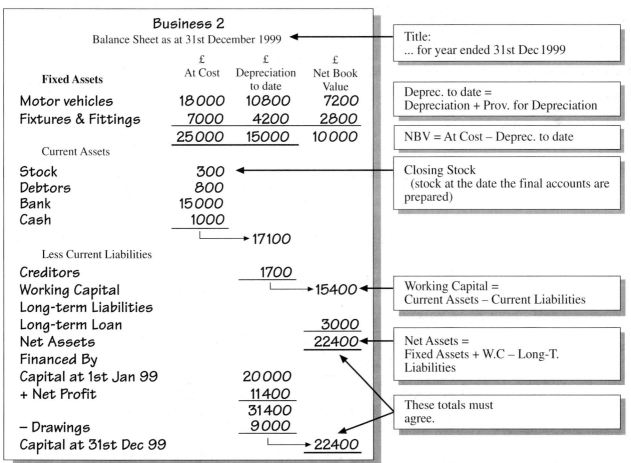

Business 2
Balance Sheet as at 31st December 1999

	£ At Cost	£ Depreciation to date	£ Net Book Value
Fixed Assets			
Motor vehicles	18000	10800	7200
Fixtures & Fittings	7000	4200	2800
	25000	15000	10000
Current Assets			
Stock	300		
Debtors	800		
Bank	15000		
Cash	1000		
		17100	
Less Current Liabilities			
Creditors		1700	
Working Capital		15400	
Long-term Liabilities			
Long-term Loan		3000	
Net Assets		22400	
Financed By			
Capital at 1st Jan 99	20000		
+ Net Profit	11400		
	31400		
– Drawings	9000		
Capital at 31st Dec 99		22400	

Title:
... for year ended 31st Dec 1999

Deprec. to date =
Depreciation + Prov. for Depreciation

NBV = At Cost – Deprec. to date

Closing Stock
(stock at the date the final accounts are
prepared)

Working Capital =
Current Assets – Current Liabilities

Net Assets =
Fixed Assets + W.C – Long-T.
Liabilities

These totals must
agree.

Revision Questions

1   The trial balance is drawn up from the balances shown on which of these?

   A books of original entry
   B documents
   C final accounts
   D 'T' accounts   (1 mark)

2   How does the trial balance prove the accuracy of the accounting recording?   (1 mark)

3   Classify the following accounts under the headings: fixed assets, current assets, current liabilities, long-term liabilities, expenses and revenues.   (6 marks)

Electricity charges	Bank overdraft	Delivery vans
Premises	Travelling costs	Petty cash
Stock for resale	Depreciation	Office cleaning
Rent	Rent received	Creditors
Debtors	Gas costs	Factory plant and machinery
Company cars	Raw materials	10-year loan

4   Identify the name of the accounts being described:

   a) customers who have been sold goods on credit
   b) suppliers from whom goods have been purchased on credit
   c) total value of all goods sold to customers
   d) total value of all goods bought from suppliers
   e) value of goods in stock at the end of the financial year
   f) total paid to weekly paid workers.   (3 marks)

5   What is the correct heading for a trading and profit and loss account drawn up on 31 December 2000 after one year's trading?

   A ... as for the month ending 31 December 2000
   B ... as at December 31 2000
   C ... for the period ended 31 December 2000
   D ... for the year ending December 31 2000.   (1 mark)

6   What is the correct heading for a balance sheet drawn up annually on 31 August 2000 – the last day of the financial year?

   A ... as for the month ending 31 August 2000
   B ... as at August 31 2000
   C ... for the period ended 31 August 2000
   D ... for the year ending August 31 2000.   (1 mark)

7   In her first year, a sole trader invested £5000 capital, made a net profit of £3000 and took out drawings of £1000. What was the owner's stake in the business at the end of the financial year?   (1 mark)

8 How much gross profit was made if goods costing £500 were sold for £800? (1 mark)

9 What is the net profit of a business with a gross profit of £1000 and expenses of £400? (1 mark)

10 What is the net profit of a business with a gross profit of £1000, additional revenues of £200 and expenses of £400? (1 mark)

11 What is the net profit or loss of a business with a gross profit of £1000, additional revenues of £200 and expenses of £1300? (1 mark)

12 How much yearly depreciation expense should be allocated for a machine which cost £5000 with an expected life of five years? (1 mark)

13 What is the expected depreciation per year on £6000 worth of equipment which is to be depreciated at the rate of 20 per cent per annum? (1 mark)

14 The following is an extract from a trial balance drawn up at the end of a financial year on 31 December 2000:

	Trial balance	
Account name	£	£
Machinery at cost	15000	
Machinery provision for depreciation		4500

Adjustments to be made:

- machinery is to be depreciated by 10 per cent per annum.

a) Calculate the 'depreciation' expense relating only to the year 2000.

b) Calculate the 'depreciation to date' (including the depreciation for the year 2000).

c) Calculate the latest 'net book value' (NBV). (3 marks)

15 The following is an extract from a trial balance drawn up at the end of a financial year on 31 December 2000:

	Trial balance	
Account name	£	£
Motor vehicles at cost	20000	
Motor vehicles provision for depreciation		10000

Adjustments to be made:

- motor vehicles are to be depreciated by 25 per cent per annum.

a) Calculate the 'depreciation' expense relating only to the year 2000.

b) Calculate the 'depreciation to date' (including the depreciation for the year 2000).

c) Calculate the latest 'net book value' (NBV). (3 marks)

CHAPTER 4

Control and Management of Cash Flow

KEY TERMS:

working capital	credit control	cash flow
stock control	aged debtor analysis	inflows
variance	budget	outflows

In this chapter you will learn how managers control and manage their assets and liabilities in order to have enough liquid funds to run their business efficiently. This will involve understanding credit control procedures and learning how to construct and interpret budgets.

Introduction

Every business must keep control of its working capital. It is vital to know what money is owed, what money is due and what the cash flow position is. It is essential to control this aspect of the business if it is to succeed.

Working capital

Working capital – current assets minus current liabilities.

This is usually the amount of current assets remaining if the creditors were to be paid off.

Current assets

- stocks of goods or raw materials
- cash balances
- bank balances
- debtors.

Current liabilities

- creditors
- bank overdraft.

If the working capital is negative (i.e. there are more current liabilities than current assets), the business will be unable to pay debts when they fall due. A negative or insufficient working capital position will create cash flow problems for the business which, if uncorrected, will cause the business to fail.

Working capital management

Stock control

Stock control – the process of ensuring that stock is always available for use or sale.

Ideally, a business should try to keep just enough stock to meet demand so that money is not tied up in excessive stock holdings. Care must be taken, however, to avoid the situation whereby insufficient stock is held because this could also create problems.

Problems associated with holding too much stock

- The costs of storing stock will increase.
- The business may have to rent space to stock the excess stock.
- The security costs of looking after excess stock will increase.
- The business may have to borrow money to pay for the stock or increase its overdraft if it has insufficient funds.

- If held for too long the stock may lose value due to it:
  - becoming unfashionable (e.g. clothes)
  - perishing (e.g. foodstuffs)
  - being superseded by a later design (e.g. computer components).

Problems associated with holding too little stock

- an inability to meet demand by the production department if raw materials are required to manufacture finished products
- an inability to meet the demand for orders from customers leading to:
  - a loss of sales and therefore profit
  - a loss of goodwill followed by the loss of repeat business as customers take their business elsewhere and find new suppliers
- Frequent reordering of small amounts of stock is uneconomical and increases the administration costs of controlling the stock.

JIT (Just In Time)

This is a stock control system which relies on suppliers to deliver stocks of raw materials only when they are required by the production process of their customers. This reduces storage costs and costs associated with the ordering process. It relies on the suppliers always having stock available to meet the demands of the customer. This system works best when there are computerised links between the supplier and the customer so that the supplier has direct access to the stock usage records of the customer in order to ensure that replacement stocks are delivered on time. Ideally the supplier should be close to avoid transportation delays.

Debtors

Debtors – customers who are sold products on credit.

Some students think that having **debtors** is a 'bad thing'. Having debtors, however, is normal, since buying and selling goods on credit is the usual method of trade. Debtors are assets which will be turned into cash assets when they pay the amounts owing for goods or services sold to them. A problem arises only when

the debtor becomes a 'bad debtor', i.e. when it will not or cannot pay when the amount owed is due.

Credit control

Credit control – the process of ensuring that debtors pay for goods or services.

The first stage in the process is to try to ensure that only reputable, reliable and creditworthy customers are allowed to open credit accounts.

The credit controller should:

- ask potential customers to supply trade references – suppliers who have supplied goods to the customer on credit before.
- ask the potential customer's bank for a credit reference
- refer to a credit reference agency which will supply information about the creditworthiness of the potential customer. A fee is charged for this service.

Once a customer has been given an account the credit controller must:

- set the credit limit beyond which goods will *not* be supplied
- determine the credit period (30 days is normal).

During the operation of the account the credit controller must ensure:

- that credit limits are not exceeded without authorisation
- that debts are paid within the credit period.

Aged debtor analysis

In order to monitor customer credit, the credit controller will often draw up an **aged debtor analysis**.

Aged debtor analysis – list of amounts owed by customers, analysed by the number of days the debts have been outstanding.

An example of an age analysis for one debtor is shown in Figure 5.4.1:

Figure 5.4.1a Statement of Account

Universal Office Supplies Ltd

35 High Street, Stanford, Herts EN4 7RY

Tel: 094 763   Fax: 0947745   E-mail: uos@marsnet.org   Web: www.uosup.co

STATEMENT OF ACCOUNT

To

Office Shop Shop 5, Lee Retail Park Roystam Staffs RO4 8PY	

Date	31/05/00
Credit Terms	30 days
Credit Limit	£6000

Date	Details	Ref.	Debit £	Credit £	Balance £
01/04/00	Balance				4000
04/04/00	credit note	cn527		❶200	3800
09/04/00	sales invoice	1245	❸800		4600
25/04/00	sales invoice	1288	❹600		5200
16/05/00	cheque rec'd	884		❷3700	1500
29/05/00	sales invoice	1350	❺4600		6100

The last figure in the Balance Column is the amount owing. Please pay promptly.

VAT Registration Number 4570121

Figure 5.4.1b Debtor aged analysis (assumes that oldest invoices are paid off first)

Owing for more than 2 months

Balance owing from March	Credits on account (Payments/Credit Notes)	Owing for more than 2 months (i.e. from March)
£4000	❶ £200 + ❷ £3700 = £3900	£4000 – £3900 = £100

Owing from 1 to 2 months

Sales Invoices	Credits on account (Payments/Credit Notes)	Owing from 1 to 2 months (i.e. from April)
❸ £800 and ❹ £600 = £1400	£0.00	£1400 – £0 = £1400

Owing for up to 1 month

Sales Invoices	Credits on account (Payments/Credit Notes)	Owing for up to 1 month (i.e. from May)
❺ £4600	£0.00	£4600 – £0 = £4600

This customer has broken the agreed terms in two ways:

1 The credit period is 30 days yet £100 worth of goods sold to the customer in March and £1400 worth of goods sold to the customer in April had not been paid for by the end of May.

2 The credit limit is £6000 yet the sales transaction on May 29th took the balance to £6100, which was £100 above the agreed limit.

The credit controller should check the analysis regularly to take action to retrieve debts before they become too old. This action can include:

- withholding new orders for goods or services until the account is operated according to the terms of the credit agreement

- sending reminders

- sending statements

- sending warning letters

- 'taking the customer to court'.

Suppliers, however, have to be careful when carrying out credit control operations, because if relations between the supplier and the customer become strained the customer may withdraw its custom and seek an alternative supplier. For this reason, suppliers usually involve the law only when they have tried all other methods first. Going to court is usually considered as a last resort when a business feels that this is the only way to recover due debts.

If the customer becomes bankrupt or can no longer be contacted, the supplier will 'write off' the debt as irrecoverable and an entry is made in the 'bad debts' account (an expense account). Expenses appear in the profit and loss account and reduce the profits of the business. For this reason, credit controllers will try to keep bad debts to a minimum.

Current liabilities

Creditors – suppliers from whom products are purchased on credit.

A business can improve its cash flow by withholding payment to **creditors** for as long as possible. It is therefore in customers' interests to arrange extended credit periods with their suppliers, if possible.

An aged creditor analysis, similar in operation to the debtor analysis, can be drawn up, which lists the amounts owed to suppliers and how long these debts have been outstanding. This enables a business to pay suppliers on the due date and not before. In some cases it may be possible to take advantage of weak credit control procedures operated by suppliers in order to delay payment beyond the agreed credit period.

Care must be taken, however, to ensure that suppliers do not take action to penalise late-paying customers. Suppliers are now allowed by law to charge interest on overdue accounts. In extreme cases a supplier may stop supplying goods or services. A business decision has to be taken on how much unauthorised 'extra credit' will be tolerated by the supplier.

Cash/bank balances

Cash or bank balances should not be too high. They should be sufficient to enable the business to pay creditors, wages and other running expenses when they are due. Having too much money in a bank current account, earning little or no interest, is not, however, making the best use of these funds. It may be better to put this money to better use. For example, a manufacturing business could use excess cash to buy additional or replacement fixed assets like machinery. In this way it may be possible to increase production and reduce staff, thus increasing profitability.

Budgeting and cash flow

Budget – a financial forecast which enables a business to plan for the future, control activities and evaluate performance.

Budgets can be prepared for almost all areas of business operations but most businesses will at least prepare the following budgets:

- sales budget: forecasts income derived from selling goods or services

- cash budget (cash flow forecast): forecasts cash inflows and outflows

- capital expenditure budget: forecasts expenditure on fixed assets.

Accurately prepared budgets allow businesses to allocate their resources effectively and take remedial action where necessary. By monitoring the budgeted figures against actual figures, action can be taken either to get the budget back 'on track' or to modify the budget based on the latest information.

Budget variance

Budget variance – difference between forecast figures and actual figures

An important part of the budgeting process is to identify the reasons for any differences between the budgeted, planned figures and the actual figures. By analysing the reasons for the differences, the business can plan more accurately and effectively for the following year.

Budgets relating to costs (e.g. capital expenditure budget)
Adverse variance: actual costs are more than budgeted costs
Favourable variance: actual costs are less than budgeted costs.

Budgets relating to income (e.g. sales budget)
Adverse variance: actual income is less than budgeted income
Favourable variance: actual income is more than budgeted income.

Budget variances can arise for the following reasons:

1 **Inaccurate** or **unreliable information** is used in the construction of the budget.

2 **Internal factors** (within the business)
Example: a manufacturing business producing metal parts for a car assembler.
If lower quality sheet steel is bought this may lead to a higher than expected wastage rate, thereby increasing costs and creating an adverse variance.

3 **External factors** (outside the control of the business)
Example: A retail shop selling souvenirs to the public at a seaside holiday resort.
Cold and wet summer weather will deter tourists and lead to a reduction in sales revenue and therefore an adverse variance.

Cash budget (cash flow forecast)

All businesses need to make sure that they have enough money to pay their debts when they fall due.

A cash flow forecast is useful because it shows the estimated revenues and costs for a future time period – usually a year ahead.

If the initial starting capital is known, then future **bank balances** can be estimated to see if the business will have enough money to make payments when they are due. If the cash flow forecast shows bank balances regularly below zero then it may be better:

- to try to increase revenue
- to try to decrease costs
- not to produce the new product or service at all.

If the cash flow forecast shows occasional times when the bank balance becomes **overdrawn** it may be possible to arrange an **overdraft** for this period or to take out a **bank loan**. Most banks will ask to see the cash flow forecast before they will grant overdraft facilities or a bank loan because they want to be sure that the business is able to afford any interest payments and be in a position to repay the loan.

The bank will, however, charge interest on both an overdraft and a bank loan and these costs will add to the existing outflows.

The importance of the cash flow forecast

Although it is called a *cash* flow forecast, it does not record just the flows of coins and banknotes. The cash flow forecast will record any flows that will affect the bank account. Cheques received and paid out will also be recorded on the cash flow forecast.

A cash flow forecast will tell the business:

- when in the year money will be required
- the amount of money that will be required.

The business can thereby take action to ensure that money is available to make payments when they are required.

Effects of incorrect forecasting

If the cash flow forecast is not completed accurately, decisions by the managers of the business, based on this incorrect information, may create problems for employees, customers, suppliers, providers of finance (e.g. banks) and owners.

For example:

- Money may be borrowed from a lender when it isn't required. This will involve unnecessary costs to the business in the form of interest payments to the lender.

- The business may unexpectedly run out of money. In this situation, the bank may:
    - refuse to 'honour' cheques already issued (not make the payment to the supplier)
    - allow these cheques to be processed (make payments to the supplier) but charge a penal (extra high) rate of interest on the amount overdrawn because an overdraft has not been arranged beforehand
    - write a letter to the business asking funds to be placed in the bank to cover the amount overdrawn. This will create an additional cost to the business since many banks will charge at least £15 for sending the letter.

If the business has insufficient money to pay suppliers, these suppliers may:

- withhold existing orders of goods until outstanding invoiced have been paid
- refuse to accept new orders from the business.

If suppliers stop supplying then the business has no products to sell, and without sales profits cannot be made. Poor forecasting can, in some cases, lead to the failure of the business.

Figure 5.4.2 A cash flow forecast

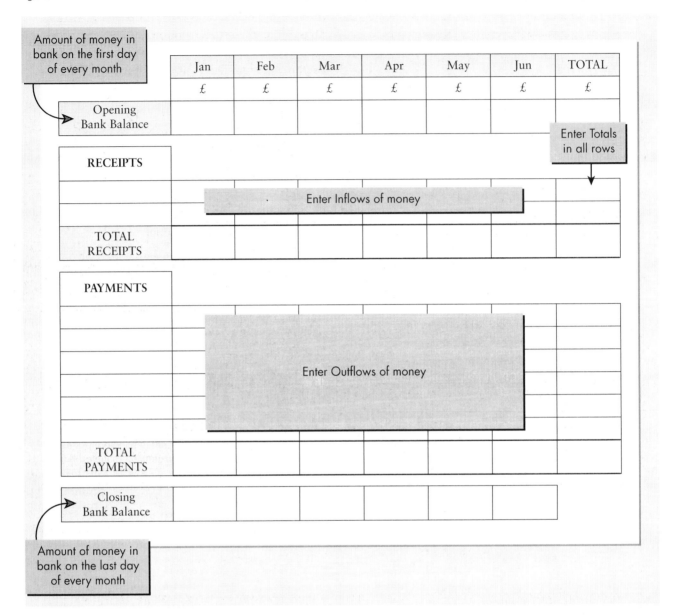

Calculating the 'opening bank balance' and 'closing bank balance'

Figure 5.4.3

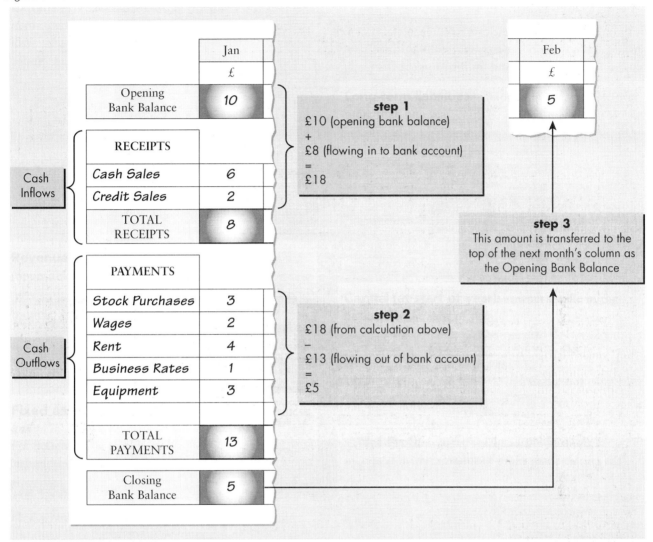

The closing bank balance shows only how much money is in the bank. Money in the bank and profit are not the same thing.

Profit figures can be found only by constructing a trading and profit and loss account.

> The closing bank balance is not the profit!

Entering amounts when a credit period is given

Amounts are only entered in the cash flow forecast in the month in which they are actually *received* or actually *paid*. In most cases it is a simple matter of entering payments or receipts in the month for which you have data. For example, if the wages for January are £3000 then £3000 would be entered in the January column where it meets the 'Wages' row.

Customers and suppliers, however, often give periods of credit which allow goods or services to be obtained but not paid for until one, two or even three months later.

In these cases you must take care to enter the inflows or outflows only when the money is actually paid out to suppliers or actually received from customers.

Inflow – receipt of money ('money coming in').

Outflow – payment of money ('money going out').

Figure 5.4.4 Checking the accuracy of the cash flow forecast

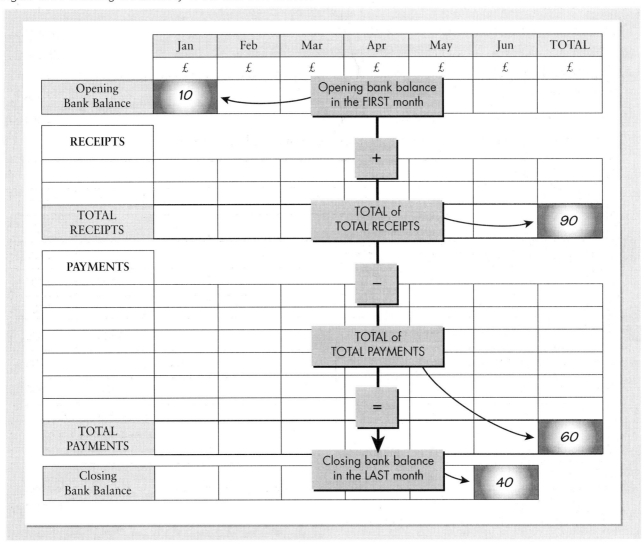

Revision Questions

1 Calculate the working capital given the following information: (1 mark)

stock of goods £500	creditors £50	bank overdraft £80
cash £100	debtors £60	

2 Why is it important to have adequate working capital? (1 mark)

3 Give two reasons for not holding too much stock. (2 marks)

4 Give two reasons for not holding too little stock. (2 marks)

5 Which form of stock control management ensures that stock is received only when it is required for the production process? (1 mark)

6 What is the job of a credit controller? (1 mark)

7 On 1 June 2000 the following statement was sent to Business C Ltd, a debtor.

Statement of Account for Business C				
2000		Debit	Credit	Balance
		£	£	£
Apr 1	balance owing from previous month			3500
Apr 4	credit note C457		100	3400
Apr 9	sales invoice 0008574	400		3800
Apr 25	cheque received		2400	1400
May 16	sales invoice 0008671	300		1700
May 29	cheque received		150	1550
			The last figure in the balance column is the amount due	

Draw up the aged debtor analysis for this customer by completing the grid below (assume earliest invoices are paid off first). (3 marks)

Business C Ltd – age analysis as at 1 June 2000

Owing for up to 1 month	Owing from 1 to 2 months	Owing for more than 2 months

8 Explain two ways in which a business can improve its cash flow position. (2 marks)

9 A cash flow budget identifies profit for the year: true or false? (1 mark)

10 What is meant by the term 'budget variance'? (1 mark)

11 If actual sales are less than budgeted sales is the variance adverse or favourable? (1 mark)

12 If actual costs are less than budgeted costs, is the variance adverse or favourable?　　　(1 mark)

13 Gift Supplies is a new firm which will supply holiday resort gift shops with cheap souvenirs for resale to the public.

The owner has put £17,000 (capital) of her savings into this business and this money has been deposited in the firm's bank account.

She intends to trade on a credit basis and therefore there will be **no cash sales**.

Her expected sales and purchases for the first six months of trading are as follows:

	SALES of goods to retailers	PURCHASES of stock from manufacturers
	£	£
JAN	12 000	6 000
FEB	9 000	7 000
MAR	11 000	7 000
APR	10 000	5 000
MAY	12 000	5 000
JUN	13 000	4 000

i) Prepare a cash flow forecast covering the first six months of this business.

In the **receipts** section of the first column enter the label: 'Sales'.

In the **payments** section enter the following expenditure labels:

'Purchases', 'Salaries', 'Rent', 'Running Costs', 'Vehicles'.

Notes:

a) Customers will be asked to pay for goods two months after they were sold to them.

b) Stock purchases from the manufacturers have to be paid for one month after purchase.

c) Salary payments are £450 every month.

d) The rent of her premises is £1,200 per month – every month. The landlord, however, demands an additional deposit equal to two months' rental, to be paid in January. (This deposit has to be paid only once.)

e) Other running expenses are about £800 every month, payable one month in arrears (i.e. one month after the month in which they occur).

f) She intends to buy a delivery van in January for £5,000.

(continued over page)

Figure 5.4.5 Cash flow forecast for Gift Supplies Jan–Jun

	JAN	FEB	MAR	APR	MAY	JUN	TOTAL
	£	£	£	£	£	£	£
Opening balance at bank							
Receipts							
Total receipts							
Payments							
Total payments							
Closing balance at bank							

ii) **Identify:**

- Total forecast **income** from sales for the six-month period (*i.e. not including debtors*).
- Forecast total **sales** for the six-month period (*this will include debtors*).
- Debtors at 30th June.
- Total forecast **expenditure** on stock purchases for six-month period (*do not include creditors*).
- Forecast total 'stock purchases' for the six-month period (*include creditors*).
- Creditors for stock purchases at 30th June.
- The month in which the bank account becomes overdrawn.

(11 marks)

Interpreting Financial Information

In this chapter you will learn how to calculate and interpret common accounting ratios. You will also learn why ratios change and how they are used by different stakeholders. In addition, you will gain an understanding of the limitations of financial information based on historical records.

Introduction

In order to plan, control and take action it is important for stakeholders to have information relating to the effectiveness of a business in a form which allows evaluation to take place.

Stakeholders who may be interested in this information are:

- managers – who need information in order to take action to maintain or increase the performance of the business

- shareholders – when considering the future profitability of the business since they will receive the profits of the business in the form of dividends

- potential shareholders – when considering the purchase of shares in the business

- providers of finance (e.g. banks) – when receiving applications to provide or maintain loans or overdrafts to the business

- government authorities, such as the Inland Revenue and Customs and Excise – in order to assess tax liabilities

- employees and trade unions – when considering pay claim levels and changes in working conditions

- suppliers and customers – since their future prosperity may depend upon the success or failure of the business.

Most of the information used to assess performance can be obtained from the final accounts of the business.

The main records used are:

- the trading and profit and loss account

- the balance sheet.

Performance, however, cannot be identified by looking at a single set of final accounts as, on their own, they give only limited information.

Stakeholders, therefore, assess a firm's performance by looking at:

- how the business performed in *previous years*

- the trends in performance

- the *planned* (forecast) performance

- the performance of *similar* firms in the *same* industry.

Financial ratios

To enable comparison and to view trends, the raw data from the final accounts is used to construct ratios. (The term ratio is used even when the results of calculations are given as percentages.) These ratios are expressed in terms of formulae as given in the following section.

The three main areas to be monitored are:

Figure 5.5.1

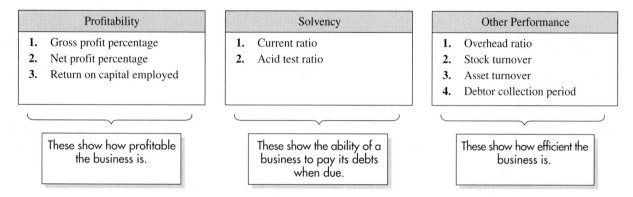

Profitability

Most businesses are set up in order to make profits. How good the business is at making profits is shown by the profitability ratios as follows.

Gross profit percentage

This shows how much gross profit is made on every £100 worth of sales.

- A gross profit percentage of 5% means the firm makes £5 gross profit on every £100 of goods sold.

- A gross profit percentage of 85% means the firm makes £85 gross profit on every £100 of goods sold.

Formula:

$$\text{Gross profit percentage} = \frac{\text{gross profit}}{\text{sales}} \times 100$$

There is no ideal level for this percentage – it depends on the type of business. A fall in this percentage from previous years should be investigated.

Possible reasons for a fall in the gross profit percentage could be:

- cash losses – theft from sales takings

- stock losses – theft by staff, shoplifting or wastage

- price reductions (e.g. having 'Sales')

- increase in cost of goods purchased from suppliers without a corresponding increase in prices of these goods sold to customers

- change in the 'product mix' – more goods being sold which have a lower gross profit percentage than other goods in the range

- stocktaking errors.

It is important to note that selling more goods will not increase the 'gross profit percentage'. Indeed, by reducing selling prices to achieve an increase in sales volume, it is possible for the gross profit to increase but gross profit percentage to decrease.

Net profit percentage (profit margin)

If this ratio decreases without a corresponding decrease in the gross profit percentage it will be due to an increase in one or more expenses. Controlling expenses is an important element in maintaining profitability and this change should be investigated and action taken. For example, if more staff have been employed in order to increase sales, but they have not been successful, then the net profit percentage will decline.

Formula:

$$\text{Net profit percentage} = \frac{\text{net profit}}{\text{sales}} \times 100$$

Return on capital employed (ROCE)

This percentage shows whether the owners of businesses are obtaining a reasonable rate of interest (return) on their investment (their capital). Owners could invest their money elsewhere, in 'safe' areas like bank or building society accounts, so they will expect a reasonable reward for risking their capital. The profits of a business belong to the owners of the business, not the business itself.

Formula:

$$ROCE = \frac{net\ profit}{capital\ employed} \times 100$$

Note: capital employed = (opening capital + closing capital) ÷ 2

Solvency/Liquidity

Solvency ratios indicate the ability of businesses to pay debts when they fall due. In order to pay creditors they will need liquid assets like cash.

Current ratio
Formula:

$$Current\ ratio = \frac{current\ assets}{current\ liabilities} : 1$$

Traditionally 2:1 has been cited as a satisfactory ratio. This means that the business should have twice as many current assets as current liabilities. Care should be taken, however, since a 'satisfactory level' is difficult to specify in practice and can vary depending on the type of business. The important point is that a business should have a ratio which allows it to pay its debts when they are due.

Acid test ratio (liquid assets ratio)
This ratio is considered to be a more reliable indicator of a business's ability to repay debts.

Formula:

$$Acid\ test\ ratio = \frac{current\ assets\ \textbf{less}\ stock}{current\ liabilities} : 1$$

It is similar to the current ratio but it omits stock. Stock cannot be used to pay debts and it is difficult to turn it quickly into cash (liquid funds). Before it can be turned into cash it has to be sold and the money collected from debtors. By removing stock from the formula the

business can get a better idea about its ability to pay debts when they become due.

1:1 is often regarded as a satisfactory ratio but, as before, care should be taken since many businesses with ratios of less than 1:1 are quite able to pay their creditors when due.

Other performance ratios

Expense (overhead) ratio
Any business expense can be expressed as a percentage of sales.

Since expenses reduce net profit, these ratios should be kept as low as possible.

Formula:

$$'Named\ expense'\ ratio = \frac{'Name\ of\ expense'}{sales} \times 100$$

e.g.

$$Wages\ ratio = \frac{wages}{sales} \times 100$$

Stock turnover

Profit is made every time an item is sold, so all firms try to 'turn over' or sell their stock as quickly as possible.

The more frequently the goods are sold, the higher the profit for the year. In addition, the longer stock is held the more likely it is to perish or become out of date.

Formula:

$$Stock\ turnover = \frac{cost\ of\ goods\ sold}{average\ stock} = \text{number of times per year all the stock is sold}$$

Note: average stock = (opening stock + closing stock) ÷ 2

A stock turnover of 12 times per year means that stock is kept for about one month before being sold.

A stock turnover of 24 times per year means that stock is kept for about two weeks before being sold.

The rate of stock turnover is often looked at together with the gross profit percentage.

- Businesses with a *low* gross profit percentage (e.g. food retailers) require a high level of stock turnover because they make only a small gross profit on each item they sell.

- Businesses with a *high* gross profit percentage (e.g. shipbuilders) survive on lower levels of stock turnover since they make a large gross profit on every ship they sell.

Asset turnover

This ratio shows how well the business uses its assets to produce sales value and should not go down from year to year – the higher the better.

Formula:

$$\text{Asset turnover} = \frac{\text{sales}}{\text{net assets}} : 1 = \begin{array}{l} \text{value of sales} \\ \text{created by each} \\ \text{£1 of net assets} \end{array}$$

For example a ratio of 7.5:1 means that the business produces £7.50 worth of sales from each £1 of assets held.

Debtor collection period

This ratio does not indicate the agreed credit period but shows how long, on average, debtors take to pay for goods sold to them.

Credit controllers should ensure that the debtor collection period does not exceed the agreed credit period – the lower the better.

Formula:

$$\begin{array}{l} \text{Debtor} \\ \text{collection} \\ \text{period} \end{array} = \frac{\text{debtors}}{\text{credit sales of year}} \times 365 \text{ days} = \begin{array}{l} \text{days} \\ \text{debtors} \\ \text{take to pay} \end{array}$$

Notes

- An **increase** in the debtor collection period is a **declining** trend. For example, a change from 35 days to 43 days indicates that customers are taking eight days longer to pay their debts.

- The ratio refers only to 'credit sales' not 'cash sales'. This ratio is not, therefore, useful to retailers who will sell most of their goods on a cash basis (i.e. receiving immediate payment for goods or services).

Investment

Limited Companies

Those interested in investing in public limited companies (plc) can buy shares through the stock exchange. Indicators used to show the performance of public limited companies include:

- share prices
- dividends
- price earnings ratio.

Share prices

Anyone wishing to own part of a public limited company can buy shares in that company from others who are willing to sell them. Shares are like any other commodity in that the price of the shares varies with the demand for those shares. The price increases if many existing shareholders wish to keep their shares and there are few shares available for sale. Alternatively, if lots of the existing shareholders wish to sell their shares, the price will decrease. Movements in share prices are, therefore, an indicator of perceived future performance since if investors think the company will perform well, the price of the shares rises, and if investors think the company will perform less well, they will try to sell their shares and the price will drop accordingly.

Dividends

Dividends are the share of the profits of a public limited company which are distributed to shareholders, usually twice yearly. Although not all the profits of the company will be given to the shareholders, the size of the dividend is a rough indicator of performance since, in general terms, the higher the profits, the higher the dividend payout. Badly performing companies may pay no dividends for several years. Some companies, however, may pay low or no dividends for a few years in order to 'plough back' profits into the business to achieve fast growth.

Price earnings ratio (P/E ratio)

This ratio allows the investor or potential investor to compare company performance over time since an increasing P/E ratio indicates that the company's profits are expected to rise in the future. Since this ratio is linked to the price of shares, the higher the P/E ratio is the greater the demand for the shares.

Formula:

$$P/E = \frac{\text{price per share (\textit{on the stock exchange})}}{\text{earnings per share}}$$

Formula:

$$\text{Earnings per share (EPS)} = \frac{\text{net profit after tax}}{\text{number of shares issued}}$$

Limitations of accounting statements and ratio analysis

The financial data used relates only to what has happened in the past. The information is, therefore, only a guide to what may happen in the future

In addition, since no two businesses are exactly the same it is difficult to compare them merely by looking at their financial data.

Information which could be useful to stakeholders but which cannot be obtained from the financial records of the business includes:

- **future plans** – the business may be expanding into new markets which may improve its performance

- **quality of staff** – staff are a non-financial asset which cannot be shown in financial statements. They are, however, very important to the future success or failure of the business

- **condition of fixed assets** – old, inefficient assets may be close to the end of their useful lives and funds will be needed to replace them

- **the location of the business** – for example, a retail business is more likely to do well if it is located in a prime site near to lots of potential customers

- **the amount of competition in the industry** – businesses with lots of competitors are less likely to do well than those with no or few competitors

- **quantity and quality of suppliers** – over-dependence on a single supplier may leave the customer short of stock. Some suppliers are more reliable than others

- **quality and quantity of customers** – it is more desirable to have many, reliable customers. If most of the sales are to one customer, the supplier may have problems if that customer ceases trading or decides to use other suppliers

- **types of products or services sold** – there is a greater risk for businesses which sell items, currently popular, which may not remain so in the future. Businesses manufacturing technological products, for example, may find that innovations by competitors leave them with no product to sell

- **future economic events** – changes in legislation or tax rates may make a business's products more or less desirable to customers.

Revision Questions

1 Calculate the gross profit percentage for each year. (1 mark)

	1999	2000
Gross profit	£25,000	£40,000
Sales	£100,000	£200,000

2 In which year is profitability better? (1 mark)

3 In which final account would you find the gross profit and sales figure? (1 mark)

4 Calculate the net profit percentage. (1 mark)

	1999	2000
Net profit	£15,000	£12,000
Sales	£100,000	£60,000

5 In which year was the net profit percentage better? (1 mark)

6 In which account would you calculate the net profit? (1 mark)

7 a) Calculate Marlin's return on capital employed.

Net profit for sole trader Marlin for the year:	£25,000
Opening capital Marlin: £190,000	Closing capital Marlin: £210,000
Building society interest rate:	6% p.a.

   b) Calculate the total yearly interest which could have been earned if the money had been invested in the building society.

   c) Which organisation is offering the best financial return? (3 marks)

8 List the four most common current assets. (1 mark)

9 List the two most common current liabilities. (1 mark)

10 Why should a firm try to have more current assets than current liabilities? (1 mark)

11

Stock: £20,000	Debtors: £6,000	Bank: £3,000	Cash: £1,000
Creditors: £50,000			

   a) Calculate the current ratio.

   b) What problem faces this business?

   c) Calculate the acid test ratio.

   d) Why is the acid test ratio a more accurate indicator of ability to pay debts than the current ratio?

   (4 marks)

12

> 1999 Administration expenses were £10,000 and sales were £100,000.
>
> 2000 Administration expenses were £25,000 and sales were still £100,000.

   a) Calculate the administration expense ratios for 1999 and 2000.

   b) Has the additional money spent on administration helped to increase sales?

   c) What action could management take as a result of this information?

   d) Why might sales decrease if management takes the action you recommend?   (4 marks)

13 What is the stock turnover if stock is kept for four months before being sold?   (1 mark)

14 If the stock turnover is 52, for how long is stock kept before being sold?   (1 mark)

15 If a business has a *low* gross profit percentage, what level of stock turnover will it need to survive (high or low)?   (1 mark)

16 If a business has a *high* gross profit percentage, what level of stock turnover is enough to survive (high or low)?   (1 mark)

17 Classify the following types of business as likely to need either 'high' or 'low' levels of stock turnover in order to stay in business:

   a) supermarket

   b) luxury car manufacturer

   c) aircraft manufacturer

   d) pencil maker

   e) button manufacturer.   (2 marks)

18 How do you calculate net assets?   (1 mark)

19 a) Calculate the asset turnover ratio.

	1999	2000
Net assets	£150,000	£200,000
Sales	£100,000	£175,000

   b) What is the value of sales created by each £1 of assets

   c) Is the business using its assets *more* or *less* efficiently in 2000?   (3 marks)

20

	1999	2000
Debtors	£10,000	20,000
Credit sales	£100,000	150,000
Credit terms period	30 days	30 days

   a) Calculate the debtor collection periods for each year.

   b) Has performance improved or declined?   (4 marks)

21 Why might the following stakeholders be interested in the financial data?

a) The managers

b) The Inland Revenue

c) Potential investors

d) Shareholders

e) Employees/trade unions.   (5 marks)

22

		1999	2000
A	debtor collection period in days	35	37
B	current ratio	1.15:1	0.25:1
C	asset turnover	1.56:1	1.85:1
D	return on capital employed	15%	14%

Which ratio shows that, in 2000:

a) assets were used more efficiently?

b) the credit control department was working less efficiently?

c) the business is less able to pay its debts?

d) the business was less solvent?   (4 marks)

23

		1999	2000
A	gross profit percentage	25%	25%
B	net profit percentage	4.5%	4.25%
C	return on capital employed	14%	15%
D	stock turnover (no. of times per year)	15	14

Which ratio showed that in 2000:

a) expenses increased?

b) profitability increased?

c) fewer goods were sold?

d) owners earned more on their investment?   (4 marks)

UNIT 5

End of Unit Revision Test

All numerical answers should be entered with the correct units.

1   An invoice for goods has been sent by J Roker to a credit customer Munns Ltd. Complete the **shaded** boxes with the correct book or account, chosen from the list below, to show how this invoice would flow through the accounting system of Munns Ltd.

- Creditor account
- Debtor account
- Purchases Day Book
- Sales Day Book
- Sales Account
- Purchases Account

Note: if an entry is not required in any book or ledger write 'not entered' in the appropriate box

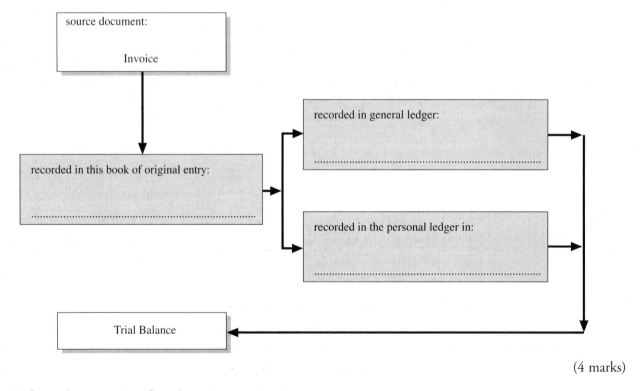

(4 marks)

2   Refer to the accounting flow shown in question 1.

   a) Why is it necessary to record the entry in both the book of original entry and the personal ledger?

   (1 mark)

   b) Explain the feature of the trial balance which allows managers to check the accuracy of the bookkeeping entries.

   (1 mark)

3 Errors in the accounts may affect other parts of the accounting system.
In each case below consider the accounting flows and state the revised Net Profit when the error is corrected.

	Original Net profit	**Error**	**Net profit after correction**
a)	£ 10 000	A cheque received for £50 had not been entered into the cash book	£
b)	£ 15 000	A sale of stock costing £500 had been recorded as a purchase of stock	£
c)	£140 000	The purchase of a motor vehicle for £15000 had been recorded as a purchase of stock	£

(3 marks)

4 a) Complete the invoice by entering figures in the **shaded** sections.   (4 marks)

Invoice No : 00478			
DriveComputer Supplies, 146 High Street, Ely, Cambs CB5 6RT			Date: 1st June 2000
To: Rand Ltd, 78 Market St, Whittle, Hants HA4 8FU			

Quantity	Description	**Price per Item**	Total Price
1	swivel chairn	£30.00	£30.00
2	Hi–keypads	£25.00	£50.00
2	17" monitors	£150.00	£300.00
			£380.00
		trade discount 20%	
		subtotal	
		VAT @ 17.5%	
1.5% cash discount is offered for payment with in 14 days of invoice date.		**Total to Pay**	

(4 marks)

b) How much should Rand Ltd pay if they settle the invoice within 14 days?   (1 mark)

i) Before the invoices are paid Rand will cross-check related documents.
Identify the three related documents Rand should check before they pay the invoice.   (2 marks)

ii) How are the three documents you identified used in the check?   (2 marks)

5 On 1st June 2000, the following statement was sent to Shorts Ltd. from Farock & Co.

Statement of Account from Farock & Co					
Customer Account Name		Shorts Ltd			
Customer Account Number		45			
Credit Terms		30 days			
Customer Credit Limit		£10000			
2000			Debit £	Credit £	Balance £
Apr	1	Balance owing from previous month			8000
Apr	6	Credit note		400	7600
Apr	8	Sales invoice 0062	1600		9200
Apr	26	Sales invoice 0096	1200		10400
May	14	Cheque received		7400	3000
May	30	Sales invoice 0192	3400		6400
				The last figure in the balance column is the amount owing	

a) Draw up the aged debtors' analysis for this customer by completing the **shaded** grid below (assume oldest invoices are paid off first).

Shorts Ltd – Age analysis as at 1st Jun 2000

Owing for up to 1 month	Owing from 1 to 2 months	Owing for more than 2 months

(3 marks)

b) This account has not been run properly. Identify the problems and suggest an initial appropriate course of action by Farock's credit controller justifying your advice. (4 marks)

6 a) Complete the Trading and Profit & Loss account and Balance Sheet prepared on 31st December 1999 by referring to the information given below on that date:

This space for your notes/workings	Name of Business: Honesk (sole trader)	£
	Stock valuation at 1 Jan 1999	500
	Stock valuation at 31 Dec 1999	400
	Owner's stake in the business at 1st Jan 1999	40000
	Total payments to weekly paid employees	20000
	Machinery purchase price	5500
	Machinery provision for depreciation	1100
	Amounts owing to suppliers	4400
	Value of goods bought from suppliers	8000
	Money in bank	13000
	Cash in office till	100
	Amounts owing by credit customers	3400
	Value of goods sold to customers	39000
	Business rates payable for the year	1500
	Cost of rent of premises	3000
	Telephone bills	400
	Original cost of fixtures & fittings	12000
	Fixtures & Fittings Depreciation provision	2400
	Long-term Loan	3000
	Drawings	22500

Make adjustments for depreciation as follows:

Machinery is to be depreciated by 10% of original purchase price.
Fixtures & Fittings are to be depreciated equally over 10 years, based on original cost.

Notes:

- Make your entries on the dotted lines in the shaded sections.
- Both the names of accounts and their values need to be entered.

Honesk Trading and P and L Account

............................31st Dec. 1999

	£	£
Sales		....
Opening stock	....	
Purchases	....	
	....	
Closing stock	....	
Closing stock		....
Closing stock		....

Expenses

....		
....		
....	....	
....	....	
Depreciation Machinery	....	
Depreciation Fix & Fitt	....	
		....
Net Profit		

Honesk Balance Sheet

............................31st Dec. 1999

Fixed assets	£ At Cost	£ Depreciation To Date	£ N.B.V
....	....	....	....
....	....	....	....
	....	....	....

Current assets		
....		....
....		....
....		....
.		....
		....

Current liabilities		
....	....	

Working Capital ....

Net Assets ....

Financed By

Capital at 1st Jan. 1999	....
Net Profit	....
	....
Drawings	....
Capital at 31st Dec. 1999	....

Long Term liabilities

....	....
	....

(10 marks)

b) Why is it necessary to show the depreciation in the profit and loss account? (1 mark)

c) What are the typical causes of machinery depreciation? (1 mark)

d) Why don't Honesk write off the full cost of the machinery and fixtures and fittings in the year in which these assets was purchased? (1 mark)

e) State two possible external stakeholders of Honesk and identify the financial information which would be of most interest to them. Justify your answers. (2 marks)

f) How would the interests of Honesk's owner and its employees differ when interpreting the performance of the business. (2 marks)

7 A business plans to start up with £8000 in the bank on 1 January 2001.
Customers' credit period will be 1 month.
Suppliers' credit period will be 0 months.

Forecast Sales and Purchases are as shown in the table on the right.

	Sales	Purchases
Jan	5000	2000
Feb	6000	3000
Mar	7000	4500

a) Complete the business's Cash flow forecast for three months, January – March, by filling in the **shaded** sections. (4 marks)

	Jan	Feb	Mar
Opening Bank balance:			
Income from Sales:			
Payments for Purchases:			
Cash Expenses:	500	500	500
Closing Bank Balance:			

b) What is the expected value of the debtors at the end of March? (1 mark)

8 Hellas Engineering is a sheet-metal-working business making a range of engineering products. As an aid to management control the managers have previously worked out the amount, quality, type and cost of sheet metal that should be used on each of the products they manufacture. For job 453 these budgeted predetermined amounts and costs were:

Budgeted	Amount of sheet metal to be used:	Cost of sheet metal:	Budgeted cost of Job
	25 metres	£3.50 per metre	£

Once job 453 was finished it was discovered that the actual amounts used and costs incurred were:

Actual	Amount of sheet metal actually used:	Cost of sheet metal:	Actual cost of Job
	28 metres	£3.25 per metre	£

a) Complete the shaded sections for the budgeted and actual cost of job 453. (2 marks)

b) What is the amount of the variance? (1 mark)

c) Is the variance adverse or favourable? (1 mark)

d) From the information supplied analyse and suggest a likely reason for the variance. (2 marks)

e) Why do Hellas engineering analyse the variances? (2 marks)

9 a) Complete the ratio column for 1999 given the following data for that year. (Round all your answers to 2 decimal places.)

	£
Sales	84 000
Gross Profit	62 400
Net profit	48 000
Capital at 1st January 1999	70 000
Drawings	19 400

	£
Current assets	22 600
Current liabilities	14 000
Stock at 1st January 1999	1 600
Stock at 31st December 1999	10 000
Debtors	12 000

Notes:

- There were no long term liabilities and no additional capital was injected.
- Some of the figures you require need to be derived.

		1998	1999
Gross Profit Percentage	$\dfrac{\text{Gross Profit}}{\text{Sales}} \times 100$	72.14%	
Profit Margin	$\dfrac{\text{Net Profit}}{\text{Sales}} \times 100$	55.78%	
Return on Capital Emplyed (ROCE)	$\dfrac{\text{Net Profit}}{\text{Average Capital}} \times 100$	54.33%	
Current Ratio	$\dfrac{\text{Current Assets}}{\text{Current Liabilities}} : 1$	1.73 : 1	
Acid Test Ratio	$\dfrac{\text{Liquid Assets}}{\text{Current Liabilities}} : 1$	1.00 : 1	
Stock Turnover	$\dfrac{\text{Cost of goods sold}}{\text{Average Stock}}$	4.13 times/year	
Asset Turnover	$\dfrac{\text{Sales}}{\text{Net Assets}} : 1$	0.98 : 1	
Debtors collection period	$\dfrac{\text{Debtors}}{\text{Sales}} \times 365$	41.85 days	

b) Identify the 2 solvency ratios and indicate if they show an improving or declining trend. (2 marks)

c) Identify 3 profitability ratios and indicate if they show an improving or declining trend. (2 marks)

d) The business decides to 'write off' any debts which are more than one year old. The usual credit terms are 60 days.

   i) What would be the justification for this policy? (2 marks)

   Explain the effect of this policy on:

   ii) the calculated working capital. (2 marks)

   iii) the profitability of the business. (2 marks)

e) Explain the possible effects on two appropriate identified stakeholders if the value of the acid test ratio fell persistently to a level less than 0.2:1. (4 marks)

f) Explain how one stated policy of your choice could improve the acid test ratio of this business. Justify the changes to business practice which would be necessary by examining the advantages and drawbacks of your policy. (4 marks)

10 A bank considering a loan application requires access to the financial ratios and the accounts of the borrower. Other significant information about the business would also be useful to the bank in its decision whether to grant the loan. Under the headings below, explain how the situations given would support the loan application.

a) Retail shop in a prime shopping area. (2 marks)

b) Fixed assets in excellent condition. (2 marks)

c) Loyal, well-motivated staff. (2 marks)

UNIT 6

Business Planning

KEY TERMS:

timescale	marketing strategy	cash flow projections
planning	financing the idea	start-up balance sheet
monitoring	producing the product	evaluation of project

In this unit you will learn how to prepare comprehensive details in relation to a new business venture. To achieve success in such an exhilarating project, you will need to pay attention to detail, maintain high levels of motivation and have a keen interest in making money. The way to make sure that this happens is to put into practice all the information covered in each of the sections of this unit.

New business ventures can be set up in any of the three main industrial sectors and future entrepreneurs will make a choice based on their own personal expertise plus their ability to spot a gap in the market.

Introduction

Although this is the final unit in your Vocational A Level Business course, it includes the use of knowledge gained in all other units studied. Each of those units concentrated on specific detail related to a particular topic and you will need to extract the key points from this extensive detail that relate to business planning. Of particular importance are the units covering:

- marketing
- finance
- human resources.

Guidance from your tutor about the nature of the business venture you intend to set up is crucial at an early stage. A brief outline of this activity should be prepared before you engage in an initial discussion with your tutor to agree the validity of the proposal.

One of the most important points to consider is the timescale you have available in which to complete the whole project. In the normal course of events a business plan is prepared with the intention of setting up a business to run on a permanent basis. If this is your goal, very careful preparation is required at each stage, particularly the presentation of data to a financial source in an attempt to persuade it to back your idea.

Most high street banks provide assistance to would-be entrepreneurs by offering a business start-up pack. Not only does this contain examples of the financial data you will need to compile, it also gives a considerable amount of advice on the generation of sales, monitoring of cash flow and insurance requirements. Once you have decided on an idea, collect this material to help you prepare accurate documentation.

> **Remember:**
> **YOU** ⇒ have to **convince** ⇒ the bank manager that your proposition is worth backing.

An agreement will be reached only if you have carefully analysed *all* aspects of your proposal and can answer any questions put to you during an interview. Using Barclays as an example, the following extract gives you an idea of the help available from similar financial sources:

Figure 6.1.1

Take a look at the
summary
of what we can offer you ...

Money saving deals already negotiated, by Barclays, for business customers:

- In association with Rocom Network Services, customers can save up to 48% on their fixed line calls and 5% on mobile calls plus an additional 20% on a wide range of telecommunications products

- Barclays and Powergen have negotiated savings for our business customers' electricity and gas supplies. 9 out of 10 businesses will save money by switching to Powergen and there is no need to replace meters, pipes or wiring. In addition, customers will receive £25.00 cash back for each business supply that is switched

- Additional discounts of up to 25% have also been negotiated on products and services, from other leading suppliers, including MYOB, Rymans, Prontaprint and the AA

Up to 18 months free banking[†]

Direct access to your own Relationship Manager and local Small Business team for practical expertise and information

Free, 24-hour Business helpline for advice on a wide range of issues

Business Information Factsheets on different markets and key aspects of running a business, plus Business Opportunity Profile information on nearly 400 different businesses

Free Online Banking[*] for a year, excluding call charges, including free Internet access and unlimited e-mail addresses

Free telephone banking for 24 hour[**] access to your account

Free business letter writing booklet

Access to Barclays Small Business Seminars and Events for both new and established small businesses

... talk to your local Barclays Small Business team

[†] *Free banking is available for up to 18 months if you are opening your first business account and you, or one of the proprietors of your business, has or transfers their main personal account to Barclays. The offer covers everyday sterling credit or debit transactions and our maintenance fee, provided the account stays in credit or within an agreed overdraft facility. This offer does not apply if you are moving an existing business account to Barclays from a competitor. Free banking will not apply to business accounts where the annual debit turnover is more than £100,000 or an exceptional number of transactions are made.*

[*] *Online Banking is not currently available in Guernsey, Jersey and Isle of Man.*

[**] *Businesscall operates during normal office hours in Guernsey, Jersey and Isle of Man.*

Members of the team are trained to help your business get off the ground and succeed. They will tailor these business offers to your requirements as part of our ongoing programme to offer the best possible support to start-up businesses.

BARCLAYS

You will note from this extract that **free banking** is available for up to 18 months. This is a critical time period and, in the normal course of events, the business should be in **profit** by this time. Take advantage of the other free services on offer such as:

- small business legal helpline
- one year on-line banking
- telephone banking
- business letter writing booklet.

Other facilities should also be utilised to assist you, e.g. information factsheets, opportunity profiles and small business seminars and events – all of which will give you access to specialist knowledge related to your business venture. Note that a 25 per cent discount is offered on a range of products and services and no wise entrepreneur will allow such opportunities to pass him/her by. In the case of Barclays, examples of such discounts are given in Figure 6.1.2:

Figure 6.1.2

Small Business Fact Sheet

Support for new small businesses

SUMMARY OF FEATURES AND BENEFITS

Practical expertise and support from your own Relationship Manager and local Small Business team

Up to 18 months' free banking*

Information on different markets and various aspects of running a business

Free telephone banking for 24 hour access to your account

Free Online Banking for a year, including free Internet access (excluding call charges)

Free, 24-hour legal helpline

Barclays Seminars and events

Discounts from major suppliers of business products and services

Barclays Business Letters – practical help with letter writing

* Free banking is available for up to 18 months if you either hold or transfer your main personal account to Barclays, and are opening your first business account. The offer applies to every day Sterling debit or credit transactions and the maintenance fee, provided the account stays in credit or within an agreed overdraft facility, and the account debit turnover does not exceed £100,000 per annum. This offer does not apply if you are moving an existing business account to Barclays from a competitor.

If you are starting up a new business, you can draw on practical expertise and experience from your local Barclays Small Business team. You also qualify for a range of special offers to help you get the best possible start.

DEDICATED SUPPORT

The people you will be working with deal with hundreds of new businesses each year. They have undergone training in most aspects of running a business, understand different challenges you will face and know how to identify and find any specialist advice required.

Your Relationship Manager is responsible for taking care of your banking needs. You will also have the support of a dedicated Small Business team - a source of practical expertise and information.

PRACTICAL INFORMATION

If you want background information on different aspects of running a business or on the market you are selling into, you will find our Business Information Factsheets and Business Opportunity Profiles useful. These are available free of charge from your local Barclays Small Business team. In addition, your Relationship Manager will be able to introduce you to other Small Business Support Agencies when you require their help.

FREE BANKING* FOR UP TO 18 MONTHS

To help you make a start, we offer free banking* - for the first 18 months if one of the proprietors operates or opens a Barclays personal account, and for 12 months in all other cases.

WIDE CHOICE OF BANKING SERVICES

We want to ensure that you get support and information as and when you need it, with minimum disruption to the running of your business. That's why we continually invest in initiatives to match our service to the needs of businesses such as yours. Your local Small Business team or our website at www.smallbusiness.barclays.co.uk will give you details.

When you open an account, you will receive a Welcome Pack which tells you how to make the most of banking with Barclays and details of how to make full use of your account, from managing your finances through to the processing of payments.

Deposits

There is also a selection of interest-earning accounts to ensure that you make the most of any surplus funds. These are available in Sterling, euro and other currencies.

BARCLAYS

Telephone banking

Barclays Businesscall allows you to access information about your account 24 hours a day for the price of a local telephone call. You can check the balance of your account and give instructions for a number of transactions, including paying bills. You have a membership number and passcode to ensure security.

Online Banking

You can also manage your finances from your own PC or laptop, using Barclays Online Banking. Again, you can check the balance of your account, transfer money between accounts and pay most bills. Online Banking comes complete with free Internet Service Provision* and access to our new Internet based, Barclays Business Park. This provides business-related services and information tailored to Small Businesses.

Branch facilities

Most Barclays branches offer 24-hour automated machines, places to have a confidential discussion with your Relationship Manager, and in our larger branches the facility of special business tills.

Cards

When you open your Barclays Business Account, you will be able to apply for a Business Barclaybank Card. This allows you to make cash withdrawals direct from your account through a cash machine (provided there are cleared funds available), balance enquiries and statement requests. You can also obtain mini-statements showing up to the last eight entries on your account since your last statement. After six months, you can also apply for up to four Barclays Business Cards. This is a charge card that can be used at VISA outlets in the UK and overseas to buy business goods and services.

Borrowings

If you need finance to help your cash flow, purchase equipment or property, or to fund an initiative, you have a choice of facilities including overdrafts, business loans and mortgages.

International trade services

If you plan to export or import you will be able to get full support. Barclays has the most extensive European Network of any UK Bank, a wide range of euro and other foreign currency products and significant worldwide banking resources.

OTHER SPECIAL BENEFITS

The enclosed sheet lists the current range of discounts, available to you as a new business customer, from several leading suppliers of business supplies and services.

Legal helpline†

The Barclays Small Business Legal Helpline offers legal advice by telephone 24 hours a day, 365 days a year (for the duration of your free banking period).

*Local call rates with no subscription fees.

Barclays Seminars and Events

Access to our Seminars and Events programme for both new and established small businesses. For details of planned events in your area, speak to your local Small Business team or visit our website at www.smallbusiness.barclays.co.uk/seminars_events

Discounts

We have negotiated discounts with major suppliers of products and services (see enclosed sheet).

Barclays Business Letters

A booklet providing you with examples and practical help with the main business letters you are likely to use. Helping you to create the right impression with customers and suppliers.

Retirement Planning

Our advisers provide a free, no-obligation review of your current pension plans to check that they will provide what you want for your retirement planning.

Business Protection

You can also obtain advice on how to protect your business from a wide range of risks, such as fire, flooding and theft. We can also protect you against the effects of the temporary or permanent loss of a key member of your team.

ONE-STOP BANKING

We offer an extensive range of personal banking services for business customers.
Our aim is to provide a simple, easy-to-use and consistent service to cover all your banking requirements.

YOUR NEXT STEP

If you would like to discuss your needs in more detail please contact your local Barclays Small Business team.

Small Business
Legal Helpline

0870 2 433 433

BARCLAYS

Details of the legal helpline are shown on the handy reminder card attached.
†Barclays Small Business Legal Helpline is provided by DAS Assistance Limited.
Calls made to the Small Business Legal Helpline may be recorded or monitored.

If you are participating in activities such as Young Enterprise or the Prince's Trust, these will prove to be valuable experiences carried out during the school/college year. The planning and preparation for these may be carried out in a group and you will gain a practical insight into how groups work. This will mean that you are not in total control of the situation and negotiation and compromise will be two personal qualities needed to achieve success. It will also mean that you have a limited timescale in which to fulfil all the requirements of the activity. This is a very critical factor and requires tight control procedures at each stage of the process because there is only a short time in which to create a profit margin before the company is wound up and the examination is taken (YE).

Your tutor can arrange for talks to be given to a group of interested students by people from various financial institutions, and local expertise can be provided through the Small Business network, TECs and LECs and the Young Enterprise/Prince's Trust advisers. Assistance can be gained from this network of advisers during the whole course of your project and you should refer to them for guidance in problem solving, alternative strategies and new sales creation.

Figure 6.1.3

Idea generation

This is obviously the first step along the route to creating your own business. The idea should be linked to your own creative abilities or the main skills of the group of which you are a member. It has to be viable – that is, capable of happening within the timescale you have available (this is limited if at school or college but ongoing if you intend to carry on the business once it has been established) and to generate sales which will earn profit.

Think about this carefully and note down all the **strengths** and **weaknesses** that already exist, either individually or within a group, to help you make a decision. If the strengths outweigh the weaknesses and these can be easily improved, then you have made the first decision in a logical manner. It is best to keep emotion out of the frame and use only hard facts to guide you! Many more critical decisions will be made along the route and this initial action should be used each time you are called upon to reach a definite conclusion.

manufacturing mouse mats

painter and decorator

cleaning patios

designing websites

software training courses

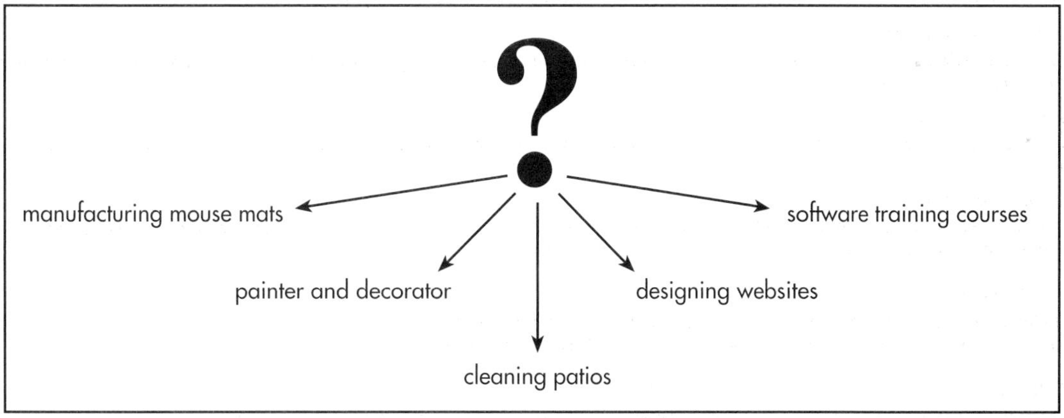

You will need many qualities to be successful and the decision to set up a business should not be taken lightly. Much personal effort will be needed to maintain the level of activity required to meet deadlines. Your communication skills will be utilised on many occasions when dealing with staff, clients/ customers, suppliers and supporting services. The key points you will need to consider are shown below.

Table 6.1.1

Personal qualities	Notes
Self-sufficiency	As a sole trader or owner/manager, you will need to use your previous experience and have strong character – major decisions are now your responsibility.
Initiative	You will need to be a self-starter who can spot opportunities and is prepared to take advantage of them.
Determination	This is required at all stages, particularly when the going gets tough and things do not go according to plan.
Resilience	Linked with determination, this factor will get you through any setbacks by finding a different way to solve problems.
Responsibility	As the owner of a business, you shoulder the responsibility if difficulties arise and this means taking critical decisions to move forwards.
Imagination	As well as the original idea, you will need to anticipate the needs of your customers, motivate staff, use your initiative to solve problems, be innovative when changing direction and be willing to learn.

Additional skills:

- management of time, people and resources
- financial understanding and knowledge
- marketing strategies
- manufacturing and distribution of finished products
- technical knowledge and expertise.

If you feel you are able to confirm you meet all of the above points, Barclays offers a further self-assessment questionnaire which you might like to complete. This will show your level of **commitment** to the task you are about to embark upon.

This self-analysis is essential to establish your determination to involve yourself in, and to complete, a business venture – individually or in a group. Any minor weaknesses identified in this questionnaire can be corrected by additional effort on your part and assistance from your tutor. If the will to succeed is there, this small setback will prove no deterrent to your inner determination to own and run your own business.

A **business opportunity profile** is a useful starting point to describe your idea because it will identify several key points you need to consider. An example of such a profile from the range offered by Barclays (Figure 6.1.5) uses the newsagents pictured at the beginning of this unit. Similar details can be written to cover your own business idea.

Figure 6.1.4

Self-assessment questionnaire

1   I often feel I'm the victim of outside forces I cannot control.

Yes   No

2   I often work later than planned.

Yes   No

3   Some days seem to go by without me having achieved a thing.

Yes   No

4   Given a bad situation, I'll always try to get something out of it.

Yes   No

5   I think a well ordered pattern of life with regular hours suits me best.

Yes   No

6   I'm much happier not having to rely on other people.

Yes   No

7   I'm prepared to take risks only when I've carefully thought through all the consequences.

Yes   No

8   There's no point starting something unless you're going to see it through.

Yes   No

9   People often tell me how good I am at seeing things from their point of view.

Yes   No

10   I tend not to be too ambitious to avoid being disappointed.

Yes   No

11   It's very important to me that people recognise my success.

Yes   No

12   When I find myself talking to a telephone answer machine, I usually hang up.

Yes   No

13   I've never been one to follow the crowd.

Yes   No

14   All that matters is how much I earn regardless of how hard I work to get it.

Yes   No

How to score

Score 2 points if you answered Yes to questions 2, 4, 7, 8, 9, 11 and 13, and zero points for questions 1, 3, 5, 6, 10, 12 and 14. Score 2 points if you answered No to questions 1, 3, 5, 6, 10, 12 and 14, and zero points for questions 2, 4, 7, 8, 9, 11 and 13.

The maximum score is 28 points. The higher your score, the better equipped you are likely to be for your future business venture.

Figure 6.1.5

Business Opportunity Profile

NEWSAGENTS   No 120

Market

Traditional newsagents sell confectionery and tobacco as well as newspapers and magazines. For this reason, they are often referred to as CTNs (Confectioners, Tobacconists, and Newsagents). Whilst many newsagents in town centre locations continue to concentrate on this type of stock, outlets in residential areas and high streets have moved towards the 'corner shop' model, stocking general groceries and the type of goods which customers need between their main shopping trips. Newsagents can also sell stamps, telephone cards and offer photocopy services. They can also be combined with other services such as video hire, off-licence or sub-post office. Demand for other products and services, provided from the premises, should be researched and assessed (see the relevant BOP).

The National Lottery has had a major impact. Most people prefer to purchase tickets at newsagents, and this in turn has lead to additional impulse purchases. Lottery Instants are also popular although interest is beginning to wane. Lottery outlets earn approximately 5% commission on ticket sales. This amounts to roughly 15% of sales each year for the independent retailer. Shops which do not provide lottery tickets are losing business.

Newspapers and magazines are supplied by wholesalers, normally on a sale or return basis. Wholesalers require a certain level of sales to be achieved to make the relationship pay. It will be essential to demonstrate the level of sales which the shop will be able to achieve, and to understand the wholesaler's terms and conditions before proceeding with the venture. Wholesalers must supply new retailers if their weekly order is at least 50% of the local average and they pay a returnable deposit equal to at least three week's supplies. If the shop changes hands, the wholesaler is not obliged to continue supply. The two largest wholesalers are WH Smith News and John Menzies PLC. Many now offer extended credit along with sales and marketing support for magazines. Some local newspapers are supplied direct. Wholesalers often have exclusive distribution rights to certain titles. Whilst newspaper rounds are declining, they remain a major source of income and also promote good customer relations. Most newsagents give credit on newspaper accounts. It is advisable to set a maximum number of weeks in which the customer can settle their bill. New customers should be asked for a week's advance to ensure payment.

Newspaper circulation is decreasing and recent price wars have resulted in reduced margins for retailers. Magazine sales, on the other hand, are on the increase. Since the deregulation of news supply in October 1994, outlets other than newsagents can sell newspapers, eg. garage forecourts and supermarkets. Deregulation has not increased sales, it has only further fragmented the industry by increasing the number of outlets. This trend is set to continue and a number of independent newsagents have closed as a result. On the other hand, convenience store retailing and the lottery have helped to offset the decline. Moreover, the numbers and locations of newsagents make them competitive and the industry continues to be dominated by independents. CTNs also tend to be quite recession resistant as their goods are low-cost necessities. Confectionery sales are rising marginally. Tobacco sales are in decline due to health risks and 'smuggling' from overseas. The future lies with the expansion of products and services in the convenience store line, exploiting the customers need for emergency purchases. A new system is being proposed which would allow people to settle bills eg. BT, British Gas, with cash at a newsagents. This could greatly increase custom. It is likely that newsagents will begin to open for longer hours, eg. some stores in the T&S chain now have 24-hour opening.

Activity

Prepare brief notes covering:

1 Your idea on the nature of a business activity you would like to develop.

2 Compile a strengths and weaknesses analysis of your personal abilities.

3 Match the strengths and weaknesses analysis with the results of the self-assessment questionnaire and consider how well these could be used in the business activity defined in 1.

4 Summarise your proposal before discussing the idea with your tutor for approval to proceed with the venture.

Planning

Careful thought must be given to any idea you are considering as a business proposal. One of the first points is the **timescale** you have available to carry out this proposition. Unlike a normal business venture, you may have only one year or less in which to complete the whole task for this unit:

Figure 6.1.6

A useful tool to show the scale of this activity is a **time schedule chart**. This will give a clear picture of where you need to be at each stage of the project. Regular monitoring of progress is essential for several reasons:

- checking you are on course
- monitoring cash flow
- making new decisions, particularly if the income and market share have not reached expectations

- revising originally planned activities
- changing advertising strategy
- altering production techniques
- searching for new outlets.

It is wise to prepare the time schedule chart first while trying to decide on the nature of the product/service the business will offer for sale. An example is given below:

Figure 6.1.7 Time schedule for a new business

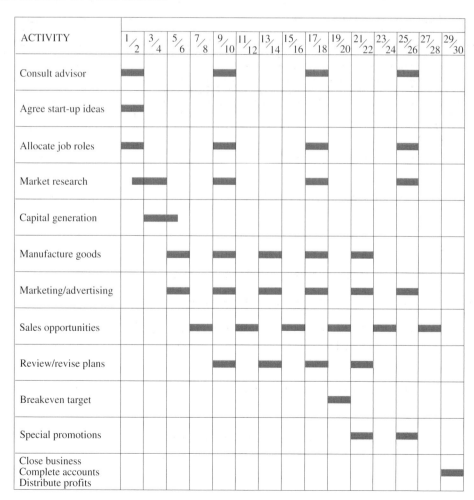

This time schedule chart should be referred to on a regular basis and placed in a prominent position as a reminder to yourself or the group of where you need to be at set points. **Monitoring** procedures should be agreed at the outset and the times when these should occur marked on the chart in a bright colour so that they are not missed. More frequent monitoring is required at the beginning of a project because critical decisions may be needed to change direction, increase advertising or alter production techniques.

In addition to the monitoring schedule, team meetings need to be arranged so that updates and reviews of current activities are passed to all participants. If a problem happens in one area, other members of the team may be able to suggest alternative solutions. In a team environment, it is useful to have fresh input from your colleagues and their suggestions can be discussed in an open communication pattern. Outside advice can be gained from any of the advisers available to you – use them wisely – and you should try to take into account any ideas that can resolve current problems amicably.

Remember:

- Decisions should be taken after carefully weighing up *all* the information available.

- These are *not* personal issues and should not allow the team environment to be affected.

Record all such discussions and decisions so that everyone can see what has been agreed. The communication pattern used between team members, both verbal and written, is very important and this can be agreed at an early meeting to ensure everyone is kept informed.

Generally, the planning and monitoring cycle covers eight stages but the timescale will vary according to the reason for setting up the business in the first place, e.g.:

- 9–12 months for a school/college project

- 5 years for a short-term profit gain with a view to disposing of the company once this has been achieved

- 25 years as a long-term permanent business.

The eight stages can clearly be identified as:

Figure 6.1.8 The eight-stage business start-up cycle

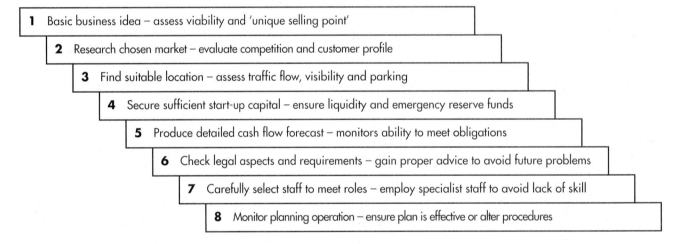

1 Basic business idea – assess viability and 'unique selling point'

2 Research chosen market – evaluate competition and customer profile

3 Find suitable location – assess traffic flow, visibility and parking

4 Secure sufficient start-up capital – ensure liquidity and emergency reserve funds

5 Produce detailed cash flow forecast – monitors ability to meet obligations

6 Check legal aspects and requirements – gain proper advice to avoid future problems

7 Carefully select staff to meet roles – employ specialist staff to avoid lack of skill

8 Monitor planning operation – ensure plan is effective or alter procedures

To keep the company on track, a **mission statement** can be written and prominently displayed as a constant reminder of the reason for starting up in the first place. As the business grows, it is likely that additional members will become part of the management team and, in particular, the board of directors. This will devolve power from one person to a group of people and will alter the decision making format. At this point, businesses often change direction and you will need to prepare yourself for this eventuality. Personal control is no longer your own prerogative and you may have become immersed in heavy managerial responsibilities rather than the practical aspects of your original business idea.

This factor became evident at the beginning of 2000 when Bill Gates, originator of Microsoft, announced he was stepping down as Managing Director to return to the practical aspects of designing the software itself. On this occasion, however, the lure of a link-up with Sir Richard Branson proved too exciting to ignore and this new venture has prompted Bill Gates to review his current role within the organisation he has created. On a personal basis, this is a far more challenging activity than the managerial role he had adopted as the business expanded.

Within your planning cycle, it is essential that you take time to check on any training needed before starting up, and the legal implications attached to the type of business activity you will be following. Both of these areas will be described in any business opportunity profile issued by a financial institution. Training needs can be very specific to the job, e.g. a pub landlord must learn how to look after the cellar so that the beer and soft drinks always meet the quality standards of both the customer and the brewery. In other cases, procedures for ordering stock and recording faults may be carried out in a certain way and accounting records always require accurate presentation.

The detail provided by Barclays in relation to the newsagents draws attention to the seven-day working week and other sources of help to ensure the service offered to customers remains first-class:

Figure 6.1.9

Training and Qualifications

Taking on a newsagent business locks you into a commitment to open seven days a week and work long hours (usually from 5am) 364 days a year (Christmas is the only holiday). It is hard work; not to be considered as an easy retirement job. A lot of the work is physical, so you need to be in good health. Tenacity, numeracy and an ability to communicate well with others are also required. No specific qualifications are needed to become a newsagent. NVQs in Retailing are available, but industry specific courses are more important. Training courses are available from The National Federation of Retail Newsagents: an induction, introductory information package and continual sessions are available to 'signed up' members only. They also produce a video and learning booklet at a cost of £14.99 (including postage and VAT). The best way to train is through work experience. Many of the multiples offer training programmes, eg. Martins and T & S Stores, alternatively, try to get work, paid or unpaid, in a local independent.

Legal advice is exceedingly important so that you get off to a good start and know exactly what you are allowed to do. In the case of the newsagents, it is illegal to employ children under 13 years of age; education authorities should be notified and cycling proficiency certificates are advisable. Several specific Acts cover this type of business and insurance policies are needed for protection, such as business premises (material damage), goods for sale (product liability), customers (public liability) and staff (employers' liability).

Figure 6.1.10

Legal

The main legal consideration will be with the employment of staff. Newspaper boys/girls must be over 13 and can only work between 7.00 and 8.00 am and not after 7.00 pm. Check local by-laws which can differ on juvenile employment. All news deliverers must be registered with the local Education Department. Make sure they possess a cycling proficiency certificate and are aware of road safety. They should also wear reflector strips.

The following legislation should be observed: the Shops Act 1950; the Sunday Trading Act 1994; the Sale and Supply of Goods Act 1994; the Offices, Shops and Railway Premises Act 1963; Consumer Protection Act 1987; and the Price Marking Order 1991. If food is being sold, food regulations will apply, including Food Safety Regulations 1990. Note also; the Children and Young Persons (Protection from Tobacco) Act 1991; the National Lottery Act 1993; and National Lottery Regulations 1994. Comprehensive insurance, covering the premises and its contents should be taken, as should Public Liability Insurance. If employing staff, Employers' Liability Insurance will also be needed. It is important to employ an accountant both before buying, in assessing the business, and in helping to run it after buying, eg. with VAT. It is necessary to register with the local authority at least 28 days before handling food (no fee will be charged): contact the local Environmental Officer. If you plan to operate in conjunction with an off-licence or Sub-Post Office, you must obtain a separate licence for each one as they are granted to the person and not the shop. The NFRN supplies a series of information leaflets covering a variety of subjects, which are free to members.

Other recommended insurance cover for long-term protection are:

- motor insurance
- engineering plant
- special risks
- business interruption
- money
- goods in transit
- key person
- professional indemnity
- share and loan protection
- pensions

Additional details need to be covered.

For all business projects:

- If you are employing staff, you have to calculate and deduct income tax and national insurance.
- VAT may need to be added to your goods or services.

These all need to be paid to the relevant collection agencies at regular intervals.

For long-term business projects:

- Capital Gains Tax is payable for profit levels over £7,100 (currently) when disposing of a capital asset, particularly if you are running the business from your home.
- Inheritance Tax may have to be paid if the value of your estate exceeds more than £231,000 (currently).
- Corporation Tax is levied on the profits of limited companies.

Legal advice is needed to help you assess these correctly.

To help you get off to a good start, read the following article from a local newspaper. This gives a summary of useful points about the value of planning and has been written by an adviser from a NatWest Business Centre.

Figure 6.1.11

BUSINESS

Planning is key to successful start-up

Janette Whitney, business manager at NatWest Horsham Business Centre.

IN these tough trading times, you'd expect people would be more cautious about starting up a new small business.

But ten per cent more small businesses started up in 1998 than in 1997 or 1996, *writes Janette Whitney, business manager at NatWest Horsham Business Centre.*

Sounds encouraging? Well, it is. But starting up your own business is one of the biggest challenges you'll ever face and you'll need to get a firm grip on it from the very beginning.

Firstly, you have to ask yourself why you're going into business. Is it to make money? Or because it really interests you? For the independence? Or is it a combination of these?

Whatever the reason, you must be clear about your personal aims and set yourself business goals.

Do you have the drive, training and skills to make a success of it? Have you thought what it will mean for your family or partner, especially when working hours could be very long?

The NatWest SBRT Quarterly Survey of Small Businesses in Britain showed that an average 51 hours was worked each week by business owners, with 29 per cent working between 50 and 59 hours and a quarter working 60 to 69 hours.

It also revealed that a quarter of owners took no more than one week's holiday in one go and only 12 per cent regularly took a lunch break.

These are things that as a small business owner you have to take into account. You need to discuss the impact of what you are doing and get the support of your family or partner.

Ask yourself whether you're prepared for this lifestyle and the commitment it needs.

But, as tough and demanding as it sounds, the same survey also found that only five per cent of small business owners weren't happy or would prefer to be paid employees.

Not a day goes by without someone asking me ''What makes a successful small business?'' I wish there was a magic formula but quite simply there isn't.

However, research for NatWest has highlighted factors that give businesses a greater chance of making it.

■ The age of the owner (the over-50s have double the survival rate of those in their 20s).

■ The number of owners (greater number, greater prospect of survival).

■ A specific vocational qualification.

■ Previous work experience in the same sector you're starting up in.

Gender doesn't matter at all – male and female entrepreneurs have just as much chance of being successful.

But there are certainly practical ways in which you can help your chance of success.

Planning is key – a business plan is the first step, offering a ''dry run'' to see how viable your idea really is and providing you with the opportunity to sort out any problems before they happen.

Small businesses that succeed have certain things in common – careful thought, planning and guidance. For instance, could you answer the following questions about your business?

● Do you know the difference between profit and cash? Could you draw up a cashflow forecast?

● Do you know how to price goods?

● Do you know who your competitors are?

● Do you know what your customers want?

● Do you know who your customers are going to be?

● Why should customers want to buy from you or choose your product or service above somebody else's?

● How much money do you have to make to break even?

You should be pretty clear about all these before you start. Also, bring it down to basic common sense.

If you are thinking of opening a coffee shop, for example, and there are already three of them in the same high street, you have to seriously ask yourself whether there's room for your business there.

Checking that out can be as simple as going down to the high street and watching the foot-flow – see how many are going in and out of those shops, at what times and watch what they are buying.

On the other hand, if there are no coffee shops whatsoever around then you need to ask yourself why not, and more importantly, find out why not, and whether there will be a future in you opening one there.

The more preparation you can do before you start the better, and with training being of paramount importance, get as much of it as you can.

Your local advice organisations can help you choose the right training course for you.

The last but most important point is to seek all the advice and help you can get.

The good news is that there is plenty out there and much of it is free.

Your local Business Link should be able to provide you with free information and advice about training, getting grants, planning your business, marketing innovation... just about everything you need to know.

Advice is also supplied by Training and Enterprise Councils (TECs), Local Enterprise Agencies (LEAs) and Chambers of Commerce — and the easy thing is that all these agencies can be found in the telephone book.

Also, of course, talk to your bank. Not just from the day you need to open a business account or take out a loan but, more importantly, from the day you first come up with the idea you want to turn into a successful business.

Source: Horsham Advertiser

Activity

To cover the planning and monitoring areas of your business plan:

- prepare a time schedule chart showing all activities planned within the timescale available to you for completion of your project

- agree points at which monitoring will occur

- arrange any team meetings which need to be held on a regular basis

- identify any training needs you must attend to

- list all the legal obligations you must comply with in the course of your business operations

- identify each area where insurance cover must be organised.

Market analysis and marketing planning

Units 2 and 3 offer specific detail of each area that covers the market for your chosen product or service. Refer to these units for any additional information you may need.

Now that the initial planning stages have been completed and you have made a firm choice of product or service, the collection of data to confirm there is in fact a market for your product needs to be carried out. This will involve a survey of all the surrounding factors that are likely to have an impact on your level of sales. The key areas to consider are:

Figure 6.1.12

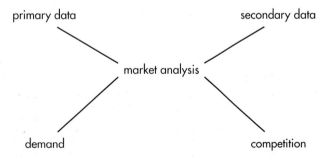

Primary data

The first decision is the format to be used to carry out the research needed to establish the size of the market for your product. Talking to people and assessing their reactions to your proposals may give you an initial feel for the market. This is not definite information on which to start planning, however, as many people will not follow through with purchases once they see the item. This indicates that potential customers, no matter how enthusiastic at the outset, need to *see* the actual product before agreeing to buy it.

Several prototypes should be made up as soon as possible and the colour range, size and prices should all be available for use during a discussion. The USP can be **highlighted** and the **benefits** of **owning** the product need to be stressed. This approach gives you a better start with potential customers and you will have **created the need** to own the product.

In some cases, a number of the prototype products could be issued for **sampling** by carefully selected clients. A considerable amount of information can be gained from this activity, e.g.:

- The quality of the product can be assessed by use and this will allow you to make changes if it does not stand up to wear and tear.

- The client can show the product to other potential customers and do some marketing for you.

- Colours and sizes requested can be added to the range.

A survey form should accompany the item so that feedback is gained to help in product development.

Another feature to set up and distribute is a questionnaire which will give you hard facts to collate and analyse. This is one of the best ways to reach a decision because it takes your own personal bias out of the frame. Prepare a spreadsheet analysis and graphs to help you assess the responses. Be careful to read the results of your analysis *correctly* and do *not* overlook any sections of the questionnaire. Minor points at the top and bottom of the scale of answers can pinpoint issues that may cause problems in the future.

The timescale for all of these activities should be tightly controlled so that a minimum number of days/weeks is used from the available time frame. While this research is being carried out and you are awaiting the results, the next stage can be undertaken.

Secondary data

Access to a range of data already collated can be gained from libraries, the internet, government publications, trade associations, specialist magazines, the local Business Link or Chamber of Commerce. It is essential that you find out as much detail as possible about the buying habits of your future customers. Previous research by similar organisations will help you to compile a profile of your customer base, their behaviour patterns, their preferences, level of sales and how they are likely to react to a new product entering the market.

Collect as much data as possible and spend time studying the details. This will help to determine the level of **demand** for your product. This information is needed to set the quantity of production required to meet the demand and the time period in which customers *expect* to be able to purchase the item. With so much choice available from many outlets, customers soon lose interest if they cannot find the item easily and will then purchase substitute products. This is not a situation you would willingly create and timing is crucial.

During the school/college year, several selling opportunities may have been identified such as a school fete or a Christmas bazaar. You *must* have sufficient stock available for these planned events otherwise the reputation of the business will be seriously damaged. It is difficult to attract back customers who have been lost after they have been let down and this generally results from bad planning in the first place. This is the time to 'start as you mean to go on' and finding out about

customer preferences is an essential part of the initial stages of marketing.

As well as looking at customer buying patterns, a survey of *competitor* activities is needed. These can be observed and assessed to help you identify your USP. The analysis will also determine the market segment in which your competitors operate and the market share they already possess – statistics are likely to be available which give this information and efforts should be made to study them. What is being considered here is the possible reaction of your main rivals when your product is launched. This will assist in determining the amount that should be budgeted for advertising to propel your product into the public eye and raise customer awareness.

Use the information sources that best match your chosen product or service and will help you to reach **logical** decisions. This may even mean changing one or two areas of your original idea if the research shows your product is not acceptable in its current format.

If your business venture requires the use of premises, the choice of location is very important. Visit several sites and note the type of customers who use the existing facilities. Assess the car parking situation and, in particular, review the type of business activity and level of competition in the area. Consider the nature of the business that has recently vacated the property you are inspecting and check the legal status of the premises, e.g. if the previous occupant was running a bookshop and you intend to set up a coffee shop the change of use must be approved by the local authority. Business rates must also be investigated.

An example of similar points are noted in Barclays information about the newsagents:

Figure 6.1.13

Promotion

The location of the shop is important in maintaining a competitive edge, eg. a corner shop is a good position for a newsagents, as it is easily noticeable. The shop front should be attractive. Accentuate the exterior with prominent signs; illuminated shop signs are particularly effective. Good point-of-sale material is essential and is available from publishers or sales reps. Leaflet drops in the local area are another way to attract customers to the shop, especially if the shop has opened recently. Ascertain the needs of the local community, either in general conversation or through questionnaires. Cultivate good relations with customers to encourage them to come back on a regular basis. Many commuters see the trip to the newsagents as part of their daily routine - it should be a pleasant experience.

The location will have repercussions on the success or failure of your company. Setting up in an area where there are already several other coffee shops, for instance, will only antagonise other operators and set off a price war. Existing businesses will have already established a customer base and it is extremely difficult to prise loyal customers away from such fixed buying habits. In this case, the best way to succeed is to have completely different food on offer and that way both businesses can survive in the same location by appealing to different market segments.

A useful example offered by Barclays in their Start-up Pack is the research carried out by Tom Star when trying to set up a mini-cab firm:

Figure 6.1.14

Here's an example of how this could work. Tom Star was planning a mini-cab business, so he compared his proposed service with two existing ones in the area.

	Tom Star	Ace Cars	L. Brown
Price	Average £ per mile	Average £ per mile	Average £ per mile
Quality	Good	OK	Very good
Availability	5.30am-2.00pm 7 days a week	24 hours 7 days a week	24 hours 7 days a week
Customers	Mostly domestic	Domestic and account work	New
Staff skills		Local businesses	
Reputation	Good	Mixed	New
Advertising	Newsagents/super markets/door to door cards	Cards door to door	Ad in Thompson Directory
Delivery	n/a	n/a	n/a
Location	Local and airports	Local and airports	Local/airports/ weddings etc.
Special offers	None	None	?
After sales service	n/a	n/a	n/a

Tom concluded from this comparison that Ace Cars wouldn't pose much of a threat. Their charges were slightly lower, but the cars were older and rundown. However, he noticed that their parcel delivery service got them some business customers and he decided to investigate offering a similar service.

The other competitor, Len Brown, was new to the area, had high standard cars and charged higher rates for special occasions, such as weddings. Tom felt he couldn't compete with this service, but could use his better cars for chauffeuring business people. This led him to include stepping-up contacts with businesses in his plan, to reduce his dependence on the less predictable domestic trade.

A final point to consider is how far away the business is situated from the suppliers of components, stock or fresh produce:

- a china manufacturer will need raw materials, paints and glazes, packaging materials and equipment

- a newsagents will need a variety of newspapers and magazines, cards and stationery, confectionery and tobacco, and possibly groceries

- a coffee shop will need fresh bread, sandwich fillings, cakes/pastries, tea/coffee/sugar and milk etc.

- a mini-cab business will need somewhere to park the vehicles when not in use, an office to take calls and allocate drivers and possibly a vehicle repair section.

All of these factors must be resolved to help you meet customer requirements and provide a satisfactory and reliable service. That is the key feature that will gain you **repeat sales**.

Marketing models are available to help you piece together a comprehensive analysis of your intended activity. All aspects surrounding the business idea should be investigated to ensure you have not missed any important features. The most useful tools are shown in Table 6.1.2.

Although there is a vast amount of research to be carried out *before* your business can start operating, there is no short cut to this process. If you are not in possession of *all* the facts, poor decisions will be made, the competition will quickly find the weak points in your operation and things will soon begin to go wrong. Knowledge of internal and external factors should be a continual process and be carried out regularly to check that you are still occupying the position that creates confidence in customers and therefore profit rather than losing market share and falling into debt. It is an exciting and stimulating process to stay one jump ahead of the competition and sail off into high profit levels, but it takes effort to maintain this position.

Table 6.1.2

Marketing tool	Brief description
SWOT analysis	This will help you to identify the USP and other features that distinguish your product from that of your competitors. It can establish new opportunities which you should take as soon as possible. Weaknesses and threats should be tackled in a positive manner by improving weak abilities and finding ways to overcome these minor setbacks.
PEST analysis	An assessment of the external environment will allow you to review any restraining factors over which you have no control but which you do need to observe, e.g. new laws, particularly on health and safety; economic factors, such as interest rates; social issues, such as demographic trends; and technological influences, such as new equipment or more sophisticated IT systems.
Ansoff matrix	This gives you an opportunity to evaluate methods of gaining market penetration and a continual supply of new products, the process of searching for new markets and when to diversify the existing product range.
Product life cycle	This is an easy tool to use to assess the stage your product has now reached and links closely with new product development and advertising budgets.
Boston matrix	This will assist the long-term business operation to piece together a number of goods that can be marketed and sold from within the portfolio of products available across the company.
Marketing mix	This gives a beneficial planning strategy that will help you to plan the profile for each product offered to customers. It covers pricing, promoting, placement, the physical environment, customer service and the training and motivation of staff.

Marketing planning

Once you have completed all the necessary research for your chosen business activity, you must prepare a detailed plan of the marketing strategy you will use to attract the potential customers that your research has shown exist. The plan should cover:

Figure 6.1.15

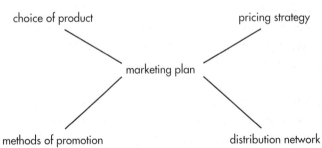

Choice of product

Information collected may cause you to amend the original idea you started with if the data shows insufficient customers are willing to purchase your product or service in its present format. These details should now be finalised so that you are clear about the item you intend to start with. This has to be fully explained to a financial source, along with your comparison of competitors in the locality.

This is the time to describe the USP of your business. If you refer to the mini-cab operation proposed by Tom Star (page 390), information revealed that his better quality cars would gain domestic trade against Ace Cars because their vehicles were older and rundown. However, he noted that it would not be possible to compete equally with Len Brown because his cars were of superior quality. This led Tom to focus on chauffeuring business clients and he planned to target these people specifically with an advertising campaign. Once a reputation has been gained from this action, the reliability and standard of service provided will develop into a strong USP for this business.

Justification of the reasons for choosing a particular product are helpful to yourself as confirmation that you have selected a potential winner, but also to convince the financial source that you approach for help that it will gain a good return on its investment.

Where the time period is short, such as the school/college year, it would be advantageous to choose several small products. This will give you wider scope than if you concentrate on a single product. If one product does not live up to expectations, there is unlikely to be enough time to start again with another item. A range of complementary products could be a wise decision made by the group and this would give the company the chance to push the more successful items and balance out the investment by the end of the financial year.

Pricing strategy

Your competitor analysis is extremely important in this area because it allows you to set the price of your item in relation to other products on the market. A new business cannot set itself up as a market leader because it has no reputation on which to build customer confidence. This has to be earned over a period of time

and this means that, to some extent, you are a market follower until you can assess the level of constant sales that allow you to move up to a higher status.

Long-term businesses can pinpoint a time slot in the plan when this is likely to be achieved and this is an excellent goal to aim for in your strategy. Tom Star decided to promote the middle range of prices but may well have set his sights on upgrading the vehicles and offering additional services once sufficient profit levels have been achieved through his reputation for reliability.

Other pricing factors to consider are:

- **Penetration**   used at the launch of a new product, it is generally lower than the main price identified and aims to attract customers away from competitors.

- **Skimming**   sets out to gain sales from people who want to be the first to own new products and prices are higher to offset research and development costs.

- **Cost plus**   calculates the costs of producing and distributing the product and adds on a small profit margin.

- **Value**   if your product is of a superior quality and you can prove that it is a 'brand' or 'designer' product, a part of the price is allocated to the 'value' of the item purchased.

- **Competitor based**   this matches the prices charged by your competitors and customers must decide for themselves which item gives the best value.

Your pricing strategy is dependent upon the quality of the item and the part of the **product life cycle** it has reached. Prices will be altered as the product passes through each stage and there will be distinct differences at **introductory**, **maturity** and **decline** levels. Regular monitoring should be carried out to check that current prices reflect the extent of customer demand for it.

Methods of promotion

The budget allocation will control the extent of your promotional activities. A new business has limited finance and must select the best methods of reaching a maximum number of potential customers. The first question to ask is 'Where are my potential customers likely to find out about my product?' Advertising can then be placed in the correct position to attract trade. This can be in the local newspaper, on the local radio, at the supermarket or various public premises. Tom Star may also have a leaflet printed for delivery by the Post Office or local free newspaper; a sign on the vehicles will be a good advertising opportunity as the cars drive around the community and business cards handed out to every passenger will help spread the company name.

Long-term businesses can afford more extreme methods, such as various sales promotions, e.g. two-for-one offers, direct mail to regular customers, sponsorship deals, improved packaging, direct selling for specific products that meet individual needs and brand awareness campaigns. Reference is always made to the stage the item has reached in the product life cycle and the success rate of previous strategies.

All of these activities will be monitored and the records consulted as to the increased volume of sales they have created. Customers will often be asked: 'Where did you find out about this product?' and the results of this research will be fed back to the marketing, sales and production departments. A new business with limited funds for advertising must monitor the best returns on its new campaign. This will give definite information to help missing clientele to be better targeted, while constant customers will not be entirely ignored but will receive regular reminders about the product or service. Tom Star will need to find out quickly which method is providing the best return and concentrate on that source until sufficient customers have been attracted to maintain a steady source of income.

Distribution network

This is the entire process of getting the actual product to the consumer. All parts of the business community have to consider the logistics involved in moving goods from one place to another and the difficulties experienced in moving different types of product. A manufacturer must deliver the finished items from the factory to a wholesale warehouse or customer depot. These goods will then pass through the various stages of retailing until they eventually arrive in the home of the customer.

For example, Tom Star has to move the mini-cabs from the depot to the customer contact points and then to the prescribed destination. He may have to face the possibility of the vehicle completing the return journey empty, and the price charged will have to reflect this point. While the newsagent may have to go to the cash and carry for some supplies, others will be delivered to the premises and some newspapers/magazines will have to be delivered to customers' addresses.

Fresh food items are trickier to deliver to customers and the method of conveyance will have to conform to health and safety regulations to ensure the produce arrives in peak condition. Large pieces of equipment or bulk cargo need special lifting gear and delivery handling, but a service offered to customers at a building society or via electronic outlets must be 100 per cent accurate every time.

Some businesses will have to consider their customer service policy in relation to the return and refund of price on unsatisfactory merchandise, or a complaints procedure to deal with poor quality service. A business offering washing machines or computers will need to ensure that packaging material is suitable to protect the

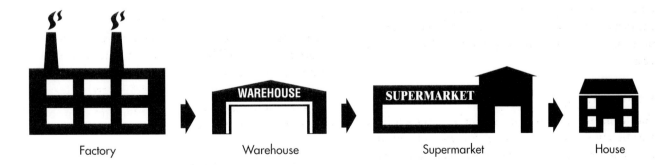

Factory   Warehouse   Supermarket   House

item in transit and what procedure it will offer the customer for installation and testing. In the case of the washing machine, this will mean correctly attaching it to plumbing and electricity supplies before the customer uses it.

The distribution network does not always end once a purchase has been made. Even if a customer bought items in a coffee shop and then consumed them on the premises, there would still be a responsibility if the consumer then fell ill with food poisoning and claimed negligence. Full protection for these occurrences should be carried out and the legal obligations attached to the type of business operated should be checked out.

Where possible, advantage should be taken of the prospect of gaining sales using modern technology. On-line shopping is now part of the distribution network and an extensive range of products can be bought through this facility. Tesco has recently introduced an on-line ordering and delivery service, which means that customers do not have to leave the comfort of their own homes to purchase basic daily essentials. A small charge is made for this service and it is particularly useful for house-bound customers since it relieves the pressure of the 'battle of the shopping trolleys' as well as the waiting time in a queue at the checkout to pay for goods selected. Home shopping catalogues also offer customers a range of products, from clothes, furniture, household appliances and accessories to children's toys and jewellery. The customer has a considerable range of outlets to use and each business will select the distribution network that best supports its range of products.

Activity

Complete both sections of this activity in relation to your marketing strategy.

1 Carry out a full market analysis to determine the extent of the likely sales for your product or service. This should include the collection of primary and secondary data, an assessment of the level of demand for your product and an evaluation of competitor activities.

2 Prepare a detailed marketing plan of each area identified at the analysis stage. This should include a qualitative description of your product and its USP, your pricing strategy, the methods you will use to promote the product and an indication of how you will distribute the goods or service to the customer.

Production and resource requirements

Additional details about both of these topics can be found in Unit 1 – Business at Work, which contains information about production requirements and quality measurement techniques, and Unit 4 – Human Resources, which draws your attention to the need for skilled staff and training to ensure that quality products and services are produced.

Some businesses will only buy in finished goods and do not get involved in their actual production schedules. Other businesses may not manufacture goods but will send their own inspectors to check quality levels. Firms engaged in manufacturing any product – whether it is bread and cakes, clothes or furniture – will co-ordinate all the features of the production operation to meet customer deadlines. This will require careful planning so that the specific details of a range of products can be met exactly and the machinery is fully used to meet timescales and the quantities needed.

For this to work successfully, a strong link must be forged between the marketing, sales and production departments of an organisation. It is pointless manufacturing too many goods just to keep equipment busy if the sales department is not selling them. Some goods become out of date quickly and to stockpile large numbers of these is using valuable capital and resources in an unsatisfactory manner. Many organisations use an integrated resource planning system to control the levels of production to meet sales orders.

Figure 6.1.16

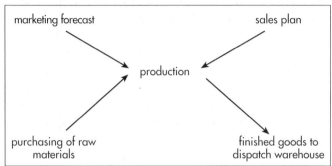

Again the stage at which the item is located in the **product life cycle** will be checked so that a constant number of products will be manufactured at the **maturity** stage and it will be possible to identify when the item is slipping into the **decline** stage so that production levels can be altered accordingly. All the manufacturing activities are planned in connection with heavy or light advertising campaigns by the marketing department.

It would be a good idea to visit a factory to see the operation at first hand. Your tutor or adviser will have contacts with people in manufacturing units in the locality who will be pleased to conduct a tour of their facilities. Prepare a list of questions before the visit, particularly in connection with any product you have decided to adopt. Try and find out any problem areas that require extra effort, the system of quality control used in the operation and any health and safety precautions you should take during the process.

If it is not possible to arrange such a visit, a talk can be organised, when a manufacturing specialist will come and outline the various procedures used to produce goods. A similar list of questions can be prepared for use in the discussion period at the end of the talk.

Production requirements

The main areas of production to cover are:

- the quantity to be produced
- the plant, machinery and equipment needed
- the quality control or quality assurance system

- the stages of the production process
- the time available to complete the manufacturing process.

Quantity

Reference to the time schedule chart you prepared at the beginning of this unit (page 383) will be of assistance at this point. This will give you an initial guide as to the quantity of products you need at set periods of time. If you have planned a special sales drive, you will need to **estimate** how many items you are likely to sell and then have *more* than that available. If you are producing products only in response to orders taken, you will need to give a **specified delivery date** and ensure production is geared up to this system. If you intend to operate **both** systems at the same time (instant sales + pre-booked orders), your production schedule will need to be set to meet both these timescales.

A final point to consider is that you must bear in mind that if you plan to make only the *exact* number required, difficulties will be experienced if the equipment breaks down, your raw materials do not arrive on time or your staff do not carry out their jobs correctly. In these circumstances you will not be able to meet a sudden rise in demand for your product. **Contingency planning** is an essential part of your scheduling arrangements, so you should consider any likely problems that may occur and have a **back-up plan** prepared.

Plant, machinery and equipment

This will help you to plan the number of staff and pieces of equipment you need to keep pace with the pre-booked orders and instant sales you have estimated. Check the length of time it takes each piece of equipment to produce a batch of products and use this figure to assess the number of machines needed and the total time required to produce the stock required. This will help you to work out the delivery dates for pre-booked items.

The building in which the equipment is housed is also a consideration because of noise levels and safety issues. The design of the production unit should be carefully organised to avoid too much wasteful movement between functions. Minimum transport between sites or processes is best but some procedures need a period of 'rest' time between stages to allow operations to take effect, e.g. glue to set, chemicals to react or paint to harden.

The health of the workforce carrying out these procedures must be given a high priority and provision of suitable equipment is a legal requirement, e.g. earmuffs for noise, protective clothes and goggles for chemicals and dust, etc. Opening windows and using extractor fans can keep clean air circulating and extract unpleasant fumes and dust. Moving and lifting gear needs to be available to shift heavy items, including boxes of finished products.

Quality levels

Discussions need to be carried out *before* production starts to agree the quality standards the products must meet. These can be written down so that *all* staff know they exist. The methods that will be adopted to meet these standards must be explained and training given, if necessary, to ensure they are fully met. A checking and monitoring procedure is key to this operation and this can be carried out as a **quality control** system after products have been manufactured *or* during the process if quality circles have been introduced.

The aim is to have a very small percentage of rejects from any batch since it is expensive to throw away finished goods that are not up to standard. More and more organisations use the **Zero defects** approach which aims to have 0 per cent errors/faults at all times. To help this operate successfully, **quality circles** or **ISO9000 procedures** may be set up. This places the responsibility on each employee to check his/her own part of the process and not pass it on to the next stage *unless it is perfect.* This is a more cost effective approach and also places the onus on the employer to ensure high quality raw materials are purchased and that all equipment is carefully maintained to assist staff in their work.

Whichever method is used, a monitoring technique is still needed to check that all the parts of the process are meeting quality standards.

Stages of production

In this area, decisions will need to be made about how to divide up the stages in the production cycle. A small easy-to-produce item will require only a few stages, whereas a highly complex item will need many more stages. It will also depend upon the number of functions one machine can complete. Compile a breakdown of these requirements for your product using a similar format to the example shown in Table 6.1.3.

This analysis will help you to set up a well controlled operation, manufacture a steady flow of finished goods, reduce wastage and maintain specified quality standards to meet customer requirements.

Timing

All of the above factors are part of the timing of the whole production process. The starting point is obviously the time schedule chart drawn up at the beginning of your operation and the resource planning control system. These clearly show:

- the number of goods needed at specified time periods within the year
- the capacity of equipment and machinery
- the number of staff needed to maintain production levels
- the pre-booked orders to be met
- the estimated sales you are attempting to meet
- the expectations and requirements of your customers.

Table 6.1.3

How many raw materials?	How many steps in the production cycle?	How many pieces of equipment?	How many packaging items?	How much storage space?
These are:	These are:	These are:	These are:	These are:
1	1	1	1	1
2	2	2	2	2
3	3	3	3	3
4	4	4	4	4

The schedules you have already detailed can be used in conjunction with any monitoring techniques you have set up to provide feedback on how well the operation is meeting its targets. Changes can be made at any stage in the procedure to avoid either under-production or over-production of items. The last thing you want to have to do is apologise to customers who are demanding your product because you have grossly underestimated their needs!

Resource requirements

Although the production unit is central to the success of your business activity, there are other factors to be taken into account. These are:

- financial
- physical
- human
- time
- legal.

Each of these will differ according to the volume of goods needed at various periods during the year. Most points have been mentioned within this section but of particular importance are the legal constraints of operating a manufacturing plant in various locations. The surrounding neighbourhood has rights and these include controlling external pollutants that issue into the atmosphere and the number of heavy vehicles moving in and out of the plant. You will need to ensure these are tightly controlled otherwise pressure groups will form and the legal process will combine to force changes on your processes.

Extensive coverage has been given in all the other five units of your course to assist you with these factors. A reminder of the main issues to consider is shown in Table 6.1.4.

Whatever the nature of your product, all the factors that surround its manufacture must be thoroughly investigated. Several courses of action should be set out in detail so that you have prepared solutions to possible problems before they occur. Managing a production process will require continual involvement and good decision making skills as well as the ability to form harmonious working relationships with staff members. The end result of all your efforts will be clearly seen by the quality levels of manufactured items and the extensive demand for your products by customers.

Environmental pollution

Table 6.1.4 Resource requirements

Resource	Points to consider
Finance	• start-up capital • break-even point • work in progress • operating costs: fixed and variable • departmental budgets: particularly production, marketing/sales • distribution of profits
Physical	• location and size • equipment and machinery • accessibility for raw materials and staff • costs: rent, lease or buy
Human	• communication pattern • job roles and departmental functions • team building and problem solving
Time	• delivery period of raw materials • production process • customer delivery date • break-even point • realistic target setting • measurement of quality levels
Legal	• any law/obligations relating to the product • health and safety procedures and facilities • ethical and moral standards • employment requirements • business operation: sole trader, partnership or limited company • local authority: licences, type of production, location and grants • tax and National Insurance

Activity

Prepare a comprehensive analysis of all the requirements needed at each stage of your production schedule.

1 Calculate the number of goods to be produced at set time periods.
Assess the capacity of equipment/machinery used in the production cycle.
Work out the number of machines, staff and hours required to manufacture the goods.

2 Produce an additional set of notes covering further resource requirements to assist the production schedule.

Financial analysis and planning

This area is fully described in Unit 5 – Finance and will give you many different methods of calculating all the funds you need for your business venture. This is clearly linked to the type of business you want to set up but you should also check any legal obligations you have to meet for your chosen operation.

In the area of finance, five key features need to be prepared before approaching anyone for assistance. These should cover:

- sources of finance
- budgets, including start-up and working capital
- a break-even forecast
- a cash flow forecast
- a projected profit and loss account and balance sheet.

Sources of finance

There are numerous sources that you can approach for help but detailed accounts will be required by all of these if you are to convince them that you are fully committed to the business idea and intend to make it succeed.

Your best plan would be to save up sufficient money to be the largest stakeholder in the firm. This will free you from having to make continual interest payments to several sources at a time when you can least afford it. Investigate any assistance that may be forthcoming from friends and family before contacting external sources. External sources will require collateral to cover the loan and many sole traders unwisely use their homes as security because they are not prepared to wait until they have saved up sufficient capital to manage without such assistance.

If a partnership is considered, careful selection of the other partners will establish their determination to make the firm successful. In this organisation, complementary skills can be brought in to cover a wider range of activities, and different amounts of capital can be contributed. Legal documents should be prepared governing the running of the partnership and what will happen if it fails.

Limited companies require much more investment, and this also means loss of control to the different categories of shareholders. A private limited company will have only a small number of shareholders, likely to be family members, who will retain full control and will take their rewards in accordance with the number of shares held. On the other hand, a public limited company may have thousands of shareholders who all own the company and all require dividend payments each financial year. This type of company normally grows out of a previous organisation and is thoroughly investigated by the Stock Exchange before it is granted this status.

Other sources of finance that could be consulted are the various high street banks and loan institutions, each of which will have a set of criteria which you must meet before your request will be granted. Visit any one of the high street banks and collect their Start-Up Pack for Small Businesses, which gives you a clear indication of these requirements. Complete all the documents in full and begin with a detailed breakdown of each of your sources of finance to make up the full amount needed. If you are asking the bank for help, they will require details of how and when you plan to pay back the loan.

It is worth investigating any grants that may be available from government sources, as well as the EU, and checking out schemes offered by the local council that allow premises to be rented at reduced rates for a set period of time to help new businesses in the region.

A combination of several of these sources may be your best course of action and these should be carefully listed, together with pay-back arrangements.

Budgets

These are a useful indication of estimated expenditure in each section of your business operation. Of particular interest to financial institutions are the estimates of start-up costs and working capital.

Figure 6.1.17

Start-up costs

These should cover all the expenses needed to begin trading, such as premises, fixtures and fittings, stock, vehicles, wages for any staff to be employed and potential sales levels.

The amount needed will vary according to the size and nature of the business. If you start up at home, no expense will be incurred for renting premises but you will need permission from the householder and extra insurance cover. If the business does require premises, the costs will be considerably higher than this and you should be certain you can cover all of these expenses.

The example given by Barclays relates to the start-up of a newsagents.

NEWSAGENTS

Start Up Costs

Normally entry into the market is achieved by purchasing an existing shop. Some of the biggest newsagency chains are selling off many of their shops, eg. T& S Stores, GT News. This is a good opportunity, but a thorough programme of research will be required before buying. Contact the chains or a business transfer agent for the availability of shops for sale. Make enquiries to the local authority to find out if there are any plans for development in the area that might affect the shop or its trading potential. High street outlets are normally branches of multiples, eg. WH Smith. Independent shops tend to be in secondary locations. Kiosks are also an option, but these are unable to hold a large amount of stock. The main thing is to assess if the business can provide decent income for the work required - the minimum turnover of a CTN should be between £3,000-£4,000 a week and normally requires between 400 and 600 square feet of retail space. If however, more than 20% of the business mix is in tobacco/cigarette sales, which show a lower profit margin, a higher turnover should be aimed at.

Starting a shop from scratch will involve purchasing premises, fixtures, fittings and stock. The total cost can be anything from £70,000 to £100,000, but prices will vary considerably and depends on the type of premises, stock levels, location, size and value of the business etc. A full EPOS system will cost around £4,000. A refrigerated cabinet will cost around £700 for a fairly small unit. A stainless steel chest freezer will cost from £500. White freezers are cheaper and will cost around £170. If planning to sell fresh fruit and vegetables a set of scales will be needed, costing from £20-40. Computerised scales cost around £500 and should be able to weigh in metric measurements. These items can be purchased second-hand but should be in good working order. Transport may be needed for stock. A small van can cost from £10,000. Security fittings and alarms will also be required eg. mirrors, CCTV, shutters, etc. If it is possible to manage without employing staff, do so: if not, target the busiest times so that extra staff are only employed when needed; ie. early mornings, school lunch times etc. The newsagent should also be present at these times in order to serve the public quickly and to prevent theft.

Note that a **minimum of £84,890** has been estimated, and this is before trading commences. Compare this figure with the start-up costs of a small business venture started by Rachel Wells, selling children's videos:

CASE STUDY

Rachel Wells trading as KIDS-VIDS

Start-up capital   £1,875

Opening stock value   £1,500   Cost price   £750

– all further purchases will be made from suppliers who allow one month's credit. She will replace stock sold each month to maintain opening stock value £1,500.

Cost price of stock = 50% of selling price.

Rachel has estimated that a quarter of sales each month will be to video shops and they will be allowed one month's credit.

Estimated sales: Jan   £750   April   £1,500

                   Feb   £1,200   May   £3,000

                   March £1,350   June £1,800

Additional costs:		
Advertising	£250 per month
Stand at exhibition (May)	£350 to be paid in April
Sundry expenses	£150 Jan, Feb, March
	£175 April, May, June
Office equipment	£500 with 5-year life span
Drawings	£150 per month

Using the above data, the first cash budget prepared by Rachel Wells will look like this:

Figure 6.1.18 Cash budget Jan-June 2000

Item	January	February	March	April	May	June	Totals
Cash sales	563	900	1,013	1,125	2,250	1,350	
Cash from debtors	–	187	300	338	375	750	
Capital introduced	1,875	–	–	–	–	–	
Total receipts	2,438	1,087	1,313	1,463	2,625	2,100	11,026
Stock purchased	1,500	–	–	–	–	–	
Payments to creditors	–	375	600	675	750	1,500	
Advertising	250	250	250	250	250	250	
Stand at exhibition	–	–	–	350	–	–	
Sundry expenses	150	150	150	175	175	175	
Office equipment	500	–	–	–	–	–	
Drawings	150	150	150	150	150	150	
Total payments	2,550	925	1,150	1,600	1,325	2,075	9,625
Opening bank balance	–	–112	50	213	76	1,376	
Add receipts	2,438	1,087	1,313	1,463	2,625	2,100	
Less payments	2,550	925	1,150	1,600	1,325	2,075	
Closing bank balance	–112	50	213	76	1,376	1,401	1,401

This shows a gradual improvement in the overall situation for the first six months' trading and will be very encouraging to the financial source approached by Rachel. There seems to be no need at present to borrow money but, once trading begins, these targets may not be met or the video shops may not pay their accounts on time. Continual monitoring of this initial cash budget will spot any discrepancies and remedial action can be taken swiftly.

A close working relationship with any financial source will benefit the business by keeping it informed of progress against targets and consulting it for advice on the best course of action to take to cover any shortfalls to your original estimates. When the time comes to expand the operation, this link will prove valuable and a quick decision is more likely to be reached in your favour.

As well as preparing such a cash budget, make frequent checks on the everyday trading position to ensure money is coming in fast enough to cover continual expenditure.

Working capital

This refers to the short-term financial position of the business and should be checked every week (the difference between current assets and current liabilities).

The main factors to check are:

- **debtors** – money owed by customers for goods bought on credit
- **creditors** – money owed by the firm to suppliers for stock purchased on credit
- **stock** – the value of materials you have purchased for immediate resale or use in the production process
- **cash or overdraft** – the money held in a bank account.

The aim of this regular check on your working capital is to ensure there is sufficient money available to replace stock and keep pace with sales. Meeting high sales levels means using vital cash to ensure stock is available. If customers do not pay their accounts within the stated time period, you may end up with insufficient money to meet daily expenses. Such over-trading will lead to business failure and therefore working capital should be calculated carefully on a weekly basis:

Stock + debtors – creditors = working capital

If a business wants to increase sales levels by 25 or 50 per cent, working capital requirements will need to increase by approximately the same percentage rate. Accepting orders that cannot be fulfilled because there is not enough money to purchase new stock will seriously damage the reputation of the business. A better strategy is to negotiate future delivery dates that are realistic and recoup any money that is owing to the business as fast as possible to allow the purchase of new stock to meet these delivery requirements.

To assist in the monitoring of working capital, the **cash book** is an essential recording system to show all receipts and payments, together with the method used to settle each account. A good example of such a cash book is provided in the Barclays Start-up Pack covering the transactions for a trader who is not registered for VAT (currently based on a sales threshold of £51,000) (see Figure 6.1.19).

Along with these records, set up a system to check out the creditworthiness of potential customers who request goods but indicate that they will pay later. State the time period within which payment should be made, e.g. 14 days or 30 days (your own suppliers will operate a similar checking system on your business) and send out your invoices promptly to encourage a positive response. Small businesses are now entitled to charge interest on overdue invoices to help their cash flow position. Your bank will advise you on these policies and give guidance on other debt collection procedures. Consult the bank as soon as you note a difficulty has arisen and do not let it continue unchecked because it will cause serious problems if your business cannot meet its financial commitments.

Break-even forecast

This useful analysis gives a calculation of the point at which you expect to reach an equilibrium between sales generated and the cost of gaining those sales. When it has passed this point, the business will start earning profit and you will be able to see the result of all your previous hard work. The cost of sales is calculated by plotting the fixed and variable costs against sales income.

Fixed costs

These remain constant for the whole of the trading period and are easy to set aside because they do not change. They are:

- rent of premises
- business rates
- insurances
- heating and lighting.

Variable costs

These change according to the volume of business activity to meet demand or an alteration in operational costs. They are:

- salaries
- fuel/energy
- raw materials/components
- packaging.

An example of a break-even chart is shown below, using a firm manufacturing calculators.

Units	Variable costs (£12 per unit)	Fixed costs	Total costs	Sales income (£18 per unit)
–	–	0	0	0
2,000	24,000	15,000	39,000	36,000
4,000	48,000	15,000	63,000	72,000

The break-even point occurs when 2,500 units have been sold but this will be achieved only if all facts originally estimated by the owner remain the same. Profit is then earned for all sales in excess of this figure. Regular monitoring of all costs will be carried out to control expenditure within agreed limits and any deviation from this needs to be spotted so that critical decisions can be made to avoid serious loss of production.

Figure 6.1.19 Example of cash book entries

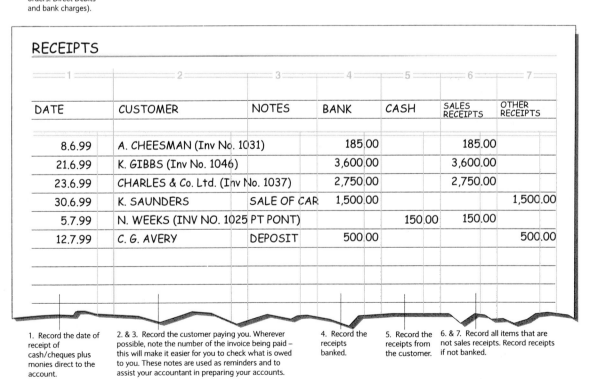

PAYMENTS

	1	2	3	4	5	6	7	8
DATE		SUPPLIER	INVOICE/ NOTES	CHEQUE No.	BANK	CASH	DRAWINGS	MATERIALS/ STOCK
4.6.99		QUIRKS ESTATE AGENTS	(RENT)	000105	300.00			
10.6.99		H.A.B.C	(RATES)	D/D	150.00			
10.6.99		ALBERT REED	(10697)	000106	354.50			354.50
10.6.99		J. PLANT & Co.	(AC7965)	000107	28.90			
15.7.99		B.T.	(TO 28/5/99)	000108	164.90			
19.7.99		VODAPHONE	(TO 19/5/99)	D/D	36.85			
19.6.99		B. SCOTT	(L59671)	000109	152.70			152.70
25.6.99		POST OFFICE	(REG. LETTER)			20.00		
30.6.99		HARTLEY SERVICES	(FUEL)			25.90		
1.7.99		STAGECOACH	(TO LONDON)	000110	16.49			
1.7.99		LUNCH/TUBE				15.60		
5.7.99		G. KEEN	(B9624)	000111	46.72			
12.7.99		SELF & P/C		000112	1050.00		1,000.00	

1. Record the date of payment, use date of cheque for cheque payments and the date on your bank statement for bank generated payments (eg. standing orders. Direct Debits and bank charges).

2. & 3. Record the name of the person/business being paid and, wherever possible, include invoice numbers and/or notes where relevant.

4. Record the type of payment: cheque number, standing order or Direct Debit.

5. Record total payment from bank account.

6. Record total payment in cash.

7–14. These columns are used to record and provide the basis for an analysis of the type of expense being paid. The number of columns you will need will depend upon the nature of your business.

RECEIPTS

	1	2	3	4	5	6	7
DATE		CUSTOMER	NOTES	BANK	CASH	SALES RECEIPTS	OTHER RECEIPTS
8.6.99		A. CHEESMAN (Inv No. 1031)		185.00		185.00	
21.6.99		K. GIBBS (Inv No. 1046)		3,600.00		3,600.00	
23.6.99		CHARLES & Co. Ltd. (Inv No. 1037)		2,750.00		2,750.00	
30.6.99		K. SAUNDERS	SALE OF CAR	1,500.00			1,500.00
5.7.99		N. WEEKS (INV NO. 1025 PT PONT)			150.00	150.00	
12.7.99		C. G. AVERY	DEPOSIT	500.00			500.00

1. Record the date of receipt of cash/cheques plus monies direct to the account.

2. & 3. Record the customer paying you. Wherever possible, note the number of the invoice being paid – this will make it easier for you to check what is owed to you. These notes are used as reminders and to assist your accountant in preparing your accounts.

4. Record the receipts banked.

5. Record the receipts from the customer.

6. & 7. Record all items that are not sales receipts. Record receipts if not banked.

	9	10	11	12	13	14	15	16	17	18
	WAGES PAYE/NI	RENT/RATES INSURANCE	ELECTRICITY GAS WATER	PRINTING POSTAGE STATIONERY	TELEPHONE ORD./ MOBILE	MOTOR EXPENSES	TRAVEL/ SUBSISTENCE		SUNDRY OTHER EXPENSES	CHEQUE NO.
		300 00								
		150.00								
				28.90						
					164.90					
					36.85					
				20.00						
						25.90				
							16.49			
							15.60			
									46.72	COMPUTER REPAIR
									50.00	PETTY CASH

Use the second to last column for sundries and make note in the last column for items which do not fall under specific column headings. The total of columns 7 onwards must equal the total of columns 5 and 6.

Figure 6.1.20 Break-even chart

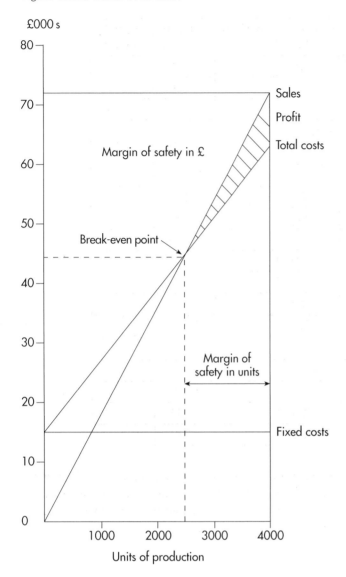

Cash flow forecast

Once you have prepared the original cash budget as part of the start-up costs, this will be brought forward each month to check the current position against budget. If you are lucky enough not to need a loan at the outset, your cash flow situation will be healthier. Look back to the case study for Rachel Wells (page 401) and note that the business was able to survive without external assistance at the beginning. Rachel will now monitor the original cash flow projections to check that no difficulties are arising. At the end of each month the totals will be recorded using a spreadsheet format. Details will be checked against the **receipts and payments book** to see that debtors are paying their accounts on time and sufficient money has come in to pay creditors and bills. The cash flow forecast will now look like this:

Figure 6.1.21 Cash flow forecast monitoring schedule Jan–Feb 2000

Item	January Budget	January Actual	February Budget	February Actual	March Budget	March Actual
Cash sales	563		900		1,013	
Cash from debtors	–		187		300	
Capital introduced	1,875	1,875	–	–	–	–
Total receipts	2,438		1,087		1,313	–
Stock purchased	1,500	1,500	–	–	–	–
Payments to creditors	–	–	375		600	
Advertising	250		250		250	
Stand at exhibition	–	–	–		–	–
Sundry expenses	150		150		150	
Office equipment	500	500	–		–	–
Drawings	150		150		150	
Total payments	2,550		925		1,150	
Opening bank balance	–		–112		50	
Add receipts	2,438		1,087		1,313	
Less payments	2,550		925		1,150	
Closing bank balance	–112		50		213	

Barclays Start-up Pack gives an example of a larger business operating as a printing firm. This shows a quite different position from Rachel Wells's new business and includes payments not being made by her. It is a useful comparison because there are expenses for VAT, interest and salaries which larger organisations need to cover. The larger the business, the greater range of expenses are incurred in running it.

Figure 6.1.22

Cash flow forecast

Name of Business   O'Brien Brothers Printers

Period covered   April 1998 to March 1999

	Month April		Month May	
Receipts	Budget	Actual	Budget	Actual
Cash sales				
Cash from debtors			14200	14980
Capital introduced	5000	5000		
Total Receipts (a)	5000	5000	14200	14980
Payments				
Payments to creditors	2200	2943	18320	12622
Salaries/Wages	1500	1112	1700	1134
Rent/Rates/Water				
Insurance	80	79	80	79
Repairs/Renewals				
Heat/Light/Power				
Postage/Printing/Stationery	20	50		
Motor & Travel				24
Telephone			200	271
Professional fees				
Capital payments	1500	1498	1600	1586
Interest & charges	100	119	100	285
Other				
VAT Payable (refund)			2100	2060
Drawings			1000	800
Total Payments (b)	5400	5801	25100	18861
Net cash flow (a-b)	(400)	(801)	(10900)	(3881)
Opening Bank Balance			(400)	(801)
Closing Bank Balance	(400)	(801)	(11300)	(4682)

Profit and loss forecast

This will indicate whether or not you expect to make a profit in a particular period of time. Rachel Wells has produced a forecast for six months but is likely to check this each month against the cash flow forecast to see if everything is going according to plan.

Figure 6.1.23 Forecast trading and profit and loss account for six months ending 30 June 2000

	£	£
Sales		9,600
Opening stock (initial purchase)	1,500	
Add purchases	4,800	
	6,300	
Less closing stock	1,500	
Cost of goods sold		4,800
Gross profit		4,800
Less expenses		
Advertising	1,500	
Stand at exibition	350	
Sundry expenses	975	
Depreciation of office equipment	50	
		2,875
Net profit		1,925

Anything can happen between starting the business and the end of a set trading period and a monthly check will find out the exact position at that time. Refer to the O'Brien Brothers Printers provided by Barclays (Figure 6.1.24) and you will see quite a different picture.

Figure 6.1.24

Profit and loss forecast

Name of Business   O'Brien Brothers Printers

Period covered   April 1998 to March 1999

	Month April Budget	Month April Actual	Month May Budget	Month May Actual
Sales (net of VAT) (a)	12300	11475	12000	8480
Less: Direct costs				
Cost of materials	7900	7034	7700	5928
Wages	1000	882	1000	889
Gross Profit (b)	3400	3559	3300	1663
Gross Profit Margin ($^b/_a$ x100%)	27.6	31.0	27.5	19.6
Overheads				
Salaries	500	230	700	245
Rent/Rates/Water	100	100	100	100
Insurance	50	79	50	79
Repairs/Renewals	300	256	400	145
Heat/Light/Power	50	70	50	70
Postage/Printing/Stationery		50		
Motor & Travel				24
Telephone	200	271	200	254
Professional fees			500	500
Interest charges	10	13	10	11
Bank charges	50	106	50	274
Other	240		140	42
Total Overheads (c)	1500	1175	2200	1744
Trading Profit (b) - (c)	1900	2384	1100	(81)
Less: Depreciation	100	73	100	73
Net Profit before Tax	1800	2311	1000	(154)
Cumulative Net Profit	1800	2311	2800	2157

Heavier expenditure generally takes its toll on levels but a reduction in expenses will work in favour of the business. Preparing an initial forecast gives the business a goal to aim for and the regular monitoring will avoid failure in the first year.

Balance sheet

This will summarise the position at the end of the six- or twelve-month period and will be useful to any investors, including the owner and financial institutions. Look at the forecast balance sheet for Rachel Wells and you will see that she has a healthy balance at the end of her first period of trading. This could indicate even greater success in the second six-month period and may encourage her to seek a wider variety of outlets to sell her stock.

Figure 6.1.25 Forecast balance sheet as at 30 June 2000

	£	£
Fixed assets		
Office equipment		500
Less depreciation		50
		450
Current assets		
Stocks	1,500	
Debtors	449	
Bank	1,401	
	3,350	
Less current liabilities		
Creditors	900	
Working capital		2,450
NET ASSETS		2,900
Financed by		
Opening capital		1,875
Add net profit		1,925
		3,800
Less drawings		900
		2,900

...tivities

...ready prepared, other ...to help you carry out the ...ing process and check that the business can pay debts as they fall due. If you have built up a successful business quickly you may decide to sell it and move on to something else. Select the calculations that will help you to determine several current aspects of your enterprise but do not forget to work out the level of dividend you will need to pay back to your investors from the profit the business has earned. They will expect a return for their faith, even at the end of the first year's trading. As a reminder to yourself, show these evaluation checks on your **time schedule**. Many business firms use the following formulae as part of their evaluation procedure:

Figure 6.1.26 Calculations table

Quick ratio	$\dfrac{\text{Debtors}}{\text{Current liabilities}}$
Working capital ratio	$\dfrac{\text{Current assets}}{\text{Current liabilities}}$ Note: a ratio of less than 1 shows insolvency
Net working capital as a percentage of sales	$\dfrac{\text{Net working capital}}{\text{Sales}} \times 100 = \%$
Rate of stock turnover	$\dfrac{\text{Cost of stock sold}}{\text{Average stock at cost}}$
Gross profit margin	$\dfrac{\text{Gross profit}}{\text{Sales}} \times 100 = \%$
Net profit as a percentage of the sales	$\dfrac{\text{Net profit}}{\text{Sales}} = \%$
Profit as a percentage of the capital used	$\dfrac{\text{Net profit}}{\text{Net assets}} \times 100 = \%$
Return on capital employed	$\dfrac{\text{Net profit}}{\text{Capital employed}} \times 100$
Liquidity or acid test	$\dfrac{\text{Current assets excluding stock}}{\text{Current liabilities}}$
Debtor collection period	$\dfrac{\text{Debtors}}{\text{Credit sales for year}} \times 52 \text{ weeks}$
Creditor collection period	$\dfrac{\text{Creditors}}{\text{Credit purchase for year}} \times 52 \text{ weeks}$

Contingency planning

This is a natural extension of all other business preparations and will look at potential difficulties that could arise within the trading period. It is a good idea to list common situations that occur in many businesses. Solutions to these problems can be identified so that time is not wasted because you have already noted ways to overcome them. Below is a list of some of these problems:

- sales levels do not meet targets and stock builds up in the warehouse
- sales levels have exceeded targets but production is not keeping pace
- too many faulty goods are being manufactured
- high percentage of customer returns due to faulty goods
- too many refunds or replacement items
- cost of raw materials has increased
- more raw materials have been used than forecast
- interest rates have increased
- credit payment period from suppliers has been shortened
- customers not paying bills on time affecting working capital
- invoicing and deliveries have not matched sales.

Each of these points can be resolved by a specific course of action, e.g.:

- poor sales levels – increase advertising to raise customer awareness
- customers not paying on time – implement debt collection procedures.

In some cases you may need to talk to an external adviser to confirm that the decision you have reached is the best course of action.

Summary

The material in this unit brings together a considerable amount of knowledge and information gained through studying all other units on the course. Business planning requires you to participate actively in the setting up of a business organisation and, from this involvement, to learn about the difficulties of running a profitable company.

In the early stages, owning your own business can be a tempting attraction to aid your personal esteem. This will quickly lead to the realisation that a wider set of skills is needed to cope with all the issues that arise on a daily basis – determination, problem solving, good communication and meticulous planning.

The principal aim of this unit is to draw your attention to the detailed analysis of a potential idea and the procedures required by financial institutions to justify their involvement. Guidance is available from a range of sources to help you prepare the documentation needed to establish the viability of your project. Use this assistance wisely because it comes from experienced personnel in the field of new business ventures. Other opportunities will no doubt present themselves during the course of future years when this consultation process should again be approached to help you decide on diversification or expansion.

The range of work available on a small business or self-employed basis is endless and it is a growing trend in the UK for more and more people to take the decision to set up on their own. Self-fulfilment and the ability to determine one's own future are two basic ideals cited by people who have taken the option to leave paid employment. A greater variety of work and more flexibility are also key factors in this new phenomenon. The following article (Figure 6.1.27) confirms many of these reasons and makes the point that you have a better choice about the tasks to accept.

The final point of importance is that if you do have a really good idea, do something about it and do not leave it to someone else to reap the rewards of your innovative scheme. Carry out an extensive investigation into its potential, prepare detailed documents and

go for it!

Figure 6.1.27

YOU AND YOUR MONEY

Earn more – go solo

EARNING more, being your own boss and doing things your way – sounds good? That's why more and more people are going freelance.

Millions of workers say they would love to throw in their jobs if it meant they could start working for themselves. New research shows that over 11.5 million people, that's more than 40 per cent of the workforce, would like to give it all up and become their own boss.

A survey by First Direct bank reveals an increasing number of people are becoming self-employed, leaving the nine to five routine behind and going solo.

There are currently about 3.7 million freelancers, and the self-employment economy is worth more than £51 billion. Experts say this is expected to rapidly increase. Of those wanting to go it alone, 35 per cent will run their own businesses and 30 per cent will go freelance. The remainder are undecided which route to take.

There are a number of reasons for the surge in interest in freelance work. For a start, computers are cheaper than ever before – giving ordinary people access to the high-tech machines needed to run their own firms. Of those who have taken the plunge and worked for themselves, more than three-quarters said their quality of life has improved since making the switch.

And insiders say freelancers earn comparatively more than staff working for a company and earning a regular salary.

For example, one of the most popular freelance careers nowadays is website design. Average pay for employed staff is about £25,000, while freelance designers get over £33,000 a year on average. Freelance architects can earn over twice as much as those on regular salaries.

Commenting on the freelance phenomenon, Peter Simpson of First Direct said: "People are increasingly seeking more control and balance in their jobs – and that's at the heart of this surge in these freelance trends.

"Relatively few people say they only work for money – most want fulfilment and flexibility too. A growing desire for independence is sweeping the country with people preferring to live and work alone."

GOING solo: TV presenter Gaby Roslin gets to choose the jobs she does – so could you

Source: Horsham Advertiser

Activity

Before approaching a financial source, prepare the following data:

1 A breakdown of all sources of finance to fund the business operation

2 A cash budget analysis and estimate of working capital

3 A profit and loss forecast and balance sheet estimate

4 Decide on the monitoring procedures you will use and the calculations that are suitable to help in the monitoring check

5 Outline your back-up plan to give responses to particular problems that may occur during the first year of trading.

UNIT 6

End of Unit Assignment

At the end of each section within this unit, the activity details have clearly identified all the preparatory documents you should complete as part of your **business plan**. To help you check that there are no gaps in your evidence, use the following checklist to collate your material.

Item No	Details	Completed	Date
1	Description of business idea		
2	Self-assessment completed		
3	Approval gained		
4	Time schedule chart prepared		
5	Monitoring dates identified		
6	Legal obligations checked		
7	Insurance cover requirements listed		
8	Market analysis completed		
9	Marketing plan prepared		
10	Production requirements analysed		
11	Additional resources identified		
12	Start-up costs and budgets prepared		
13	Cash flow forecast prepared		
14	Profit and loss and balance sheet forecasts completed		
15	Evaluation procedure identified		
16	Contingency planning outlined		
17	Portfolio containing business plan completed		

Your portfolio will now be ready for assessment by your tutor or, if you are going to set up your own business, by the financial institution you have selected to approach. Good luck!

Index

Acknowledgements

We are grateful to the following for permission to reproduce copyright material:

The Abbey National Group for p. 22; Barclays Bank PLC for pp. 376, 377 to 378, 404 to 405, 408 and 409; *The Economist* for 'At the coal face – Tower Colliery workers take control' p. 25 © *The Economist*, London (5 January 1995); Horsham District Council for pp. 299 to 306; News International Syndication Ltd for p. 26 'Charities to get investment boost' by Gavin Lumsden in *The Times* of 20 October 1999 and p. 211 'Keep in touch: give a dog a phone' by Robert Whyman in *The Times* of 27 October 1999 © Times Newspapers Limited; Prontaprint Ltd for p. 26; Trinity Hospice for p. 26; WH Smith Europe Travel Retail for p. 267.

We are grateful to the following for permission to reproduce copyright photographs:

BMW (GB) Limited for p.283*br*; British Red Cross for p.249; Corbis for pp 289, 290, 291; Sylvia Cordaiy Photo Library/Chris Parker for p.284; Leslie Garland Picture Library for p.3; Gettyone Stone/Adam Lubroth for p.64; Gettyone Stone/Michael Rosenfeld for p.106*l*; Gettyone Stone/Glen Allison for p.108; Gettyone Stone/Walter Hodges for p.283*l*; Life-File Photographic Library/Emma Lee for p.283*tr*; Panasonic UK Limited for p.106*r*; 'PA' News Photo Library for p.374*tr*; Pictor International for pp.374*br*, 385*b*; Ariel Skelley/The Stock Market for p.248*l*, Paul Barton/The Stock Market for p.385*t*; 'Tesco Photographic Unit' for p.98; Special Collections, J. Willard Marriott Library, University of Utah for p.293; John Walmsley Photography for pp. 248*r*, 374*l*, 386; Yamaha Motor (UK) Limited for p. 90.

IMPRINT

IMPRESSUM

KODAK. Celebrating the brand
Creative corporate scenography
Publisher/Authors Herausgeber/Autoren
Friedrich O. Müller/Uwe R. Brückner
Editor Redaktion
Klaus Tiedge
Design/Concept Gestaltung/Konzeption
Birgit Koelz
Translations Übersetzungen
Rolf Fricke, Prof. George Burden
Printing Druck
Studiodruck, Nürtingen

Bibliographic information published by Die Deutsche Bibliothek
Die Deutsche Bibliothek lists this publication in the Deutsche
Nationalbibliographie, detailed bibliographic data is available on
the Internet at www.ddb.de
Bibliographische Informationen der Deutschen Bibliothek
Die Deutsche Bibliothek verzeichnet diese Publikation in der
Deutschen Nationalbibliographie, detaillierte bibliographische
Daten sind im Internet über www.ddb.de abrufbar

International distribution Vertrieb international
avedition GmbH
Verlag für Architektur und Design
Publishers for architecture and design
Königsallee 57, D-71638 Ludwigsburg
contact@avedition.com
www.avedition.com

Published independently by **av**edition GmbH courtesy of
Eastman KODAK Company and KODAK GmbH, Stuttgart.
KODAK and other KODAK trademarks and trade dress are
the property of Eastman KODAK Company and affiliated
companies and are used with permission. Advertisements,
press releases, trade show exibition displays and other KODAK
historical materials are copyrighted by KODAK and are used with
permission.
Von **av**edition unabhängig herausgebracht mit freundlicher
Genehmigung von Eastman KODAK Company und KODAK
GmbH, Stuttgart. KODAK und andere KODAK Marken und
Ausstattungen sind das Eigentum der Eastman KODAK
Company und deren verbundenen Firmen und werden mit
Genehmigung benutzt. Werbung, Presseveröffentlichungen,
Messe-Ausstellungsmaterial und andere historische KODAK
Materialien sind von KODAK urheberrechtlich geschützt und
werden mit Genehmigung benutzt.

This work, including all its parts, is subject to copyright. It may
not be reproduced in any form in whole or in part without the
express written permission of the publisher and authors.
Das Werk einschließlich aller seiner Teile ist urheberrechtlich
geschützt. Nachdruck und jegliche Art der auszugsweisen Wie-
dergabe bedürfen der schriftlichen Zustimmung des Verlages
und der Autoren.

KODAK and Easyshare are registered trademarks
KODAK und Easyshare sind eingetragene Schutzmarken

ISBN 10: 3-89986-062-4
ISBN 13: 978-3-89986-062-7

© 2006/2007 by **av**edition GmbH, Ludwigsburg
Printed in Germany
© by Eastman KODAK Company, Rochester
© by the relative Authors and Photographers